The
DEFINITIVE GUIDE
to the
BEST
and
WORST
OF EVERYTHING

Les Krantz

PRENTICE HALL
Paramus, New Jersey 07652

To Billy,
The Best of All
The Bests in This Book

The following images are courtesy of Click Art ® Incredible Image Pack; © 1996, T-Maker Company, a wholly owned subsiderary of Broderbund Software, Inc. All rights reserved. Used by Permission. Pages: 55, 80, 99, 101, 106, 116, 119, 125, 128, 131, 132, 139, 141, 143, 145, 159, 162, 173, 180, 182, 188, 190, 210, 213, 215, 256, 257, 262, 264, 267, 269, 272, 274, 277, 281, 284, 303.

©1997 by Les Krantz

Acquisitions Editor: Susan McDermott

Printed in the United States of America

10 9 8 7 6 5 4 3 2 1

ISBN 0-13-861410-5

PRENTICE HALL
Career & Personal Development
Paramus, NJ 07652
A Simon & Schuster Company

On the World Wide Web at http://www.phdirect.com

Prentice Hall International (UK) Limited, *London*
Prentice Hall of Australia Pty. Limited, *Sydney*
Prentice Hall Canada, Inc., *Toronto*
Prentice Hall Hispanoamericana, S.A., *Mexico*
Prentice Hall of India Private Limited, *New Delhi*
Prentice Hall of Japan, Inc., *Tokyo*
Simon & Schuster Asia Pte. Ltd., *Singapore*
Editora Prentice Hall do Brasil, Ltda., *Rio de Janeiro*

CONTENTS

RESEARCH DIRECTOR	Adrienne Brown
SPORTS EDITOR	Mark Mravic
MANUSCRIPT EDITOR	Mark Scheffler
CONTRIBUTING WRITER	Jackie Laks Gorman
CONTRIBUTING WRITER	Bob Kalish
CONTRIBUTING EDITOR	Melissa Ulloa
PROOFREADER	Christine Nielsen-Craig

SPECIAL ACKNOWLEGEMENTS: Many thanks to my editor Susan McDermott, whose enthusiasm was contagious; Gene Brissie, who put us together; Yvette Romero, Sally Hertz and Donna Gould, who were assets to the project and a pleasure to work with.

L ots of attention-hungry organizations take it upon them-selves to point to their versions of the best and worst, ranging from silly things like the "Worst Dressed," the "Most Beautiful," or the "Sexiest Alive."

Journalistically speaking, this sort of fluff annoys me. So, I thought someone should take the task of finding the *real* bests and worsts; that is, write a book filled with ratings that could be taken somewhat seriously and be practical for readers to act upon, if so desired. So here it is, my *Definitive Guide to the Best and Worst of Everything.*

The measurements I used to arrive at my conclusions had to meet several criteria before I accepted them. I sought measure-ments from reliable sources that based their judgments on numeri-cal data, not opinion. I also sought the most current available data compiled by reliable sources. These sources were quite diverse, including agencies of the U.S. government, trade associations, authoritative publications, broad-based opinion polls and hun-dreds of other organizations. I required that the data be based on a large sampling of the category in question. In most cases I demanded a world-wide or national sample. Once in a while—when the subject was more fun than practical—our group of publishing professionals (see the adjacent page) simply cast votes, but only after we studied the information at hand, and only when there was absolutely no quantitative data to consider. The text clearly states which ratings are based on this balloting process. They're on the lighter side, but you're likely to enjoy learning, for example, who's the best or worst admiral, the most influential rock 'n roller, or the very best American citizen in history. You never know what cocktail party you can use these gems at.

Sometimes there were more serious things I wanted to rate, but I could not find quantitative measurements to consider. For exam-ple, who can reasonably measure the best hamburger? Matters of taste are hard to rate. But even with the absence of hard data, I thought at least some objective evaluation might suffice. In such cases, I relied on several methods. Expert opinion was one, but it had to come from someone with impeccable credentials. For example, in the case of wines, I used the opinion of Frank Schoonmaker, a world renowned wine connoisseur and author of one of the most respected references on wine ever published. I also used the opinion of the editors of the London-based magazine the *Economist*, who rated the most influential gurus on money matters. Scores of other expert opinions are given on the pages that follow, though in the main, most bests and worsts are based on numerical data that would be hard to argue with.

In many instances, formulas or criteria were devised for measuring the best and worst, which were dubbed "Best and Worst Original" as its source. This endeavor, was primarily the work of my long-time researcher and editor Mark Mravic, now an editor at *Sports Illustrated*, though his work in this book is his own and not the magazine's. Mark's exhaustive knowledge of sports was the basis of how we used established sports facts and numerical data to arrive at our conclusions for such things as the best sports stars and teams. We also used quantitative data to determine some of the most influential writers, books and other hard-to-measure phenomena.

Perhaps the best parts of this book are the things you'd never expect to find in print—things like where you'll find "the most asses" (the four-legged variety), the worst generals, the most overpaid CEOs, the worst advice, the highest and lowest salaries, not to mention the best stocked libraries, the most obese people, the most claustrophobic jobs and lots more things you've wondered about your whole life.

I hope you'll have as much fun reading it as I did writing it.
Les Krantz

PEOPLE

A CTORS AND ACTRESSES

Most Popular Stars

As the decade opened in 1990, Eddie Murphy, that year's top-grossing star, must have sent a message to Hollywood—audiences would rather have their funny bone tickled than their intellect challenged. This latest list has four comedic actors, whereas Murphy was the only comedic actor to make the top-ten list in 1990. Still on the list are Sylvester Stallone and Arnold Schwarzenegger, proving that the public's tastes may be fickle, but they still like action-packed thrills from the same purveyors. The following are the stars who have grossed the most over the two-year period of 1995-1996, along with their astronomical takes.

Star	Two-year Gross, 1995-96
1. Arnold Schwarzenegger	**$74 million**
'95: $22 million; '96: $52 million	
2. Jim Carrey	**$63 million**
'95: $29 million; '96:$34 million	
3. Jerry Seinfeld	**$59 million**
'95: $31 million; '96: $28 million	
4. Tom Hanks	**$50 million**
'95: $36 million; '96: $14 million	
5. Tom Cruise	**$46 million**
'95: $19 million; '96: $27 million	
6. Harrison Ford	**$44 million**
'95: $19 million; '96: $25 million	
Clint Eastwood	**$44 million**
'95: $18 million; '96: $26 million	
Sylvester Stallone	**$44 million**
'95: $34 million; '96: $10 million	
9. Robin Williams	**$42 million**
'95: $15 million; '96: $27 million	
10. Roseanne	**$40 million**
'95: $19 million; '96: $21 million	

Source: *Forbes*, September 23, 1996.

A DMIRALS

Judging the "best" naval commanders is a difficult task and is open to much speculation and further discussion; in the following rating, the best commanders are judged not just by statistics, but by their stories as well. Factors in this assessment include relative force (offense vs. defense) in armament, ship number, men and guns available, weather conditions of battles, tactical planning and execution, and importantly, success. The following are the editors' selections for the greatest naval commanders of modern times.

BEST ADMIRALS

Admiral/Significant Battle

1. **Horatio Nelson**
   Nile, 1798
   Defeats well-positioned French fleet despite overwhelming odds of 3 to 13, goes on to greater glory and fame.

2. **Don John of Austria**
   Lepanto, 1570
   Unites multi-national force, even numbers match, destroys Turkish foe.

3. **Sir Francis Drake**
   Spanish Armada, 1588
   Facing much larger force, tough weather, deters foe; Drake's early daring raids delayed Spanish fleet departure.

4. **Martin Tromp**
   The Downs, 1639
   Takes initiative, attacks with 17 vs. 77 while rest of his fleet is elsewhere. Indecisive enemy and the arrival of reinforcements were responsible for his victory.

5. **Chester Nimitz**
   Midway, 1942
   Turning point in WWII in Pacific: Nimitz defeats Japanese fleet despite significant losses. Nimitz earns command of Pacific fleet, goes on to win control of entire Pacific. Father of "Nuclear" Navy.

6. **George Monck**
   Four-day battle, 1666
   Splits fleet, takes initiative anyway, attacks with less than 50 ships against an enemy of 90. Forces enemy to alter plan; reinforcements arrive—victory.

7. **Edward Hawke**
   Quiberon Bay, 1759
   Hawke makes bold move, pursues French fleet in a gale, defeats French in their own home waters, losing only two ships to seven for the French.

8. **Heimachoro Togo**
   Tsushima, 1905
   Togo's well-planned and executed battle results in a massive victory over the slower but larger Russian fleet.

9. **Pierre-Andre de Suffren**
   East Indies, 1782-83
   This master tactician's excellent planning helped keep British away from French territory in the Caribbean until his departure.

10. **David Farragut**
    Mobile Bay, 1864
    Strapped himself to the mast of his flagship to steady himself in battle. Loses one ship early to a sea mine, but gives famous order, "Damn the torpedoes, full speed ahead." Takes Mobile Bay from the hands of the Confederates.

Source: *Great Sea Battles.*

WORST ADMIRALS

The following worst admirals are rated by magnitude of their loss—the more lost in a single battle, the higher on the list.

Admiral /Significant Battle

1. **Admiral Bruey**
   Nile, 1798
   Has incredible superiority and position over Nelson, manages to lose entire fleet (only two ships escape), signals beginning of end for French empire.

2. **Admiral Rojdestvensky**
   Tsushima, 1905
   Commits gravest mistake a commander can make—goes into battle against Togo of Japan *expecting to lose!* Expectations realized—he loses entire, numerically superior fleet.

3. **Duke of Medina**
   Spanish Armada, 1588
   Loses Spanish Armada. Deterred by Drake from attacking England, makes bad call to go to North Sea: six ships sink in battle, loses 64

more ships and 10,000 men to weather. Only 50% of fleet returns to Spain.

4. **Ali Pasha**
   Lepanto, 1570
   Lost Turkish fleet to Don John of Austria: 300 ships, 3200 men, all previously captured European prisoners serving as rowers on Turkish ships are freed.

5. **Admiral d'Oquendo**
   The Downs, 1639
   Loses early initiative, his 77 ships are attacked by Admiral Tromp's 17 and Tromp wins encounter. Further bad planning, no tactics, allow Tromp to get reinforced. D'Oquendo loses.

6. **Admiral Buchanan**
   Mobile Bay, 1864
   Poor planning, execution and equipment allow Farragut to take Mobile Bay easily.

7. **Sir Richard Pearson**
   Flamborough Head, 1779
   Clear advantage over John Paul Jones in fight, bad maneuvering allows ships to grapple; subsequently British lose.

8. **Comte de Toulouse**
   Gibraltar, 1704
   Inexperienced commander (king's son) does not take initiative; first encounter a draw, next encounter, roundly defeated.

9. **Prince of Denmark**
   Copenhagen, 1801
   Foe of Nelson. Danes have harbor position, inflict much more damage against a stronger fleet under Nelson, but bad luck and weak will cause surrender of Danish fleet.

10. **K.G. Wrangel**
    The Sound, 1658
    Has numerical advantage, but loses wind. Bad luck in a fierce fight and Wrangle loses.

Source: *Great Sea Battles.*

ADVISORS WITHIN THE FAMILY

Does Father Still Know Best?

Though the nuclear family is declining percentage-wise as a familial situation, the traditional role of parent as advisor is still strong. In a recent public opinion poll, mothers ranked somewhat ahead of fathers as the best advisor. One might surmise that this is a result of women gaining more power and equality in American society. The image of the omnipotent father gradually has given way to a more realistic, more fallible perception of the father as "human," rather than an all-knowing authority figure. Another possible interpretation of the recent poll's findings is that there may be a bit of Oedipal influence at work: males named their mothers as the best advisors, while females said their mothers and fathers were tied for first place. The following tabulations represent the percentage of poll respondents who gave the following answers to the question: *"Overall (meaning on most matters), which one family member is most likely to give you the best advice?"*

Family Member	Percent
1. Mother	15.84%
2. Father	13.82%
3. Wife	9.63%
4. Husband	5.67%
5. Sister	5.38%
6. No answer	5.35%
7. Brother	4.08%
8. Grandfather	2.55%
9. Grandmother	2.34%
10. Aunt	1.85%

Source: The Peoplepedia Opinion Poll, 1996.

PEOPLE

GREATEST AMERICAN CITIZEN OF ALL TIME, Abraham Lincoln.

A MERICAN CITIZENS

Greatest of All Time

Who's the greatest American ever? Lincoln? Kennedy? Martin Luther King, Jr.? In order to make a determination, Americans of historical significance were scored from 1 to 10 in four categories: leadership, power or influence on his or her contemporaries, influence in changing the course of history, and lasting stature in history. According to our editors, Lincoln scores slightly higher than Washington in his influence on the course of history, because the editors felt that preserving the Union presented an even more challenging and, in the long run, historically significant, task than founding it. Washington helped start the country, but Lincoln saved it and allowed it to become

great. Edison scored highest in the "contemporary influence" and "course of history" categories—receiving perfect 10s in both—for the profound effects his inventions had on the daily lives of Americans as well as people throughout the world.

American	Score
1. Abraham Lincoln	36
2. George Washington	35
3. Franklin D. Roosevelt	31
4. Thomas Edison	27
5. Benjamin Franklin	24
6. Martin Luther King, Jr.	21
7. Henry Ford	19
8. Theodore Roosevelt	18
9. Clara Barton	16
Eleanor Roosevelt	16

Source: *Best and Worst* original.

A MERICANS, WEALTHIEST

John Kluge, formerly the wealthiest individual in the United States, has had his share of disappointments—his net worth advanced a paltry $2 billion since 1990. While the smartest investors—namely speculators who put their fortunes in fledgling companies—tripled and quadrupled their investments, Kluge's more modest appreciation might be enough to make him look for a better way to make a living. His less than spectacular performance is contrasted with men of lesser fortunes when he was number one. Bill Gates, head of Microsoft, barely had $3 billion then. Today, Gates' fortune has reportedly increased over tenfold to $36.4 billion. Warren Buffett, American's second richest in 1990 behind Kluge, dropped a notch on the list—he's now only number three. He needn't worry that his wealth is stagnating—his net worth is now $23.2 billion, up from $3.8 billion. Life for billionaires has its share of headaches and heartaches. Below are some of the biggest sufferers in the limo line at the bank's drive-up window.

Name/Source	Net Worth (millions)
1. **Gates, Bill** Microsoft Corp.	$36,400
2. **Walton Family** Inheritance (Wal-Mart Stores)	$27,600
3. **Buffett, Warren Edward** Stock market	$23,200
4. **Allen, Paul Gardner** Microsoft Corp.	$14,100
5. **Haas Family** Levi Strauss	$12,300
6. **Mars Family** Mars Candy Company	$12,000
7. **Newhouse, Samuel and Donald** Media Holdings	$9,000
8. **Cargill Family** Cargill Co.	$8,800
9. **Ballmer, Steven** Microsoft Corp.	$7,500
10. **Kluge, John Werner** Metromedia Co.	$7,200

Source: *Forbes* magazine, July, 1997.

AMERICA'S WEALTHIEST, Microsoft Chairman Bill Gates.

ATHLETES, DECEASED

Most Notable Deaths

One of the most tragic events one can witness is a great athlete being struck down in the prime of his career by a debilitating illness or sudden fatal accident. The editors of this book have compiled a list of what we consider the most notable athletes' deaths of the century. Some of the deaths are the result of accidents or injuries caused by play on the field, while others are less related to athletics. But, perhaps, the saddest are those of Len Bias and Sonny Liston, both of whom fatally succumbed to the temptations of drugs.

1. **Lou Gehrig**
   The Pride of the Yankees, a man who became known as the "Iron Horse" for his remarkable record of more than 2,100 consecutive games played, is forced to retire after being diagnosed with a mysterious muscle disorder. Gehrig succumbs two years later, in 1941, to the disease that now bears his name.

2. **Len Bias**
   Drafted number two in the 1986 NBA draft by the Boston Celtics and projected as a huge NBA impact player, Bias parties the night he's drafted and dies of a cocaine overdose.

3. **Roberto Clemente**
   While shuttling relief supplies to Nicaraguan earthquake victims on

PEOPLE

New Year's Eve, 1972, the Pittsburgh Pirate great—batting champ, 1971 World Series MVP, Puerto Rican national hero—is killed in a plane crash. Clemente's last hit of the '72 season, and the last of his career, was his 3000th.

4. **Hank Gathers**
The highest scoring college hoopsters of all time, Gathers faints on the court in a game against UC-Santa Barbara; diagnosed with an irregular heartbeat, Gathers gradually reduces his intake of the drugs that were prescribed to combat his condition. Three months after his first attack, in a game against the University of Portland, Gathers collapses on the court after a slam dunk; he dies a short time later.

5. **Lyman Bostock**
The California Angels star is mistaken for someone else and killed by a shotgun blast while sitting in his car.

6. **Knute Rockne**
The legendary Notre Dame football coach is killed in a plane crash.

7. **Thurman Munson**
The Yankee catcher is killed when the plane he is piloting crashes in Ohio during the 1979 season.

8. **Spider Savage**
Skiing star Savage is shot to death in a lover's tiff by Claudine Longet.

9. **Sonny Liston**
The former heavyweight champ, once considered the strongest and meanest man alive, dies of a heroin overdose shortly after losing his second heavyweight championship bout with Cassius Clay (Muhammad Ali).

10. **Flo Hyman**
Star of the U.S. women's gold medal volleyball team in the 1984 Olympics, Hyman succumbs on the court shortly after the Games to Marfan's Syndrome, a disease that strikes unusually tall persons.

Source: *Best and Worst* original.

A THLETES, ENDORSEMENTS

Top Endorsement Contracts

Many of the best jocks are not the highest paid players in their respective sports leagues, even though they are often the best performers. Until 1996, Michael Jordan was not the highest paid hoopster and Dennis Rodman wasn't even near the top. Though both of them got spectacular raises, they apparently didn't worry too much about their paychecks for many years. Why have top athletes been relatively unconcerned about their salaries? Endorsements. That's where the *real* money is in sports. Below are the top *men*—unfortunately, even when women's endorsements are considered, there's absolutely no comparison to what the men pull down from companies eager to associate their goods and services with them.

Athlete	Annual Endorsements
1. Michael Jordan	$40 million
2. Shaquille O'Neal	$17 million
3. Arnold Palmer	$15 million
4. Andre Agassi	$13 million
5. Tiger Woods	$10 million
6. Dale Earnhardt	$8.5 million
Dennis Rodman	$8.5 million
8. Michael Schumacher	$8.0 million
Pete Sampras	$8.0 million
Jack Nicklaus	$8.0 million

Source: *Business Week*, April 28, 1997.

A THLETIC PERFORMANCE

Best All-Sports Achievements

To rate the greatest athletic feats of modern times, we looked at record-setting performances in baseball,

8

basketball, football, hockey, golf and the Olympics, and judged the records according to the percentage by which the new mark surpassed the old. For instance, Babe Ruth's remarkable home run record of 54, set in 1921, surpassed the existing single-season standard (set by Ruth himself in 1919) by 25, or an astounding 86 percent. By this standard, Ruth's 1921 home run mark is by far the most groundbreaking athletic performance in a major sport during this century. (For Bob Beamon's 1968 long jump performance, we normalized the numbers by taking the difference in inches beyond 23 feet; for Michael Johnson's 200 meter time, we used seconds above 18.)

Ath.—Event /Yr.—Prev. Rcrd.	% Diff.
1. **Babe Ruth**—54 Home Runs, 1921—29 Home Runs	86.2%
2. **Bob Beamon**—74.5' Long Jump, 1968—52.75'	41.2%
3. **Dan Marino**—48 Touchdown Passes, 1984—36 T.D. Passes	33.3%
Tiger Woods—12 Point Margin in Masters Tourn., 1997—9 strokes	33.3%
5. **Wilt Chamberlain**—4029 Pt. Season, 1962—3033 Pts.	32.8%
6. **Wayne Gretzky**—212 Pt. Season, 1982 —162 Pts.	30.9%
7. **Wilt Chamberlain**—100 Pt. Game, 1961—78 Pts.	28.2%
8. **Joe Dimaggio**—56-Game Hitting Streak, 1941—44 Hts.	27.3%
9. **Bill Russell**—1564 Rebounds, one season, 1958—1256 rebounds	24.5%

TOP-PAID ATHLETE FOR ENDORSEMENTS, Michael Jordan (See Page 8).

10. **Michael Johnson**—.34 second lowering of 200 Meter Record, 1996 —19.32 Seconds   20.5%

Source: *Best and Worst* original.

BASEBALL MANAGERS

Greatest Managers of All Time

Baseball managers were measured on two criteria: regular-season winning percentage and World Series championships. The formula used for this measurement was to multiply their winning percentage times 1,000 then to add their world championships times 100. Not surprisingly, the top two managers on our list are associated with the most successful franchise in baseball history: the New York Yankees. Joe McCarthy directed the powerhouse Yankees of the 1930s and early '40s to seven World Series titles; shortly after he left the Yanks, Stengel took over the team and led it to seven more. Sixth-best manager Miller Huggins also earned his stripes in Yankee pinstripes. Stengel would have challenged McCarthy for the top spot in this rating if not for the four seasons he spent with the expansion New York Mets, with whom his winning percentage was a meager .300. Two less familiar names make the list: Billy Southworth, who managed the St. Louis Cardinals to two championships in the 1940s, and Danny Murtaugh, who directed the Pittsburgh Pirates to two titles, in 1960 and 1971. Following are the top 10:

Mngr.	Win.%	W.S. Champs	Score
1. **Joe McCarthy**			1,315
	.615%	7	
2. **Casey Stengel**			1,208
	.508%	7	
3. **Connie Mack**			986
	.486%	5	
4. **Walter Alston**			958
	.558%	4	
5. **John McGraw**			887
	.587%	3	
6. **Miller Huggins**			855
	.555%	3	
7. **Sparky Anderson**			845
	.545%	3	
8. **Billy Southworth**			797
	.597%	2	
9. **Frank Chance**			793
	.593%	2	
10. **Danny Murtaugh**			740
	.540%	2	

* scores based on data through 1996

Source: *Total Baseball.*

BASEBALL PLAYERS

Greatest Players of All Time

To judge the greatest baseball players of all time, we employed *Total Baseball's* formula, called the Total Player Rating. TPR is a complex combination of a player's offensive production, fielding prowess and base-stealing ability, and takes into account his position and how his home park affects the average player's productivity. In general, the formula reflects a player's relation to the average player during his day. The results certainly argue for the validity of the process, as Babe Ruth himself tops the list, with a TPR of 105.2, more than 10 points beyond the next player on the list, Napoleon Lajoie. Indeed, the difference between Ruth and Lajoie is more than twice that between any other two players. As usual, the Bambino stands head and shoulders above the rest. These are the top 10 greatest baseball players, as measured by *Total Baseball's* Total Player Rating:

Player	TPR
1. Babe Ruth	105.2
2. Nap Lajoie	94.9
3. Ty Cobb	92.8
4. Ted Williams	92.4
5. Tris Speaker	88.5
6. Willie Mays	86.4
7. Hank Aaron	84.6
8. Honus Wagner	82.6
9. Mike Schmidt	80.3
10. Rogers Hornsby	79.8

Source: *Total Baseball.*

BASEBALL PLAYERS, BASES PRODUCED

Most All-Time Bases Produced

There are innumerable measures of a baseball player's offensive performance—the traditional batting average, runs batted in and home runs—as well as more elaborate statistics, such as slugging percentage, ratio of bases to outs and runs produced. But the intricate analysis of stats undoubtedly doesn't stop there. Want to know how many times a particular batter has knocked in a runner from second with two outs after the seventh inning against a left-handed pitcher on astroturf in his home stadium? Some number-cruncher somewhere can tell you. The following is an interesting measure of an player's offensive productivity. The formula used to derive the list below adds together a player's total number of bases gained through hits, walks and steals over his career, then divides that number by the total number of games played. The result yields the average number of bases gained per game for each player, and multiplying that number by 150 gives an index of the offensive productivity of a player over the course of a regular season. The statistic favors powerful home run hitters, since a homer earns four bases for every swing of the bat, while a single accounts for only one base. The list is led by three power hitters—Ruth, Gehrig and Williams—but the interesting members of this top 10 club are Rickey Henderson and Ty Cobb, players shorter on power but longer on speed. The prowess of Henderson

HIGHEST-PAID YANKEE, First Baseman Cecil Fielder is among the top-ten highest paid in the game. (See page 12)

and Cobb in swiping bases adds greatly to their offensive threat.

Player Bases Produced/150 Games	
1. Babe Ruth	478
2. Lou Gehrig	462
3. Ted Williams	453
4. Rickey Henderson	436
5. Jimmy Foxx	421
6. Mickey Mantle	400
7. Ty Cobb	396
8. Willie Mays	394
9. Stan Musial	387
Hank Aaron	387

Source: *The New York Times*.

BASEBALL PLAYERS, BATTING AVERAGES

Highest Career Averages

A ball no larger than a fist speeds at a man holding what looks like a dowel. In a fraction of a second the man pivots and brings the wood into contact with the ball. The collision of bat and ball resounds in the park and is immediately followed by a roar from the crowd. A rush of activity follows, and within moments the batter is standing on base brushing the dust from his uniform. Some say hitting a baseball is the most difficult feat in all of sports. Even the most accomplished baseball players can scarcely get a hit more than once in three chances, and fewer still can retain that average over the course of an entire career. These are the players with the highest lifetime batting averages.

Player	Lifetime Average
1. Ty Cobb	.366
2. Rogers Hornsby	.358
3. Joe Jackson	.356
4. Ed Delahanty	.346
5. Tris Speaker	.345
6. Ted Williams	.344
Billy Hamilton	.344
8. Dan Brouthers	.342
Babe Ruth	.342
Harry Heilmann	.342

Source: Major League Baseball, 1997.

BASEBALL PLAYERS, EARNINGS

Highest Paid Players

Today's baseball contracts—at least when it comes to the superstars—often cover several years of play. Mike Piazza of the Los Angeles Dodgers, for example, recently signed a contract for two years of service. His pay? $15 million. In order to compare his salary to the annual salary of other players, one must use an "average salary,"

which is simply the average compensation per year, based on the total monetary amount of the contract, divided by the years of play covered by the contract. In Piazza's case, his average salary was computed as $7.5 million per year. In the big leagues of today, million-dollar salaries are common and the stars of many teams earn multimillions, at least for the better teams in the bigger cities like New York, Chicago and Los Angeles. Players in lesser baseball domains such as Cleveland, Milwaukee and Seattle often suffer salary-wise not from their play on the field but from geography—there simply aren't enough ticket buyers or TV viewers in the market to generate the big bucks that teams in the major metropolitan areas do. The following were the highest paid players in 1996.

Player/Team	Average Salary
1. **Barry Bonds**, San Fran. Giants	$11.45 million
2. **Albert Belle**, Chicago White Sox	$11.00 million
3. **Ken Griffey, Jr.**, Seattle Mariners	$8.50 million
4. **Roger Clemens**, Toronto Blue Jays	$8.25 million
5. **John Smoltz**, Atlanta Braves	$7.75 million
6. **Mike Piazza**, L.A. Dodgers	$7.50 million
7. **Frank Thomas**, Chicago White Sox	$7.25 million
8. **Cecil Fielder**, N.Y. Yankees	$7.24 million
9. **Alex Fernandez**, Florida Marlins	$7.00 million

Source: *Los Angeles Times*, January 22, 1997.

BASEBALL PLAYERS, FIELDING

Greatest Fielders of All Time

A statistical analysis of baseball players' fielding prowess is problematic. Comparing a player from one position to one at another is akin to comparing apples to oranges—third basemen naturally commit more errors than second basemen, since balls to third are on average harder hit (hence the name "the hot corner"); and third basemen also often play closer-in than their infield colleagues. In addition, judging a fielder on fielding percentage (percentage of chances that are error-free) alone hurts the player with better range, as he takes more chances and therefore has more opportunity for error. To compile our list, we compared assists to errors—that is, the number of times a player threw a runner out in relation to the number of errors committed. Ratios varied widely among positions—a ratio of 10 to 1 for first basemen was above average, while the standard of excellence for outfielders (who get an assist only when they throw out a runner trying to advance) seemed to be a ratio of 1.75 to 1. An interesting sidelight to our ratings was seeing how dramatically fielding has improved over the years (thanks in no small part to larger, better constructed gloves, and probably to artificial surfaces as well). For instance, Hall of Fame shortstop Honus Wagner, who played in the early decades of the century, had an assist to-error ratio of 8.94 to 1, more than three times worse than the top-rated shortstop, Larry Bowa, who played in the 1970s and

GREATEST FIELDING SECOND BASEMAN OF ALL TIME, Chicago Cub Ryne Sandberg.

'80s. This is our all-time best fielding lineup, by position, measured by the ratio of assists to errors.

Position/Plr.	Assts.	Errors	Assts./Err.
Catcher: Lance Parrish			
	914	88	10.39
First Baseman: Keith Hernandez			
	1,682	115	14.63
Second Baseman: Ryne Sandberg			
	5,096	84	60.67
Third Baseman: Brooks Robinson			
	6,205	263	23.59
Shortstop: Larry Bowa			
	6,857	211	32.50
Outfielder: Johnny Callison			
	175	57	3.07
Outfielder: Dwight Evans			
	157	59	2.66
Outfielder: Mel Ott			
	256	98	2.61

Source: *Best and Worst* original.

BASEBALL PLAYERS, HITTING

Most Hits of All Time

The list below has some of the most ironic statistics in all of baseball. Pete Rose, a player with more hits than anyone, cannot even get his name in the Baseball Hall of Fame. Rose is ineligible because of his past conviction for gambling and was banned from the game for life, even though he retired as a player many years before his troubles with the law and the baseball commissioner. Surprisingly, Babe Ruth, the man who did more than any other player to make baseball America's national pastime, is not on the list. In order to include the Bambino, the list would have to be extended to 32 places, which is where Ruth's 2,873 hits positioned him.

Player	Hits (lifetime)
1. Pete Rose	4,256
2. Ty Cobb	4,189
3. Hank Aaron	3,771
4. Stan Musial	3,630
5. Tris Speaker	3,514
6. Carl Yastrzemski	3,419
7. Cap Anson	3,418
8. Honus Wagner	3,415
9. Eddie Collins	3,315

Source: *Total Baseball*, 1996.

BASEBALL PLAYERS, PINCH HITTING

Greatest Pinch Hitters of All Time

Pinch hitting is one of those hard-to-understand baseball vagaries which leave many observers confused. Pinch hitters sit on the bench for almost the entire game. Then, when their team desperately needs a run, they are called upon to replace batters whose averages are often little lower than their own. Pinch-hitting specialists are often older players who can still connect with the ball but whose legs are not quick enough to compete with their younger teammates—Manny Mota, for instance, extended his career by years through his ability to come off the bench and whack a base hit. In creating this ranking, the editors took into consideration both the player's total number of pinch hits and his pinch-hitting average. The following are the top 10 pinch hitters of all time. Note that none are Hall of Famers—the pinch hitter's art has yet to be recognized in that hall of immortals.

Player	Pinch Hit Average
1. Tommy Davis	.320
2. Frenchy Bordagaray	.312
3. Frankie Baumholtz	.307
4. Sid Bream	.306
5. Mark Carreon	.306
6. Chip Hale	.304
7. Red Schoendiens	.303
8. Bob Fothergill	.300
9. Dave Philley	.299
10. Manny Mota	.297

Source: *Total Baseball*, 1996.

BASEBALL PLAYERS, PITCHING

Greatest Pitchers of All Time

If there's any doubt that Cy Young should have an award named after him, read on. Our rating of baseball's greatest pitchers is the sum of winning percentage (times 1,000), number of 20-win seasons (times 100), earned run average (10 minus ERA, then x 100), strikeouts per season, and—to normalize scores for modern-day pitchers, who pitch fewer innings and play in an offense-heavy era—Cy Young awards won. Topping the list is Cy Young; his remarkable career has set the standard. The top southpaw on the charts is Warren Spahn. (For Greg Maddux, the only active player on the list, 20-win seasons were prorated over a 20-year estimated career, and adjustments were made to take into account the 1994 players strike.) Below are the top 10.

Pitcher	Score
1. Cy Young	2,982.3
2. Christy Mathewson	2,899.2
3. Warren Spahn	2,811.0
4 Walter Johnson	2,750.1
5. Jim Palmer	2,568.4
6. Greg Maddux	2,476.4
7. Grover Alexander	2,395.9
8. Steve Carlton	2,324.3
9. Lefty Grove	2,307.3
10. Tom Seaver	2,299.0

* scores based on data up to 1996
Source: *Best and Worst* original.

BASEBALL PLAYERS, PURE HITTING

Greatest "Pure Hitters" of All Time

By a "pure hitter" we mean a batter who can make contact with the ball at will, as opposed to a "power hitter," who can hammer a pitch out of the park, but who invariably has a much higher strike-out rate. A lesser known Hall of Famer tops our list of the best pure hitters in the history of baseball: Joe Sewell. A 14-year veteran of the Cleveand Indians and New York Yankees from 1920 to 1933, Sewell was the best contact hitter the game has seen, striking out just once every 63 at-bats. In 1925, Sewell logged 608 at-bats for the Indians and whiffed

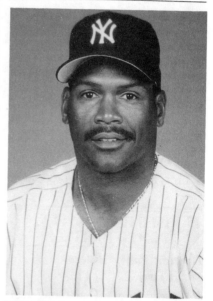

TOP-TEN ALL-TIME BASE STEALER, New York Yankee Tim Raines. (See page 16)

just four times—showing an astounding ability to put bat on ball. In two other seasons he had just three strikeouts (though with fewer at-bats). Sewell, who played primarily shortstop and third base, retired with a .312 batting average and was elected to the Hall of Fame by the Veterans Committee in 1977. These are the best pure hitters in baseball history, measured by the ratio of at-bats to strikeouts.

Player/AB/SO's	AB/SO's
1. **Joe Sewell**	
7,132 / 114	62.6
2. **Lloyd Waner**	
7,772 / 173	44.9
3. **Nellie Fox**	
9,232 / 216	42.7
4. **Tommy Holmes**	
4,992 / 122	40.9
5. **Andy High**	
4,400 / 130	33.8

6. **Sam Rice**
9,269 / 275   33.7
7. **Frankie Frisch**
9,112 / 272   33.5
8. **Dale Mitchell**
3,984 / 119   33.5
9. **Johnny Cooney**
3,372 / 107   31.5
10. **Frank McCormick**
5723 / 189   30.3
* scores based on data up to 1996

Source: *Best and Worst* original.

BASEBALL PLAYERS, POWER HITTING

Greatest Power Hitters of All Time

Believe it or not, we are living in the second great age of the home run hitter in baseball. The first, heralded by Babe Ruth, lasted from the early 1920s until the late '30s, when the ball became deadened and World War II diluted the talent pool. In the past decade, with expansion weakening the quality of pitching, home run hitters have feasted like they haven't in years—three of the 10 players on our rating of greatest power hitters in baseball history are active: Mark McGwire and Jose Canseco of the Oakland A's, and New York Yankees slugger Cecil Fielder. Over the course of his career, McGwire has hit home runs at a rate surpassed only by Ruth himself; in fact, if he can stay clear of injuries that have plagued him, McGwire may even challenge Hank Aaron for the all-time home run record. This rating measures power hitting by the ratio of at-bats to homers. Ruth went long once every 11.76 at-bats; McGwire has

averaged a dinger once every 12.36. Following are the top 10:

Player	AB	HR	AB/HR
1. **Babe Ruth**	8,399	714	11.76
2. **Mark McGwire**	414	335	12.36
3. **Ralph Kiner**	5,205	369	14.11
4. **Harmon Killebrew**	8,147	573	14.22
5. **Ted Williams**	7,706	521	14.79
6. **Dave Kingman**	6,677	442	15.11
7. **Mickey Mantle**	8,102	536	15.12
8. **Mike Schmidt**	8,352	548	15.24
9. **Cecil Fielder**	4,453	289	15.41
10. **Jose Canseco**	5,134	330	15.56

Source: *Best and Worst* original.

BASEBALL PLAYERS, BASE STEALING

Most Stolen Bases of All Time

Stolen base kings are the fleet-footed wonders of the baseball world. Thieves with fast feet and the instinctive ability to read the pitchers moves, these denizens of the base paths can take a simple single or a walk and turn it into a quick run. Many a game with Rickey Henderson involved has led off with Henderson walking, stealing second, advancing to third on an infield out and scoring on a sacrifice fly. Thus the pitcher, untouched in the hit column, already finds himself down where it counts—the score. Three of the top 10—Rickey Henderson, Tim Raines and Vince Coleman—were active during the 1996 season.

Following are the most larcenous men ever to get on base.

Player	Steals
1. Rickey Henderson	1,186
2. Lou Brock	938
3. Billy Hamilton	912
4. Ty Cobb	892
5. Tim Raines	787
6. Vince Coleman	752
7. Eddie Collins	744
8. Arlie Latham	739
9. Max Carey	738
10. Honus Wagner	722

Source: *World Almanac*, 1997.

BASKETBALL COACHES

Most NBA Wins

There are coaches who have had more championships, coaches who have had more glory, coaches who have had more superstars, but no coach in NBA history had more victories than Lenny Wilkens. Coaching for Seattle and Atlanta, Wilkens' record of wins surpasses all the great coaches, including legendary Celtics coach Red Auerbach and Phil Jackson of the Chicago Bulls. For a while Pat Riley was thought to stand a chance of catching him. The well-coiffed Riley signed on with the Los Angeles Lakers in the early 1980s, just as the Lakers began to flourish. With such stars as Magic Johnson and Kareem Abdul-Jabbar, Riley was stepping into championship shoes with a team that just needed some fine-tuning. Certainly, Riley's four championships with the Lakers have added impressively to his list of wins. With the New York Knicks, it was thought he'd be pro-

MOST NBA WINS OF ALL TIME, Coach Lenny Wilkens is the only coach to win over 1,000 games (1,014). Photo: Andrew D. Bernstein © NBA Photos.

WINNINGEST PERCENTAGE OF ALL TIME IN THE NBA, Coach Phil Jackson of the Chicago Bulls.

BASKETBALL COACHES

Best NBA Winning Percentage

Basketball teams never cease to amaze aficionados of sports statistics. At one time, the Boston Celtics' amazing championship streak was thought unbeatable. Their stats were generally regarded as permanent highs in the annals of the sport. The Celtics won *ten* NBA championships from 1959 to 1969, including eight in a row. Their coach, Red Auerbach, won almost two of every three games he coached. Then Pat Riley, who's bounced around the sport, boasted a winning average of .733, triumphing in almost three of four games his teams would play. But he only had the Knicks. Then came Phil Jackson. Respected, though unproven, when he came to coach the Chicago Bulls, his record would soon establish him as the winningest NBA coach of all time. In 1995-96 his Bulls won almost *nine of every 10* games played, and they did it again in 1996-97. Like all good coaches, Jackson has had some superstars on his side, namely Michael Jordan, Scottie Pippen and Dennis Rodman.

pelled to the top of the all-time winning list. Then the Bulls came along, which, under Jackson, stole his team's thunder. Ironically it was Wilkens who breached the 1,000 win barrier, leaving Auerbach—and Riley—in the dust.

Coach	Wins
1. Lenny Wilkens	1,014
2. Red Auerbach	938
3. Dick Motta	918
4. Bill Fitch	891
5. Jack Ramsey	864
6. Don Nelson	851
7. Cotton Fitzsimmons	832
8. Pat Riley	798
9. Gene Shue	784
10. John MacLeod	707

Source: NBA, 1997.

Coach	Percent
1. Phil Jackson	.721%
2. Pat Riley	.702%
3. Billy Cunningham	.698%
4. K.C. Jones	.674%
5. Red Auerbach	.662%
6. Rick Adelman	.620%
7. Tom Heinsohn	.619%
8. Jerry Sloan	.601%
9. Chuck Daly	.598%
10. Larry Costello	.589%

Source: NBA, 1997.

BASKETBALL COACHES

Greatest College Coaches of All Time

One name stands above all others in the annals of college basketball coaching: John Wooden of UCLA. "The Wizard of Westwood" led his UCLA Bruins—which boasted the likes of Lew Alcindor (later Kareem Abdul-Jabbar) and Bill Walton—to 10 NCAA national championships in 12 seasons, from 1964 to 1975. Wooden thus easily tops our rating of the greatest coaches in the college game, measured by the sum of winning percentage (times 1000) and national championships (times 100). Kentucky placed two of its coaches, Adolph Rupp and Rick Pitino, in the top 10.

Coach	Pct.	Titles	Score
1. John Wooden	.804	10	1,804
2. Adolph Rupp	.822	4	1,222
3. Bob Knight	.733	3	1,033
4. Dean Smith	.775	2	975
5. Jerry Tarkanian	.783	1	930
6. Mike Krzyzewski	.694	2	894
7. Nolan Richardson	.748	1	848
8. Al McGuire	.739	1	839
9. Rick Pitino	.728	1	828
10. John Thompson	.727	1	827

* scores based on data up to 1996

Source: *Best and Worst* original.

BASKETBALL COACHES

Greatest NBA Coaches of All Time

Our rating of the all-time great NBA coaches combines winning percentage during the regular season with the number of championships won. This formula yields a final score that reflects a coach's dual mission: to get his team into a position to win a championship, and then win it. The best at that, by far, in the 50-year history of the NBA, is Red Auerbach, who led the Boston Celtics to nine championships in the 1950s and '60s. Close on Auerbach's heels, however, are two active coaches—Phil Jackson of the Chicago Bulls, and Pat Riley of the Miami Heat, who won his four titles with a Los Angeles Lakers team that featured Magic Johnson and Kareem Abdul-Jabbar. A less familiar name pops up in fourth place: John Kundla. He coached the Lakers to five titles when the team was still in Minneapolis. Here are the top 10.

Coach	Pct.	Titles	Score
1. Red Auerbach	.662	9	1,562
2. Phil Jackson	.721	4	1,121
3. Pat Riley	.702	4	1,102
4. John Kundla	.583	5	1,083
5. K.C. Jones	.674	2	874
6. Tom Heinsohn	.619	2	819
7. Chuck Daly	.598	2	798
8. Lester Harrison	.620	1	720

9. Larry Costello

| | .589 | 1 | 689 |

10. Billy Cunningham

| | .587 | 1 | 687 |

* scores based on data up to 1996
Source: *Best and Worst* original.

BASKETBALL PLAYERS

Greatest Players of All Time

When Wilt Chamberlain wasn't up to snuff in a few games, a sports writer asked him why he wasn't getting the usual accolades from the Los Angeles fans, he lamented, "Nobody cheers for Goliath." Twenty-five years later, another basketball quote surfaced, this time from an ad slogan, not a player: "I wanna be like Mike." That Mike is Michael Jordan and the quotation is exclaimed by millions of young basketball fans. Though many players would like to be like Mike too, some wouldn't—because Michael Jordan isn't *that* good, at least compared to a few players in particular. One such player is Wilt Chamberlain. No matter how you look at the basketball greats, the plain fact is that "Wilt the Stilt," not Michael Jordan, is the most dominant basketball player ever. At least that's what the sports statistics reveal. This assessment is based on a simple formula: the sum of a player's points, rebounds and assists per game, plus NBA championships, Most Valuable Player Awards and All-Star selections. Although Jordan does hold the NBA record for scoring average, and Bill Russell

FOURTH GREATEST BASKETBALL PLAYER OF ALL TIME (at right), Chicago Bull Michael Jordan. Jordan is also the highest paid in the game.

played on a record 11 championship teams with the Boston Celtics, Wilt the Stilt brought to the court an incomparable package of scoring, rebounding and even assists, a category in which he actually led the league one season. These are the 10 greatest basketball players in NBA history.

Player /Pts./RPG/APG/C/MVP/AS						Score
1. Wilt Chamberlain						**76.4**
30.1	22.9	4.4	2	4	13	
2. Bill Russell						**69.9**
15.1	22.5	4.3	11	5	12	
3. Kareem Abdul-Jabbar						**66.4**
24.6	11.2	3.6	6	6	15	
4. Michael Jordan						**62.1**
32.0	6.4	5.7	4	4	10	
5. Bob Pettit						**59.6**
26.4	16.2	3.0	1	2	11	
6. Larry Bird						**58.6**
24.3	10.0	6.3	3	3	12	
7. Magic Johnson						**57.9**
19.5	7.2	11.2	5	3	12	
8. Elgin Baylor						**57.2**
27.4	13.5	4.3	0	0	12	
9. Oscar Robertson						**56.7**
25.7	7.5	9.5	1	1	12	
10. Julius Erving						**54.8**
24.1	8.5	4.2	1	1	16	

    * scores based on data up to 1996
Source: *Best and Worst* original.

BASKETBALL PLAYERS

Greatest College Scorers of All Time

What sport did you play in college, Wilt? One might just as easily ask that of Michael Jordan and other NBA greats who were not superstars in the NCAA like they were later in the professional ranks. Great play in college basketball

GREATEST COLLEGE SCORER OF ALL TIME, "Pistol Pete" Maravich. Photo: Wen Roberts. © NBA Photos

4. **Calvin Murphy, Niagara**
   ('68-'70) 2,548   33.1
5. **Dwight Lamar, S.W. Louisiana**
   ('72-'73) 1,862   32.7
6. **Frank Selvy, Furman**
   ('52-'54) 2,538   32.5
7. **Rick Mount, Purdue**
   ('68-'70) 2,323   32.3
8. **Darrell Floyd, Furman**
   ('54-'56) 2,281   32.1
9. **Nick Werkman, Seton Hall**
   ('62-'64) 2,273   32.0
10. **Willie Humes, Idaho State**
    ('70-'71) 1,510   31.5

Source: *World Almanac*, 1997.

BASKETBALL PLAYERS

Highest Paid NBA Players,

When John "Hot Rod" Williams signed for $5 million with the Cleveland Cavaliers in 1990—twice the then-younger Michael Jordan's salary—it set a precedent. Big bucks became the watchwords of salary negotiations. But Williams didn't earn his top-salary, while many lesser-paid players like Jordan, Earvin "Magic" Johnson of the Los Angeles Lakers and Charles Barkley of the Philadelphia 76ers did. They became the top players in the sport, and yet earned half of what other players "in their league" were earning. Ironically, there was not the pressure one might expect to raise their salaries. These stars were already earning huge sums from product endorsements. As the most valuable commercial endorser in the pantheon of sports, Jordan's stock has risen even further with the five NBA championships he and the Bulls won. But today, big endorsement money won't suffice for the superstars. Team owners now feel

does not necessarily indicate a great future in the pros. Many college superstars, fresh out of college programs in which they excelled, are shocked to find the level of competition so much higher in the NBA. Some of the top all-time collegiate scorers indeed went on to pro stardom—Pete Maravich, Oscar Robertson, Elvin Hayes, and Larry Bird. But other top college scorers are destined to struggle for a few years on an NBA bench, in the Continental Basketball Association or even in Europe before they realize that there may be more to life than throwing a ball through a hoop.

Player/Univ./Yrs./Tot./Pts./Pts. per Game

1. **Pete Maravich, L.S.U.**
   ('68-'70) 3,667   44.2
2. **Austin Carr, Notre Dame**
   ('69-'71) 2,560   34.6
3. **Oscar Robertson, Cinncinnati**
   ('58-'60) 2,973 33.8

pressure to pay their players commensurate with their ability to win games. With it, salaries—and ticket prices—soared.

Player/Team	Salary, 1996-97
1. Michael Jordan Chicago Bulls	**$30.0 million**
2. Horace Grant Orlando Magic	**$15.0 million**
3. Reggie Miller Indiana Pacers	**$11.0 million**
4. Shaquille O'Neal Los Angeles Lakers	**$10.7 million**
5. Gary Payton Seattle Supersonics	**$10.2 million**
6. David Robinson San Antonio Spurs	**$10.0 million**
7. Juwan Howard Washington Bullets	**$9.8 million**
8. Hakeem Olajuwan Houston Oilers	**$9.7 million**
9. Alonzo Mourning Miami Heat	**$9.4 million**
10. Dikembe Mutombo Atlanta Hawks	**$8.0 million**

Though Dennis Rodman of the Chicago Bulls signed a contract for over $9 million, it is heavily dependent on performance bonuses. Rodman also lost over $1 million when he was suspended for various violations during the 1996-97 season, including kicking a cameraman in plain view of stadium fans and millions in the television audience.

Source: NBA Players Association, 1997.

BLACK AMERICANS

Percentage of the U.S. Population

Though the percentage of the U.S. population composed of blacks has declined, recent census data indicates that their numbers are on the upswing again. When the United States was founded in 1776, nearly one in five inhabitants of the new country was an African slave. The black population in the U.S. has grown to more than 30 million in the years since, but due to waves of immigration from various parts of the globe over the ensuing years, the Black percentage of the total population has never been as high as it was in 1800. In the mid-19th century it dropped to below 10 percent, and in the most recent census their numbers constituted 12.3 percent of the total population. The black population increased 18.6 percent from 1980 to 1990, twice the rate of white population growth. Nevertheless, by the year 2010, the Census Bureau projects that Blacks no longer will be the largest minority group in the country; Hispanics will outnumber blacks by that time. Following is a ranking of the years in which blacks constituted the largest percent of the U.S. population.

Year	Pop.(1,000s)	% U.S.
1. 1800	1,002	18.9%
2. 1850	3,639	15.7%
3. 2000*	35,006	13.1%
4. 1990	30,486	12.3%
5. 1980	26,683	11.8%
6. 1900	8,834	11.6%
7. 1970	22,581	11.1%
8. 1960	18,872	10.5%
9. 1920	10,463	9.9%
10. 1940	12,866	9.8%

* projection

Source: U.S. Census Bureau.

BOXERS

Top-Earning Prize Fighters

With big-time heavies like Don King still running things on the financial end, the Sweet Science still

HIGHEST-PROFILE BUSINESS MOGUL, Steve Forbes.

has not caught the smell of the rose. The purses, however, have swelled considerably, and the publicity attending the sport has created a somewhat more equitable situation for the fighters. Today's heavyweight champs, for example, earn about $30 million per fight, even if they get disqualified for biting a piece or two of their opponent's ear off, as Mike Tyson did on June 28, 1997. Following are the earnings (including endorsements) of the top professionals.

Fighter	Earnings, 1996 (millions)
1. Mike Tyson	$75.0
2. Evander Holyfield	$15.0
3. Roy Jones Jr.	$12.0
4. Riddick Bowe	$11.5
5. Oscar de la Hoya	$11.0
6. Julio Cesar Chavez	$9.0
7. George Foreman	$8.0

Source: *Jet Magazine*, December 12, 1996.

BUSINESS MOGULS

Highest Profile

Judging notoriety is always dicey. But every year *Forbes* puts its fingers to the computer keyboard and quantifies the amount of press coverage various business moguls received in the period. *Forbes* admits the list may not be the most precise measuring stick because it is based on only one criterion: the number of articles in the Nexis databases that mention a mogul's name during the year. Since this is a list of "business" persons, it is limited to those whose main reputation is for their business acumen. Interestingly, Michael Jordan, star of the Chicago Bulls, might get enough press to make the list, but his main occupation is basketball, and he therefore doesn't qualify. Following are the 1996 top 10 and their Nexis citations.

Businessperson	Nexis Citations
1. Steve Forbes	**26,250**

Among the press he received was a 7,000 word article in *Fortune* estimating his net worth at $440 million.

2. Rupert Murdoch	**12,957**

As the owner of many newspapers in England, Murdoch always gets a boost in these rankings. However, he also gets a lot of coverage in New York, the media capital of America.

3. Bill Gates	**8,433**

The richest man in America always gets a lot of ink.

4. Steven Spielberg	**7,485**

Much of his press revolved around *Schindler's List* and *The Lost World*.

PEOPLE

5. George Steinbrenner 6,851
This object of much vilification got less of it than usual in 1996 because the team he owns, the New York Yankees, won the World Series.

6. Ted Turner 6,683
Most of his press pertained to merging his TV holdings with Time Warner. It also didn't hurt that he publicly compared Rupert Murdoch to Hitler, or that he's married to Jane Fonda.

7. Donald Trump 3,544
Most members of the press who tried to get to "the Donald" were successful. Unlike other busy moguls he's known to take phone calls if it means his name will get in the newspaper.

8. Yasuo Hamanaka 3,262
Japanese businessmen who lose $1.8 billion are considered "good copy," so his fiasco with unauthorized copper transactions was big news.

9. Michael Eisner 2,762
Not only did Disney have a good year, but when Eisner got rid of his pal Michael Ovitz, paying him tens of millions to leave, the press picked up on it, and how.

10. George Soros 2,474
Self-made, an immigrant, a mega-philanthropist and an author, Soros is a good story and a cooperative interviewee who always has something meaningful to say.

Source: *Forbes*, February 3, 1997.

CELEBRITIES, DECEASED

Top Stiff Stars

Elvis is alive! And he has been spotted, not at a supermarket in Michigan, but at the top of our list of the most popular dead celebrities. What inspired such a revelation? A few years back, a professor named E.D. Hirsch wrote a book called *Cultural Literacy*, in which he described the ideas, events, and historical personages with which a person must be familiar in order to be "culturally literate." But we think Hirsch didn't go far enough, limiting himself to the stuff of history, philosophy and high culture. We, the "Best and Worst" editors, wanted to know what celebrities who have run their entire course in the public eye—that is, dead and gone—have the most indelible image in pop-culture. So, we developed a "pop-culture index" of the highest-profile, most important, most media-genic and totally breathless stars. In order to do so, we searched the periodicals in the several magazine databases, which were full-text, on-line services offering articles from over 100 magazines for the period from 1987 to mid year 1997. We wanted to see how often each celebrity was mentioned in magazines ranging from *The Atlantic* and *Cosmopolitan* to *Playboy* and *Working Woman*. The final score is the overall number of articles in the database in which the deceased celebrity is mentioned. So who's the most popular star in the cemetery? The King, of course. Elvis is so big, in fact, he received almost twice the number of hits of the second most cited celeb, Marilyn Monroe. Other dead celebrities who scored well, but did not make the top-ten list, are Humphrey Bogart, Greta Garbo, Alfred Hitchcock, and surprisingly, Frank Capra, the director of the ubiquitous Christmas classic *It's a Wonderful Life*. Several more recently deceased celebrities got many hits and would almost certainly have been among or close to

TOP DECEASED CELEBRITY: Elvis Presley, still lives . . . at the top of the list of the most written about deceased celebrities. Photo courtesy David Beckwith, Rogers & Cowan.

the top-ten had a shorter time period been used in the search. They are George Burns, Jerry Garcia, Greta Garbo, Dean Martin, and Kurt Cobain. Following are the top-ten deceased celebrities in the search of American magazines, half of whom are, perhaps not so coincidentally, from England, the mother of American pop-culture.

Artist	Celebrity Index
1. Elvis Presley	594
2. Marilyn Monroe	296
3. John Lennon	282
4. John Wayne	241
5. Laurence Olivier	204
6. Charlie Chaplin	200
7. Fred Astaire	172
8. Cary Grant	161
9. Orson Welles	129
10. Peter Sellers	101

Source: "Best and Worst" original.

CELEBRITIES AS PRESIDENT

Some celebs have political aspirations, some don't. Nonetheless, many non-politicians seem popular enough to get elected. In this context, a recent public opinion survey asked which non-politician would be the best President. The answers were mixed—evangelists, talk show hosts, poets and basketball players all made the list. The surprising roster of potential White House inhabitants is led by Colin Powell, but also includes such unlikely candidates as Oprah Winfrey, David Letterman, Maya Angelou and Charles Barkley. The tabulations below represent the percentage of poll respondents who gave the following answers to the question: *"What one public figure who is not a politician would make the best President of the United States?"*

BEST PRESIDENTS

Potential Candidate	% Who Favor
1. Colin Powell	13.74%
2. Rush Limbaugh	5.03%
3. Oprah Winfrey	2.75%
4. Robert Redford	2.55%
5. David Letterman	2.26%
6. Steve Forbes	2.22%
7. Maya Angelou	1.97%
8. Walter Cronkite	1.56%
9. Bill Gates	1.44%
10. Charlton Heston	1.44%

And the Worst President? "President Limbaugh" was the overwhelming non-choice for the Oval Office, according to the poll, which also asked who the worst President might be among non-politicians. Though Rush Limbaugh, Ross Perot (No. 2) and even Howard Stern (No. 3) have expressed interest in political office, it's highly unlikely that some other names that made the list—O.J. Simpson, Courtney Love or Dennis Rodman—will be appearing on the ballot anytime soon. The tabulations below represent the percentage of poll respondents who gave the following answers to the question: *"What one public figure who is not a politician would make the worst President of the United States?"*

WORST PRESIDENTS

Potential Candidate	% Who Favor
1. Rush Limbaugh	7.61%
2. Ross Perot	5.93%
3. Howard Stern	4.11%
4. Barbra Streisand	3.09%
5. Madonna	2.34%
6. Louis Farrakhan	2.26%
7. Jesse Jackson	1.85%
8. O.J. Simpson	1.65%
9. Hillary Clinton	1.56%
10. Charlton Heston	1.36%

Source: The Peoplepedia Opinion Poll, 1996.

CHIEF EXECUTIVE OFFICERS

Highest Paid CEOs

Lawrence Coss, CEO of little-known Green Tree Financial, was the highest paid CEO in 1995 at $65.6 million. The company, which loans money to mobile home buyers, had $254 million in net income. Overall in the business world, earnings growth has averaged 44 percent since 1990. CEO salaries soared an average of 30 percent last year to $3.75 million. Perhaps it is even well deserved—their company profits rose 75 percent since 1990. However, during the same period, factory workers' pay rose only 16 percent. This will do little to calm anti-business sentiment and a backlash against downsizing. Adding insult to injury, the pay of white-collar professionals rose a mere 4.2 percent in 1995, while factory employees received only a one percent raise. CEO pay at the 20 companies with the largest announced layoffs last year rose 25 percent over 1994. Warren Buffett, chairman of Berkshire Hathaway, gave shareholders the most return for pay over the last three years. Michael Eisner, CEO of Walt Disney, gave shareholders the least return for his $228 million pay over three years.

CEO/Co. Salary/Bonus	Earnings *
1. Lawrence Coss	**$65.6**
Green Tree Financial $65.6 None	
2. Sanford Weill	**$49.8**
Travelers Group $5.6 $44.2	
3. Jack Welch	**$22.1**
General Electric $5.3 $16.7	
4. Gordon Binder	**$20.5**
Amgen $1.5 $20.0	
5. James Donald	**$19.2**
DSC Communications $5.6 $13.6	
6. Casey Cowell	**$18.6**
U.S. Robotics $2.8 $15.8	
7. Floyd English	**$17.7**
Andrew Corp. $1.7 $15.9	

TOP-TEN BUSINESS MOGUL, George Steinbrenner (See page 24). In addition to having the fifth-highest public profile among businessmen, he also has the New York Yankees, the number one sports franchise of all time (See page 307).

8. **Howard Solomon**   **$17.0**
Forest Laboratories
$0.6 $16.4
9. **Stanley Gault**   **$16.6**
Goodyear Tire & Rubber
$2.2 $14.3
10. **Edward Brennan**   **$16.4**
Sears Roebuck
$3.1 $13.3
* figures in millions and for 1995
Source: *Business Week.*

C HIEF EXECUTIVE OFFICERS

Who's Earning Their Pay?

Is it possible to "feel sorry" for someone who's earning too little? What if "too little" still means over a million dollars annually? Some CEOs are millionaires, when they should be *multi*millionaires. And there are the multimillionaire CEOs whose performance is so poor they should only be millionaires. Sound crazy? Not to corporate analyst Graef Crystal, who compares actual CEO compensation with the level he says a CEO would have earned in 1995 if the market were more rational and the pay level reflected the firm's size and performance. Below is his interpretation of what the "best and worst" paid CEOs should really be earning, if they were paid competitively. "Actual pay" in the tables below include salary, bonus, free stock shares and the present value of option grants and other long-term incentives.

HIGH PERFORMANCE— LOW PAY

Crystal says these executives had much smaller paychecks than they merited based on their firms' size and performance.

CEO/Co.—Compet. Pay	Actual Pay
1. **Steven A. Burd** Safeway, Inc.—$8,086,000	**$1,356,000**
2. **John H. Dasburg** Northwest Airlines—$10,771,000	**$1,081,000**
3. **O.G. Richar** Columbia Gas—$4,266,000	**$604,000**
4. **Richard Moley** Stratacom, Inc.—$2,983,000	**$564,000**
5. **George Perlegos** Atmel Corp.—$2,424,000	**$404,000**
6. **Bill Gates** Microsoft Corp.—$5,464,000	**$416,000**

7. **Warren E. Buffett**   **$324,000**
Berkshire Hath-
away—$6,143,000
8. **John F. Gifford**   **$264,000**
Maxim
Integrated—$2,271,000

LOW PERFORMANCE— HIGH PAY

These executives below earned far more than they deserved based on their firms' size and performance.

CEO/Co.—Compet. Pay	Actual Pay
1. **Clyde T. Turner** Circus Circus—$1,940,000	**$23,396,000**
2. **John C. Malone** Tele-Comm TCI—$3,674,000	**$13,591,000**
3. **William Farley** Fruit of the Loom—$2,097,000	**$7,766,000**
4. **William Smithburg** Quaker Oats Co.—$2,978,000	**$4,787,000**
5. **James Woods** Baker-Hughes, Inc—$2,438,000	**$4,625,000**
6. **Paul R. Charron** Liz Clai- borne—$2,033,000	**$4,400,000**
7. **Ronald Richey** Torchmark Corp.—$2,242,000	**$3,795,000**
8. **Daniel Crowley** Foundation Health—$1,734,000	**$3,396,000**

Source: *U.S. News & World Report,* June 17, 1996.

COMPOSERS, GREATEST ALL-TIME

Who's the most influential composer of all time? We used to bandy about the phrase "the three B's"— Bach, Beethoven and Brahms— which seemed to be based on an outmoded sense of popular recognition. But a more telling indication of influence is the sheer number of recordings of a composer's works, as well as the amount of scholarly and popular writing about the composer's life and music. One way of ascertaining this information is to check the number of records under a given composer in the Online Computer Library Center database, the most comprehensive information science database available on published and recorded material. As it turns out, those "three B's" should really be "two B's and an M," since the top three composers of all time as judged by OCLC method are Bach, Mozart and Beethoven. In fact, the two top composers led the list by a wide margin over their nearest rival. Bach checked in with approximately 17,640 database records, and Mozart came in a close second with 17,150 records. Beethoven dropped a relatively distant third with 13,622, while that pretender to the third spot, Brahms, tallied a mere 8,133. No rock stars came close, so Beethoven has no reason to roll over.

Rank/Composer

1. Johann Sebastian Bach
2. Wolfgang Amadeus Mozart
3. Ludwig van Beethoven
4. Johannes Brahms
5. Joseph Haydn
6. Franz Schubert
7. George Handel
8. Peter Tchaikovsky
9. Robert Schumann
10. Richard Wagner

Source: "A Guide to Special Collections in the OCLC Database," OCLC Online Computer Library Center, Dublin, Ohio.

PEOPLE

CONGRESSPERSONS,

Most Conservative Voting Records

With the Republicans controlling the House of Representatives, the conservative block of voters swing a mighty bat with or without Newt Gingrich, whose popularity swings like branches in a storm. The statistics in the following table represent the percentage of times each politician voted in accordance with the American Conservative Union on selected votes in 1995.

REPRESENTATIVES

Politician	Voting Record Percent
Boehner (R-OH)	100%
Bonilla (R-TX)	100%
Buyer (R-IN)	100%
Dreier (R-CA)	100%
Fields (R-TX)	100%
Hastings (R-WA)	100%
Lightfoot (R-IA)	100%
Livingston (R-LA)	100%
McCrery (R-LA)	100%
Skeen (R-NM)	100%
Thornberry (R-TX)	100%
Vucanovich (R-NV)	100%
Wicker (R-MS)	100%

SENATORS

Politician	Voting Record Percent
Cochran (R-MS)	100%
Lott (R-MS)	100%
Ashcroft (R-MO)	98%
Gramm (R-TX)	98%
Grams (R-MN)	98%
Hutchinson (R-TX)	98%
Murkowski (R-AK)	98%
Burns (R-MT)	98%
Coverdell (R-GA)	96%
Craig (R-ID)	96%
Thurmond (R-SC)	96%

Source: *Congressional Quarterly Almanac, 1995.*

CONGRESSPERSONS

Occupational Breakdown

The world might not need more lawyers, but it's possible that the founding fathers of the U.S. thought their new country did. John Adams was an attorney, as was Thomas Jefferson. And so were 12 other signers of the Declaration of Independence. Fourteen out of the first 56 representatives of the fledgling democracy were lawyers. The legal profession, even back then, was far ahead of the second most common profession among the signers of the Declaration of Independence—merchants. Not much has changed in the past 200 years. Lawyers still make up the majority of occupations for the 105th Congress, followed by business or banking. Following is a list of those occupations enjoyed by our political representatives.

Occupation	Total
1. Law	225
2. Business or Banking	214
3. Public Service	126
4. Education	87
5. Agriculture	30
6. Real Estate	28
7. Journalism	21
8. Medicine	14
9. Law Enforcement	10
10. Engineering	8

Source: *Congressional Quarterly,* 1997.

CRIMINALS, MOST WANTED

The FBI's Ten Most-Wanted Fugitives From Justice

Want to earn some extra money? You could try robbing a bank. If

PEOPLE

your mother taught you never to point guns at honest people, there's a better way—point them at some *dishonest* people. You'll find pictures of some who are alleged to be on the Internet, and you could get a reward from the FBI. Some of the more dangerous fugitives have a handsome price on their heads. So be careful if you meet up with them. They're rough boys. (Sexist though it may be, no women are to be found on the FBI's Web Page [www.fbi.gov]) Complaints can be sent to Gloria Steinem. Following is some information about them which was culled from the FBI page at press time.

1. Lamen Khalifa Fhimah
(Reward: $4 million)
aka: Lamen Khalifa Al-Fhimah; Al Amin Khalifa Fhimah.
Lamen Khalifa Fhimah is being sought for his participation in the December 21, 1988 bombing of Pan Am Flight 103 which exploded over Lockerbie, Scotland. A total of 259 passengers and crew members and 11 Lockerbie villagers were killed.

2. Victor Manuel Gerena
aka: Victor Ortiz, Victor M. Gerena Ortiz, Victor Manuel Gerena Ortiz.
Victor Manuel Gerena is being sought in connection with the September 1983 armed robbery of approximately $7 million from a security company in West Hartford, Connecticut. He took two security employees hostage at gunpoint then handcuffed, bound, and injected them with an unknown substance in order to further disable them.

3. Glen Stewart Godwin
aka: Michael Carmen, Glen Godwin, Glen S. Godwin, Dennis H. McWilliams, Dennis Harold McWilliams.

Photograph taken 1993

Agustin Vasquez-Mendoza

THE $50,000 REWARD will not be paid for this "capture" (screen capture, that is) of Mendoza on the FBI's home page on the Internet.

In March 1981, Godwin was convicted of murder and sentenced to 25 years to life. On June 30, 1987, he escaped from Folsom State Prison by accessing the main storm drain and thereby reaching the American River where a raft was waiting. He is one of only three prisoners to ever escape from this prison.

4. Mir Aimal Kansi
(At press-time Kansi was captured and was not replaced on the list.)
aka: Mir Aimal Kanci, Mir Aimal Kasi, Mohammed Alam Kasi, Mir Aman Qazi, Mir Amial Qansi, Amial Khan.
Mir Aimal Kansi is being sought in connection with the shooting of five individuals with an AK-47 assault rifle. The January 1993 shooting occurred outside CIA Headquarters in Langley, Virginia, and resulted in the killing of two individuals and the wounding of three others.

PEOPLE

5. Abdel Basset Ali Al-Megrahi
(Reward: $4 million)
aka: Ahmed Khalifa Abdusmad; Abdelbaset A. Mohmed; Abdelbaset Ali Ibaset Ali Mohmed Al Megrahi; Abdelbaset El Azzabi; Abd Al Baset Ali; Abd Al Basset.

Abdel Basset Ali Al-Megrahi is being sought for his participation in the December 21, 1988 bombing of Pan Am Flight 103, which exploded over Lockerbie, Scotland. A total of 259 passengers and crew members and 11 Lockerbie villagers were killed.

6. Agustin Vasquez-Mendoza
(Reward: $50,000)
aka: Augustin Vasquez-Mendoza, Fernando Cruzziniga, Anisito Cruzziniga, Rogelio Cruz-Sunica, Augustin Mendoza, Fernando.

Agustin Vasquez-Mendoza is being sought for his alleged participation in a drug conspiracy involving a Drug Enforcement Administra-

tion Special Agent who was killed on June 30, 1994, during an undercover drug transaction in Glendale, Arizona.

7. Thang Thanh Nguyen
aka: Thanh Thang Nguyen, Thang T. Nguyen, T. T. Nguyen

Thang Thanh Nguyen is being sought for the January 26, 1992, burglary, armed robbery, and "execution-style" murder of a Vietnamese businessman at his residence in Irondequoit, New York.

8. Andrew Phillip Cunanan
aka: Andrew Phillip DeSilva

Cunanan, a suspect in the murder of David Madson, Lee Miglin and Gianni Versace, died from a self-inflicted gun shot at press-time (July 23, 1997). His spot on the FBI's Ten-most Wanted List has not yet been filled.

9. Arthur Lee Washington, Jr.
aka: Azikikwe Ekundayo Onipedo, Arthur L. Washington. Jr.

THE FBI's TEN MOST-WANTED can be accessed on the Internet on the Bureau's home page on which one clicks a mouse on the portraits below in order to get more information about the fugitives. Pictured below is a screen capture of the page.

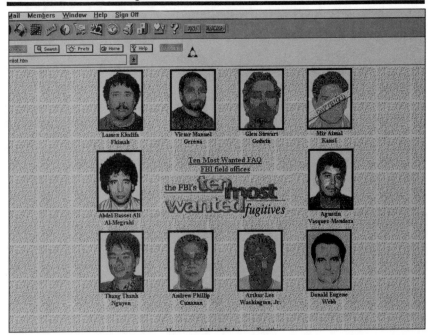

Arthur Lee Washington, Jr. is being sought in connection with the April 1989 attempted murder of a New Jersey state trooper wherein a .45 caliber semi-automatic handgun was used.

10. Donald Eugene Webb

aka: A.D. Baker, Donald Eugene Perkins (true name), Donald Eugene, Pierce, John S. Portas, Stanley John Portas, Bev Webb, Eugene Bevlin Webb, Eugene Donald Webb, Stanley Webb, and others.

Donald Eugene Webb is being sought in connection with the December 1980 murder of a Saxonburg, Pennsylvania, police chief who was shot twice at close range after being brutally beaten about the head and face with a blunt instrument.

Source: FBI, 1997.

EDUCATORS

Most Influential Educators

The pragmatic philosophy of John Dewey, itself an outgrowth of the thinking of 19th-century American philosophers C.S. Pierce and William James, had reverberations not only in philosophic discourse but in wide-ranging fields, including psychology, sociology and, perhaps most forcefully, education. His doctrine: that experience is the most effective tool in education—"learn by doing"—continues to play an integral role in educational theory up to the present day. The three most influential contemporary educators on our list—William Bennett, E.D. Hirsch and Allan Bloom—all are proponents of a traditional education stressing a fundamental core of knowledge basic to an informed and enlightened citizenry. Bennett made his influence felt most strongly while Secretary of Education under Reagan; Hirsch published a widely discussed book titled *Cultural Literacy*; while Bloom expounded on what he thought was wrong with modern post-secondary education in his controversial book *The Closing of the American Mind*. In order to rate the relative influence of educators, the editors searched for references to each individual in the Educational Research Information Center (ERIC) database, a CD-ROM service offering abstracts from tens of thousands of articles, surveys and other education research sources; educators received one point for each reference to them, the final score being the total number of references for each educator.

Educator	Score
1. John Dewey	380
2. Thomas Hopkins Gallaudet	238
3. Carl Rogers	115
4. William Bennett	114
5. E.D. Hirsch	85
6. Horace Mann	64
7. Allan Bloom	40
Marshall McLuhan	40
9. Maria Montessori	39
10. Friedrich Wilhelm Froebel	38

Source: *Best and Worst* original.

ENTERTAINERS

Most Lucrative Concert Tours

My, how things have changed. Or have they? Seven years ago, The New Kids on the Block were the most successful act on the road. Now they're nowhere to be seen (there is a God). But a quick glance at the list below shows that the 1970s, horrifying as they may seem, are back. With the Grateful Dead disbanded (literally) and the bodacious, bigtime stars like Madonna, the Rolling Stones and Pearl Jam off the big-buck list, concert-goers have spent their concert dollars on the following.

Act	Gross Receipts, 1996
1. Eagles	$60,312,265
2. KISS	$36,576,533
3. Garth Brooks	$33,584,636
4. Bob Seger	$26,308,693
5. Neil Diamond	$25,266,088
6. Rod Stewart	$23,078,252
7. Reba McEntire	$21,580,965
8. Alanis Morissette	$19,521,727
9. Jimmy Buffett	$18,380,000
10. Ozzy Osbourne	$17,662,091

Source: *Amusement Business*, "BOXSCORE," December 16, 1996.

ENTERTAINERS

Highest-Earning

As far back as 1990, if you couldn't sing or tell jokes, you didn't have a ghost of a chance of earning much more than $60 million annually. Back then, few other than top comics or crooners made the top-10 list of earners. That has changed. The latest top-10 list of super earners in the entertainment industry has its share of the unfunny, "unsung" heroes of the entertainment world, namely Oprah and Steven Spielberg, the giants who top the list. Another noncomic, nonperformer makes the new list, screenwriter/author Michael Crichton. Off the list is Bill Cosby who, in 1989-90, earned the most of anyone in show business, $115 million. His fortunes have fallen down to the $50 million range. If the young

woman who allegedly claimed to be his illegitimate daughter had been successful in the $40 million extortion attempt the police reported, Cosby would have a paltry $10 million left.

Entertainers	Earnings, 1995-96
1. Oprah Winfrey	$171 million
'95: $74 million; '96: $97 million	
2. Steven Spielberg	$150 million
'95: $120 million; '96: $30 million	
3. The Beatles	$130 million
'95: $100 million; '96: $30 million	
4. Michael Jackson	$90 million
'95: $45 million; '96: $45 million	
5. Rolling Stones	$77 million
'95: $71 million; '96: $6 million	
6. The Eagles	$75 million
'95: $43 million; '96: $32 million	
7. Arnold Schwarzenegger	$74 million
'95: $22 million; '96: $52 million	
8. David Copperfield	$74 million
'95: $52 million; '96: $22 million	
9. Jim Carrey	$63 million
'95: $29 million; '96: $34 million	
10. Michael Crichton	$59 million
'95: $22 million; '96: $37 million	

Source: *Forbes*, September 23, 1996.

ETHNIC GROUPS

Composition of the U.S.

America is a funny place. We have almost 40 million "Irish," yet in its entire history, Ireland has never had a population exceeding nine million. And most of our "Irish" have ancestors not primarily from Ireland, but from England, Scotland, Italy and elsewhere. The pot has melted! There are many other ironies about ethnicity in the U.S. One of the most curious ones is that we have fought more wars with the country from which most Ameri-

PEOPLE

cans trace their roots, Germany, than with any other nation. And in World War II, the supreme commander was, in fact, a German ethnic, General Dwight D. Eisenhower. It's been said that he proved to the world that America had even better Germans than Germany. In addition to the major ethnic groups listed below, the U.S. has some smaller ethnic groups that are uncounted due to their small numbers—Gypsies and Amish, to name a few. Following is an estimate of the sizes of ethnic groups whose numbers in the U.S. are greater than one million.

Group	Population
1. German	57.9 million
2. Irish	38.7 million
3. English	32.7 million
4. African-American	23.8 million
5. Italian	14.7 million
6. Mexican	11.6 million
7. French	10.3 million
8. Polish	9.4 million
9. Dutch	6.2 million
10. Jewish*	6.0 million
11. Scotch-Irish	5.6 million
12. Scottish	5.4 million
13. Swedish	4.7 million
14. Norwegian	3.9 million
15. Russian	3.0 million
16. French Canadian	2.2 million
17. Welsh	2.0 million
Spanish	2.0 million
Puerto Rican	2.0 million
20. Slovak	1.9 million
21. Danish	1.6 million
Hungarian	1.6 million
23. Chinese	1.5 million
Filipino	1.5 million
American Indians	1.5 million
26. Czech	1.3 million
27. Portuguese	1.2 million
28. Greek	1.1 million
29. Swiss	1.0 million
Japanese	1.0 million

* about 80 percent of American Jews trace their ancestry to Germany, Poland and Russia

Source: U.S. Census Bureau.

FEAR ITSELF

Scary Guys

Yes *guys*! Since no females made the list of who we really are scared of, though no gender was applied to the question. A recent poll indicates that fear is linked to a concern over the amount of power people wield—or have the potential to wield—and what they may do with that power. The poll indicated that Hillary Clinton, who has no specific executive duties, is feared by a significant portion of the American populace. The first lady ranks fourth overall in a recent poll of the most feared public figures. The poll's results differ widely from women to men. Women fear conservative Republicans who wield actual power over such issues as abortion rights and workplace equality much more than they do the First Lady; in contrast, Ms. Clinton ranks third overall among male respondents. Following are the percentages of poll respondents who fear various public figures as indicated by their answer to the question:
"What one public figure do you find the most frightening?"

Most Feared	Percent*
1. Newt Gingrich	11.02%
2. Bill Clinton	7.86%
3. Pat Buchanan	6.83%
4. Hillary Clinton	5.81%
5. O.J. Simpson	4.11%
6. Louis Farrakhan	3.70%
7. Rush Limbaugh	3.12%

8. Phil Gramm 2.63%
9. Jesse Helms 2.63%
10. Dick Gephardt 1.85%
* data is compiled from all poll respondants

Source: The Peoplepedia Opinion Poll, 1996.

FOOTBALL COACHES, COLLEGE

Greatest College Football Coaches of All Time

To qualify for our ranking of the best college football coaches of all time, a coach had to first accrue more than 200 wins, a bench mark adjudged as the threshold of greatness. That narrowed the crop down to 15; not surprisingly, no college coach with 200 wins has a losing record. We then ranked the qualifiers by overall winning percentage. Longtime Nebraska coach Tom Osborne comes out on top by this measure; in his 23 years of coaching in Lincoln, his Cornhuskers have won more than 80 percent of their games. That's better than Joe Paterno, Bear Bryant, Woody Hayes or any other great name in college coaching. And yes, Osborne does have a national championship; his Huskers won the title in both 1994 and 1995. These, then, are the top 10 college football coaches.

Coach	Wins	Winning %
1. Tom Osborne	231	.827
2. Joe Paterno	278	.792
3. Paul (Bear) Bryant	323	.780
4. Bo Schembechler	234	.775
5. Woody Hayes	238	.759
6. Bobby Bowden	259	.759
7. Glenn (Pop) Warner	319	.733
8. LaVell Edwards	214	.726
9. Vince Dooley	201	.715

10. Lou Holtz 208 .689
* scores based on data up to 1996
Source: *Best and Worst* original.

FOOTBALL COACHES, COLLEGE

Most Wins, as Percent of Games Played

The previous entry dealt with coaches who won more than 200 games. Here we look at coaches overall. Winning percentage is the best measure of success, but Knute Rockne's position atop the rankings is secured by more than that. Notre Dame's domination of the college game during most of this century traces directly to the pioneering efforts of Rockne and those of his disciple, Frank Leahy, who played tackle on Rockne's last three teams in South Bend. The Fighting Irish won six national championships and put together five unbeaten and untied seasons under "Rock." He not only helped popularize the sport by making Notre Dame the first team to play a national schedule, but he also helped change the way it was played. Rockne often used his so-called "shock troops," a full team of second stringers, at the start of games, presaging the day of two-platoon systems. Imitating the precision and timing of a chorus line, he put his backfield in motion before the snap of the ball, a scheme that would be outlawed by the rulemakers of his day, but eventually accepted and employed by just about every team, college and pro, playing the game today. He recognized the potential of the forward pass, then in its infancy, and used it to great advantage while most of his counterparts stubbornly kept the ball on the ground. Rockne was inducted into the National Football Foundation Hall of Fame in 1952, the first year of induction. For all their fame, none of the first five names on the all-time coaching victories list—Paul "Bear" Bryant (323 wins); Amos Alonzo Stagg (314); Glenn "Pop" Warner, 313; Wayne "Woody" Hayes (238); and Glenn "Bo" Schembechler (234)—managed to crack the list of top winning percentages.

Coach	Winning Pct.
1. Knute Rockne	.881
2. Frank Leahy	.864
3. George Woodruff	.846
4. Barry Switzer	.837
5. Percy Haughton	.832
6. Robert Neyland	.829
7. Fielding Yost	.828
8. Bud Wilkinson	.826
9. John Sutherland	.812
10. Tom Osborne	.809

FOOTBALL COACHES

Greatest NFL Coaches of All Time

The Green Bay Packers' Super Bowl XXXI victory warmed the hearts of many football fans, not only because Green Bay is the smallest town in the NFL, but because it heralded a return to the team's glory days, the 1960s, when Vince Lombardi's powerhouse clubs won five football championships, including the first two Super Bowls. Indeed, in our rating of NFL coaches, Lombardi comes out on top, besting even legendary Chicago Bears coach George Halas. The rating below is a coach's career winning percentage (times 1000) plus the number of league champi-

GREATEST NFL COACH OF ALL TIME, Knute Rockne.

onships won (times 100); it thus rewards success both in the regular season and when it matters most, with a title on the line. To qualify, coaches had to have at least 100 wins. Here are the NFL's all-time best coaches:

Coach	Winning%	Titles	Score
1. Vince Lombardi	.740	5	1240
2. George Halas	671	5	1171
3. Paul Brown	609	4	1009
4. Joe Gibbs	.683	3	983
5. Chuck Noll	.572	4	972
6. Don Shula	.665	3	965
7. Curly Lambeau	.623	3	923
8. Bill Walsh	.617	3	917
9. John Madden	.731	1	831

10. Weeb Ewbank

.507   3   807

* scores based on data up to 1996

Source: *Best and Worst* original.

FOOTBALL PLAYERS

Greatest Players of All Time

Today's football fans should consider themselves lucky—over the past decade they've been able to watch four of the greatest players in the history of the game compete at the same time. The NFL's explosion in offense since the mid-1980s has come courtesy of players like Emmitt Smith of the Dallas Cowboys, Barry Sanders of the Detroit Lions, Thurman Thomas of the Buffalo Bills and the San Francisco 49ers' incomparable wide receiver, Jerry Rice. These four are among the six most productive offensive players the game has seen, judged by total yardage per season. In Smith's seven NFL seasons through 1996, he has averaged 1,766 yards rushing, receiving and returning the ball. Sanders is just behind him over his eight years. Both stand a chance of breaking Walter Payton's all-time total yardage record in the next five seasons. These are the greatest offensive players in NFL history, judged by productivity:

Player	Seasons/Yds.	Yds./Season
1. Emmitt Smith		**1,766**
7	12,360	
2. Barry Sanders		**1,756**
8	14,052	
3. Jim Brown		**1,742**
9	15,676	
4. Walter Payton		**1,677**
13	21,803	
5. Thurman Thomas		**1,626**
9	14,638	
6. Jerry Rice		**1,417**
12	17,007	
7. Eric Dickerson		**1,405**
11	15,459	
8. Tony Dorsett		**1,361**
12	16,326	
9. Gale Sayers		**1,348**
7	9,435	
10. O.J. Simpson		**1,306**
11	14,368	

Source: *Best and Worst* original.

FOOTBALL PLAYERS

Highest Paid

One can only wonder why the best football players earn so little compared to their counterparts in other sports; that is, if you consider $5 million "little." There are several factors at work, one of which is the NFL policy dictating that teams must, in some instances, determine a player's salary with a formula based on what other teams pay. This "franchise/transition" system is explained in the entry immediately following, which is concerned with pay by positions. The other factor is simply that NFL teams don't play as many games as teams in other sports. The regular season in the NFL consists of only 16 games—contrast that with the NBA's 82 games and Major League Baseball's 144. Hence, NFL team owners just don't have the revenue stream that owners in other sports do. Football stars, however, supplement their salaries with endorsements in a fashion that far exceeds athletes in other sports. Nonetheless, paychecks in the NFL—for the stars as well as the regular starters—aren't too shabby. Below are the top earners in the sport.

Player/Team	1996 Salary
1.Troy Aikman Dallas Cowboys	$5.371 million
2. Dan Marino Miami Dolphins	$5.327 million
3. Steve Young San Francisco 49ers	$4.975 million
4. Scott Mitchell Detroit Lions	$4.317 million
5. John Elway Denver Broncos	$4.266 million
6. Brett Favre Green Bay Packers	$4.175 million
7. Drew Bledsoe New England Patriots	$4.093 million
8. Barry Sanders Detroit Lions	$4.347 million
9. Emmitt Smith Dallas Cowboys	$4.001 million
10. Troy Vincent Philadelphia Eagles	$4.600 million

Source: SportsLine USA, NewsWire, February 14, 1997.

FOOTBALL PLAYERS

Greatest Quarterbacks of All Time

There are many ways to measure an NFL quarterback's performance. The NFL's convoluted "passer rating" system takes the three standard figures—touchdowns, total passing yards and completion percentage—plus a quarterback's interception percentage, and combines the stats using a near-mystical algorithm to produce a quarterback's rating. Although the formula does a decent job of evaluating a quarterback's efficiency—i.e., his ability to complete passes, avoid interceptions and score—it fails to take into account other aspects of a field general's job: directing the offense to the prime objective, a victory. As a

result, numerous mundane quarterbacks—Neil Lomax? Dave Krieg?—appear on the top 20 "passer rating" list, while Hall of Famers such as Bart Starr, Terry Bradshaw and Johnny Unitas are far down the list. Our system employs the NFL's passer rating, but goes a step further by incorporating the purest measure of a quarterback's leadership skills: his ability to direct his team to the NFL championship game, and win it. The scores below are the sum of a quarterback's career passer rating, plus his league championship or Super Bowl appearances (times three) and championship victories (times eight). These are the NFL's best:

Rating	CA [1]	CW [2]	Score*
1. Joe Montana			136.3
92.3	4	4	
2. Bart Starr			135.5
80.5	5	5	
3. Otto Graham			128.6
86.6	6	3	
4. Terry Bradshaw			116.6
72.6	4	4	
5. Troy Aikman			116.0
83.0	3	3	
6. Johnny Unitas			114.2
78.2	4	3	
7. Roger Staubach			111.4
83.4	4	2	
8. Sid Luckman			108.1
61.1	5	4	
9. Steve Young			107.2
96.2	1	1	
10. Sammy Baugh			103.3
72.3	5	2	

* scores based on data up to 1996
[1] CA: league championship game or Super Bowl appearances
[2] CW: league championship or Super Bowl victories

Source: *Best and Worst* original.

FOOTBALL PLAYERS

Pay By Position

As if the game wasn't complicated enough, pay scales are even worse. The National Football League has set a minimum pay scale based on average earnings of the top players in the sport. There are two designations: "Franchise Players" and "Transition Players." Franchise Players are free agents who cannot get paid less than the top-five players at their position in the NFL. Transition Players are also free agents who cannot get paid less than the top-10 players at their positions. Below is a list of the minimum that each designation can earn.

PAYSCALES (millions)

Position	Franchise	Transition
Quarterback	$4.851	$4.365
Runningback	$3.086	$2.553
Wide Receiver	$2.774	$2.450
Tight End	$1.515	$1.360
Offensive Line	$3.037	$2.800
Defensive End	$3.182	$2.974
Defensive Tackle	$2.792	$2.502
Linebacker	$3.448	$3.131
Cornerback	$3.362	$2.787
Safety	$2.420	$2.094
Punter/Kicker	$0.869	$0.778

Source: NFL Players Association, 1997.

FOOTBALL PLAYERS

Greatest Wide Receivers of All Time

Our rating of NFL receivers takes into account receptions, yardage and touchdown catches—but any way you combine the numbers, the San Francisco 49ers' Jerry Rice will come out on top. In his 12 NFL seasons, Rice has shattered the records for career receptions, receiving yards and touchdowns; by the time he hangs up his spikes, he most likely will have scored a once-unthinkable 200 touchdowns. Our formula is the sum of three receiving factors: average receptions per season, average yards per catch (times five) and career touchdowns. Though Rice's per-catch yardage mark is unspectacular (New York Jets legend Don Maynard is highest among the top 20 all-time receivers), his uncanny knack for hauling in the ball and his undying determination to reach the endzone set him far above the rest of the receiving pack. Here are the NFL's 10 all-time best wide receivers.

Yrs./Recs./Yds./Avg./TDs	Score *
1. Jerry Rice	**319.5**
12 1050 16,377 15.6 154	
2. Steve Largent	**238.5**
14 819 13,089 16.0 100	
3. Don Maynard	**223.7**
15 633 11,834 18.7 88	
4. Sterling Sharpe	**218.5**
7 595 8,134 13.7 65	
5. James Lofton	**214.3**
16 764 14,004 18.3 75	
6. Andre Reed	**209.8**
12 766 10,884 14.2 75	
7. Gary Clark	**206.0**
11 699 10,856 15.5 65	
8. Cris Carter	**205.2**
10 667 8,367 12.5 76	
9. Henry Ellard	**201.4**
14 775 13,177 17.0 61	
10. Charley Taylor	**198.9**
13 649 9,110 14.0 79	

* scores based on data up to 1996

Source: *Best and Worst* original.

GENERALS, THE BEST

Greatest Generals of All Time

History's greatest generals proved to be masters not only of war, but of politics as well. Since the dawn of mankind, the safety and prosperity of one's tribe has always been of utmost importance. The art of generalship stems from this very principle, with the strongest individual rising to the leadership position. As civilized societies began forming, strength of body was no longer enough. Leaders had to have strength of will as well. With this in mind, the generals rated on this list were judged according to the following criteria: battles won, territory captured and secured, and the legacy they left behind. Alexander the Great emerges as the best general. Representing the society and culture of Greece, he captured and securely established great swaths of territory. Sweeping into the Persian empire, Alexander took over much of Egypt and India. The stamp he left has reverberated through history and still affects us today. (Is there not a current debate about "core" curriculums which still employ texts on Greek philosophy and ideas? Not to mention our system of democratic government, which also finds its origins in early Greek culture). By conquering and assimilating other cultures (rather than attempting to subjugate them), Alexander not only influenced his immediate subjects (he did become king), but also history itself.

GREATEST GENERAL OF ALL TIME, Alexander The Great.

Rank/General/Major Accomplishment

1. **Alexander the Great**
   Defeats Persian Forces, assimilates populations, fundamental in the spread and persistence of Greek cultural and political traditions.

2. **Napoleon Bonaparte**
   Gains control of France after leading revolutionary armies against rest of Europe; masterful tactics in Battle of Austerlitz leaves him de facto ruler of Europe; only his own ego defeats him in vain attack on Russia. Nearly regains European dominion at Waterloo.

3. **Ulysses S. Grant**
   First "modern" general. Created the "American way of war"—destruction of enemy's warmaking capability. Realized the power of the Union's industrial and manpower resources. Eschewed nonsense of "accepted" theories. Hard-headed refusal to accept or admit defeat results in victory over Lee's armies.

ONE OF THE GREATEST GENERALS OF ALL TIME (at left), Robert E. Lee.

4. Duke of Wellington
Defeats Napoleonic forces in Spain. At Waterloo, maintains cool head and defeats Napoleon himself. Claims "the Battle of Waterloo was won on the playing fields of Eton."

5. Hannibal
Master tactician in the mold of Alexander. Pincers envelopment of enemy at Cannae achieved one of the most remarkable victories in the history of warfare. Greatest achievement for any general to this day is to win his own "Cannae."

6. King Henry V
Victor at Battle of Agincourt, stunning defeat of French. Henry forces French into ill-conceived attack for which English forces, a mere one-fifth the size of the French, are well-prepared and entrenched. Casualties: several dozen English, several thousand French.

7. George Washington
Against great odds, unites colonies and inspires American Revolutionary forces to victory over British. First American President.

8. Erwin Rommel
First, and perhaps greatest, master of tank warfare. Daunted Allies throughout Second World War. Lead German spearhead through France; commanded vaunted "Afrika Korps." Respected even by foes.

9. George S. Patton
Charismatic American General in WWII. Disengages entire army in midst of major battle, turns 90 degrees and travels 100 miles in 48 hours to relieve besieged Bastogne during Battle of Bulge.

10. Robert E. Lee
A great leader of men, even in defeat by the better-equipped North. Consistent victories over numerically superior Northern forces in-

clude Chancellorsville, where he divides his forces, and, with Stonewall Jackson, rolls up the staggered Union General Hooker's right.

Source: *Best and Worst* original.

GENERALS, THE WORST

Worst Generals of All Time

A bad commander is the worst possible thing to inflict on a corps of soldiers. It is said that some men are born mediocre, some men rise to mediocrity and other men have mediocrity thrust upon them. The following generals have gone down in history as the worst figures at the head of an army. Not only are all of them losers of battles, many either died (some by their own hands) or were relieved of command so they could not inflict further damage on their own forces.

Rank/General/Major Blunder

1. **Marcus L. Crassus (c. 115-53 BC)** Lost two-fifths of force of 50,000 and was himself killed in a single battle in the Roman-Parthian War.
2. **Philip VI of France (1293-1350)** Loses 4,000 (one-third of his force) to a mere 100 English in the Battle of Crecy.
3. **Horatio Gates (c. 1728-1806)** More concerned with politics than command. Ineffective leader, his underlings took charge (luckily); later relieved of command.
4. **William H. Winder (1775-1824)** Battle of Stony Creek, snatches failure from the jaws of victory, loses battle with three to one advantage over foe.
5. **A. Lopez de Santa Anna (1795-1876)** Lost two wars for Mexico. In Mexican-American War, lost every battle he waged.
6. **George McClellan (1826-1885)** Diminutive commander of Union Army for first two years of Civil War. "Little Napoleon" turns out to be Big Chicken, continually overestimating opposing Confederate forces by factors of two to three. Indecisiveness and inability to take risks led to decisive defeat to Lee in Peninsular Campaign, and draw at Antietam; does not pursue weak and vulnerable Southern forces after that battle; relieved of command by Lincoln.
7. **Sir Ian Hamilton (1853-1947)** Losing commander at Gallipoli, one of the bloodiest battles in WWI; 250,000 dead/wounded.
8. **Robert Nivelle (1856-1924)** Continues to order fruitless attacks in WWI. Relieved of command.
9. **Aleksander Samsonov (1859-1914)** Beaureaucrat thrust into command. Hopelessly confused, loses battle of Tannenberg and commits suicide.
10. **Maurice Gamelin (1872-1958)** Held Maginot Line believing the Blitzkrieg was a "diversion." Bad call, Germany overruns France.

Source: *Book of Lists*.

GOLFERS, MALE

Top-Earning Men

"The Shark," Australian Greg Norman, topped the list of golf's super winners for many years, though he was not as dominant as his predecessors of the 1970s and '80s, Jack Nicklaus and Arnold Palmer. Last year Norman didn't even make the top 10. Whatever the future holds for golf, one thing is clear—in 1997, and perhaps for many years thereafter, a new name, Tiger Woods, will be at or near the top of the list of money winners. The following list, then, is likely to be the last of the millennia in which Woods' name does not appear.

Player	Earnings, 1996
1. Tom Lehman	$1,780,159
2. Phil Mickelson	$1,699,799
3. Mark Brooks	$1,429,396
4. Steve Stricker	$1,383,739
5. Mark O'Meara	$1,255,749
6. Fred Couples	$1,248,694
7. Davis Love III	$1,211,139
8. Brad Faxon	$1,055,050
9. Scott Hoch	$1,039,564
10. David Duval	$977,079

Source: PGA, 1997.

GOLFERS, FEMALE

Top-Earning Women

For many years no one came even close to Beth Daniel, who in 1990 won an astonishing $863,578. Back then, most followers of the sport thought it was a foregone conclusion that very soon, some lucky lady would surpass the magic mark of a million dollars. In ensuing years, the top-earning women of golf didn't even come close . . . until Karie Webb got hot. In 1996, Webb broke the barrier, though just barely.

Player	Earnings, 1996
1. Karie Webb	$1,002,000
2. Laura Davies	$927,302
3. Annika Sorenstam	$808,311
4. Liselotte Neumann	$625,633
5. Dottie Pepper	$589,401
6. Kelly Robbins	$562,458
7. Meg Mallon	$510,209
8. Michelle McGunn	$498,561
9. Emilee Klein	$463,793
10. Val Skinner	$413,419

Source: LPGA, 1997.

GOOD LOOKS

The Family Beauty Contest

Vanity, vanity. All is vanity. When asked who the most attractive member of the family is, the largest number of respondents among both sexes, 11 percent, maintained *they* were. Among female respondents, twice as many, 20 percent, answered that they were the best-looking member of the family. Vanity, we have long been told, is one of seven deadly sins. A more current theory espoused by psychologists is that a strong self-image is essential for good mental health. However, Americans may have taken the idea of a positive self-image a bit overboard. At least that's what a recent Internet poll suggests. The tabulations that follow represent the percentage of poll respondents who gave the following answers to the question:
"Which one family member is the best looking?"

MOST VOTES

Fam. Member	% Voted Best-looking
1. Self/Me	11.14%
2. Brother	10.00%
3. Wife	8.93%
4. Sister	8.85%
5. Daughter	7.32%
6. No answer	5.35%
7. Cousin	4.89%
8. Husband	3.82%
9. Mother	3.50%
10. No one	2.14%

LEAST VOTES*

Fam. Member	% Voted Best-looking
1. Father	1.94%
2. Son	1.44%
3. Brother-in-Law	1.07%

4. Niece	0.58%
5. Uncle	0.49%
Children	0.49%
Nephew	0.49%
8. Equal	0.29%
Grandmother	0.29%
Other relative	0.29%
Sister-in-Law	0.29%

* list is in descending order

Source: The Peoplepedia Opinion Poll, 1996.

Gurus

Who Can You Trust?

Is a "guru" really someone who can advise you? Especially when it comes to things like money? Yes, according to the *Economist*, one of the most respected financial magazines in the world. The British-based publication believes in gurus and thinks those who follow financial markets should too. The magazine maintains that gurus do, in fact, impact the outcome of investments and global markets. But what makes a guru? According to the *Economist*, gurus tend to come from a variety of fields and disciplines; they also have "follow power," which is what economics is all about. In measuring the gurus' power, *The Economist*, looked at four basic characteristics: *Influence, Originality, Intellectual Coherence* and *Devotion of Followers*. *The Economist* rates each of these traits on a scale of 1 to 5, with 5 being the high end. Below are their results. The "Points" immediately below the gurus' names represent—in order—the measurements for the four previously stated criteria.

MOST TRUSTED "GURU" OF ALL when it comes to matters concerning the economy, Milton Friedman. Photo: University of Chicago-News Office.

Rank/ Individual	Score
1. Milton Friedman	**20**

Points: 5, 5, 5, 5
Often cited as the "greatest economist in the 20th century," Dr. Friedman is the father of "monetarism"; a top debater, speaker, teacher and best-selling author; the originator of a monetary ideology that impacted the world, especially in the 1980s.

2. Peter Drucker	**17**

Points: 5, 5, 4, 3
Notable author credited with "virtually inventing the serious study of management." Central European immigrant to the U.S., first published in 1939.

3. Edward Teller	**15**

Points: 3, 4, 3, 5
Physicist participant in Hydrogen Bomb creation; leader in weapons laboratory development (Lawrence Livermore); spreading ideas and influencing policy.

Jeffrey Sachs	**15**

Points: 5, 3, 5, 2

Foreign government advisor; advocate of "shock therapy" economics in Poland and Russia; Harvard University economist.

5. Jacques Derrida   14
Points: 5, 4, 0, 5
French academic noted as "father of deconstruction"; attacker of hierarchy of "great books" giving strength to "empowering" minorities idea; leading voice in "political correctness."

Octavio Paz   14
Points: 2, 5, 4, 3
Nobel winner for literature; former ambassador to India; poet/intellectual, leading Latin American voice against repressive regimes.

Lee Kuan Yew   14
Points: 4, 3, 4, 3
Former Prime Minister of Singapore; strong Asian voice for autocrats and anti-welfare state ideology.

Rush Limbaugh   14
Points 5, 1, 3, 5
Populist conservative broadcaster/best-selling writer, weekly audience of over 20 million.

9. Ayn Rand   13
Points: 3, 3, 2, 5
Best-selling author; institute founder promoting strength of individualism and capitalism as positive world forces.

Sathya Sai Baba   13
Points: 5, 2, 1, 5
True and Holy Father in India, message of "peace and love" spreading without his traveling worldwide; outlived or outpaced critics, currently wealthy philanthropist.

Michael Porter   13
Points: 4, 3, 3, 3
Energetic management lecturer/writer, notable thrust on changing globalization & technological issues that reshape the gauging of businesses.

Nicholas Negroponte   13
Points: 4, 3, 4, 2

Founder and director of M.I.T. media lab; prescient advocate of multimedia computing (in 1975!), futuristic researcher and shaper in the converging technologies of phone-TV- computer.

13. Tom Peters   12
Points: 3, 2, 2, 5
Management lecturer/best selling writer, currently commands $50,000 lecture fees; notable work: "In Search of Excellence."

14. Kenichi Ohmae   11
Points: 2, 4, 3, 2
Best-selling author's "The Mind of the Strategist" introduced the West to Japan's art of business practice.

15. George Soros   10
Points: 5, 1, 1, 3
Billionaire investor, created "Quantum fund," reputation as "man who broke the Bank of England."

16. Vaclav Havel   9
Points: 1, 2, 2, 4
Philosopher/playwright/poet currently leading Czech Republic, former imprisoned dissident, noted for calm decency handling the "velvet divorce" between Czech and Slovak republics.

17. Noam Chomsky   8
Points: 1, 2, 1, 4
Celebrated professor of linguistics; leading voice of the "left"; critic of ruling government and corporate elite, promulgator of "multinationals control the world" idea.

Source: *The Economist*, January 7, 1994.

HOCKEY COACHES

Greatest Coaches of All Time

To evaluate the all-time greatest NHL coaches, the editors multiplied the coach's winning percentage by 1000 and the number of Stanley Cups the coach won in his career by 100, then added the two numbers together for an overall score. Using this formula—which rewards regular-season excellence and postseason success in equal parts—the top-rated coach of all-time turns out to be, not surprisingly, associated with the Montreal Canadiens. Toe Blake coached the fabled Habs to a remarkable eight NHL championships during his 14 seasons behind the bench. Following are the top 10 coaches of all time, according to the formula.

Coach/Pct.	Cups	Score
1. Toe Blake		
.634	8	1434
2. Scott Bowman		
.663	6	1263
3. Hap Day		
.549	5	1049
4. Glen Sather		
.616	4	1016
5. Al Arbour		
.564	4	964
6. Dick Irvin		
.559	4	959
7. Pete Green		
.656	3	956
8. Punch Imlach		
.534	4	934
9. Tommy Ivan		
.587	3	883
10. Jack Adams		
.513	3	813

Source: *Best and Worst* original.

HOCKEY PLAYERS

Highest Paid

With "the Great One," Wayne Gretzky, past his peak, a new name dominates hockey, or at least the Pittsburgh Penguins' payroll—Mario Lemieux. His astronomical $11 million salary was well-earned, however. Though he hasn't even come close to Gretzky's record 92 goals in one season,

Lemieux has many things to boast about; for one, having a salary that is almost double the number-two man in the NHL. Money aside, "Super Mario's" 1996 league-leading figures include the most points scored (161), the most goals (69), the most power-play goals (31) and the most shorthanded goals (8). And Lemieux has one other achievement that no one in the sport can lay claim to—he earns over twice as much as the Great One, whose earnings fell to number three last season.

Player/Team	Salary
1. Mario Lemieux	**$11,321,429**
Pittsburgh Penguins	
2. Mark Messier	**$6,000,000**
New York Rangers	
3. Wayne Gretzky	**$5,047,500**
New York Rangers	
4. Pavel Bure	**$5,000,000**
Vancouver Canucks	
5. Pat LaFontaine	**$4,600,000**
Buffalo Sabres	
6. Steve Yzerman	**$4,492,349**
Detroit Red Wings	
7. Patrick Roy	**$4,455,944**
Colorado Avalanche	
8. Brett Hull	**$4,400,000**
St. Louis Blues	
9. Dominik Hasek	**$4,200,000**
Buffalo Sabres	
10. Sergi Fedorov	**$4,200,000**
Detroit Red Wings	

* figures are for 1996-97 season
Source: National Hockey League Players Association, 1997.

INTELLIGENCE

Who Gets the Votes for Brains?

America has always respected those with knowledge, be they public figures, friends or family members. But who do Americans think are the smartest? A recent public opinion poll sought to find out for sure. According to the results, Americans believe the most intelligent public figures are the proven movers and shakers, whether they're loved or vilified—Newt Gingrich, Colin Powell and Hillary Clinton, to name a few. Within the family, however, Americans voted for *themselves* as the smartest. According to the tally of male responses, the top three votes for the "most intelligent family member"are males: self/me, father and brother, respectively. According to females polled, their mothers' intellect was not highly esteemed—mother ranked 14th among women who voted. Only 1.33 percent thought mom was the smartest in the family, which places the father's rank in the family almost 20 times higher. Following are the percentage of poll respondents who gave the following answers to the question: *"What one public figure is the most intelligent?"*

SMARTEST PUBLIC FIGURES

Individual	Percent of Votes
1. Newt Gingrich	9.10%
2. Colin Powell	5.50%
3. Hillary Clinton	4.81%
4. Bill Clinton	3.91%
5. Rush Limbaugh	3.50%
6. Bill Gates	3.21%
7. Stephen Hawking	2.14%
8. Jimmy Carter	1.77%
9. Bob Dole	1.48%
10. Al Gore	1.48%

Other pubic figures who made the list include Noam Chomsky (1.07%), William Bennett (0.87%), William Buckley (0.87%) and Ralph Nader (0.58%).

SMARTEST FAMILY MEMBERS

Individual	Percent of Votes
1. Self/Me	15.30%
2. Father	15.13%
3. Brother	6.67%
4. No answer	6.13%
5. Sister	5.26%
6. Husband	3.99%
7. Mother	3.09%
8. Son	2.63%
9. Uncle	2.55%
10. Grandfather	2.26%

Source: The Peoplepedia Opinion Poll, 1996.

LIARS IN THE FAMILY

The Biblical brothers Jacob and Esau vied with each other, and distrust between siblings apparently didn't stop there, according to the findings of a recent Internet poll. The poll asked which family member is most likely to tell a lie. Brothers and sisters topped the list of both male and female respondents. Could it be due to battles over who broke the vase or put the dent in the family car? On a positive note, a good number of respondents— nearly nine percent—said no one in the family is most likely to tell a lie, making it the third most frequent response regarding the issue of familial deception. The following tabulations represent the percentage of poll respondents who gave the following answers to the question: *"Which family member is most likely to tell you a lie?"*

Liar	Percent of Votes
1. Brother	18.02%

2. Sister	10.04%
3. No One	8.56%
4. Mother	7.32%
5. No Answer	6.13%
6. Son	3.99%
7. Father	3.82%
8. Daughter	3.70%
9. Self/Me	1.56%
10.Cousin	1.44%

Source: The Peoplepedia Opinion Poll, 1996.

MOVIE STARS

Highest Paid per Film

For better or worse, the movie industry is a fair reflection of society—both have been reluctant to fully embrace the Equal Rights Amendment. According to box office receipts, Arnold Schwarzenegger's *Terminator* was more popular than Demi Moore's *Striptease*, and in the bottom line-based brain of Hollywood, that means Arnold is worth more than Demi. However, even when an actress's movies are more popular than those of her male counterpart, she'll still make less than him. Go figure. The following are estimates of what the top ten stars command for a picture. Note that some stars, in addition to the base pay shown here, also have deals that give them a percentage of the movie profits; although how much Stallone's recent duds will yield the Italian Stallion is hard to determine.

HIGHEST PAID ACTORS

Actor	Pay per Film (millions)
1. Jim Carrey	$20.0
Arnold Schwarzenegger	$20.0
Mel Gibson	$20.0
Sylvester Stallone	$20.0
Harrison Ford	$20.0
Tom Cruise	$20.0
7. John Travolta	$17.0
8. Bruce Willis	$16.5
9. Robin Williams	$15.0
Kurt Russell	$15.0

HIGHEST PAID ACTRESSES

Actress	Pay per Film (millions)
1. Demi Moore	$12.5
2. Julia Roberts	$12.0
3. Sandra Bullock	$10.5
4. Whoopi Goldberg	$10.0
Whitney Houston	$10.0
6. Jodie Foster	$9.0
Michelle Pfeiffer	$9.0
8. Meg Ryan	$8.0
9. Sharon Stone	$7.0
10. Alicia Silverstone	$5.0

Source: *Premiere* magazine, 1996.

OLYMPIANS, AMERICAN

Greatest of All Time

Mark Spitz and Carl Lewis are tied for most gold medals by an American Olympian, but Spitz outdistances Lewis by three points in our ratings thanks to his one bronze medal. If Lewis had run in the 4x100 relay in Atlanta in 1996 and picked up a silver with the U.S. team, he would have passed Spitz to become the most decorated American Olympian. Following are the Americans with at least 50 points on our Olympic rating system (10 points for gold, five for silver, three for bronze).

	Gold	Silver	Bronze	Score
1. Mark Spitz– Swimming				
	9	1	1	98
2. Carl Lewis—Track				
	9	1	0	95
3. Matt Biondi—Swimming				
	8	2	1	93

4. Carl Osburn—Shooting

5	4	2	76

5. Jenny Thompson—Swimming

5	0	0	50

Shirley Babashoff—Swimming

2	6	0	50

Bonnie Blair—Speed Skating

5	0	0	50

Eric Heiden—Speed Skating

5	0	0	50

Source: *Best and Worst* original.

OLYMPIANS, INTERNATIONAL

Greatest of All Time

Of all the great athletes to partake in the Olympic Games, both summer and winter, the most decorated is a woman from the Ukraine, gymnast Larissa Latynina. In three Olympic Games—1956 in Melbourne, 1960 in Rome and 1964 in Tokyo—she won a record total of 18 medals, including nine golds. The greatest Olympian not involved in gymnastics or swimming is Finnish distance runner Paavo Nurmi, who earned nine gold medals in the 1920s. The top American is swimmer Mark Spitz, who earned nine golds, including a record seven at Munich in 1972, plus a silver and a bronze. Our rating awards 10 points for gold, five for silver and three for bronze. Latynina's overall score for her nine golds, five silvers and four bronzes comes to 127.

Gold	Silver	Bronze	Score

1. Larissa Latynina, USSR
Gymnastics

9	5	4	127

2. Vera Caslavska, Czech
Gymnastics

7	4	10	120

3. Paavo Nurmi, Finland
Track

9	3	0	105

4. Nikolai Andrianov, USSR
Gymnastics

7	53	104

5. Mark Spitz, USA
Swimming

9	1	1	98

Sawao Kato, Japan
Gymnastics

8	3	1	98

7. Boris Shakhlin, USSR
Gymnastics

7	4	2	96

8. Carl Lewis, USA
Track

9	1	0	95

9. Matt Biondi, USA
Swimming

8	2	1	93

10. Edoardo Mangiarotti, Italy
Fencing

6	5	2	91

Source: *Best and Worst* original.

PHILOSOPHERS

Top Modern-Day Philosophers

For all its dubious merit, the literary-philosophical theory of deconstruction, developed by the French philosopher Jacques Derrida, has been perhaps the most influential philosophical idea of the post-war era. Derrida's concept—i.e., that a reader's response to a text, as opposed to the author's intentions when writing the text, is the real element for philosophical analysis—has been expanded to a wide range of other critical fields, from literature, art and architecture to political science and law. Thus, though Anglo-American academic philosophers would hesitate to include Derrida among their ranks, he is, according to our formula, the most influential living philosopher in the world. Our rating method is based on an analysis of the Arts and Humanities citation index. Interestingly, accompanying Derrida at the top of the list are two more philosophical gadflies—Noam Chomsky and Richard Rorty. We hesitate to include Chomsky on this list, since his philosophical output in the last decade has declined considerably, as he pursues ever more entrenched left-wing political causes. Yet, since Chomsky has written some of the most influential treatises on philosophy and linguistics, the final decision was for inclusion on this list of philosophers. Of the Anglo-American philosophers working within the traditions of 20th-century mathematico-linguistic philosophy, the leader is David Lewis, whose main tenet is that of modal realism: the idea that our world and its inhabitants are only one of an infinite number of worlds containing an infinite number of conceivable objects that actually exist; or, as Lewis puts it, "There are so many worlds, in fact, that absolutely *every* way that a world could possibly be is a way that some world in fact *is*."

Philosopher	Score
1. Jacques Derrida	405
2. Noam Chomsky	284
3. Richard Rorty	178
4. David Lewis	118
5. Paul Ricoeur	108
6. John Rawls	104
7. Donald Davidson	99
8. Nelson Goodman	83
9. Thomas Nagel	76
10. Bernard Williams	74

Source: *Best and Worst* original.

PLAYBOY PLAYMATES

May the Best Man Win Her Over

Controversial though the magazine may be in some circles, *Playboy* has changed how American men think about and act around women. More than any other periodical, men have read it for years to get insight into what turns their "dream girl" on or off; that is, if they could only get a date with *that* ideal woman—a playmate. What male hasn't fantasized about a date with one? Or even just a "cover girl;" that is, if she's on the cover of *Playboy*. In your wildest dreams the naked nymph would surely be putty in your hands. But that's in your dreams. What would *really* happen if you got a date with one? Would you turn her

WHAT TURNS HER ON? The magazine above may have some answers.

on, or turn her off? That depends what you'd do or say on your date. Some things will really light her up. Other things will repulse her. The original mission to find out what will do which was the idea of the editors of *Spy*, a humor magazine that analyzed centerfolds' likes and dislikes based on the text that accompanied their pictorials. In addition to determining what turned them on or off, they also averaged the girls' vital statistics. In the 1990 analysis, they found the average height was 5' 6"; weight 113 lbs.; and the impressive measurements 35-23-34. More recently in 1996, *Playboy* did their own analysis of top turn-ons and -offs of playmates. Following is a list men should put in their pocket next time they have a date with one. Consult it frequently on your date, it will increase your chances of being a hit, as opposed to striking out.

TOP TURN-ONS

Rank/Turn-on

1. Music
2. Animals
3. Eating
4. Clothes
5. The beach
6. Dancing,
   Speed (tied with dancing)
8. Rain or thunderstorms
9. Flowers
   Sense of humor (tied with flowers)

TOP TURN-OFFS

Rank/Turn-on

1. Egotists
2. Liars
3. Jealousy
4. Rudeness
5. Getting up early, tobacco (tie)
7. Pollution
8. Traffic

9. Waiting
10. Judgmental people
Source: *Playboy* Magazine, November, 1996.

PROTESTANTS

If you think the Catholic Church is complicated with a saint for this, and saint for that (not to mention rules for about everything from sex to how you're supposed to get to heaven), try to figure out what's what among Protestants. There are approximately 200 denominations in America. Twenty-one preach the Baptist faith, 14 the Methodist, 30 the Pentecostal, 14 the Lutheran and four the Latter-Day Saints. Total membership in Protestant churches in the U.S. is approximately 101.4 million in 337,556 congregations. And that's the easy part. Among Baptist churches, the Southern Baptist Convention is the largest Protestant church in the country, with 15 million members. It has 37,922 local congregations and 124,316 clergy. Three of its churches—the National Baptist Convention, USA, Inc. (7.8 million members), the National Baptist Convention of America (7.8 million members) and the Progressive National Baptist Convention (2.7 million)—are predominantly black churches. Together, the three black churches account for more black churchgoers than any other family of churches. Now, for the Methodists: the United Methodist Church counts 8.9 million members, more than two-thirds of the family's total membership. Its two "African" churches, with a total of 3.4 million members account for almost all of the remaining third of the group. And the Pentecostals? Really complicated! Suffice to know the major Protestant denominations in the U.S., which are ranked in the following list.

Denomination	Membership
1. Baptist	36.4 million
2. Methodist	14.2 million
3. Pentecostal	10.3 million
4. Lutheran	8.3 million
5. Latter-Day Saints (Mormons)	4.7 million
6. Presbyterian	4.3 million
7. Churches of Christ	3.7 million
8. Episcopal	2.5 million
9. Reformed Churches	2.1 million
10. Adventists	800,000

Source: *Yearbook of American and Canadian Churches, 1995.*

P UBLIC DISTRUST

Believe it or not, Americans are united on one matter of opinion: when asked who they distrust the most among public figures, a recent Internet poll found that politicians dominated the list. According to the poll's overall rankings, President Clinton got the most votes for the "least trusted public figure"— more than 27 percent of respondents named him as the most distrusted. Women clearly find Clinton's Republican counterpart, Speaker of the House Newt Gingrich, less trustworthy than the President. Ironically, O.J. Simpson is less distrusted—and therefore *more* trusted—than many prominent politicians. Below are the tabulations representing the percentage of poll respondents who gave the following answers to the question: *"What one public figure do you trust the least overall?"*

Most Distrusted	Percent of Votes
1. Bill Clinton	27.17%
2. Newt Gingrich	20.31%
3. Bob Dole	4.11%
4. Rush Limbaugh	2.14%
5. Ted Kennedy	1.85%
6. O.J. Simpson	1.77%
7. Phil Gramm	1.56%
8. Hillary Clinton	1.07%
9. Dick Gephardt	1.07%
10. Pat Buchanan	0.78%

Source: The Peoplepedia Opinion Poll, 1996.

P RESIDENTS

Biggest Presidential Victories

Modern presidential elections, with their third party candidates, have provided that the winner does not always get the clear majority that past presidents have received. In 1996, President Clinton trounced

BIGGEST WINNER IN PRESIDENTIAL HISTORY, Warren G. Harding captured almost two-thirds of the popular vote in 1920.

his main opponent, Bob Dole, with the president getting about 20 percent more popular votes (45,590,703 to 37,816,307). Nonetheless, Clinton received only about 50 percent of the popular vote, not a wide victory margin compared to other presidents who thoroughly beat the major opposing-party candidate. President Kennedy, certainly one of the most popular U.S. presidents, also was voted into office with nearly half of the popular vote.

Most of the truly spectacular wins have come in this century, as political parties have become more settled than they were in the 1800s. Interestingly enough, this list of presidential landslides reveals the prevalence of truly mediocre, even downright terrible, presidents on the winning end of some of the biggest landslides in American history—Warren Harding, who ran one of the most corrupt administrations ever, died ignominiously in office; Richard Nixon, who, even while celebrating his crushing of McGovern, was plotting the Watergate cover-up that eventually led to his downfall; Herbert Hoover, who in 1932, four years after his large mandate from the people, received an even smaller percentage of the votes than the man he defeated in 1928; James Buchanan, who did nothing during his term to prevent the country from plunging into civil war; Lyndon Johnson, who, four years after his overwhelming defeat of Barry Goldwater, was driven from office by the tragedy of Vietnam; and even Ronald Reagan, who, despite all the good times America seemed to be having, left

office under the cloud of the Iran-Contra affair and a general feeling that the country would soon have to start paying for the high-flying, free-spending, fun-filled 1980s.

Below are the most one-sided presidential victories in history, along with the losers shown below.

Year: Winner	Percent of Votes
1. 1920: **Warren G. Harding**	**63.84%**
James M. Cox	36.16%
2. 1936: **Franklin Roosevelt**	**62.46%**
Alfred Landon	37.54%
3. 1972: **Richard M. Nixon**	**61.79%**
George McGovern	38.66%
4. 1964: **Lyndon Johnson**	**61.34%**
Barry M. Goldwater	38.66%
5. 1904 **Teddy Roosevelt**	**60.01%**
Alton B. Parker	39.99%
6. 1984: **Ronald Reagan**	**59.17%**
Walter Mondale	40.83%
7. 1932: **Franklin Roosevelt**	**59.15%**
Herbert Hoover	40.85%
8. 1982: **Herbert Hoover**	**58.76%**
Alfred E. Smith	41.24%
9. 1836: **Martin Van Buren**	**58.19%**
William H. Harrison	41.81%
10. 1956: **Dwight Eisenhower**	**57.75%**
Adlai E. Stevenson	42.25%

Four years after winning by 17 percentage points, Herbert Hoover lost by almost 19 percentage points. Franklin D. Roosevelt appears twice winning by 18.3 points in 1932 and bettering that mark with the second-best victory margin of 24.9 percent in 1936. History now has to look back at the efforts of Richard Nixon to secure his 1972 election as overkill, since he won handily by 22.7 points. Did his re-election committee really need to break into the Democratic office in the Watergate Hotel? Perhaps it was Nixon's loss to Kennedy by a narrow margin that made them so paranoid. Like Hoover, Van Buren was rewarded after a large mandate with losing to the man he defeated William "Tippicanoe" Harrison. In 1836 Van Buren won handily by 17 points; in 1840 Van Buren lost to Harrison by seven points.

Source: Federal Election Committee.

PRESIDENTS

Lowest Percentage of Popular Vote

You may not be able to please most of the people most of the time, but you can still get elected to the presidency. Maybe that's why we've all grown up believing that one day even we could become president, even though the majority of the nation doesn't want us. John Quincy Adams was one such president. He didn't even come close to a majority. To be fair, in the election of 1824 there were four candidates. In fact, all the candidates listed below except the last two—Rutherford B. Hayes and Benjamin Harrison — were involved in races that had more than two candidates. There seems little correlation to a president's stature in history and his popular vote when elected. Lincoln, for example, only won about 40 percent of the popular vote, but is generally considered one of our greatest presidents. With Bill Clinton (43 percent in 1992), the jury is still out.

Year	Winner	% of Votes
1. 1824	John Quincy Adams	29.92%
2. 1860	Abraham Lincoln	39.91%
3. 1992	Bill Clinton	43.28%
4. 1968	Richard M. Nixon	43.56%
5. 1912	Woodrow Wilson	44.95%
6. 1856	James Buchanan	45.99%

CLINTON received the lowest percentage of the popular vote in modern history, yet is now enjoying one of the highest approval ratings of any Post-War president.

7. **1892** Grover Cleveland 47.18%
8. **1848** Zachary Taylor 47.35%
9. **1876** Rutherford B. Hayes 48.49%
10. **1888** Benjamin Harrison 49.56%
Source: *World Almanac*, 1997.

PRESIDENTS

Narrowest Victory Margin

"The winner by an eyelash is ..." America is a nation of winners. As a country, we emphasize winning, paying little attention to the margin of the victory. But often the more interesting facts lay just behind the bottom line, inside the result. For example, when looking at presidential elections, it's much more interesting to look at election victories from the standpoint of the smallest margin of victory rather than the landslides. Three of our presidents were elected despite garnering less "popular votes" than their opponent. In 1824 none of the four candidates could gain a majority of the popular vote, so Congress voted in the one who nearly lost by a two to one margin, John Quincy Adams. In 1876 Rutherford B. Hayes received a majority of electoral votes, despite losing the popular vote to his opponent. The way the system works, it's not how big you win, but what states you win. A landslide in New Hampshire is not nearly as good as a squeaker in New York. Grover Cleveland tried for the White House three times, winning the popular vote each time. Yet he won only two elections. More recently, Richard Nixon experienced close races in his first two attempts, losing to John F. Kennedy by 0.17 percentage points and defeating Hubert Hum-

phrey in a three-way race by 0.70 percentage points in 1968.

Following are the smallest margins of victory in presidential races. Below the winners are the losers with their percentage of votes.

Year: Winner	Percent of Votes
1.**1824: John Q. Adams**	**29.92%**
Andrew Jackson	44.27%
Henry Clay	13.23%
William Crawford	12.58%
2. **1876: Rutherford Hayes**	**48.49%**
Samuel J. Tilden	51.51%
3. **1888: Benj'n. Harrison**	**49.56%**
Grover Cleveland	50.44%
4. **1880: James A. Garfield**	**50.04%**
Winfred S. Hancock	49.96%
5. **1960: John F. Kennedy**	**50.09%**
Richard M. Nixon	49.91%
6. **1884: Grover Cleveland**	**50.32%**
James G. Blaine	49.68%
7. **1968: Richard M. Nixon**	**43.56%**
Hubert H. Humphrey	42.86%
8. **1844: James K. Polk**	**50.72%**
Henry Clay	49.28%
9. **1976: Jimmy Carter**	**51.05%**
Gerald R. Ford	48.95%
10. **1829: Grover Cleveland**	**47.18%**
Benjamin Harrison	44.09%

Source: *World Almanac*, 1997.

PRESIDENTS

Most Public Appearances

In the good old days, the presidency seemed lofty and removed. Unless you actually saw the president during a public appearance, you didn't know what he sounded like or how he really appeared. Technology changed all that. With the advent of radio in the 1920s, major public events began to be broadcast live. President Franklin D. Roosevelt in the 1930s and 1940s became the first chief executive to make wide use of radio, and he was a master, embracing the medium as a way to communicate, person-to-person, with all citizens. His fireside chats were "must-hear radio" for all Americans. Television took over from radio after World War II, and John Kennedy proved to be the next master of the mass media, using TV to go directly to the people to promote his policies. Television has since become an indispensable part of the political process, with politicians using it to reach huge numbers of people with the appeal of intimacy. Americans now expect their presidents to appear on TV—and often. Today, we live in an age of sound bites and 24-hour TV news coverage, a time when the president has even gone on TV to discuss his preference in underwear. That may not have been quite the message FDR intended his successors to carry to the American people, but no one can say Bill Clinton hasn't been public with his public. This list gives the most TV and public appearances by presidents since Harry Truman, counting nonpolitical speeches, news conferences, and other U.S. appearances.

President	Number of Appearances
1. Bill Clinton (1993-1994)	357
2. Gerald Ford	344
3. George Bush	311
4. Ronald Reagan (1st term)	299
5. Lyndon Johnson	293
6. Jimmy Carter	262
7. John Kennedy	219
8. Ronald Reagan (2nd term)	211
9. Richard Nixon(1st term)	159
10. Harry Truman (2nd term)	130
11. Richard Nixon (2nd term)	113
12. Dwight D. Eisenhower (2nd term)	85
13. Dwight D. Eisenhower (1st term)	83
14. Harry Truman (1st term)	62

THE MOST RECLUSIVE PRESIDENT IN MODERN HISTORY, President Dwight D. Eisenhower, in his combined two terms, made fewer public appearances (168) than any Chief Executive.

Source: Vital Statistics on the Presidency.

RACE CAR DRIVERS

Top-Earning NASCAR Drivers

He has never won the Indianapolis 500, an Indy Car Championship or the Daytona 500, but boy, has he won some money. Jeff Gordon, who drives a Chevy, has run circles around Ford's top driver, Dale Jarrett. Racing rivals Gordon and Jarrett battled it out last season on the Winston Cup circuit with Gordon winning 10 Winston Cups to Jarrett's five. Nonetheless, Jarrett earned almost as much money on

PEOPLE

the track; his Daytona 500 winnings put him incredibly close to Gordon's $2 million-plus winnings.

Driver	Winnings, 1996
1. Jeff Gordon	$2,484,518
2. Dale Jarrett	$2,343,750
3. Terry Labonte	$1,939,213
4. Dale Earnhardt	$1,725,396
5. Mark Martin	$1,550,558
6. Ernie Irvan	$1,480,167
7. Bobby Labonte	$1,362,415
8. Sterling Martin	$1,315,050
9. Rusty Wallace	$1,296,912
10. Ricky Rudd	$1,213,373

Source: *Chicago Tribune*, 1996.

REPRESENTATIVES

Top Campaign Contributions from Individuals

Campaign finance reform seems to be a perennial issue, blossoming every two years during elections, and lying dormant in between. On the one hand, we have a right to support any candidate we want with however much money we can afford. On the other hand, some candidates, especially incumbents, seem to have an advantage in attracting large political donors. Add to that the sheer expense of campaigning—especially TV advertising, which costs hundreds of thousands of dollars—and you have a situation that very few political watchdogs are happy about. Below is a listing of the top politicos in the House and Senate who excel at attracting individual contributions, with the amounts through November 1996.

Representative	Contribution*
1. Newt Gingrich (R)	$5,077,414
2. Charles Schumer (D)	$2,621,512

3. Ronald E. Paul (R)	$1,773,203
4. Joseph Kennedy II (D)	$1,701,737
5. John R. Kasich (R)	$1,349,282
6. Richard Gephardt (D)	$1,220,700
7. Martin R. Hoke (R)	$1,202,310
8. William V. Hilleary (R)	$1,194,062
9. John Eric Ensign (R)	$1,188,759
10. Rod Blagojevich (D)	$1,150,623

* individual contributions through November 1996

Source: Federal Election Committee, 1996.

REPRESENTATIVES

Top PAC Congressional Contribution Recipients

To take, it must be noted, is not necessarily to be taken. It is quite conceivable than most politicians who accept large donations from self-interested PACs and lobbyists maintain their integrity and objectivity. Others, however, most assuredly, are unduly influenced by the wants and wishes of their largest campaign contributors, and ultimately the public interest is compromised. Below are the House members who have received the most in campaign contributions from political action committees. Despite their griping about the Republicans as the party in which money talks most powerfully, the list of well-financed House members is dominated by Democrats.

Representative	PAC Contributions*
1. Victor H. Fazio (D)	$1,362,728
2. Jonas M. Frost III (D)	$1,126,345
3. Richard Gephardt (D)	$1,101,282
4. Newt Gingrich (R)	$1,078,732
5. Thomas Delay (R)	$1,059,024
6. John Dingell (D)	$899,842
7. David Bonior (D)	$878,546
8. Barton J. Gordon (D)	$766,070

MOST INFLUENTIAL ROCK 'N ROLLER OF ALL, (at right) Chuck Berry.

9. Rick White (R) $740,976
10. John Eric Ensign (R) $734,741
    * contributions through November 1996
Source: Federal Election Committee, 1996.

Rock Musicians

Most Influential of All Rockers

One of the first things any kid who ever picked up an electric guitar learned is the opening riff from Chuck Berry's classic "Johnny B. Goode." For that alone, Berry could merit top honors as rock 'n roll's most influential figure. But perhaps the real proof of the pudding is that almost every rock guitar player from John Lennon and Keith Richards to Eddie Van Halen and U2's The Edge and countless other greats have said at one time or another that he owes a deep debt to Berry's style. Berry, then and now, gives an electric jump-start to rock music and places his guitar squarely at front and center as *the* instrument of the rock era. The following are the 10 most influential rock musicians of all time, as determined by the *Best and Worst* editorial staff which took into account all the aforementioned when the votes were cast.

Rank/Artist

1. Chuck Berry
2. John Lennon
3. Buddy Holly
4. Bob Dylan
5. Jimi Hendrix
6. Eric Clapton
7. Jimmy Page

8. Keith Moon
9. The Ramones
10. Jim Morrison
Source: *Best and Worst* original.

ROLE MODELS, FAMILIAL

Though he is viewed in a different light than in years' past, the American father is still the top role model in the family, according to a recent Internet poll. More than 20 percent of the poll's respondents named their father as their role model—though, interestingly, more women than men view their fathers as role models. The responses below amply indicate the existence of a male role model, even though he may not necessarily be living with his family. The following tabulations represent the percentage of poll respondents who gave the following answers to the question: *"Which one family member is best identified as your role model?"*

Family Member	% Who Voted for
1. Father	20.82%
2. Mother	13.53%
3. No one	7.66%
4. Grandmother	4.31%
5. Sister	3.74%
6. Grandfather	3.50%
7. Brother	2.51%
8. Husband	2.26%
9. Aunt	1.65%
Wife	1.65%

Source: The Peoplepedia Opinion Poll, 1996.

SENATORS

Top PAC Congressional Contribution Recipients

Senator John Warner was always a man with expensive tastes. After all, what other kind of a man would marry Elizabeth Taylor? Like his ex and all her jewels and expensive perfumes, Warner, too, had his share of riches, namely a wad of contributions from political action committees. While the Republicans make an issue of how President Clinton and Vice President Gore raise their election funds, it's the GOP who has eight in 10 Senators on the top 10 list of PAC recipients.

Senator	PAC Contributions, 1995-96
1. John Warner (R)	$1,473,796
2. Larry Pressler (R)	$1,466,772
3. Max S. Baucu (D)	$1,355,135
4. Theodore Stevens (R)	$1,202,128
5. Mitch McConnell (R)	$1,187,233
6. Dick Zimmer (R)	$1,179,138
7. Pat Roberts (R)	$1,177,711
8. Richard J. Durbin (D)	$1,153,496
9. Phil Gramm (R)	$1,079,873
10. A. Wayne Allard (R)	$1,050,036

Source: Federal Election Committee, 1996.

SENATORS

Lefties: Most Liberal Senators

One thing's for sure in American politics: there is a brood of senators you can count on to make a lot of speeches about caring for the downtrodden, insuring the nation, funding education and cutting the defense budget. Compiled by the liberal interest group Americans for Democratic Action, this ranking represents the percentage of times each senator voted in accordance with the ADA position on 20 selected votes during the 101st Congress. Space prohibits listing the large number of Representatives who vote liberal, but in the Senate there's a smaller, though almost as predictable, lot who—if the rules permitted it—would raise their *left* hand every time a liberal issue was voted on.

Senator	Liberal Voting Record
1. Carl Levin (D-MI)	98%
2. Barbara Boxer (D-CA)	95%
Russell Feingold (D-WI)	95%
4. Bill Bradley (D-NJ)	94%
Paul Simon (D-IL)	94%
6. Frank Lautenberg (D-NJ)	93%
Paul Wellstone (D-MN)	93%
8. Patrick Leahy (D-VT)	91%
Clairborne Pell (D-RI)	91%
Paul Sarbanes (D-MD)	91%

Source: *Congressional Quarterly Almanac*, 1995.

SENATORS

Biggest Senate Race Winners

The U.S. Senate has often been called a millionaire's club and a men's club. Both are still fairly apt nicknames. It is also a club in which the members with the fattest wallets can be the most popular with their constituents, and doubly so if they can give the appearance of independence while at the same time taking contributions from special interests. Those who can put up a good front have stellar election records. The Senators on the following list carried the highest percentage of the popular vote in their respective states.

Senator	Percent of Votes, 1996
1. Ted Stevens (R-AK)	77%
2. Jay Rockefeller (D-WV)	77%
3. Thad Cochran (R-MS)	71%
4. Pete Domenici (R-NC)	64%
5. John Reed (D-RI)	63%
6. Pat Roberts (R-KS)	62%
7. Fred Thompson (R-TN)	61%
8. Joseph Biden (D-DE)	60%
9. Carl Levin (D-MI)	58%
10. James Inhofe (R-OK)	57%

Source: Federal Election Committee, December 31, 1996.

TELEVISION VIEWERS

Most Hooked

Despite the constant complaints from parents that "kids are watching too much TV," it is, in fact, the older generations that are most glued to the tube. Teenagers, it seems, have other things on their agendas, like the telephone and the Internet, today's hot new trend. The popularity of the Internet is, to be sure, firmly entrenched in the under-35 crowd, and the hours they spend online are clearly taking time away from their television viewing. And for that reason, some are even saying that the Internet is a greater evil than the Boob Tube. It's a matter of opinion—as well as a matter of time—as to which medium will win the honor of the "vastest wasteland."

Group	Hours/Minutes (weekly)
1. Women 55 and over	25:47
2. Women 25-54	21:35
3. Men 55 and over	21.27
4. Women 18 and over	20:38
5. Men 18 and over	16:10
6. Women 18-24	16:00
7. Men 25-54	15:30
8. Children 2-5	13:25
9. Men 18-24	12:10
10. Teens 12-17	11:02
11. Children 6-11	10:45

Source: Nielsen Media Research, May 1996.

TRADING PLACES

Shoes We'd Like to Be In

Would you rather be President of the United States or the head of the most powerful computer software company in the world? According to a recent public opionion survey, Bill Gates, chairman of Microsoft, outpolled the President as the public figure with whom Americans would most like to trade places. Following are tabulations representing the percentage of poll respondents who gave the following answers to the question: *"What one public figure would you most like to trade places with?"*

Public Figure	Percent Who Voted For
1. Bill Gates	7.66%
2. Bill Clinton	5.11%
3. Newt Gingrich	4.65%
4. None	4.57%
5. Hillary Clinton	2.75%
6. Oprah Winfrey	1.97%
7. Rush Limbaugh	1.73%
8. Stephen King	1.27%
9. Martha Stewart	0.99%
Cindy Crawford	0.99%

Souce: The Peoplepedia Opinion Poll, 1996. ·

WOMEN

Highest-Paid American Women in Business

If you think working women are getting the shaft in the paycheck department, you are right. But it's worse than you think. Don't buy that old-wives tale that women earn 75 cents for every dollar a man earns. That's only for women at the bottom, or the middle. At the *very* top—the CEO level—women earn about 10 to 20 cents for every dollar a male earns. Linda Wachner, the nation's top-paid female CEO, earns approximately one-thirteenth of her male counterpart, Lawrence Coss. Coss, America's top-paid CEO, earns over $65 million compared to Wachner's paltry $5 million. Below are the ten-top paid women.

Name/Position	Pay (millions)
1. **Linda Wachner,** Chairwoman, CEO and president, Warnaco; chairwoman and CEO, Authenic Fitness.	**$11.16**
2. **Jill Barad** CEO, Mattel	**$6.17**
3. **Carol Bartz,** Chairwoman, CEO and president, Autodesk	**$5.51**
4. **Sally Crawford,** COO, Healthsource	**$4.02**
5. **Estee Lauder,** Chairwoman emeritus, Estee Lauder	**$3.82**
6. **Ngaire Cuneo,** Executive VP, Conseco	**$3.68**
7. **Jane Hirsh** President, International Business, and Copley Pharmaceutical	**$3.39**
8. **Nancy Pedot,** CEO and president, Gymboree	**$3.19**
9. **Donna Karan** Chairwoman, CEO, chief designer, Donna Karan	**$2.73**
10. **Sharon Mates** President, North American Vaccine	**$2.33**

Source: *Los Angeles Times*, December 17, 1996; *Working Woman Magazine*.

WRITERS

Most Published

The author with the all-time record for the most titles published is the ubiquitous William Shakespeare, with more than 15,000 titles in a computer survey of authors in the Online Computer Center Library database. Shakespeare had almost twice as many titles as his next closest rival, Charles Dickens, who had just under 8,000 titles. The list of the top 100 authors contains only five women: Agatha Christie, George Eliot, Ellen G. White, Jane Austen and George Sand (two of whom, strangely enough, took identical male monikers). Compare this list with our list of the greatest writers of all time to see whether there is any correlation between the sheer volume of publication and an author's lasting influence.

Rank/Writer

1. William Shakespeare
2. Charles Dickens
3. Sir Walter Scott
4. Johann Wolfgang von Goethe
5. Aristotle
6. Alexandre Dumas
7. Robert Louis Stevenson
8. Mark Twain
9. Marcus Cicero
10. Honore de Balzac

Source: "A Guide to Special Collections in the OCLC Database," OCLC Online Computer Center, Dublin, Ohio.

WRITERS

Greatest Writers of All Time

Our list of the greatest writers of all time is topped, of course, by Shake-

HAMLET IS BUT ONE WORK that qualified William Shakespeare for the quadruple honor: Most Published Writer, the Greatest Writer of All Time, the Greatest Playwright of All Time and the Greatest British Writer of All Time.

speare—also the most published author the world has ever known. The rating is derived from an analysis of citations in the Modern Language Association International Bibliography; the score reflects the number of scholarly articles written about a particular author (for a complete description of the methodology, see "Writers, American, Greatest of All Time"). Eight of the top 10 writers are English or American—including T.S. Eliot, who, one might say, is both, having been born in St. Louis but adopting England as his home. This preponderance reflects not only the influence of writers in English but of Anglo-

American academia in the field of literature. Nevertheless, the list is an accurate reflection of the influence of various writers on the literary world.

Writer	Score
1. William Shakespeare	5848
2. James Joyce	1943
3. Johann Wolfgang von Goethe	1802
4. Geoffrey Chaucer	1593
5. John Milton	1445
6. Dante	1330
7. William Faulkner	1324
8. Henry James	1210
9. Charles Dickens	1080
10. T.S. Eliot	1057

Source: *Best and Worst* original.

RITERS

Greatest Novelists of All Time

The novel is the most popular and accessible of literary forms, but the greatest novelist of all time, according to our rankings, is responsible in part for turning the novel into a less accessible, more esoteric art form. James Joyce is commonly credited with creating the modern novel form, with his extensive use of stream of consciousness and other experimental techniques in his great work, *Ulysses*, the narrative of which takes place in a single day, June 16, 1904. Joyce had great difficulty publishing his first work, the *Dubliners*, a collection of short stories he described as "the moral history of his community," with which he spent years in poverty trying to get it published. After two years of unsuccessful attempts to interest a publisher he finally got it in print with a smaller, poorly financed publishing house. This first

edition had so many typographical errors it had to be republished as many as two more times before the work was finally acceptable and noticed by main stream English-language publishers, who eventually embraced his book as revolutionary. His last novel, *Finnegan's Wake*, is an even more difficult work, for in it Joyce employs an idiosyncratic language in which he uses invented words, plays on words and makes obscure allusions. The study of Joyce, especially of this last work, is a cottage industry among academics; indeed, the imposing *Finnegan's Wake* is rarely approached by the lay reader. Many of Joyce's techniques were adopted by the second writer on our list, the American William Faulkner. For the common reader, though, it is good to see the populist Charles Dickens high up on the scale. The following are the 10 greatest novelists of all time, as measured by the number of scholarly articles written about their work.

Writer/Notable Work(s)	Score
1. James Joyce *Ulysses*	1943
2. William Faulkner *As I Lay Dying*; *Absalom, Absalom*	1324
3. Henry James *The Ambassadors*	1210
4. Charles Dickens *Nicholas Nickleby*	1080
5. Miguel de Cervantes *Don Quixote*	1038
6. Herman Melville *Moby Dick*	996
7. D. H. Lawrence *Women in Love*	919
8. Fyodor Dostoevsky *The Brothers Karamazov*	901
9. Franz Kafka *The Trial*; *The Castle*	844

10. Nathaniel Hawthorne 817
The House of the Seven Gables
Source: *Best and Worst* original.

WRITERS

Greatest Playwrights of All Time

As with the ranking of the all-time greatest writers, William Shakespeare leads the list of greatest playwrights—by a wide margin indeed. But following him on the list are two twentieth-century writers known for their iconoclasm. The second greatest playwright, Bertolt Brecht, was known for his fervent commitment to Marxism, most obvious in his *Threepenny Opera* and *Rise and Fall of the City of Mahogonny*. Number three on the list is Samuel Beckett, whose *Waiting for Godot* shattered all accepted theatrical traditions and features the quintessential line that sums up both the story and Beckett's comment on life: "It's terrible. Nothing happens." (Indeed, at least one critic, not recognizing the genius of the work, used that line as his brief review of the play—something Beckett would have admired). The following are the greatest playwrights of all time, measured by the amount of influence they have had on the scholarly world (for a complete description of the methodology, see "Writers, American, Greatest of All Time").

Writer/Notable Work(s)	Score
1. William Shakespeare	5848
The Tempest; A Midsummer Night's Dream	
2. Bertolt Brecht	835
Rise and Fall of the City of Mahagonny	

DUBLINERS

JAMES JOYCE

THE FIRST WORK OF THE AUTHOR (above) laid the foundation for the writer who ranks as the Greatest Novelist of All Time.

3. Samuel Beckett	766
Waiting for Godot; Endgame	
4. Lope de Vega	509
Punishment without Revenge	
5. Ben Jonson	460
The Alchemist	
6. Friedrich von Schiller	438
The Gods of Greece	
7. Pierre Corneille	431
Horace; Le Menteur	
8. Moliere	414
Tartuffe; Le Misanthrope	
9. Gotthold Ephraim Lessing	396
Emilia Galotti	
10. Eugene O'Neill	394
Mourning Becomes Electra; The Iceman Cometh	

Source: *Best and Worst* original.

WRITER JUDY BLUME, whose book *Tales of a Fourth Grade Nothing* is one of the top-ten all-time best-selling hardcover books for children (See Books on page 222).

Greatest Poets of All Time

The influence of Goethe on the German-speaking world is hard to overestimate. He is, far and away, the first man of German letters, the leading figure of the important *Sturm und Drang* movement of the late 18th century and the German Romanticism of the early 19th. Not a poet only, Goethe, with Voltaire and Kant, was a true giant of the Enlightenment and a master of many forms—epic poetry, epistolary novel, drama. In addition, he wrote numerous scientific tracts, most notably on plant biology and optics. His works, read by every German schoolchild to this day, created a uniquely German literary style and influenced most every subsequent German author, from Karl Marx to Thomas Mann. Other poets on our list of greats include those two banes of high school English students, Chaucer and Milton.

Poet	Score
1. Johann Wolfgang von Goethe	1802
2. Geoffrey Chaucer	1593
3. John Milton	1445
4. Dante Alighieri	1330
5. T. S. Eliot	1057
6. William Wordsworth	969
7. Ezra Pound	907
8. William Butler Yeats	791
9. William Blake	732
10. Alexander Pushkin	710

Source: *Best and Worst* original.

WRITERS— AMERICAN

Greatest, 1980-1990

While the nineties is spawning many great new authors, it is too early to determine the greatest of the current decade. For the eighties, however, enough time has passed to make a reasonable determination as to the best. John Updike, whose novels deal with the superficial materialism of middle class life (just think of the Reagan years), is the clear winner in this category. His novels about the life of Harry "Rabbit" Angstrom—including *Rabbit is Rich*, about the Seventies, and *Rabbit Redux*, about the Eighties, have attained the unlikely status of both popular and critical success, the former being not only a best-seller but the winner of the Pulitzer Prize and the National Book Award. However, a writer did not have to win one of those prized to make in on the list; two novelists who didn't were Stephen King and James Michener. They earned "top writer" status because of the enormous popularity of their books—eight best-sellers each in ten years. The selections were made according to three factors: (1) Pulitzer Prize awards; (2) National Book Award; and (3) best sellers. In the first category, 50 points were awarded for a Pulitzer Prize. In category two, 40 points were awarded for a National Book Award. In category three, 30 points were awarded for a best seller that won a Pulitzer Prize, 25 points was awarded for a best seller whose author won a Pulitzer Prize for another book; and 8 points were awarded for best sellers that didn't win any prizes.

Writer	Total Points
1. John Updike	120
2. Alice Walker	90
3. Larry McMurtry	80
4. Anne Tyler	75
5. Louis L'Amour	72
6. Stephen King	64
James Michener	64
8. Tom Wolfe	56
John Irving	56
10. E.L. Doctorow	48

Source: "Best and Worst" original.

WRITERS, AMERICAN

Greatest of All Time

Who is America's greatest writer? Some say it's simply a matter of taste. Do you prefer the vernacular of Mark Twain or the esoteric intellectualism of Henry James? The strong, spare prose of Ernest Hemingway or the gothic grotesquery of Poe? Certainly no one can quantify preference, or, more importantly, greatness, in literature. But it is possible at least to judge the overall influence of a writer on his generation and on ours. The editors of *Best and Worst* have developed a method that allows us to give a quantitative score which we feel successfully reflects the overall importance of a writer across time and throughout the world. The Modern Language Association International Bibliography contains citations from articles in more than 3,000 journals and series published worldwide on literature and language. The citations include monographs, collections, working papers, proceedings of conferences, dissertations and reference works, in all modern languages. We feel that it is the most comprehensive and authoritative guide to literature in existence. Using the MLA International Bibliography, available on CD-ROM from the Wilsonline Information System, we compiled a numerical score reflecting the number of articles about a particular author. Based on this method, the following list represents the 10

GREATEST AMERICAN WRITER OF THE LAST DECADE, John Updike.

PEOPLE

most influential American writers of all time, together with one or more of their most notable works. The list includes three 20th-century writers, including the top-rated writer overall, as well as three poets, but only one woman, the tenth-rated Emily Dickinson. Interestingly, two of the top-ten American writers became expatriates. Henry James of the illustrious James family (father Henry was a noted 19th-century historian and brother William the first great American psychologist) eventually took British citizenship. The poet Ezra Pound spent a good deal of time with the American literary crowd in Paris in the 1920s; he then moved to Rome, and, in perhaps the most bizarre episode in the annals of American literature, became an avid propagandist for Mussolini. His family is still seeking the right to bury him in the United States. Our method seems a real indicator of literary greatness, unlike, say, the strange machinations of the Nobel Prize committee. Only two of our top 10 American writers were awarded the Nobel Prize in their lifetimes; but no one reads some of the other American winners of that dubious prize. The best indication of this is Pearl Buck, whose literary fame has all but vanished since being awarded the Nobel in 1932, as indicated by her score of a mere 6 in the MLA Bibliography.

Writer/Notable Work(s)	Score
1. **William Faulkner** *The Sound and the Fury*	1324
2. **Henry James** *Portrait of a Lady*	1210
3. **Herman Melville** *Moby Dick*	996
4. **Ezra Pound** *Cantos*	907
5. **Nathaniel Hawthorne** *The Scarlet Letter*	817
6. **Ernest Hemingway** *A Farewell to Arms*	810
7. **Mark Twain** *The Adventures of Huckleberry Finn*	744
8. **Edgar Allan Poe** *The Raven; The Tell-Tale Heart*	658
9. **Walt Whitman** *Leaves of Grass*	607
10. **Emily Dickinson** *Collected Poems*	554

Source: *Best and Worst* original.

WRITERS, AMERICAN

Greatest Novelists of All Time

The greatest American novelist of all time is best known for creating the imaginary Mississippi county of Yoknapatawpha, complete with its own idiosyncratic characters and a social structure that examined the burdens of Southern history, race relations, class conflict and a way of life in conflict with the progress of the twentieth century. Second on the list is a writer very much different from Faulkner in background and subject matter; where Faulkner was intrigued by the people of the American South, the anglophilic James explored the confrontation between American and European cultures and deeply probed the psychology of his characters. The list of the 10 greatest American novelists follows.

Writer/Notable Work	Score
1. **William Faulkner** *Light in August*	1324
2. **Henry James** *The Turn of the Screw*	1210

PEOPLE

Source: *Best and Worst* original.

WRITERS, AMERICAN

Greatest Playwrights of All Time

The figure of Eugene O'Neill towers above the realm of American drama. Commonly considered the founder of the modern American theater, O'Neill is one of a very few—perhaps the only other is Tennessee Williams—whose works are consistently produced in Europe and who has become a part of the international dramatic canon. O'Neill, whose parents were both actors, expressed in his work a profound interest in classical Greek drama, as seen in his trilogy *Mourning Becomes Electra*. O'Neill's works covered a wide range of topics; his early works were based on his life as a seaman, while his later works became progressively more involved psychologically. The ideas of Freud and Nietzsche played an important role in these later plays, culminating in the autobiographical *Long Day's Journey Into*

WRITER S.E. HINTON, whose book *The Outsiders* is one of the top-ten all time best-selling hardcover books for children. (See Books on page 222).

LONG DAY'S JOURNEY INTO NIGHT
EUGENE O'NEILL

WORKS LIKE THE ONE ABOVE are the reason its author ranks number-one of all American Playwrights.

2. **Henry James** *The Turn of the Screw*		1210
3. **Herman Melville** *Billy Budd*		996
4. **Nathaniel Hawthorne** *Twice-Told Tales*		817
5. **Ernest Hemingway** *For Whom the Bell Tolls*		810
6. **Mark Twain** *Life on the Mississippi*		744
7. **Vladimir Nabakov** *Lolita*		465
8. **Thomas Pynchon** *V*		364
9. **Willa Cather** *O Pioneers!*		363
10. **Saul Bellow**		362

Henderson the Rain King
Source: *Best and Worst* original.

WRITERS, AMERICAN

Greatest Playwrights of All Time

The figure of Eugene O'Neill towers above the realm of American drama. Commonly considered the founder of the modern American theater, O'Neill is one of a very few—perhaps the only other is Tennessee Williams—whose works are consistently produced in Europe and who has become a part of the international dramatic canon. O'Neill, whose parents were both actors, expressed in his work a profound interest in classical Greek drama, as seen in his trilogy *Mourning Becomes Electra*. O'Neill's works covered a wide range of topics; his early works were based on his life as a seaman, while his later works became progressively more involved psychologically. The ideas of Freud and Nietzsche played an important role in these later plays, culminating in the autobiographical *Long Day's Journey Into Night*, an emotional and psychological tour de force probing the conflicts in the playwright's own family. The work, written in 1941, was so disturbing that O'Neill did not allow it to be produced in his lifetime. The following are the 10 most influential American playwrights of all time, based on the number of citations of their works in the MLA International Bibliography.

Playwright/Notable Work	Score
1. **Eugene O'Neill** *Long Day's Journey Into Night*	394

4. Emily Dickinson   554
5. William Carlos Williams   486
6. Wallace Stevens   427
7. Robert Frost   304
8. H.D. (Hilda Doolittle)   196
9. Marianne Moore   165
10. Robert Penn Warren   145

Source: *Best and Worst* original.

WRITERS, AMERICAN

Greatest Females of All-time

The greatest American woman writer never published a word of her work in her lifetime. Emily Dickinson wrote more than 1,000 poems, but the reclusive poet withdrew entirely from society before the age of 30. Her works, typified by spare lyricism in an idiosyncratic diction and meter, were discovered only after her death. Below are the 10 most important female American writers of all time, as determined by the number of citations in the MLA International Bibliography (for a complete description of the scoring methodology, see the description under "Writers, American, Greatest of All Time"). Other women writers scoring highly include the poets Alice Walker with 124 citations, Sylvia Plath (115) and Anne Sexton (90), and the novelist, short story writer and essayist Joyce Carol Oates (82).

Writer/Notable Work	Score
1. Emily Dickinson *Collected Poems*	**554**
2. Willa Cather *One of Ours*	**363**
3. Flannery O'Connor *A Good Man is Hard to Find and Other Stories*	**338**
4. Eudora Welty *The Optimist's Daughter*	**254**

5. Edith Wharton *House of Mirth*	**209**
6. H.D. (Hilda Doolittle) *Red Shores for Bronze (poetry)*	**196**
7. Toni Morrison *Beloved*	**170**
8. Gertrude Stein *The Autobiography of Alice B. Toklas*	**166**
9. Marianne Moore *Collected Poems*	**165**
10. Kate Chopin *The Awakening*	**126**

Source: *Best and Worst* original.

WRITERS, BRITISH

Greatest of All Time

Although not really considered a poetic people, the list of the 10 greatest English writers contains five poets, while there are four novelists and only one playwright, the ubiquitous Shakespeare, on the list. Another interesting aspect of this compendium of British writers is that two—T.S. Eliot and Joseph Conrad—were not English-born. Eliot hailed from the mundane American midwestern town of St. Louis, while Conrad's native tongue was Polish. The scores here reflect the amount of scholarly work produced on a particular author's work, as measured by the number of citations in the MLA International Bibliography.

Writer/Notable Work(s)	Score
1. William Shakespeare *Hamlet, Macbeth*	**5848**
2. Geoffrey Chaucer *The Canterbury Tales*	**1593**
3. John Milton *Paradise Lost*	**1445**
4. Charles Dickens *A Tale of Two Cities*	**1080**

5. **T.S. Eliot**   1057
   The Waste Land
6. **William Wordsworth**   969
   The Prelude
7. **D.H. Lawrence**   919
   Lady Chatterly's Lover
8. **Joseph Conrad**   771
   Heart of Darkness
9. **William Blake**   732
   Songs of Innocence
10. **Virginia Woolf**   673
    To the Lighthouse

Source: *Best and Worst* original.

WRITERS, CLASSICAL

Greatest of All Time

Although the Greek poet Homer is widely regarded as the first true literary figure, his Roman counterpart Vergil is seen here as the writer from classical antiquity with the most influence on modern-day literary forms. Vergil employed Homer's style of epic poetry in his *Aeneid*, but, unlike Homer, mastered other poetic forms as well, as can be seen in his *Bucolics* and *Georgics*. His acceptance by the early Christians, moreover, made him extremely popular during the Middle Ages. Whereas Homer gave life to the classic literary form, Vergil was its greatest proponent and greatest practitioner. The following are the ten most influential Greek and Roman writers, measured by the amount of scholarship on their works.

Writer/Notable Work(s)	Score
1. **Vergil**	402
The Aeneid	
2. **Ovid**	344
Metamorphoses	
3. **Homer**	309
The Iliad; The Odyssey	

4. **Horace**   158
   Odes
5. **Sophocles**   114
   Oedipus Rex
6. **Euripedes**   83
   Medea
7. **Aeschylus**   46
   The Oresteia
8. **Catullus**   44
   Attis
9. **Lucretius**   43
   De rerum natura
10. **Plautus**   41
    Amphitruo

Source: *Best and Worst* original.

WRITERS, FRENCH

Greatest of All Time

Gustave Flaubert edges out Marcel Proust by a scant two points in our ranking of the greatest French writers of all time. Flaubert was master of the naturalist style, of depicting object and event in a precise, impersonal way; but his dedication to an artistic ideal in the depiction of reality was intense. A highly disciplined writer, he is legendary for spending hours contemplating the sound of a particular phrase or searching for the *mot juste*, the right word. Proust, too, was a literary perfectionist, and the last years of his life were spent in the cork-lined bedroom of his Parisian apartment, writing and revising his monumental *Remembrance of Things Past*, an ode to memory, thought and emotion.

Writer/Notable Work	Score
1. **Gustave Flaubert**	720
Madame Bovary	
2. **Marcel Proust**	718
Remembrance of Things Past	

WRITER JAMES REDFIELD, whose book, *The Celestine Prophecy*, has had the longest run ever on *Publisher's Weekly's* Bestseller list. (See Books on page 223).

3. Stendahl   668
The Red and the Black

4. Honore de Balzac   628
The Human Comedy

5. Charles Baudelaire   615
Flowers of Evil

6. Michel de Montaigne   604
Essays

7. Victor Hugo   534
Les Miserables

8. Emile Zola   504
Les Rougon-macquart;
"J'accuse"

9. Andre Gide   434
The Immortals

10. Pierre Corneille   431
Le Cid

Source: *Best and Worst* original.

WRITERS, GERMAN

Greatest of All Time

As we said before, Johann Wolfgang von Goethe is the towering figure of German literature; indeed, of the nine other writers on the list of greatest German authors, none preceded Goethe, and only one, Schiller, was his contemporary. The two were fundamental in founding Weimar Classicism, which led eventually to the German Romantic movement, whose influence spread from music to philosophy. We include in this list authors and poets who wrote in German, and thus the Czech writers Franz Kafka and Rainer Maria Rilke appear here. The following are the 10 greatest practitioners in the German language; the score reflects the number of scholarly articles written about the author's works.

Writer/Notable Work	Score
1. **Johann Wolfgang von Goethe** *The Sorrows of Young Werther*	1802
2. **Franz Kafka** *The Metamorphosis*	844
3. **Bertolt Brecht** *The Caucasian Chalk Circle*	835
4. **Thomas Mann** *The Magic Mountain*	572
5. **Friedrich von Schiller** *The Robbers*	438
6. **Gotthold Ephraim Lessing** *Nathan the Wise*	396
7. **Heinrich von Kleist** *The Prince of Homburg*	358
8. **Hugo von Hoffmannsthal** *Der Rosenklavier*	342
9. **Rainer Maria Rilke** *Duino Elegies*	340
10. **Heinrich Heine** *Reisebilder*	330

Source: *Best and Worst* original.

WRITERS, IRISH

Greatest of All Time

The Irish literary voice has long struggled to distinguish itself from that of English literature as a whole, and the list below of greatest Irish writers presents a variety of authors who either entered into the mainstream of English literature—such as Oscar Wilde—or who held out for a more purely Irish literature, as exemplified by the proponents of the Irish Renaissance such as W.B. Yeats and John Millington Synge. Indeed, something about the conflict in the Irish soul between the

English language and that of Irish Gaelic seems to make Irish writers something of linguistic basket-cases: Joyce's *Finnegan's Wake* is written in a highly idiosyncratic, invented language; and his early apostle Samuel Beckett abandoned English after his first several novels to write mainly in French. The list below represents the ten greatest Irish writers of all time, as measured by the number of citiations in the MLA International Bibliography.

Writer/Notable Work	Score
1. **James Joyce** *Finnegan's Wake*	1943
2. **William Butler Yeats** *The Wild Swans at Coole*	791
3. **Samuel Beckett** *Waiting for Godot*	766
4. **Jonathan Swift** *Gulliver's Travels*	557
5. **Oscar Wilde** *The Importance of Being Earnest*	214
6. **John Millington Synge** *The Playboy of the Western World*	117
7. **Sean O'Casey** *Juno and the Paycock*	112
8. **Oliver Goldsmith** *The Vicar of Wakefield*	105
9. **Isabella Augusta Gregory** *The Rising of the Moon*	36
10. **Richard Brinsley Sheridan** *The Rivals*	32

Source: *Best and Worst* original.

WRITERS, ITALIAN

Greatest of All Time

As Shakespeare is the guiding force in English literature and Goethe in

PEOPLE

German, so Dante is the great figure of Italian literature. His *Divine Comedy*, completed in 1321, is based firmly on the theological writings of St. Thomas Aquinas and is an allegory of the journey of the human soul toward God, beginning in the *Inferno* to free the soul from temptation, progressing to *Purgatorio* to purge man of error, and finally to *Paradisio*, where Dante meets his Beatrice, who represents perfection and divine revelation. In its highly religious content, and in its allusions to the political and social climate of his times, Dante's masterwork is a detailed evocation of the late Middle Ages and the signal literary epic of the early Renaissance.

Writer/Notable Work	Score
1. **Dante Alighieri** *The Divine Comedy*	1330
2. **Petrarch** *Ecologues*	479
3. **Giovanni Boccaccio** *Decameron*	390
4. **Allesandro Manzoni** *The Betrothed*	298
5. **Luigi Pirandello** *Six Characters in Search of an Author*	293
6. **Giacomo Conte Leopardi** *Canzoni*	233
7. **Italo Calvino** *Italian Fables*	205
8. **Ludovico Ariosto** *Roland Mad*	196
9. **Torquato Tasso** *Jerusalem Liberated*	193
10. **Eugenio Montale** *The Offender*	186

Source: *Best and Worst* original.

WRITERS, RUSSIAN

Greatest of All Time

Although Tolstoy is considered to have created the greatest novel of all time in *War and Peace*, the literary output of Dostoevsky places him at the top of the list of greatest Russian writers. In part, this reflects the different subject matter that the two approached, as well as their stylistic variations. Tolstoy, though master at evoking a complete universe of characters and events in his larger works, still wrote in a traditional, even at times romantic, style, characterized by a deep commitment to spirituality. Dostoevsky, on the other hand, explored the darker psychological motivations of his characters—the "Grand Inquisitor" passage from *The Brothers Karamazov* is felt to be one of the main precursors to 20th-century existentialism. The yin and yang of Russian literature, Tolstoy and Dostoevsky represent, perhaps, the dividing line between the Romantic and the Modern eras. These, then, are the greatest Russian writers of all time, measured by their citation score in the MLA International Bibliography.

Writer/Notable Work(s)	Score
1. **Fyodor Dostoevsky** *Notes from Underground*	901
2. **Alexander Pushkin** *The Prisoner in the Caucuses*	710
3. **Leo Tolstoy** *War and Peace; Anna Karenina*	550
4. **Anton Chekhov** *The Cherry Orchard*	371

The Time Machine by H. G. Wells

WORKS LIKE THE ONE ABOVE are the reason that Wells ranks as the number one science fiction writer of all time.

5. Nikolai Gogol	**328**
Dead Souls	
6. Ivan Turgenev	**289**
Notes of a Hunter	
7. Boris Pasternak	**210**
Dr. Zhivago	
8. Mikhail Bulgakov	**201**
The Master and Margarita	
9. Aleksandr Blok	**185**
The Scythians	
10. Anna Akhmatova	**178**
Anno Domini	

Source: *Best and Worst* original.

W RITERS, SCIENCE FICTION

Greatest of All Time

Science fiction is one of the more recent additions to the pantheon of literary genres, although its roots go back at least to Jonathan Swift's *Gulliver's Travels*. The first truly modern science fiction writer—the one who really used scientific principles and theories to look into the future or create fantastic alternative worlds—was the Frenchman Jules Verne. But, according to our rating, which measures SF writers by the number of scholarly articles about their work in the MLA International Bibliography, H.G. Wells ranks as the all-time master of the field, with his two early 20th-century masterpieces, *The Invisible Man* and *The Time Machine*. Taking a surprising fifth position in the ratings is the late American writer Philip K. Dick, whose fame continues to increase as his works become better known. Dick's consistent theme is that of displacement; his characters never seem to be firmly entrenched in any one reality, but are always drifting, consciously or unconsciously, through different times, different universes. Dick is perhaps best known as the author of the works that were later made into the popular movies *Blade Runner* and *Total Recall*.

Writer/Notable Work(s)	Score
1. H.G. Wells	**211**
The Invisible Man; The Time Machine	
2. Jules Verne	**128**
Twenty Thousand Leagues Under the Sea	
3. Ursula Le Guin	**96**
Left Hand of Darkness	
4. Stanislaw Lem	**62**
Solaris	
5. Philip K. Dick	**58**
The Man in the High Castle	
6. Samuel Delany	**30**
Dahlgren	

7. J. G. Ballard   27
The Drowned World

8. Arthur C. Clarke   26
Childhood's End

9. Ray Bradbury   23
The Martian Chronicles

10. Isaac Asimov   24
Foundation

Source: *Best and Worst* original.

WRITERS, SPANISH & PORTUGUESE

Greatest of All Time

The greatest Iberian writer of all time is known almost entirely for his massive work *Don Quixote*, the images of which—an aging, nearly blind knight-errant, accompanied by his faithful, practical servant Sancho Panza, vainly jousting at windmills and other figments of the imagination—have become part of our common literary heritage, as well as a vivid evocation of the Spanish character. For this, Cervantes' place atop the list of greatest Spanish and Portuguese writers is well-deserved. The ratings are based on the number of scholarly articles written about a particular author's work and on the degree of the author's lasting influence in scholarly and popular circles.

Writer/Notable Work	Score
1. Miguel de Cervantes *Don Quixote*	1038
2. Federico Garcia Lorca *Lament for the Death of a Bullfighter*	534
3. Lope de Vega *The Knight of Olmedo*	509
4. Miguel de Unamuno *Mist, A Tragicomic Novel*	326
5. Pedro Calderon de la Barca *El Gran Teatro del Mundo*	308
6. Francisco Gomez de Quevedo y Villegas *The Life of a Scoundrel*	285
7. Juan Ramon Jimenez *Diary of a Recently Married Poet*	272
8. Luis Vaz de Camoes *The Lusiads*	266
9. Antonio Machado y Ruiz *Campos de Castilla*	189
10. Luis de Gongora y Argote *Soledades*	153

Source: *Best and Worst* original.

PLACES

AIRLINE ROUTES, BUSIEST

Where are all those people who flood the airports going? The facts are that the most traveled routes involve passage to or from the Big Apple—six of the 10 busiest airline routes have New York City as the point of arrival or departure. Following is a list that shows the most heavily traveled airline routes and the number of passengers who fly them annually.

DOMESTIC DEPARTURES

Route	Passengers
1. New York-Los Angeles	2,998,000
2. New York-Boston	2,948,000
3. New York-Washington	2,877,000
4. New York-Miami	2,590,000
5. Los Angeles-San Francisco	2,423,000
6. New York-Chicago	2,383,000
7. Dallas-Houston	2,306,000
8. Honolulu-Kahului (Maui)	2,055,000
9. New York-San Francisco	2,042,000
10. New York-Orlando	2,004,000

FOREIGN DEPARTURES*

Route	Passengers
1. Mexico	2,696,000
2. United Kingdom	2,273,000
3. West Germany	1,209,000
4. Bahamas	979,000
5. Japan	973,000
6. France	845,000
7. Dominican Republic	655,000
8. Jamaica	578,000
9. Italy	458,000
10. Netherlands Antilles	408,000

* from all U.S. cities

Source: *Travel Industry World Yearbook, 1995.*

AIRPORTS, BUSIEST

Busiest U.S. Airports

It's easy to complain about the density of air traffic at major international hubs, not to mention the frequency of delays. But solutions are not so easily forthcoming. In the main, major American cosmopolitan airports are hemmed in by residential neighbors and overzealous tax collectors. In most of the business world, more is more. In the over-heated airline industry, more is definitely too much. Chicago's O'Hare International Airport is the nation's busiest at the moment.

Airport	Passengers, 1995
1. Chicago O'Hare	31,433,002
2 William B. Hartsfield (Atlanta)	28,090,978
3. Dallas/Fort Worth	26,962,940
4. Los Angeles Intl.	26,133,795
5. San Francisco Intl.	17,187,766
6. Miami Intl.	16,065,673
7. Denver Intl.	14,858,763
8. John F. Kennedy Intl. (New York City)	14,601,827
9. Detroit Metropolitan Wayne	14,082,598
10. Phoenix Sky Harbor Intl.	13,738,433

Source: Federal Aviation Commisssion; Department of Transportation, 1996.

DALLAS/FORT WORTH AIRPORT (above) may be the biggest in the U.S., but not the busiest.

IRPORTS, BUSIEST

Busiest Foreign Airports

The five busiest airports in the world are all in the United States, but things are far from sluggish at the globe's other major air centers. London's Heathrow, a traditional hub for passengers traveling to and from Europe and the United States, handles the most passengers of any airport outside America. Tokyo's bustling Haneda is a close second.

Airport	Passengers, 1995
1. London, UK (Heathrow)	54,452,634
2. Tokyo/Haneda, Japan (Tokyo Intl.)	45,822,503
3. Frankfurt, Germany (Rhein/Main)	38,179,543
4. Seoul, South Korea (Kimpo Intl.)	30,919,462
5. Paris, France (Charles De Gaulle)	28,355,470
6. Hong Kong Intl.	. 28,043,338
7. Paris, France (Orly)	26,653,878
8. Amsterdam, Netherlands (Schiphol)	25,355,007
9. Tokyo, Japan (Narita)	24,210,286
10. Singapore (Changi)	23,196,242

Source: Airports Council International.

IRPORTS, ON-TIME RECORDS

Worst On-Time Records

The more crowded, overbuilt and under-thought an airport is, the more time you are likely to spend there, on a trip-to-trip basis. Our

PLACES

biggest worries are of mid-air collisions in over-trafficked skies, but the perils in the hangar, at the gate and on the ticket line are also considerable. Here are the worst examples of the sluggish side of rapid transit.

Airport	% Departures On-time, 1995
1. Atlanta, Hartsfield Intl.	68.6%
2. San Francisco Intl.	70.5%
3. Los Angeles Intl.	72.2%
4. Chicago, O'Hare	74.5%
5. Salt Lake City Intl.	74.8%
6. St. Louis, Lambert	75.7%
7. Boston, Logan Intl.	76.2%
8. New York, Kennedy Intl.	76.3%
9. Detroit, Metro Wayne	77.1%
10. Pittsburgh, Greater Intl.	77.7%

Source: U.S. Department of Transportation, Office Of Consumer Affairs, *Air Travel Consumer Report. Monthly.*

ARCHITECTURAL ACHIEVEMENTS

Best Architecture in America

To list the "best building" in the U.S. is a daunting task; how does one judge such a contest? Architecture, considered by Vitruvius to be "the Mother of the Arts," is a very personal thing, much like painting or sculpture, although buildings influence our daily lives to a much greater extent whether we are aware of it or not. Distinguished practitioners from the American Institute of Architects chose not to name the "best buildings," but rather the "proudest achievements" of American architecture. Their choices are varied in date, style, aesthetic and location. The campus of the University of Virginia, de-

ROCKEFELLER CENTER is considered by the AIA as the second-greatest architectural achievement in the U.S.

signed by Thomas Jefferson, was the most popular choice, undoubtedly for its Palladian beauty and its idyllic campus quality. The architect most represented in the top-ten list is Frank Lloyd Wright, with Falling Water, Robie House and the Johnson Wax building. Wright, by both his own opinion and that of more impartial scholars, is considered the greatest American architect of the twentieth century.

Achievement/Location
1. University of Virginia Charlottesville, VA
2. Rockefeller Center New York City
3. Dulles International Airport Chantilly, VA
4. Falling Water Mill Run, PA
5. Carson Pirie Scott Chicago
6. Seagram Building New York City
7. Philadelpha Savings Fund Society Building Philadelphia
8. Trinity Church Boston
9. Boston City Hall Boston
10. Robie House Chicago

Source: American Institute of Architects.

ART MUSEUMS

Best Attended

Twenty-four North American art museums are visited by at least 500,000 people each year. Who says Americans are philistines? Annually, 20 million visitors come to the top 10 art museums in the country to feast their eyes on the works of Picasso, Renoir, Michelangelo and ancient Greek statuary in the nation's great public collections. No doubt, the National Gallery benefits from its location in Washington, where each summer hosts of unwilling kids are subjected to a little "culture" on their family vacation before being allowed to romp through the really cool stuff at the Smithsonian. What's more, admission is free.

Museum	Number of Vistors/Year
1. National Gallery of Art Washington, DC	6,500,000
2. Metropolitan Museum of Art New York City	4,700,000
3. Art Institute of Chicago Chicago	1,300,000
4. Los Angeles County Museum of Art Los Angeles	1,000,000
5. Hirshhorn Museum & Sculpture Garden Washington, DC	908,000
6. New York State Museum Albany, NY	900,000
7. Ringling Museum of Art Sarasota–Bradenton, FL	900,000
8. Fine Arts Museum of San Francisco San Francisco	800,000
9. Museum of Fine Arts Boston	800,000
10. Carnegie Museum of Art Pittsburgh	700,000

Source: American Art Directory, 1996.

BEACHES

Best in Southern California

Heading for a vacation in sunny Southern California? Heard about the great surf, the sunny skies, the clean water and the uncrowded beaches? California is also the home of off-shore oil refineries and the largest port on the West Coast. The following rates Southern California's beaches from best to worst, taking into account, in descending order of importance, water quality, surf, sand quality, parking and access to the beach. Water quality was scored from 8 to 32 points, surf and sand from 5 to 15 points, and parking and access 2 to 6 points. The maximum score possible was 74, which was earned only by Zuma Beach, a beautiful enclave north of Los Angeles—far enough north to discourage the mere amateur beachgoer (for the exact location of these beaches, consult any map of the area). Zuma's ample parking, great surf and sand, pure water, and easy access make it the best of the Southland's many beaches. In the tie for ninth place, Cardiff has better surf, Windansea has better sand.

ZUMA BEACH (above) is Southern California's number-one rated spot for fun in the sun.

BEST BEACHES

Best Beaches	Total Score
1. Zuma	74
2. San Buenaventura	64
3. El Pescador/El Matador	61
4. Leo Carillo	60
5. Crystal Cove	63
6. La Jolla Shores	62
7. San Clemente	61
8. Bolsa Chica	59
9. Cardiff	58
Windansea	58
11. Corona Del Mar	57
Malibu	57

5. Cabrillo Beach	31
Temescal Canyon	31
7. Will Rogers	35
8. Royal Palms	38
9. Pt. Mugu	39
10. Dockweiler	40
11. Seal Beach	41

Source: *Best and Worst* original, from information in the *Los Angeles Times*.

WORST BEACHES

Worst Beaches	Total Score
1. Belmont Shore	24
2. Imperial Beach	26
3. Santa Monica	28
4. Redondo Beach	29

CITIES— ACTIVITIES

Most Things to Do

We rated the most active cities in seven categories: sun, sea, surf, snow, nature, sports and culture. Each city was assigned a point total from 0 to 100 in each category; the resulting index charts the amount of leisure and recreational activities normally available to residents of each locale. The "sun" category is a relative score based on weather conditions—Los Angeles and San Diego topped the list with perfect scores of 100. Similarly, the "sea" category reflects water-based recreation such as boating; "sand" referred to beach activities; "snow" referred to winter activities, especially skiing, and scores were determined by the proximity of major ski resorts; "nature" was a subjective evaluation of the natural beauty of the area and the number of major national parks in the vicinity; "sports" referred to major sports franchises in the area and their success; and "culture" evaluated art museums, galleries, symphonies, dance and specialty museums. The good-times capital of the U.S., according to our ranking, is sunny Los Angeles, with its abundance of sun, sand, boating, desert and even skiing opportunities.

The Top 10 Cities	Score
1. Los Angeles	596
2. San Diego	440
3. Miami	432
4. New York City	427
5. Washington	426
6. San Francisco	412
7. Boston	392
8. Seattle	387
9. Denver	358
10. Phoenix	291

Source: *Best and Worst* original.

FLORIDA—a state with many faces— is where 9 of the 10 cities with the oldest populations are located. Photo: Greater Miami Convention and Visitor's Bureau.

CITIES— AGE

Oldest Populace

As we get on in years, we reward ourselves by creating a life filled with the greatest possible comforts. For many, this means a moving away from a long-time place of residence to a more accommodating, convenient and/or inexpensive locale. Some flock to family, others to the Sunbelt. Here's where seniors have settled in greatest concentrations.

City	Median Age
1. Punta Gorda, FL	53.2
2. Sarosata-Bradenton, FL	47.3
3. Fort Myers-Cape Coral, FL	43.4

4. Naples, FL	42.3
5. Fort Pierce-Port St. Lucie, FL	41.9
6. Daytona Beach, FL	41.6
Ocala, FL	41.6
West Palm Beach-Boca Raton, FL	41.6
9. Barnstable-Yarmouth, MA	40.9
10. Tampa-St. Petersburg-Clearwater, FL	40.4

Source: *Sales & Marketing Magazine*, Survey of Buying Power, 1996.

CITIES—AGE

Where Youthfulness Reigns

Some of the cities with the youngest populace are, not surprisingly, college towns. Other youthful cities contain or are located near military bases; still others are border towns that see a good deal of immigration from Mexico. The median age in the United States is approximately 33. Following is a list of the most youthful cities in the land, as measured by median age.

City	Median Age
1. Provo-Orem, UT	22.7
2. Bryan-College Station, TX	24.6
3. Jacksonville, NC	25.0
4. McAllen-Edingburg-Mission, TX	25.3
5. Laredo, TX	26.3
6. Lawrence, KS	27.1
7. Flagstaff, AZ	27.4
8. Bloomington, IN	28.2
9. Salt Lake City-Ogden, UT	28.3
Kileen-Temple, TX	28.3

Source: U.S. Census Bureau.

CITIES—AIDS

Largest Concentrations of AIDS Victims

AIDS has simultaneously struck America deaf, dumb and blind. We listen but don't hear. We are told, but don't repeat. We see but don't understand. AIDS is an epidemic which must be cornered and destroyed; to fight it we will need all of our senses intact. Below are the cities where this epidemic has struck hardest.

City	AIDS Cases*
1. New York City	86,977
2. Los Angeles	32,859
3. Miami	17,511
4. Chicago	15,322
5. Houston	13,322
6. Newark, NJ	12,495
7. Atlanta	11,400
8. Boston	10,006
9. Baltimore	9,257
10. Dallas	9,158

* cases reported July 1994 through June 1996

Source: HIV/AIDS Surveillance Report, 1996.

CITIES—ALCOHOL

Most Spending on Alcohol

Do the gentrified country and suburban folks who live on the perimeter of America's big cities drink more than city dwellers? Or do they just spend more on their alcoholic beverages? City drinkers are way down on the list when it comes to how much they spend on booze. Following are the communities that have two-fisted drinkers, but are hardly tight-fisted when they reach

BEST ARCHITECTURE OVERALL: Chicago, with it's lakefront skyline, is one of most spectacular urban settings in the world.

for their wallets to pay for their drinking pleasures.

Area	Yearly Spending per Capita
1. Nassau-Suffolk, NY	$427
San Jose, CA	$427
3. Middlesex-Somerset-Hunterdon, NJ	$424
4. Anchorage	$420
5. Orange County, CA	$417
6. Ventura, CA	$412
7. Washington, DC (includes MD, VA, WV)	$405
8. Honolulu	$400
Bergen-Passaic, NJ	$400
Dutchess County, NY	$400

Source: Consumer Spending Survey, 1996.

CITIES— ARCHITECTURE

Best Architecture Overall

Since the late 1800s, Chicago has been America's first city of architecture. From the urban planning of Daniel Burnham, whose motto was "Make no small plans," to Louis Sullivan, Frank Lloyd Wright, Mies Van der Rohe and the architectural firm of Skidmore, Owings and Merrill, the city has been home to the country's most innovative and influential architects. An architectural competition in Chicago always manages to stir up big interest, both here and abroad. Our ratings are a subjective scoring by *Best and Worst* editors of cities in four different categories: number of im-

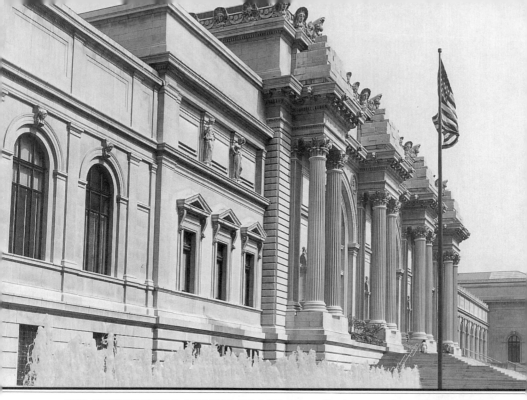

THE METROPOLITAN MUSEUM OF ART, the nation's second most-visited art museum, (See Art Museums on page 81) is one of the chief reasons New York is the number-one rated city in the arts.

portant architectural works, diversity of architecture, indigenous architectural styles and drama of skyline. Each city received a point score from 1 to 250 in these four categories. The top 10 American architectural towns based on this formula are as follows:

City	Score
1. Chicago	753
2. New York City	616
3. Los Angeles	605
4. Miami	423
5. San Francisco	395
6. Boston	382
7. Houston	344
8. Pittsburgh	317
9. Philadelphia	272
10. New Orleans	244

Source: *Best and Worst* original.

CITIES— ARTS

Best Arts Overall

This rating is derived from the rating of overall activities, and reflects the cultural opportunities of the cities in terms of art galleries and museums, dance, theater, orchestral music, and specialty museums. The scores are subjective evaluations from the editors of the *Best and Worst*. New York City, of course, comes out on top for its plethora of art galleries and museums, its specialty museums catering to a variety of artistic and cultural interests, and its large arts community. New York is indeed still the place to be for the up-and-coming artist.

PLACES

City	Score
1. New York City	97
2. Chicago	84
3. Washington, DC	82
4. San Francisco	77
5. Los Angeles	68
6. Boston	66
Philadelphia	66
8. Atlanta	56
9. Houston	44
10. Pittsburgh	42
11. Cleveland	37

Source: *Best and Worst* original.

CITIES— AUTOMOBILES

Where's New York?

Finally, here's some material to one-up a New Yorker. Alas, the Big Apple is not first in something—car sales. In fact, they are not even in the top 10. Who, after all, would want to spend money on a car in New York, a place where there's nowhere to park and no room to drive.

Metro Area	Auto Sales ($1,000s)
1. Chicago	$17,096,549
2. Los Angeles/Long Beach	$15,868,134
3. Detroit	$11,894,194
4. Philadelphia	$10,884,240
5. Washington, DC	$10,514,899
6. Houston	$10,124,731
7. Dallas	$8,820,727
8. Atlanta	$8,775,048
9. Fort Lauderdale, FL	$7,338,260
10. Minneapolis-St. Paul	$7,147,637

Source: *Sales & Marketing Magazine*, Survey of Buying Power, 1996.

CITIES—BARS AND RESTAURANTS

Wining and Dining Capitals

Where do Americans spend the most on dining out? Surprisingly, it's not New York City; rather it's the blue-collar town of Chicago. Below are the cities where folks spend the most on dining and drinking out.

City	Restaurant Sales ($1,000s)
1. Chicago	$8,076,777
2. Los Angeles-Long Beach	$7,297,208
3. New York City	$7,135,082
4. Washington, DC	$4,893,639
5. Detroit	$4,541,367
6. Atlanta	$4,019,923
7. Boston-Lawrence-Lowell-Brockton, MA	$3,909,410
8. Philadelphia	$3,903,720
9. Houston	$3,658,736
10. Phoenix-Mesa	$3,453,806

Source: *Sales & Marketing Magazine*, Survey of Buying Power, 1996.

CITIES— BIRTH RATE

Highest and Lowest

In the beginning, God said go forth and multiply. But these days, most of us are doing our procreating at or near home. And from these carnal conjurings come the young folk, who in turn stick close to the hearth for many years. In some of our cities, the blood runs hotter and heavier than in others. Herewith, the birth capitals and backwoods of these United States, measured in births per 1,000 populations.

PLACES

HIGHEST BIRTH RATES

City	Birth Rate per 1,000 Pop.
1. La Puente, CA	64.8
2. Miami	49.5
3. Gaithersburg, MD	49.2
Watsonville, CA	49.2
5. Whittier, CA	44.1
Palmdale, CA	44.1
7. Lake Worth, FL	43.0
8. Bakersfield, CA	42.4
9. Madera, CA	41.3
10. Jacksonville, NC	40.3

LOWEST BIRTH RATES

City	Birth Rate per 1,000 Pop.
1. Danville, IL	18.0
Longview, WA	18.0
Baltimore	18.0
Greenville, SC	18.0
Rochester, NH	18.0
Charlotte, NC	18.0
Manchester, NH	18.0
Worcester, MA	18.0
Jacksonville, FL	18.0
Hampton , VA	18.0

Source: U.S. Census Bureau, *County/City Data Book*, 1994. Statistical Abstract of the United States, 1996.

CITIES—BLACK POPULATION

The South is no longer home to the city with the largest percentage of Blacks. Today, Detroit is number one. Previously it was Memphis, followed by New Orleans and Norfolk, Virginia. Nonetheless, black populations are still high in the South, even though large groups have migrated north, with the greatest numbers going to New York, Chicago and Baltimore. Below are the 10 metropolitan areas with the greatest percentage of African Americans.

Metro Area	% Black Population
1. Detroit	75.7%
2. Atlanta	67.1%
3. Washington, DC	65.8%
4. Birmingham, AL	63.3%
5. New Orleans	61.9%
6. Baltimore	59.2%
7. Newark, NJ	58.5%
8. Richmond, VA	55.2%
9. Memphis	54.8%
10. St. Louis	47.5%

Source: U.S. Census Bureau, *County/City Data Book*, 1994.

CITIES— CABLE TV

Top 20 Cable TV Markets

Once upon a time, it seemed that the networks were all but invincible, and a free, clear signal was thought of as a God-given right. But progress—and commercialism—can't be stopped, and the penetration of pay cable channels have made deep inroads into traditional broadcast markets. Although cable is still looked on by many as a low-level luxury, over the next decade a battle will be played out for supremacy of the screen. The following are the towns where cable reigns most supreme.

City	% Households Wired
1. Palm Springs, CA	90%
2. Hartford & New Haven, CT	86%
Santa Barbara-Sanmar-San Luis Ob., CA	86%
Honolulu	86%
5. W. Palm Beach-Ft. Pierce, FL	83%
6. San Diego	82%
Anniston, AL	82%
Biloxi-Gulfport, MS	82%
9. Springfield-Holyoke, MA	81%
Johnstown-Altoona, PA	81%

Source: A.C. Nielsen, 1997.

CITIES—CONVENTION CAPITALS

Tops Hosts for Conventioneers

When Chicago's McCormick Place opened in early 1997, it became the largest convention center under one roof in North America, with 2.2 million square feet of space. That's a lot of room for a lot of convention goers, but it's necessary space— millions of businesspeople attend conventions or trade shows each year. Their favorite site is Las Vegas, with its many varied attractions beyond the trade show floor. The first list below shows the cities with the greatest attendance at conventions and trade shows in 1995. Not surprisingly, all are major metropolitan areas capable of supporting the many large hotels and other services necessary to host convention traffic. The second list is of the largest North American convention centers in square footage, including expansion plans.

MOST CONVENTION ATTENDEES

City Attendance	(millions)
1. Las Vegas	2.92
2. Chicago	2.86
3. Orlando	2.66
4. San Diego	1.95
5. Philadelphia	1.46
6. New York City	1.45
San Francisco	1.45
7. Washington, D.C.	1.37
8. Boston	1.21
9. Phoenix	1.10

BIGGEST CONVENTION FACILITIES

City	Square Footage (thousands)
1. Chicago	2,200
2. Cleveland	1,600
3. Las Vegas (Las Vegas Convention Center)	1,550
4. Las Vegas (Sands Expo)	1.300
5. New Orleans	1,100
Orlando	1,100
6. Toronto	1,080
7. Houston	1,000
Louisville	1,000
8. Atlanta	950

Source: Cities' convention and visitors bureaus, *Tradeshow Week.*

CITIES— CRIME

Most Dangerous Cities

Where would you feel more secure, Pine Bluff, Arkansas, or New York City? The former has the second highest crime rate in the nation. The latter—though fifth in crime in the U.S.—has a drastically reduced rate of crime compared to previous years. Crime in the U.S. has always

THE TABLES AREN'T THE ONLY REASON that Las Vegas attracts more conventioneers than any other U.S. city. Photo: Las Vegas News Bureau.

been associated with big cities in the minds of many Americans. When driving in places like Chicago or Philadelphia, we lock our doors for safety. In smaller towns of the South most people feel more secure. That may be the sentiment, but in reality, some big cities are relatively safe and some seemingly peaceful communities are places where you are most likely to fall victim to a criminal. Following are the cities in which the most crimes per capita are committed.

City	Crimes per 100,000, 1995
1. Miami	1,886.3
2. Pine Bluff, AR	1,659.4
3. Los Angeles-Long Beach	1,433.6
4. Gainesville, FL	1,416.8
5. New York City	1,392.8
6. Baton Rouge	1,386.0
7. Baltimore	1,335.9
8. New Orleans	1,334.5
9. Lawton, OK	1,330.8
10. Sioux City, IA	1,271.4

Source: FBI Uniform Crime Reports, 1996.

CITIES— DIVERSITY

Most Diverse Population

New York, the mythical melting pot, has always been the newly arrived immigrant's first glimpse of America. From the processing rooms of Ellis Island to the Customs Office at Kennedy Airport, New York holds out a somewhat dubious welcome for the tired, the poor and the huddled masses yearning to breathe free (or at least free-market). However, in recent years, such hot spots as Los Angeles and Miami have become major immigration centers for people from Latin America and the Far East. Los Angeles, with its thriving Latino population, its strong Jewish community, and its large concentrations of Armenian-Americans and other Middle Eastern immigrants, rates highly in terms of ethnic diversity, as does Miami, with flourishing communities of Cubans, Haitians, Central Americans and African-Americans, not to mention its older Jewish community. These, then, are the most ethnically diverse North American cities, based on editors' evaluations of census information.

Rank/City
1. New York City
2. Los Angeles
3. Miami
4. Chicago
5. Washington, DC
6. Toronto
7. Houston
8. San Diego
9. Seattle
10. Boston

Source: *Best and Worst* original, based on U.S. Census Bureau information.

CITIES— EDUCATION

Educational Attainment

The following list ranks cities according to the educational attainment of their populations, as measured by the percentage of the population with 16 or more years of education. The list of big cities with the best-educated populace is led by Raleigh, North Carolina, home of the University of North Carolina, and the West Coast meccas of San Francisco and Seattle. Washington,

THE LADY (at right) still has pulling power. New York today, as yesterday, has the most diverse population of any American city (See page 90).

with its preponderance of lawyers and bureaucrats, also scores high. The cities in which educational attainment is lowest are primarily northeastern urban centers that also suffer from other blights—unemployment, high crime, an entrenched underclass. These factors are part of the continued cycle of poverty that keeps educational, and ultimately social, opportunity out of reach for many inner-city residents. In Cleveland, a mere 8.1 percent of the population has reached a college-degree level of education.

MOST EDUCATED

City	% w/ 16+ Yrs. School
1. Raleigh, NC	40.6%
2. Seattle	37.9%
3. San Francisco	35.0%
4. Austin, TX	34.4%
5. Washington, DC	33.3%
6. Lexington-Fayette, KY	30.6%
7. Minneapolis	30.3%
8. Boston	30.0%
Arlington, TX	30.0%
10. San Diego	29.8%

LEAST EDUCATED

City	% w/ 16+ Yrs. School
1. Cleveland	8.1%
2. Newark, NJ	8.5%
3. Detroit	9.6%
4. Santa Ana, CA	10.6%
5. Las Vegas	13.4%
6. Miami	14.1%
Toledo, OH	14.1%
8. Milwaukee	14.8%
9. Akron, OH	14.9%
10. Stockton, CA	15.0%

Source: U.S. Census Bureau, *City and County Data Book,* 1994.

8. Pittsburgh-Beaver Valley, PA $51.59
9. Detroit-Ann Arbor, MI $48.18
10. Baltimore $47.85
  * for 500 kilowatt hours
Source: U.S. Bureau of Labor Statistics (SAUS, 1996).

THE GREAT WHITE WAY is a costly proposition (See below). Excessive power consumption in New York has caused regional blackouts that have darkened many nearby counties and states for as much as three days at a time.

CITIES— ELECTRICITY

Highest Electric Bills

A large portion of America's energy consumption volume is generated from electricity. The following lists are rankings of the cities with the highest and lowest electricity bills. The data is drawn from a field of the 75 largest cities in the U.S. and illustrates typical monthly residential electric bills.

City	Avg. Elec. Cost, 1995*
1. New York-Long Island, NY-NJ-CT	$70.74
2. Los Angeles-Anaheim-Riverside, CA	$64.95
3. San Francisco-Oakland-San Jose, CA	$62.98
4. Philadelphia-Wilmington-Trenton, PA-NJ-DE-MD	$62.09
5. Boston-Lawrence-Salem, MA-NH	$62.02
6. Chicago-Gary-Lake County, IL-IN-WI	$57.40
7. Cleveland-Akron-Lorain, OH	$54.90

CITIES— FEDERAL TAX

The "Urban Rich" and their Tax Bill

The Revenue Reconciliation Act of 1993 took an average of $23,500 from households that earned $200,000-plus annually. Nonetheless, except for minor changes, the tax increase had little effect on the spending habits of the wealthy. Most of the money generated by the one percent of Americans in the "plus" class goes toward maintaining an executive lifestyle and sending children to good schools—two spending habits upper-class folk are not likely to alter, according to the consulting firm Auricom Corporation in Bethesda, Maryland. The firm says wealthy households spend only two percent of their income on food, compared to 12 percent for the average U.S. household. In total, that one percent tax was estimated to contribute $2.2 billion to the federal budget in 1994. The tax hike hit hard in Stamford, Connecticut, where 11.7 percent of households are in the plus class— the nation's highest concentration of the category—and in nearby Norwalk, Connecticut, where 8.9 percent are in the class. It is estimated that Stamford shelled out $214 million in taxes in 1994, and Norwalk $102 million. It also is estimated that New York's Nassau and Suffolk counties, where three percent, or 25,000 households, are classed as rich, generates the most tax revenue of any area in the country: $593 million. That's due to the area's large population—2.64 million, compared to Stamford-Norwalk's 331,000. San Francisco is estimated to be second, producing $423 million, and Newark, New Jersey, third with $415 million, according to Donnelley Marketing Information Service of Stamford. Following are the places with largest share of $200,000-plus householders, "the rich" in percent, and aggregate federal income taxes they paid.

Area	% "Rich"	Tax (millions)*
1. Stamford, CT	11.7%	$214
2. Norwalk, CT	8.9%	$102
3. Lake County, IL	4.4%	$189
4. Naples, FL	3.4%	$55
5. Danbury, CT	3.0%	$49
6. Nassau-Suffolk, NY	2.9%	$593
7. San Francisco	2.8%	$423
8. Newark, NJ	2.7%	$415
9. Bergen-Passaic, NJ	2.7%	$292
10. West Palm Beach, FL	2.3%	$217

*figures are for 1994

Source: *American Demographics.*

CITIES—GOVERNMENT WORKERS

Most Government Employees

Nearly everyone complains about big government, but few in that teeming majority recognize the irony when they also complain of the scarcity of staff at public places (trains, schools, parks, prisons) and the sloth of service (at public-sector glamour spots like the departments of Motor Vehicles and Health). City workers, who engage the public mano-a-mano, are the closest link of 'us' (the citizens) with 'them' (the "leaders"). Power to those people-of-the-people! Here are the cities with the most public sector employees per 10,000 people.

City	Govt. Empl./10,000 Pop.
1. Washington, DC	709
2. New York City	520
3. Buffalo, NY	396
4. Norfolk, VA	383
5. Baltimore	380
6. Boston	366
7. Memphis	360
8. Virginia Beach, VA	356
9. Nashville-Davidson, TN	348
10. San Francisco	332

Source: U.S. Census Bureau (SAUS, 1996).

CITIES—HISPANIC

Most Hispanics

While America is a nation of immigrants, most immigrants eventually assimilate into the mainstream. Unlike America's traditional European stock, Latin American immigrants, to a large extent, maintain their unique culture and, above all, their language. The cities on the list below are where you will find the nation's largest Hispanic populations.

Metro Area	% Hispanic
1. El Paso, TX	69.0%
2. Santa Ana, CA	65.2%
3. Miami	62.5%
4. San Antonio	55.6%
5. Corpus Christi, TX	50.4%
6. Los Angeles	39.9%
7. Albuquerque	34.5%
8. Anaheim, CA	31.4%

PLACES

9. Fresno, CA 29.9%
10. Tucson 29.3%
Source: U.S. Census Bureau.

CITIES—HISPANIC

Least Hispanic Metro Areas

The neo-Hispanic bent of American urban culture is unmistakable, but unbroken bastions of Caucasian exclusionism still abound. Most often, though, the cultural purity of these metros has less to do with the discriminatory attitudes of the locals than with the desirability of the locales as far as Hispanics are concerned. These, then, are the toughest places in the U.S. in which to find a good burrito.

Metro Area	% Hispanic
1. Birmingham, AL	0.4%
2. Memphis	0.7%
Louisville	0.7%
Cincinnati	0.7%
Akron, OH	0.7%
6. Richmond, VA	0.9%
Pittsburgh	0.9%
Nashville-Davidson, TN	0.9%
9. Mobile, AL	1.0%
10. Lexington-Fayette, KY	1.1%
Indianapolis	1.1%
Columbus, OH	1.1%

Source: U.S. Census Bureau, *City and County Data Book*, 1994.

CITIES—HOMELESSNESS

Be It Never So Humble

A 1994 survey by the U.S. Conference of Mayors found that single men and families with children make up the largest groups of homeless in the nation. The report showed total requests for shelter up an average 13 percent from 1993, and food requests up 12 percent.

Single men make up the highest group, at 48 percent of the total. Families account for 38 percent, single women 11 percent, and children—family-rejects or runaways—three percent. The Department of Housing and Urban Development maintains there are 50,000 homeless people in the United States. Advocacy groups say the number is more like three million. The Census Bureau has its own count. Beginning on March 20, 1990, the Census Bureau undertook a two-day count of homelessness, visiting 11,000 shelters and 24,000 street sites. The census takers found far fewer homeless people to survey than others who have done head counts, namely those who work often with the homeless. The bureau's survey, however, is the best estimate we have of the nation's homeless population: 228,261—178,828 in emergency shelters and 49,793 at "preidentified street locations." A 1991 survey by the Census Bureau said California led the way in homeless, with 48,887, with New York second with 43,793. Far behind in third was Florida with 10,299. Blacks make up the highest percentage of the homeless population, at 53 percent, followed by whites at 31 percent, Hispanics at 12 percent, American Indians at three percent, and Asians at one percent. The mayors gave the following as characteristics of the homeless: 43 percent substance abusers, an increase of three percent from a similar report by the mayors in 1991; 26 percent mentally ill, up from 24 percent in 1991; 23 percent veterans, down from 25 percent; 19 percent employed full- or part-time,

PLACES

up from 18 percent; and eight percent with AIDS or HIV, up 1 percent. Minorities comprised the largest number of homeless in New York, Detroit, Chicago, Baltimore and St. Louis, according to a study made by the National Academy of Sciences' Institute of Medicine. Milwaukee, Phoenix, Portland and the state of Ohio accounted for the highest percentage of whites, according to the report, summarized in the *Universal Almanac*. Following are the numbers of homeless people in select American cities.

City	Population Homeless
1. New York City	55,000
2. Philadelphia	35,000
3. Los Angeles	31,000
4. Kansas City	13,000
5. Louisville	11,442
6. Cleveland	10,000
7. Washington, DC	7,500
8. San Diego	7,000
9. Chicago	6,764
10. Phoenix	6,300

Source: *USA Today*; *Universal Almanac*; U.S. Census Bureau, March 20, 1990.

CITIES— HOUSING

Most and Least Costly Homes

Statistics generated from a wide variety of fields suggest that the generation that is now approaching "adulthood" and its accompanying responsibilities will have a much more difficult time attaining the lifestyle that their parents enjoyed. The federal deficit, the strain on services, increased costs of health care, the costs of fighting social ills,

THE SMALL, POORLY FUNDED AND TOTALLY PRIVATE ENTERPRISE that publishes Streetwise, a newspaper about the plight of the homeless, has done more to help homeless people than all levels of government combined.

a declining work ethic and the slide of the middle class are just a few of the factors that will make it more difficult to maintain a middle-class lifestyle. Below are the most and least expensive housing markets for new homes in the country. The figures are based on the average cost of a new home and are drawn from a database of approximately 300 cities encompassing the largest metropolitan areas in the country.

HIGHEST HOME COSTS

Metro Area	Avg. Home Cost
1. Honolulu	$332,000
2. San Francisco	$256,800
3. San Jose, CA	$251,800
4. Santa Cruz- Watsonville, CA	$235,000
5. Stamford-Norwalk, CT	$223,500
6. Orange County, CA	$215,500
7. Bergen-Passaic, NJ	$215,000
8. Salinas, CA	$213,500
9. Long Island, NY	$210,000
10. Ventura, CA	$210,000

LOWEST HOME COSTS

Metro Area	Avg. Home Cost
1. Steubenville- Weirton, OH-WV	$58,000
2. Johnstown, PA	$58,500
3. Texarkana, TX-AR	$58,500
4. Duluth- Superior, MN-WI	$59,500
5. Pine Bluff, AR	$59,500
6. Wheeling, WV-OH	$59,500
7. Waterloo-Cedar Falls, IA	$61,500
8. Enid, OK	$62,500
9. Huntington- Ashland, WV-KY-OH	$63,500
10. Janesville-Beloit, WI	$64,500

Source: Data Quick, Inc., National Association of Realtors; from *Places Rated Almanac, 1997.*

CITIES— HOUSING

Most One-person Households

One is the loneliest number, but there's yet another downside: it's wasteful. In the U.S. we throw away millions of pounds of garbage that could be recycled. We consume most of the world's fuel supply in order to heat and transport us from our homes to our workplaces and back. One indication of just how wasteful we are is the number of houses and apartments lived in by one person. In some countries just the idea of one person having three or four rooms to themselves is unheard of. Interestingly, Washington, D.C., where "wasteful" is the latest buzz word, leads in one-person households.

City	% Households w. One Person
1. Washington, DD	41.5%
2. Denver	40.4%
3. Seattle	39.8 %
4. Cincinnati	39.5 %
5. San Francisco	39.3 %
6. St. Louis	39.2 %
7. Minneapolis	38.5 %
8. Pittsburgh	36.2 %
9. Richmond	35.9 %
10. Buffalo	35.6 %

Source: U.S. Census Bureau, *City and County Data Book,* 1994.

CITIES— JOB GROWTH

New Jobs Through the Year 2000

Finding a job is no easy task. First you have to decide just exactly what it is you want to do. Then you have to train, whether it means going to college or through some other type of preparation. Once that's completed, the most important component of finding a job is to be where the jobs are; that is, the cities in which the openings exist. Interestingly, despite the downsizing of the federal government, the most jobs available from now until the new century will be in the Washington, DC, metropolitan area, followed by the usual movement south and west. One notable exception to the geographical trend is Chicago; the city of the broad shoulders seems to thrive no matter what.

City	Projected Jobs
1. Washington, DC-MD-VA-WV	101,194
2. Atlanta	91,642
3. Orange County, CA	90,493
4. San Diego	89,682
5. Orlando,FL	83,014
6. Chicago	82,568
7. Dallas	81,873
8. Houston	78,210
9. Phoenix-Mesa	76,175
10. Tampa-St.Petersburg-Clearwater, FL	73,911

Source: Woods & Poole Economics, Inc.

CITIES—MEDICAL SPECIALISTS

Most Medical Specialists

Although there is a growing trend towards Family Practice in medical schools, the majority of American physicians still specialize. Their numbers per 100,000 tend to rise in smaller areas where medical schools and Veterans Administration hospitals are located. Also, a small city where medical care is a

COMMERICAL WASHINGTON, D.C. on Connecticut Ave. (above), where many private companies do business. With some governmental responsibilities eliminated, private companies perform roles which were once federal functions.

major industry, like Rochester, Minnesota, would play host to an anomalous proportion of medical specialists. Below are metro areas with more than 100 medical specialists per 100,000 people.

Metro Area	Specialists per 100,000
1. Rochester, MN	375
2. Boston	144
3. Iowa City, IA	133
4. Charlottesville, VA	132
5. San Francisco	118
6. Columbia, MO	107
7. Long Island, NY	104
8. Gainesville, FL	104
9. Greenville, NC	101

Source: U.S. Department of Health and Human Services.

PLACES

CITIES— MURDER

Murder Capitals, Per Capita

Murder is a familiar scene on the evening news in some of our nation's cities. People shoot their spouses with guns meant for self-defense. Drug deals go bad. Kids shoot each other over perceived slights—basketball jackets or the expensive shoes they couldn't afford. New Orleans, jazz capital of the South, is also the country's murder capital. The good news is that the murder rate is down overall in the U.S. In 1990, for example, there were over 42 murders per 100,000 population in New Orleans. By 1995, the rate was down approximately 25 percent.

City	Murders per 100,000, 1995
1. New Orleans	32.7
2. Chicago	30.0
3. Philadelphia	28.2
4. Jackson, MS	25.0
5. Oklahoma City	24.2
6. Memphis	20.0
Pine Bluff, AR	20.0
8. Shreveport-Bossier City, LA	19.7
9. Los Angeles-Long Beach	18.3
10. Rocky Mount, NC	18.2

Source: FBI Uniform Crime Reports, 1996.

CITIES— MURDER

Highest Body Count

There are not as many murders in the U.S. now as there once were. Nonetheless, some cities such as Washington are experiencing an increase in the murder rate—and it's a significant one. In 1989 there were 434 murders. By 1995 the number grew to 600. Other cities, New York in particular, have experienced a significant drop in murders. The Big Apple, for example, had over 1,900 murders in 1990. Five years later, the number fell to 1,220. The following ranking lists the 10 cities (with populations of 10,000 and over) with the most murders.

City	Murders, 1995
1. Los Angeles-Long Beach	1,682
2. New York City	1,220
3. Chicago	824
4. Washington, DC	600
5. Detroit	564
6. Houston	446
7. Philadelphia	432
8. New Orleans	431
9. Baltimore	392
10. Riverside-San Bernadino, CA	358

Source: FBI Uniform Crime Reports, 1996.

CITIES— OBESITY

Highest and Lowest Percentages of Obese Citizens

Americans have been dieting for decades, and yet we still eat too much and, consequently, weigh too much. You would think that with all the calorie-conscious information available, the custom-made diet programs, and the barrage of bulletins on healthy eating and living, the number of obese citizens would decline. But it hasn't. For example, back in 1962, 28 percent of males between the ages of 45 and 54 were considered overweight. By 1992 that percentage had risen to over 35 percent. Below are the cities with the highest and lowest percentages of obese citizens.

MOST OBESE PERSONS

City	Percent Obese
1. New Orleans	37.55%
2. Norfolk, VA	33.94%
3. San Antonio	32.96%
4. Kansas City	31.66%
5. Cleveland	31.50%
6. Detroit	31.01%
7. Columbus	30.75%
8. Cincinnati	30.71%
9. Pittsburgh	29.99%
10. Houston	29.19%

FEWEST OBESE PERSONS

City	Percent Obese
1. Denver	22.10%
2. Minneapolis	22.63%
3. San Diego	22.91%
4. Washington, DC	23.84%
5. Phoenix	24.36%
6. St. Louis	24.78%
7. Tampa	24.91%
8. San Francisco	25.16%
9. Los Angeles	25.22%
10. Atlanta	25.49%

Source: *USA Today*, March 4, 1997.

NEW ORLEANS, capital of shrimp dishes, jambalya and crawfish pie, is a hard place to live and be thin.

City	Percent
5. Las Vegas	7.6%
Memphis	7.6%
7. Nashville	7.6%
8. Portland-Vancouver, OR	7.8%
9. Charlotte, NC	8.5%
10. Greensboro-Winston Salem-High Point, NC	8.6%

Source: U.S. Census Bureau, Society of Industrial and Office Realtors, (SAUS, 1996).

CITIES—OFFICE VACANCY RATES

Room To Grow?

In some U.S. cities, it has become increasingly difficult to get office space. In a few cases, the glut is due to a slumping real estate scene; in others it's just a matter of overcrowding. Following are the cities in which there is little room for a new business— at least one that needs office space.

Metro Area	Vacancy Rate
1. Columbus, OH	4.2%
2. Salt Lake City	4.6%
3. Richmond-Petersburg, VA	5.5%
4. Birmingham, AL	7.1%

CITIES—PARKING PLACES

Where Parkers Keep Circling the Block

Can't find a place to park? Don't be ridiculous, there are plenty of spots. In fact, there are 3.4 million parking spaces available in designated parking stalls in American cities; it's just that none of them seem available when you're late for your appointment. There are also a total of 10,171 parking facilities ready to rent. Among them, 6,407 are open-air parking lots and 3,764 are multi-level parking structures. A full

8,481 of them let you park your own car while 1,687 do it for you. Parking cars can be lucrative: those 10,171 facilities took in a total of $3.7 billion in receipts. Below is a listing of those metropolitan areas with the most parking spaces. It's no surprise that the Southern California region far outpaces the rest of the country, is it?

Metro Area	Quantity of Parking Stalls*
1. Los Angeles	550,329
2. Washington, DC	190,248
3. Chicago	136,697
4. Atlanta	112,577
5. San Diego	98,043
6. Houston	96,989
7. Seattle	65,622
8. Minneapolis-St. Paul	58,155
9. Cleveland	54,463
10. Honolulu	53,677

* excludes valet parking and municipal lots, and lots operated by establishments primarily engaged in other activities (e.g., restaurants)

Source: U.S. Census Bureau, *Census and You*, July 1996.

CITIES—PEDESTRIAN SAFETY

Walk on the Wild Side

Walking is supposed to be good exercise. Then how could taking a walk be hazardous to your health? It just might be if you're strolling through the streets of Fort Lauderdale, Florida—recently rated the deadliest American city for pedestrians. It's a dubious distinction, and right behind Fort Lauderdale and rounding out the top five are Miami, Atlanta, Tampa, and Dallas—all located in the South, where cars are king and speed is the thing.

Surprisingly, pedestrians don't have to watch their steps quite so cautiously in some large cities, including New York. Those spots score as markedly safer as a result of their wide sidewalks, bus stops, and other pedestrian niceties. Although the largest cities do have the most total deaths, they are not considered the most dangerous, since the report ranked cities by number of fatalities per 100,000 population compared to the number of people walking to work each day.

MOST HAZARDOUS STREETS

Area	Average Annual Fatalities*
1. Fort Lauderdale	58
2. Miami	100
3. Atlanta	84
4. Tampa	85
5. Dallas	76
6. Houston	101
7. Detroit	107
8. Riverside, CA	92
9. Phoenix	79
10. Charlotte, NC	29

SAFEST STREETS

Area	Average Annual Fatalities
1. Pittsburgh	33
2. Milwaukee	19
3. Boston	22
4. Rochester, NY	17
5. New York City	310
6. Minneapolis	35
7. San Francisco	43
8. Philadelphia	120
9. Norfolk, VA	25
10. Columbus, Ohio	20

* Figures are for quantity of fatalities; rankings are based on fatalities per 100,000 population.

Source: Environmental Working Group, Surface Transportation Policy Project.

FORT LAUDERDALE is a good place to stay on the beach. The streets are the most dangerous ones in the U.S. for pedestrians.

CITIES—POLICE FORCES

Cop Counts

Miami must have a crime problem. The city has more cops than most *states!* In fact, about 55% of all the police officers in Florida are in Miami. In the U.S., a large population translates to a large base of law enforcement officers. More people mean more crime and more people in more crowded conditions mean even more law enforcement. So it is no surprise that the states with the most police officers are the states with the largest population and with the most crowded urban centers. New York leads the way, even though it no longer leads the country in population, and the crime rate there is dropping. Maybe all those cops are having an effect.

MOST COPS

State	Police Officers (thousands)
1. New York	68.2
2. California	65.8
3. Texas	41.3
4. Illinois	35.7
5. Florida	32.9
6. New Jersey	26.7
7. Pennsylvania	23.7
8. Ohio	20.9
9. Miami	19.6
10. Georgia	16.8

FEWEST COPS

State	Police Officers (thousands)
1. Vermont	1.0

2. Alaska	1.1
3. North Dakota	1.1
4. South Dakota	1.1
5. Wyoming	1.2
6. Montana	1.4
7. Delaware	1.6
8. New Hampshire	2.1
9. Idaho	2.2
10. Maine	2.3

Source: U.S. Bureau of Justice Statistics; *Sourcebook of Criminal Justice*, 1994. (SAUS, 1996).

CITIES— POPULATION

World's Largest Metropolitan Centers

We're running out of elbow room as the world's population continues to grow at an exponential rate. But the growth is not even. Some places are booming much faster than others, and experts are concerned about populations that outgrow their ability to feed themselves. We know about famine in parts of Africa. In fact, as of 1995, Africa comprises over 15 percent of the world's population. But that population remains mainly rural. On the continent of Asia the population continues to move from the country to the city. The entire continent holds well over half the world's population. So it's no surprise that the largest city in the world is the greater Tokyo area, followed by other Asian cities like Seoul, South Korea; Osaka, Japan; and Bombay and Calcutta, India. On the other hand, Asia is the largest land mass on earth, so why shouldn't it support more than half the world's people? Will the last one out turn off the lights?

City (1,000s)	1995	2000
1. Tokyo-Yokohama, Japan	28,447	29,971
2. Mexico City, Mexico	23,913	27,872
3. Sao Paulo, Brazil	21,539	25,354
4. Seoul, South Korea	19,065	21,976
5. New York City, United States	14,638	14,648
6. Osaka-Kobe- Kyoto, Japan	14,060	14,287
7. Bombay, India	13,532	15,357
8. Calcutta, India	12,885	14,088
9. Rio de Janeiro, Brazil	12,788	14,169
10. Buenos Aires, Argentina	12,232	12,911
* estimated		

Source: U.S. Census Bureau International Database.

CITIES—POPULATION CHANGE

Greatest Population Change in Metro Areas, 1980-1997

Though some cities *proper* have lost over 20 percent of their populations, metropolitan areas, on the other hand, are usually more stable. Here are the ones that that are not. Las Vegas is the fastest growing metropolitan area in the U.S. The ones with the largest decrease in population are in the Northeast, with metropolitan areas in Maine and Massachusetts losing the most population.

BEST GROWTH

City	Percent Growth
1. Laredo, TX	36.4%
2. Las Vegas, NV-AZ	35.3%

3. McAllen-Edinburg-
   Mission, TX   29.5%
4. Naples, FL   26.9%
5. Punta Gorda, FL   26.7%
6. Las Cruces, NM   24.4%
7. Boise City, ID   24.0%
8. Olympia, WA   22.8%
9. Orlando, FL   22.7%
10. Raleigh-Durham-
    Chapel Hill, NC   22.1%

WORST GROWTH

City	Percent Loss
1. Pittsfield, MA	-4.2%
2. Lewiston-Auburn, ME	-3.2%
3. New London-Norwich, CT-RI	-3.0%
4. New Bedford, MA	-2.9%
5. Alexandria, LA	-2.8%
Champaign-Urbana, IL	-2.8%
7. Fitchburg-Leominster, MA	-2.6%
8. Steubenville-Weirton, OH-WV	-2.5%
9. Bangor, ME	-2.3%
10. New Haven-Meriden, CT	-2.1%
Springfield, MA	-2.1%

Source: Wood & Poole Economics, Inc., Compusearch Market and Social Research Ltd., population estimates.

CITIES—POPULATION DENSITY

The Most Densely Populated Cities in America

In these, the densest of American cities, people live vertical, apartment-house lives. One gets to know the neighbor's habits, preferences and tendencies—whether one wants to or not. This life abounds in the rush of constant contact, but, also the pain of loud neighbors and street noise too. City living has its benefits: you can get coffee and a danish any hour of day or night, but the closest thing to nature you see are the rats digging through your garbage. Significantly, three of the 10 most densely populated cities are in the New York metropolitan area. Manhattan itself has a staggering density of approximately 70,000 people per square mile.

City	Persons per Sq. Mile
1. New York City	23,617
2. San Francisco	15,609
3. Jersey City, NJ	15,341
4. Chicago	12,185
5. Philadelphia	11,492
6. Boston	11,398
7. Newark, NJ	11,254
8. Santa Ana, CA	10,628
9. Miami	10,309
10. Washington, DC	9,531

Source: U.S. Census Bureau, *City and County Data Book*, 1994.

CITIES—POPULATION DENSITY

Far From the Maddening Crowd: Least Densely Populated Cities

Good fences make good neighbors, according to Robert Frost, but distance, too, brings us closer together. Where then, do all of our 250 million inhabitants live? If you're looking to get away from it all, if you want some *space* in between you and your neighbor, check out the following list. The following towns offer that wide-open American landscape to each inhabitant, while still preserving something of an urban environment. Figures are drawn from U.S. Census Bureau numbers for population density in cities with a population of 200,000 or more.

City	Persons per Sq. Mile
1. Anchorage	145
2. Oklahoma City	746
3. Lexington-Fayette, KY	817

PLACES

4. Jacksonville, FL	871
5. Nashville-Davidson, TN	1,046
6. Kansas City, MO	1,385
7. Colorado Springs, CO	1,615
8. Fort Worth, TX	1,617
9. Virginia Beach, VA	1,680
10. Mobile, AL	1,711

Source: U.S. Census Bureau, *City and County Data Book*, 1994.

CITIES—POPULATION OF METRO AREAS

Though only 10 U.S. cities have populations over one million, 43 metropolitan *areas* have over one million. This means that Americans who move out of the cities aren't necessarily going very far; many are simply choosing the suburbs as their desired place of residence. Although the cities of the South and Southwest are growing quickly, other metropolitan areas—that is, the cities and their suburbs—continue to set the pace. For instance, while San Diego (6th ranked in population), Phoenix (9th-ranked) and San Antonio (10th-ranked) all pushed their way into the top 10 American cities by population in the 1990 census, they have yet to develop into the huge metroplexes that characterize the New York, Los Angeles, Chicago and Washington-Baltimore areas. Thus they rank further down on the Census Bureau's list of "standard metropolitan statistical areas" (SMSA). Their ranks as SMSAs are as follows: San Diego 15th, Phoenix 20th and San Antonio 30th. The following lists represent the 10 largest cities in the U.S., compared to the 10 largest

LIKE A BIG CITY, BUT HATE THE CROWDS AND THE TRAFFIC? Anchorage (below) has many of the amenities of big-town America , but few of the same problems.

metropolitan areas, from Census Bureau figures.

LARGEST CITIES

City	Population
1. New York	7,322,564
2. Los Angeles	3,485,398
3. Chicago	2,783,726
4. Houston	1,630,672
5. Philadelphia	1,585,577
6. San Diego	1,110,549
7. Detroit	1,027,974
8. Dallas	1,006,831
9. Phoenix	983,403
10. San Antonio	935,927

LARGEST METRO AREAS *

City	Population
1. New York	19,640,175
2. Los Angeles	15,047,772
3. Chicago	8,410,402
4. Washington–Baltimore	6,919,572
5. San Francisco–Oaklando–San Jose	6,409,891
6. Philadelphia	5,938,528
7. Boston	5,438,815
8. Detroit	5,245,906
9. Dallas/Fort Worth	4,214,532
10.Houston	3,962,365

* the U.S. Census Bureau has changed its designation of metropolitan areas, therefore the figures may be inconsistent in this volume and elsewhere

Source: *The Peoplepedia,* 1996.

CITIES— POVERTY

Most and Least Poverty Stricken

Poverty is commonplace in America, and its symptoms pervade our bigger cities. But the true urban sad spots in this nation, the poorest of our cities, are actually concentrated in our small- and mid-sized metropolitan areas. The following are the 10 poorest and 10 richest metropolitan areas in the country out of the top 275, as judged by the percentage of people living below the poverty level. The most poverty-stricken towns are those along Mexican border, where a large number of poor immigrants from south of the Rio Grande have settled—at least for the moment. The regions with the least poverty are primarily in the upper midwest.

MOST POVERTY STRICKEN

City	% Below Poverty Level
1. Carbondale, IL	46.1%
2. State College, PA	45.4%
3. Pharr, TX	44.5%
4. Prichard, AL	44.1%
5. East St. Louis, IL	43.9%
Brownsville, TX	43.9%
7. Auburn, AL	39.9%
8. Ithaca, NY	39.4%
9. Athens, GA	39.3%
10. Del Rio, TX	38.3%

LEAST POVERTY STRICKEN

City	%
1. Bowie, MD	1.1%
Germantown, TN	1.1%
Brookfield, WI	1.1%
4. Los Altos, CA	1.2%
5. Park Ridge, IL	1.3%
6. Saratoga, CA	1.4%
7. Elmhurst, IL	1.4%
8. Upper Arlington, OH	1.4%
9. Buffalo Grove Village, IL	1.5%
10. Naperville, IL	1.5%

Source: *County and City Data Book,* 1994.

CITIES— RAINY DAYS

Rain or Shine?

Whether you're an asthmatic looking for a crisp, dry climate or a

IT'S LUSH AND BEAUTIFUL and it's where the U.S.'s rainiest cities are situated,—the Gulf Coast. More than 60 inches of rain fall annually, about 10 times more than in America's Southwest, where other snow birds of the North flock.

swamp dweller seeking moss hanging from trees, the United States has got the climate for you. The diverse shades of precipitation are striking. From the arid, desert-like climate of the Southwest to the wet, muggy cities of the Old South and the snowy streets of Juneau, Alaska, you can choose your rainfall to the tenth of an inch. If you are a backyard gardener, you might want to choose your city by the favorite climate of your favorite plant! On the other hand, you might just wonder how wet the other Americans are. Here are the soggy totals for the rainiest American cities.

RAINIEST CITIES

City	Avg. Annual Rainfall (inches)
1. Mobile, AL	64.0
2. New Orleans	61.9
3. Miami	55.9
4. Jackson, MS	55.4
5. Juneau, AK	54.3
6. San Juan, PR	52.3
7. Memphis	52.1
8. Jacksonville, FL	51.3
9. Little Rock	50.9
10. Atlanta	50.8

The driest cities in the country are for the most part located in the booming American Southwest, and at least part of that boom can be attributed to technologies that bring water to the desert. But it is a real question as to how much more development and population growth these areas can support, given the limited supplies of water available to them. One can only drain a river so much for an upstream city until the town's downstream starts drying out.

DRIEST CITIES

City	Avg. Annual Rainfall (inches)
1. Reno, NV	7.5
2. Phoenix	7.7
3. El Paso, TX	8.8
4. Albuquerque	8.9
5. San Diego	9.9
6. Los Angeles	12.0
7. Boise	12.1
8. Cheyenne	14.4
9. Denver	15.4
10. Bismarck, ND	15.5

Source: U.S. National Oceanic and Atmospheric Administration, Climatography of the United States (SAUS, 1996).

CITIES— REAL ESTATE

Highest and Lowest Rents

As recently as 1980, three quarters of us lived in metropolitan areas. That percentage has risen to 80 percent and is still moving upward. Such pressure has caused housing rentals to rise, and mortgage and rental costs are taking a bigger bite out of our income. If you are a renter, that bite is bigger than if you are paying off a mortgage on a home. For example, if you were an average renter in 1975, your rent took 23 percent of your income. In 1993 that percentage had risen to almost 30 percent, according to the U.S. Census Bureau. Of course, it depends on where you are renting. In the larger, more crowded cities on the east coast, rentals are higher than in Southern and Midwestern cities. A listing of the cities with both the highest and lowest rental rates follows.

HIGHEST RENTS

City	Rent per Sq. Ft.
1. Boston	$36.00
Washington, DC	$36.00
3. New York	$33.01
4. Stamford, CT	$30.50
5. San Francisco	$29.27

LOWEST RENTS

City	Rent per Sq. Ft.
1. Memphis	$15.20
2. St. Paul, MN	$15.50
Houston	$15.50
Denver	$15.50
5. St. Louis	$16.50

Source: NCOR International's Year-End Market Report, 1996.

CITIES— SEGREGATION

Most Segregated

Reynolds Farley, a University of Michigan researcher, has developed an index that ranks the relative degree of segregation in American cities. The study includes cities that had at least a three percent black population, or 20,000 blacks. Overall, it indicated that since the 1980s, when the measurements began, segregation declined in 191 cities of the 232 measured. The national segregation index declined overall in the U.S. from 68 in the 1980s to 64 for the most current measurement. It's no surprise that the most segregated cities are in the industrial Northeast and Midwest, the latter region having 10 of the 15 most segregated communities in the nation. The author predicts that segregation will stay this way in the foreseeable future. Below are the cities in which black populations are the most and the least segregated.

PLACES

LAKE SHORE DRIVE in Chicago (above)—one of the nation's most segregated cities— is predominantly black at its south end, and white at its north end.

MOST SEGREGATED

City	Index Score
1. Gary, IN	91
2. Detroit	89
3. Chicago	87
4. Cleveland	86
Buffalo, NY	84
Flint, MI	84
7. Milwaukee	84
8. Saginaw, MI	84
9. Newark, NJ	83
10. Philadelphia	82

LEAST SEGREGATED

City	Index Score
1. Jacksonville, NC	31
2. Lawton, OK	37
3. Anchorage	38
4. Fayetteville, NC	41
Lawrence, KS	41
6. Clarksville, TN	42
7. Fort Walton Beach, FL	43

8. Tucson	45
San Jose, CA	45
Killen, TX	45
Danville, VA	45
Charlottesville, VA	45

Source: University of Michigan, 1997.

CITIES— SIZE

Most Spaced-Out Cities

Did you ever meet a big city-slicker from Juneau, Alaska? It is, after all, the biggest city—in area—in the U.S. The biggest cities in America are not necessarily those that come immediately to mind at the mention of those words. Although Los Angeles is among the 10 geographically largest cities in the country, the remaining two of the Big Three—New York and Chicago— do not make the list. Here, then, are the most spaced-out cities in the United States.

City	Area in Sq. Miles
1. Juneau, AK	2,593.6
2. Anchorage	1,697.6
3. Jacksonville City, FL	758.7
4. Butte-Silver Bow, MT	716.2
5. Oklahoma City	608.2
6. Houston, TX	539.9
7. Nashville-Davidson, TN	473.3
8. Los Angeles	469.3
9. Phoenix	419.9
10. Suffolk City, VA	400.1

Source: U.S. Census Bureau, *County and City Data Book*, 1994.

CITIES— SNOWFALL

Snowiest American Cities

One thing every skier can count on: when the Rocky Mountains need more snow, it's always guaranteed to come down in Buffalo, New York. It might not be everybody's idea of a winter wonderland, but Buffalo, like many other cities, can be where kids tunnel like gerbils to friends' houses; where principals never cancel school because of inclement weather; and where every self-respecting citizen keeps a set of chains in the trunk of his or her car. In compiling this list, the U.S. National Oceanic and Atmospheric Administration counted ice pellets as well as snow.

City	Aver. Annual Snowfall (inches)
1. Sault St. Marie, MI	115.5
2. Juneau, AK	101.3
3. Buffalo, NY	91.0
4. Duluth, MN	78.2
5. Burlington, VT	77.5
6. Portland, ME	70.6
7. Albany, NY	63.7
8. Concord, NH	63.5
9. Denver	60.3
10. Great Falls, MT	59.0

Source: U.S. National Oceanic and Atmospheric Administration, *Comparative Climatic Data*, annual.

CITIES—SOCIAL SECURITY

Concentrations of Social Security Recipients

The aging of the American population is a widely reported phenomenon. The high rates of public pensioners in many locales are clear warnings of the difficult times ahead. Following are the major U.S. cities which have the greatest percentages of Social Security recipients.

City	Recipients as % of Pop.
1. St. Petersburg, FL	22.2%
2. Pittsburgh	17.9%
3. St. Louis	16.6%
Miami	16.6%
Louisville	16.6%
6. Honolulu	16.0%
7. Richmond, VA	15.4%
8. Philadelphia	15.2%
Seattle	15.2%
10. Akron, OH	14.9%

Source: U.S. Census Bureau.

CITIES—SPORTS

Best and Worst Sports Towns

America's best sports city isn't in the United States at all—it's located just north of the border. Montreal rates first in our ranking of sports towns thanks to the incredible success of the hometown Canadiens, who have won more than 20 Stanley Cup championships (and whose success outweighs the relative mediocrity of the other pro team, baseball's Expos). To qualify for our rating, a city had to have at least two current major league teams among the NFL, NHL, NBA and Major League Baseball. The score for a city is the sum of a town's scores for each of its teams, divided by the number of teams, yielding an average success score for a city's sports franchises. These are the 10 best and worst sports cities in North America, based on data up to 1996.

BEST SPORTS TOWNS

City	Score	Teams	Avg.
1. Montreal	3,196	2	1,598

2. Boston			
	4,743	4	1,186
3. Toronto			
	2,303	2	1,152
4. Oakland			
	2,879	3	960
5. New York			
	5,685	6	947
6. Chicago			
	4,545	5	909
7. Los Angeles			
	3,552	4	888
8. Detroit			
	3,481	4	870
9. St. Louis			
	2,587	3	862
10. Pittsburgh			
	2,566	3	855

WORST SPORTS TOWNS

City	Score	Teams	Avg.
1. Tampa			
	668	2	334
2. New Jersey*			
	890	2	444
3. Anaheim			
	972	2	486
4. Denver			
	1,952	4	488
5. Phoenix			
	1,512	3	504
6. Minneapolis			
	1,513	3	504
7. Seattle			
	1,514	3	505
8. Miami			
	2,076	4	519
9. Atlanta			
	1,570	3	523
10. San Diego			
	1,051	2	525

* part of Metro New York, home of the Nets (NBA) and the Devils (NHL)

Source: *Best and Worst* original.

CITIES— TAXES

Property Taxes

Home ownership is an integral part of the American dream, but in the towns listed below, property taxes make that dream a nightmare for most, and unattainable for the others. Here are the cities with the highest per capita property taxes, where ownership truly costs the most.

HIGHEST TAXES

City	Tax per $100
1. Milwaukee, WI	$3.60
2. Bridgeport, CT	$3.51
3. Newark, NJ	$3.46
4. Manchester, NH	$3.20
5. Des Moines, IA	$3.00
6. Providence, RI	$2.82
7. Detroit	$2.82
8. Houston	$2.73
9. Philadelphia	$2.64
10. Sioux Falls, SD	$2.55

LOWEST TAXES

America's anti-tax capitals are in the libertarian Western states, where land is plentiful and relatively cheap. Below are the cities where property taxes take the smallest bites from the checkbook.

City	Tax per $100
1. Honolulu	$0.33
2. Los Angeles	$0.67
3. Birmingham	$0.70
4. Cheyenne, WY	$0.74
5. New York City	$0.87
6. Charleston, WV	$0.92
7. Washington, DC	$0.94
8. Seattle	$0.96
9. Denver	$1.04
10. Las Vegas	$1.06

Source: Government of the District of Columbia; Department of Finance and Revenue.

CITIES— TEENS

Teen Pregnancy

With out-of-wedlock births on the rise, it's no wonder that teen pregnancies are occurring in epidemic proportions. Abortion is the most prevalent solution. If the option of abortion is eliminated, as many Americans are pushing for, it is a foregone conclusion that out-of-wedlock births will soar.

Metro Area	Teen Births, 1995
1. Los Angeles-Anaheim-Riverside, CA	36,390
2. New York-Northern New Jersey-Long Island, NY	22,950
3. Chicago-Gary-Lake County, IL-IN-WI	17,688
4. Houston-Galveston-Brazonia	10,226
5. Dallas-Ft. Worth	9,788
6. Philadelphia-Wilmington-Trenton, PA-DE-NJ	9,609
7. Detroit-Ann Arbor	9,347
8. San Francisco-Oakland-San Jose	8,753
9. Atlanta	5,955
10. Phoenix	5,643

Source: U.S. National Center for Health Statistics; Vital Statistics of the United States; and unpublished data (SAUS, 1996).

CITIES— TRAFFIC

Most Congested Metropolitan Areas

Any surprise that three out of the top five cities with the most traffic congestion are in California? Surprisingly, the most congested met-

THE MODERN LOOK OF MONACO can be deceiving. It's the ninth-oldest nation in the world (See Page 118.).

ropolitan area is not Los Angeles. It is the outlying sprawl of San Bernadino and Riverside, near the foothills of the mountains. It is here that the average person spends 76 hours in traffic every year—the equivalent of spending two work-weeks behind the wheel of an idling car. On the other hand, in laid-back Texas, commuters in Corpus Christi spend a mere seven hours a year behind an idling engine. But look on the bright side. Those people who don't have the long waits in their cars probably don't listen to as many books on tape while driving.

MOST CONGESTED AREAS

	Avg. hours per year in traffic
1. San Bernadino-Riverside, CA	76
2. Washington, DC	70
3. San Francisco-Oakland	66
4. Los Angeles	65
5. Houston	60

IT'S ALMOST ALWAYS A GREAT DAY in San Diego (above) which has the best weather in the U.S.

LEAST CONGESTED AREAS

City	Avg. hours per year in traffic
1. Corpus Christi, TX	7
2. El Paso, TX	11
3. Indianapolis	12
Salt Lake City	12
5. Memphis	13

Source: Texas Transportation Institute, Texas A&M University.

CITIES— WEALTH

Where the Money Is

Five of the top 10 cities in terms of average household income are within commuting distance of New York—though fashionably far enough away to "insulate" the affluent from the masses of working-class and poor that reside in the Big Apple. Many of the poorest cities in the country are located near the border of Mexico and contain a large number of recent immigrants from south of the border. Other bastions of "poverty"—a "financial condition" rather than a "state of mind"

as the old adage goes—are college towns. The following are the richest and poorest metro areas in the country, as measured by average household income.

RICHEST CITIES

City	Avg. Household Income*
1. Long Island City, NY	$100,200
2. Bergen-Passaic, NJ	$96,500
3. San Francisco	$93,300
Trenton, NJ	$93,300
5. Middlesex-Somerset-Hunterdon, NJ	$92,300
6. Newark, NJ	$91,500
7. San Jose, CA	$90,000
8. West Palm Beach-Boca Raton, FL	$89,700
9. Washington, DC-MD-VA-WV	$87,200
10. Anchorage	$84,900
Honolulu	$84,900

POOREST CITIES

City	Avg. Household Income*
1. Bryan-College Station, TX	$42,100
2. McAllen-Edinburg-Mission, TX	$44,200
3. Las Cruces, NM	$44,600
4. Goldsboro, NC	$45,500
5. Lawrence, KS	$45,800
6. Jacksonville, NC	$45,900
7. Hattiesburg, MS	$46,000
8. Flagstaff, AZ-UT	$46,100
9. Sumter, SC	$46,700
10. Cumberland, MD-WV	$46,900

* figures rounded to the nearest $100

Source: Woods & Poole Economics, Inc.

CITIES— WEATHER

Best and Worst Overall Days

Sunny day, chasing the clouds away! When there's nothing else to talk about, people talk about the weather. With heat waves, record snowfalls, pounding hurricanes, cresting floodwaters, and destructive tornadoes, there's a lot to talk about. And if you run out of things to say, you can tune in the Weather Channel for up-to-the-minute forecasts and conditions around the world. Some people don't have to discuss their local weather, though. In some places, the temperature is always balmy, the winds are always mild, it never seems to snow, and the rainfall is always light. Check out the first list below, of the cities worldwide with the most pleasant year-round weather. Five U.S. cities made the top ten, all in California. Perhaps it would be best to avoid the cities in the second list, with the worst year-round weather. Seven are in the United States, five of them in Alaska.

MOST PLEASANT YEAR-ROUND WEATHER

Rank/City

1. Las Palmas, Canary Islands
2. San Diego, California
3. Casablanca, Morocco
4. Port Elizabeth, South Africa
5. Oceanside, California
6. Santa Barbara, California
7. Los Angeles, California
8. Mexico City, Mexico
9. San Miguel de Allende, Mexico
10. San Luis Obispo, California

WORST YEAR-ROUND WEATHER

Rank/City

1. Nome, Alaska
2. Reykjavik, Iceland
3. Denali National Park, Alaska
4. Paradise, California
5. Valdez, Alaska
6. Yekaterburg, Russia

7. Tomsk, Russia
8. Stehekin, Washington
9. Fairbanks, Alaska
10. Anchorage, Alaska

Source: Consumer Travel Publications.

CITIES—WHITE POPULATION

Whitebread America: Most Caucasian Metropolitan Areas

In these tightly held, brightly lit, ivoried citadels, black faces are few and far between, but at least what small populations there are do not suffer the debilitations of segregation found in the major cities.

City	% Black Population
1. Wausau, WI	.1%
Bismarck, ND	.1%
3. Laredo, TX	.3%
Eau Claire, WI	.3%
4. Dubuque, IA	.4%
6. Sheboygan, WI	.5%
Pocatelo, IA	.5%
Medford - Ashford, CT	.5%
Casper, WY	.5%
10. St. Cloud, MN	.6%
Provo-Orem, UT	.6%
Lewiston - Auburn, ME	.6%
La Crosse, WI	.6%
Grand Junction, CO	.6%
Fargo - Moorhead, ND	.6%

Source: *Sales & Marketing Magazine,* Survey of Buying Power, 1996.

CITIES— WIND

America's Windiest Cities

Except for Honolulu, which looks out on Mamala Bay and the Pacific Ocean, America's windiest cities are in dusty, wind-swept Plains states, on the shores of the Great Lakes or, like Boston, on ports that

PLACES

face the rough northern Atlantic Ocean. These wind-blown metropolises may some day be surrounded by electricity-generating windmills. However, today, they gain little benefit from the tremendous energy to which they are subject. Interestingly, Chicago, which is sometimes called the "Windy City," is ranked 21st out of 68 American cities surveyed by the U.S. National Oceanic and Atmospheric Administration. Legend has it that the city got its moniker not from its atmospheric conditions, but from its wind-bag politicos.

City	Avg. Wind Speed (mph)
1. Cheyenne, WY	12.9
2. Great Falls, MT	12.7
3. Boston	12.5
4. Wichita, KS	12.3
5. Oklahoma City	12.3
6. Buffalo	11.9
7. Milwaukee	11.5
8. Honolulu	11.3
9. Sioux Falls, SD	11.1
10. Duluth, MN	11.0

Source: U.S. National Oceanic and Atmospheric Administration, Comparative Climatic Data (SAUS, 1996).

CITIES—WORKING MOTHERS

Ms. Jones, Call Your Sitter

To be a "latch-key" kid is a relatively new lot in life, though statistics show that it's one the youngsters should start getting used to. Mothers in the nation's labor force totaled six million in 1992, up

THE COWBOY below is just as likely to get blown off as bucked off at Cheyenne's Frontier Days, which is held in America's windiest city, Cheyenne, Wyoming.

Photo: The Wyoming Travel Commission.

from four million in 1978, according to Census Bureau figures evaluated in the 1993 issue of *American Demographics*. Of those six million, 5.5 million held jobs, and 535,000 were looking for work. Working moms are more likely to be found in Midwestern cities, according to U.S. Census figures. In fact, 18 Midwestern metro areas are among the top 25 places with the most working mothers, and almost half of those are in Wisconsin and Iowa. Sioux Falls, South Dakota, on the western fringe of the Midwest, tops the list, with 84 percent of its mothers working. Madison, Wisconsin, and Bismarck, North Dakota, follow, with 82.7 percent. Seventy percent of American mothers with children under the age of 18 are in the labor force. Eighty percent of working mothers in Sioux Falls have a child under age six, as do 75 percent of the working mothers in Madison. In that category, 13 metro areas in the Midwest are among the top 15 areas in the nation claiming the most working mothers of preschoolers, an average proportion of 73 percent. Far down on the scale of metro areas where mothers work are Hispanic areas in Texas: Laredo (54.3 percent); McAllen-Edinburg-Mission (56.6 percent); Brownsville-Harlingen (57.8 percent); and El Paso (58.9 percent). California metros with low percentages of working mothers include Yuba City (60.5), Visalia-Tulare-Porterville (62 percent) and Merced (62.8 percent). Following are the top 10 and bottom 10 metropolitan areas ranked by the percentage of working mothers in the labor force. The two right-most columns indicate the age of their children in 1990.

MOST WORKING MOTHERS

City	Percent of Mothers Working
1. Sioux Falls, SD	84.0%
2. Madison, WI	82.7%
Bismarck, ND	82.7%
4. Hickory-Morgan, NC	82.1%
5. Sheboygan, WI	82.0%
6. Lincoln, NE	81.7%
7. Rochester, MN	81.0%
8. Springfield, IL	80.9%
LaCrosse, WI	80.9%
10. Des Moines, IA	80.8%

FEWEST WORKING MOTHERS

City	Percent of Mothers Working
1. Houma-Thibodaux, LA	52.2%
2. Laredo, TX	54.3%
3. McAllen-Edinburg-Mission, TX	56.6%
4. Steubenville, OH-Weirton, WV	56.7%
5. Huntington, WV-Ashland, KY	57.8%
Brownsville-Harlingen, TX	57.8%
7. El Paso, TX	58.9%
8. Las Cruces, NM	59.5%
9. Yuba City, CA	60.5%
10. Beaver County, PA	60.8%

Source: U.S. Census Bureau.

CITIES— WORLD CONFLICT

Most Fought Over

If you think Dublin or Belfast have track records as conflicted cities, bone up on your history. Their troubles are just getting started, at least from a historical perspective. Some land seems to have more than its fair share of battles fought over it. Leading the way, not too surprisingly, is the city of Jerusalem, which has had

THE WAILING WALL IN JERUSALEM, was once a wall of one of the great temples in a city that has survived nine wars, making it the most fought-over city in the world.

nine major wars fought within its bounds, from the Romans and the Crusades and up through to World War I and the Arab-Israeli conflict. These only include battles that involved the city changing hands via invaders or uprisings that threw out the entrenched power; it doesn't touch on the petty skirmishes and confrontations that seem to surround that beleaguered city on a daily basis. Here, then, are the world cities that have played host to the most fighting.

City	Number of Wars
1. Jerusalem	9
2. Adrianople (Edilne)	7
Constantinople (Istanbul)	7
Rome	7
5. Warsaw	6

6. Pavia	5
Baghdad	5
8. Alexandria	4
Paris	4
Prague	4
Ravenna	4

Source: *Encyclopedia of Battles.*

CITIES—WORLD POPULATION

Projected Population

It's a small world after all—or is it? Although zero population growth is a goal of most nations, fertility rates do not reflect this fact. Many of the capitals of Catholic Latin America are speeding toward hyper-population, while others have passed that point long ago. Below are the projected most populous cities in the year 2000. The majority of the cities listed here are in third-world nations.

City	Projected Population
1. Tokyo-Yokohama, Japan	29,971,000
2. Mexico City, Mexico	27,872,000
3. Sao Paulo, Brazil	25,354,000
4. Seoul, South Korea	21,976,000
5. New York City, USA	14,648,000
6. Osaka-Kobe-Kyoto, Japan	14,287,000
7. Bombay, India	15,357,000
8. Calcutta, India	14,088,000
9. Rio de Janeiro, Brazil	14,169,000
10. Buenos Aires, Argentina	12,911,000

Source: U.S. Census Bureau International Data Base.

COUNTIES— FARMS

Most Farms

Los Angeles and St. Louis are just a few of the names of counties where you'll find farms, though not very many—most have been swallowed up by modernity. Even today, however, there are farms in some of the most settled communities in the country. So, despite our increasingly technological society, a tremendous agrarian economy still flourishes. Here are the most cultivated counties in all the land, as measured by the number of farms within county borders.

County	Number of Farms
1. Fresno, CA	7,590
2. San Diego	6,259
3. Tulare, CA	5,911
4. Lancaster, PA	4,775
5. Stanislaus, CA	4,630
6. San Joaquin, CA	4,366
7. Yakima, WA	4,239
8. Riverside, CA	3,874
9. Greene, TN	3,580
10. Stearns, MN	3,185

Source: U.S Census Bureau, *County and City Data Book,* 1994.

COUNTIES— FARMS

Small Farm U.S.A.

Despite the trend toward larger, more productive farms in the U.S., a sizable number of small, family-owned and -operated farms still exist. Small farms—defined here as those under 50 acres—are most prevalent in the land-scarce isles of Hawaii, and in Southern California, where residential areas are continuing to encroach on the farmer's traditional domain. These are the counties with the most farms under 50 acres as a percentage of all farms operating within the county.

County	Percent Small Farms
1. Piscataquis, ME	22.5%
2. Calhoun, IL	22.4%
Catahoula, LA	22.4%
Dooly, GA	22.4%
Houston, TN	22.4%
Heard, GA	22.4%
Mineral, MT	22.4%
8. Brown, WI	22.3%
Robertson, TX	22.3%
Clinton, IL	22.3%

Source: U.S. Census Bureau, *County and City Data Book,* 1994.

COUNTIES—POPULATION GROWTH

Fastest Growing

America has always had its fastest growing regions. For decades the flight was to Sun Belt cities. While it still is, a different picture emgerges when one looks at *counties*. Unlike cities, the county designation takes into account unsettled acreage. Most of this, obviously, cannot be within America's city limits. Instead it's "out in the county," as you're likely to hear, rather than the old cliche "out in the country." Below are some of the counties experiencing the American urge to pull up the stakes and move on when things start going bad. Interestingly, Colorado is feeling it more than most places.

County	Percent Change (1990-95)
1. Douglas County, CO	64.9%
2. Elbert County, CO	51.0%
3. Summit County, UT	50.1%
4. Park County, CO	47.6%
5. Washington County, UT	45.4%
6. Paulding County, GA	44.0%
7. Henry County, GA	43.9%
8. Flagler County, FL	41.6%
9. Forsyth County, GA	41.4%
10. Custer County, CO	40.3%

Source: U.S. Census Bureau, Department of Commerce, Population Change within U.S.; *Census and You*, April 1996.

COUNTIES— SIZE

Largest in the U.S.

Out of the brave, innocent explorations of Columbus and other pre-industrial seekers, an urban nation has emerged whose appearance would strike its founders dumb. The seats of political, cultural and industrial power that man has wrought in America—in a mere matter of a half millennium, a drop in time's bucket —would be utterly unintelligible to our forbears, even those from the

last century. Given the shear numbers of residents now as opposed yesteryear, following are the counties that our ancestors would be the least likely to recognize.

County	Population
1. Los Angeles	9,138,789
2. Cook, IL	5,136,877
3. Harris, TX	3,076,867
4. San Diego	2,644,132
5. Orange, CA	2,563,971
6. Maricopa, AZ	2,432,372
7. Kings, NY	2,244,021
8. Wayne, MI	2,055,500
9. Dade, FL	2,031,336
10. Queens, NY	1,963,628

Source: U.S. Census Bureau, *County and City Data Book*, 1994.

COUNTRIES— AGE

Oldest Nations on the Globe

Age is a fundamental criterion in establishing the legitimacy of nations and their governments. Of the more than 160 independent countries on Earth, a mere 45 existed in their current forms before the turn of the century. The Napoleonic wars resulted in the births of many new geo-political entities, as did the cessation of hostilities in WW I. Now, however, some of those geo-political patchwork constructions are falling apart, not the least of which is the once fearsome Soviet Union, as ethnic groups gravitate toward older associations and assert their independence. The following are the oldest continuous countries in the world.

Nation	Year Founded
1. Ethiopia	3000 B.C.
2. San Marino	c. A.D. 400
3. France	486

THE CRY *VIVE LA FRANCE!* (long live France), must be working. Paris, France's City of Lights, is the principle city of one of the ten oldest nations on the globe.

4. Japan	c. 500
5. United Kingdom	1066
6. Hungary	1101
7. Andorra	1278
8. Switzerland	1291
9. Monaco	1338
10. Spain	1492

Source: *Encyclopedia Britannica.*

COUNTRIES— AGRICULTURE

Most Agriculturally Mechanized

While many third-world farmers still use ox-drawn plows or even simple sticks to cultivate their land, farmers in the advanced nations have long since abandoned muscle power in favor of machine power. Along with the McCormick reaper and a few other mechanical advances, the tractor has freed the farmer from reliance on the ox, the horse, the mule and his own back to plow and sow his field. The most agriculturally mechanized country in the world is the United States, with almost five million tractors in use, or about one-fifth of all the farm tractors in the world. The bottom 10 in this list are places that either can't or don't have to rely on home-grown agricultural production; many of them are tourist-rich island nations or oil-rich Gulf states.

MOST TRACTORS

Country	Number of Tractors
1. USA	4,800,000
2. Japan	2,050,000
3. Italy	1,470,000
4. France	1,440,000
5. Poland	1,310,690
6. Germany	1,300,000
7. India	1,257,630
8. Russian Federation	1,147,500
9. Spain	789,747
10. Turkey	763,529

FEWEST TRACTORS

Country	Number of Tractors
1. Tuvalu	1
2. British Virgin Islands	3
3. Hong Kong	4
4. Djibouti	6
5. St. Kitts Nev	10
6. Western Sahara	11
7. Norfolk Island	12
Montserrat	12
9. American Samoa	15
10. Cape Verde	16

Source Food and Agriculture Organization of the United Nations, 1994, 1996.

COUNTRIES— AGRICULTURE

Most Agriculturally Advanced

Perhaps the truest index of the level of agricultural advancement is the comparison of mechanization with the amount of arable land. Using this criterion, Japan and Europe on average have the most advanced agricultural levels in the world. The top 10 are led by Iceland, which suffers from a veritable tractor traffic jam with 1,754 tractors per hectare. Of the countries with a large-scale agricultural industry, Japan leads with 403 tractors per hectare. European countries average about 200 tractors per hectare; by comparison, the United States has only 25 tractors for every hectare of arable land, but still manages a very high crop yield. Many African nations have no tractors for their arable land.

Country	Tractors per Hectare
1. Iceland	1,754
2. Japan	403
3. Switzerland	269
4. Austria	226
5. Netherlands	221
6. Germany	204
7. Ireland	196
8. Norway	174
9. New Zealand	158
10. Belgium	147

Source: Food and Agriculture Organization Production Yearbook.

COUNTRIES— AIR POLLUTION

Carbon Dioxide Emissions

In addition to being a major component of what we exhale, carbon dioxide is a product of the burning of fossil fuels. In earlier days, we needn't have worried much about carbon dioxide emissions, since the compound is converted by plants into life-sustaining oxygen, providing a natural system to offset the increase. But the past several dec-

ades have seen an increase in carbon dioxide emissions concurrent with the destruction of the rain forests in Asia, South America and the Pacific Northwest. These rain forests are called by many scientists "the lungs of the world"; the loss of them, combined with the continued high level of carbon dioxide emissions from the industrialized nations, could seriously upset the planet's fragile ecological balance. Below are the worst perpetrators in terms of carbon dioxide emissions from fossil fuels, ranked by tons of emissions annually.

Country Metric	Tons Annually
1. USA	4,881,349
2. China	2,667,982
3. Russian Federation	2,103,132
4. Japan	1,093,470
5. Germany	878,136
6. India	769,440
7. Ukraine	611,342
8. United Kingdom	566,246
9. Canada	409,862
10. Italy	407,701

Source: Carbon Dioxide Information Analysis Center, 1996-97.

COUNTRIES— ALLIES

Friend or Foe to the U.S.?

Among 14 countries named in a recent opinion poll, only four were regarded as more friendly to the U.S. than they had been in the early 1980s: Mexico, Russia, Haiti and Cuba. Japan took the biggest bashing in the survey, which polled 2,006 adults age 18 and older. In 1982 Japan was described as a friend or ally of the U.S. by 64 percent of Americans; but by 1993 only 38 percent of Americans felt the same way. The pollsters cited tensions in U.S. and Japanese trade practices as causing the decline. Russia rose almost one-third in favorable responses from those polled. In 1982 only four percent regarded the Big Bear as friendly to the U.S. After the breakup of the Soviet Union, that climbed to 29 percent. In 1982—just a few years after the U.S.-brokered Egyptian-Israeli peace agreement—51 percent of Americans regarded Egypt kindly, but in 1993 that percentage dropped to 29 percent. Israel fared little better, falling from 60 percent to 45 percent in favorability. According to the pollsters, China's dismal record on human rights was reflected in a drop of 10 percentage points in the estimation of those polled, from 24 percent viewing the country as friendly in 1982, to 14 percent who did so in 1993. A general feeling of growing animosity extended even to longtime ally Britain, which fell from 85 percent who regarded it as friendly to 78 percent. France, Poland and Canada also slightly declined as friends or allies in the view of Americans. Following are the percentages of those polled who agreed that the given country was a friend or ally of the U.S., along with the percentage point change since 1982. The list below is ranked by the most current percentage of respondents (the in third column) who consider the nation in question as an ally.

THERE ARE MORE IN THE U.S. than anywhere, though tractors are only one measure of agricultural advancement. The U.S. is not even among the top-ten agriculturally mechanized nations (See page 119). Photo: Georgia Bureau of Industry and Trade.

Country	1982	1993	Change
1. Canada	83%	81%	-2%
2. Britain	85%	78%	-7%
3. France	54%	50%	-4%
4. Mexico	46%	47%	+1%
5. Germany*	59%	46%	-13%
6. Israel	60%	45%	-15%
7. Japan	64%	38%	-26%
8. Russia**	4%	33%	+29%
9. Poland	33%	30%	-3%
10. Egypt	51%	29%	-22%
11. Haiti	7%	16%	+9%
12. China	24%	14%	-10%
13. Cuba	4%	6%	+2%

* 1982 data for West Germany
** 1982 data for Soviet Union

Source: Roper Starch International, 1993.

COUNTRIES—ARMS MERCHANTS

Largest Importers and Exporters of Weapons

The sale of arms has been drastically reduced, due, in part, to the demise of the cold war, as well as global pressure to end indiscriminate of lethal weapons. One of the most graphic lessons of the dangers of unchecked arms sales was Desert Storm; it provided proof that the wanton sales of leading-edge weapons to loose-cannon, third world megalomaniacs must be curtailed. Nonetheless, since there has been no major war involving the superpowers since the Persian Gulf crisis in 1991, weapons purchased prior to that year are still in inventory. And they are plentiful. The tables below give a good representation of where most of the world's existing weaponry came from and where it went.

TOP ARMS EXPORTERS

Nation	Share of World Market*
1. Soviet Union	35.0%
2. United States	32.8%
3. France	10.3%
4. Britain	5.1%
5. Germany	4.0%
6. China	2.9%
7. Netherlands	1.4%
8. Sweden	1.1%
Brazil	1.1%
10. Czechoslovakia	0.9%

TOP ARMS IMPORTERS

Nation	Share of World Market*
1. India	14.8%
2. Iraq	10.0%
3. Egypt	6.3%
4. Saudi Arabia	4.8%
5. Israel	4.6%
6. Japan	3.7%
Syria	3.7%
8. Turkey	3.4%
Czechoslovakia	3.4%
10. Angola	3.1%

* figures represent sale of arms prior to 1991 when world armament proliferation began curtailment

Source: International Peace Research Institute.

COUNTRIES— AUTOMOBILES

Most and Fewest Cars Per Person

We like to cruise! America is a car culture, make no bumpers about that. It is little surprise, then, that we lead the world in per capita car ownership. On the other hand, rush hour in such auto-deprived countries as Syria or Paraguay must be a breeze, unless you're unlucky enough to be carpooling in the same vehicle with 1,000 other of your hapless compatriots. Let's at least hope the buggy is a four-door.

MOST CARS

Country	People per Car
1. United States	1.31
2. New Zealand	1.57
3. Canada	1.71
4. Italy	1.77
5. Japan	1.91
6. Germany	1.94
7. France	1.97
8. Australia	2.06
9. Sweden	2.09
10. Netherlands	2.42

FEWEST CARS

Country	People per Car
1. Syria	55
2. Paraguay	48
3. Dominican Republic	40
4. Ecuador	22
5. Thailand	21
6. Chile	13
7. Hong Kong	12
Costa Rica	12
9. Uruguay	11
Panama	11

Source: American Automobile Manufacturers Association, Inc., Detroit; *AAMA Motor Vehicle Facts & Figures*, annual.

PLACES

COUNTRIES— AUTOMOBILES

Most Registered Vehicles

With almost 200 million cars—nearly one for every American old enough to drive—our society has at last become truly treaded-out. It is time for us to face some simple facts in America, and one of the first things that we should own up to is that we are obsessive, unyielding, sometimes wanton road hogs. All the frenzied exhortations to carpool, use mass transit, walk, bike, cut down on trips and conserve energy can't stem the most basic American desire to hit the road. And we are fast approaching the day when every American will be able to do so in his or her very own personal auto. Whether there will be anywhere to go by then is another matter.

Country	Number of Cars
1. United States	194.0 million
2. Japan	63.4 million
3. Germany	42.0 million
4. Italy	32.3 million
5. France	29.5 million
6. Canada	17.2 million
7. Australia	10.5 million
8. Poland	7.9 million
9. Argentina	6.5 million
10. Netherlands	6.4 million

Source: American Automobile Manufacturers Association, Inc., *AAMA Motor Vehicle Facts & Figures*, 1996.

COUNTRIES— BIRTH RATE

Do true-believing Catholics use birth control? Maybe the low birth rates in predominately Catholic Southern Europe says something about the Vatican's influence on the sexual habits of its followers. In non-Catholic, non-Christian nations, ironically, the birth rate is the highest in the world and it's the lowest in Spain and Italy, the bastions of Catholicism. The group of African nations which have the world's highest birth rates is the same basic group which has the world's highest infant mortality rate—and its lowest life expectancy. These countries are growing in population but not nearly as much as their huge birth rates might suggest, for they have neither sufficient health facilities nor the basic needs of food and shelter for their rapidly procreating populations. Intensive birth control counseling and education could alleviate the problem, but the puritanical U.S. opposition to abortion and other family-planning counseling means that this country's vast resources cannot be mobilized against the problems of excessive birth rates either here or in the rest of the world.

HIGHEST BIRTH RATES

Country	Birth Rate per 1,000
1. Niger	52.5
2. Uganda	51.8
3. Angola	51.3
4. Mali	50.8
5. Guinea	50.6
6. Malawi	50.5
7. Somalia	50.2
Afghanistan	50.2
9. Cote d'Ivoire	49.9
10. Yemen	49.4

LOWEST BIRTH RATES

Country	Birth Rate per 1,000
1. Spain	9.7
2. Italy	9.8

3. Germany	9.9
Greece	9.9
5. Japan	10.1
6. Bulgaria	10.3
7. Slovenia	10.5
8. Russian Federation	10.9
9. Estonia	11.0
10. Croatia	11.3
Romania	11.3

Source: *World Resources* 1996-97.

COUNTRIES— DEATH RATES

Americans die at a rate of 8.8 deaths per 1,000 inhabitants, which is contrasted by rates in Africa which are about two to two-and-a-half times greater. It's here where the desperately poor citizens have the world's highest death rates, something that we can expect in regions where medical care and sanitation are the poorest. What is a surprise, however, are the death rates in certain wealthy oil producing states. No major "developed" countries are in the top-10 list of lowest death rates. Perhaps it's the stress, the fatty-foods and other amenities of modern life that kill the more affluent westerners, who, interestingly, have death rates in the middle of the global scale, not at the top as one might expect.

HIGHEST DEATH RATES

Country	Deaths/1,000, 1990-95
1. Sierra Leone	25.2
2. Afghanistan	21.8
3. Guinea-Bissau	21.3
4. Guinea	20.3
5. Malawi	20.0
6. Angola	19.2
7. Mali	19.1
8. Niger	18.9
9. Gambia	18.8
10. Mozambique	18.5
Somalia	18.5

LOWEST DEATH RATES

Country	Deaths/1,000, 1990-95
1. Kuwait	2.1
2. United Arab Emirates	2.7
3. Costa Rica	3.7
4. Solomon Islands	4.4
5. Fiji	4.5
6. Venezuela	4.7
Saudi Arabia	4.7
8. Belize	4.8
Oman	4.8
10. Malaysia	5.1

Source: United Nations Population Division, United Nations Children's Fund; the World Bank.

COUNTRIES— DEVELOPMENT

Most Developed Nations

While America may be unmatched in industrial development, its lack of progress in other areas prevent it from being a complete success story as a country. Overall, America is only second on the "Human Development Index," published for the United Nations Development Program by the Oxford University Press, and authored by Robert M. Solow, Nobel laureate in economics. Solow's index measures the average human capabilities in countries, ranking them according to a combination of life expectancy, educational attainment and basic purchasing power. America is second strongest in the world in overall education and second in college attendance, with 39 per cent of college age Americans in school. Our second rank reveals that though Americans have solved many problems of socialization and development, other nations have too, and some have devised even better solutions than we have. Hence, in *hu-*

man terms, the U.S. is doing pretty well, but could do even better. For example, we have considerable problems in health care and financing. The U.S. is first in AIDS cases among industrial nations, with 22.7 cases per 100,000 people, compared with an average of nine cases per 100,000 in other countries of high human development. In life expectancy, the U.S. ranks 18th among industrial countries and 18th in preventing maternal deaths, suggesting that improvement in health care lags behind economic growth. Below are the nations with the best Human Development Index (HDI) scores.

HDI Rank/Nation

1. Canada
2. USA
3. Japan
4. Netherlands
5. Norway
6. Finland
7. France
8. Iceland
9. Sweden
10. Spain

Source: UNDP, Human Development Report, 1996.

COUNTRIES— DEVELOPMENT

Most Underdeveloped Nations

In the previous entry, we listed the most developed countries in the world—those that enjoy the highest life expectancy, educational attainment and basic purchasing power. Here we list the other side of the coin, the true developmental backwaters of the world, where life expectancy is low, literacy is uncommon and economies are primitive. Africa, in the main, is

IF YOU WERE HERE and didn't know where you were (the Gas Town section of Vancouver) you'd never know that you were in the most developed nation in the world — Canada.

where these least developed countries are found. Clearly the nations of the Third World have far to go in the most basic areas of nutrition, education, health care and economic development before they can hope to improve their lot. This would be the greatest peace dividend one could imagine—the developed nations of the world ceasing their petty squabbling over trade and ideology and lending a helping hand to the less-privileged around the world. Below are the lowest ranked nations of the 174 that were included in the Human Development Index project described in the previous entry.

HDI Rank/Nation

165. Angola
164. Burundi

167. Mozambique
168. Ethiopia
169. Afghanistan
170. Burkina Faso
171. Mali
172. Somalia
173. Sierra Leone
174. Niger

Source: UNDP, Human Development Report, 1996.

COUNTRIES—EXPATRIATES

Love It Not, Leave It, for . . . ?

Where Expatriates Go

Living abroad is a right of passage for people who want to experience another lifestyle before eventually returning to live permanently in their own country. But the true expatriates never come back. Some leave the U.S. to escape a country to which they feel no particular affection or allegiance. For others, it's necessitated by military service or career factors. Many expatriates simply choose the romance of another country and another culture as a means of enriching their life experience and expanding their horizons. The following list represents the quantity of U.S. citizens residing abroad in selected countries, in 1994.

Nation	U.S. Citizens
1. Mexico	539,000
2. Germany	354,000
3. Canada	296,000
4. United Kingdom	259,000
5. Israel	112,000
6. Italy	104,000
7. Dominican Republic	97,000
8. Spain	79,000
9. Australia	62,000
10. France	59,000

Source: U.S. Census Bureau.

COUNTRIES—FISHING

Fishy Places

The most prolific fishermen in the world are the Chinese, who rely on fish as a major protein source in their diet, much as Americans used to rely on beef. The following rating lists the countries where the most and fewest fish are caught.

MOST FISHY COUNTRIES

Country	Fish Catch (tons)
1. China	18,983,730
2. Peru	8,450,600
3. Japan	8,129,670
4. Chile	6,037,990
5. USA	5,958,040
6. Russian Fed.	4,461,380
7. India	4,324,230
8. Indonesia	3,637,700
9. Thailand	3,330,770
10. Korea Rep.	2,648,980

LEAST FISHY COUNTRIES

Country	Fish Catch (tons)
1. East Timor	0
Gaza Strip*	0
3. Monaco	3
4. Pitcairn	8
5. Lesotho	35
6. America Samoa	50
7. Jordan	62
8. Montserrat	110
9. Swaziland	110
10. Niue	120

*unincorporated Israel

Source: Food and Arigulture Organization of the United Nations, 1993, 1996.

COUNTRIES—"FOREIGN" FARMS

Most U.S. Agricultural Land Holdings by Foreign Owners

Despite all the recent Japan-bashing concurrent with the sale of popular

PLACES

American entities—i.e. Rockefeller Center or Hollywood film studios like Columbia Pictures—the nationalistic zealots of America might look down on the farm, rather than at urban and cultural icons. The following rating represents the countries who own the largest chunks of the U.S. agricultural property measured in acreage.

Country	Acres
1. Canada	1,687,398
2. United Kingdom	1,024,718
3. Germany	867,626
4. Netherlands	363,882
5. Switzerland	323,510
6. Japan	284,860
7. France	271,571
8. Mexico	252,485
9. Luxembourg	234,551
10. Netherlands Antilles	212,250

Source: U.S. Department of Interior, 1996.

COUNTRIES—FOREIGN TRADE

America's Biggest Customers

Americans are flocking to buy the cars, television sets and shoes a myriad of producers and importers have brought from Asia, Europe, Canada and Mexico. No longer are our imports limited to novel and inexpensive dolls, pottery and Christmas decorations. America is still the world's largest economy, but it has transferred much of its own manufacturing to Mexico and the Far East where labor is cheaper. Below are the nations that buy the most American goods with the dollar amount each one purchases.

MOST EXPORTS (TO)

Country	Exports, 1995
1. Canada	$127,226 million
2. Japan	$64,343 million
3. Mexico	$46,292 million
4. United Kingdom	$28,857 million
5. South Korea	$25,380 million
6. Germany	$22,394 million
7. Taiwan	$19,209 million
8. Netherlands	$16,558 million
9. Singapore	$15,333 million
10. France	$14,245 million

Americans perceive Japanese goods, particularly cars and electronics, to be of the highest quality. Korean products are regarded as good bargains. Germans are masters of engineering. Italians have a flair for style. America is the largest market for the world's goods. Adding to our balance of payments is the trend of American companies manufacturing overseas and in Mexico, buying "our own goods," from foreign nations. Below are the nations from which we buy our foreign-made merchandise.

MOST IMPORTS (FROM)

Country	Exports, 1995
1. Canada	$145,349 million
2. Japan	$123,479 million
3. Mexico	$61,685 million
4. China	$45,543 million
5. Germany	$36,844 million
6. Taiwan	$28,972 million
7. United Kingdom	$26,898 million
8. South Korea	$24,184 million
9. Singapore	$18,561 million
10. Malaysia	$17,453 million

Source: U.S. Census Bureau, U.S. Merchandise Trade, Series FT 900 (SAUS, 1996).

COUNTRIES— HEALTH CARE

Highest Percentage of GNP Spent on Health Care

With the median age of the population in steady ascent, America faces

PICTURES OF HEALTH? These Americans should be! Almost one of every $8 of GNP in the U.S. is spent on health care, the highest proportion of any world nation.

an imminent health care crisis. Despite the fact that we do not provide national health insurance or nearly adequate Medicaid care, the U.S. has already committed more of its gross national product to health care than any other nation on Earth. Mustering our resources for effective treatment of those in need of health care—especially in view of the coming crunch of aging baby-boomers—is our most pressing national imperative.

Nation	% Spent on Health Care
1. United States	13.3%
2. Canada	9.9%
3. France	9.1%
Germany	9.1%
5. Finland	8.9%
6. Sweden	8.8%
7. Netherlands	8.7%
8. Nicaragua	8.6%
Australia	8.6%
10. Burkina Faso	8.5%
Austria	8.5%

Source: United Nations Population division, United Nations Children's Fund; the World Bank. *World Resources* 1996-97; Mortality and Nutrition, 1970-95.

COUNTRIES— U.S. IMMIGRANTS

Birth Nations of Legal Aliens

Whereas Europe served as the source of most of America's immigrants during its first two centuries, the new breed of immigrants is made up predominantly of Asians and Latin Americans. Much is said of our uninvited guests from South of the Border, but we hear little about the half million or so Latin Americans granted legal admittance to our country. Nor has the great wave of Philippine immigration been much noted. The co-mingling of old immigrants with new has catalyzed the history of America—the time is now here for a new stew from the melting pot. The country should be in for some very interesting changes as the demographic make-up continues to shift from European predominance to a more globally representative ethnic mix.

Nation U.S.Immigrants' Origins, 1995	
1. Mexico	327,891
2. Philippines	167,976
3. China	155,026
4. Vietnam	142,711
5. Dominican Republic	135,121
6. India	109,520
7. Poland	69,718
8. Ukraine	56,758
9. Korea	50,084
10. Jamaica	47,988

Source: U.S. Immigration and Naturalization Service, 1996.

COUNTRIES—INFANT MORTALITY

Infant mortality is a pretty good indication of a health-care system's quality and its reach to *every* level of society. For instance, while the white minority in South Africa might get excellent health care, the same is not true for the black majority who live with substantially less access to health care. The result is 46 infant deaths per 1,000 live births, whereas for whites the figure is more in line with rates in the more developed western world, about 10 per 1,000. The industrialized countries listed below all have excellent

health care systems, which reach to every level of society. Most of these societies are homogeneous and very well off. In the United States there are eight infant deaths per 1,000 live births.

LOWEST INFANT MORTALITY

Country	Inf. Deaths/1000 Live Births
1. Japan	4
2. Finland	5
Iceland	5
Sweden	5
5. Belgium	6
Germany	6
Switzerland	6
Singapore	6
9. Austria	7
Denmark	7
France	7
Ireland	7
Netherlands	7
Spain	7
United Kingdom	7
Canada	7
Australia	7

HIGHEST INFANT MORTALITY

Country	Infant Deaths/1000 Live Births
1. Sierra Leone	166
2. Afghanistan	163
3. Mali	159
4. Mozambique	148
5. Malawi	143
6. Guinea-Bissau	140
7. Guinea	134
8. The Gambia	132
9. Burkina Faso	130
10. Liberia	126

War, famine and lack of pre-natal care, sanitary conditions and proper obstetrical care—the reasons for infant mortality are many. Yet while larger societal problems loom, the fact is most young children die from diseases which are readily treatable in the West, such as diarrhea, whose dehydrating effects can usually be kept at bay with fluids. Except for Afghanistan, which borders on Pakistan and the former Soviet Union, the countries with the highest infant mortality rate are in Africa. While many of these countries have recently been involved in wars, others merely struggle with dismal living conditions.

Source: *World Resources 1996-97.*

COUNTRIES— LEPROSY

Highest Incidences of Leprosy

Leprosy is on the rise again, though it has been virtually eradicated in the United States and Europe; with that eradication, the disease has all but vanished from the public eye of westerners, save those in Brazil where there is an alarming number of new cases. The few who are still afflicted by the illness in the U.S. are cared for just as any other patients. However, leprosy, which calls to mind the darkest images of the Middle Ages, still constitutes a major public health problem in Asia and Africa.

Country	Registered Cases
1. India	542,511
2. Brazil	137,806
3. Indonesia	40,232
4. Myanmar	21,071
5. Nigeria	17,371
6. Nepal	12,764
7. Bangladesh	12,434
8. Philippines	11,674
9. Mozambique	11,072
10. Ethiopia	9,627

Source: World Health Organization, 1996.

COUNTRIES—LIFE EXPECTANCY

With a life expectancy of 75.8 years, America is not even in the top 10 of the rankings. In Japan, which has the longest life expectancy, an individual born now can expect to live almost 20 years longer than the average human, who can expect to live only slightly past the age of 60. Unfortunately, the disparity between life expectancy in the industrialized world and that in the rest of the world indicates more about the generally awful nutritional, sanitary and economic conditions most humans live with than it does about the good living conditions in a few advanced countries.

LONGEST LIFE EXPECTANCY

Country	Life Expectancy (years)
1. Japan	79.5
2. Sweden	78.2
Iceland	78.2
4. Switzerland	78.0
5. Spain	77.6
Greece	77.6
Australia	77.6
8. Italy	77.5
9. Netherlands	77.4
Canada	77.4

SHORTEST LIFE EXPECTANCY

Country	Life Expectancy (years)
1. Sierra Leone	39.0
2. Guinea-Bissau	43.5
Afghanistan	43.5
4. Guinea	44.5
5. Uganda	44.9
6. Gambia	45.0
7. Malawi	45.6
8. Mali	46.0

9. Mozambique   46.4
10. Niger   46.5
Source: *World Resources*, 1996-97.

COUNTRIES—
LIVESTOCK

Most Asses

The world population of asses is over 40 million. Judging simply from American political campaigns and network television programming, one might get the impression that the United States is home to the most asses in the world. The four-footed variety, however, are most numerous in China, where many people still rely on beasts of burden as the basic means of transport and cultivation.

Country	Ass Population
1. China	10,923,000
2. Ethiopia	5,200,000
3. Pakistan	3,901,000
4. Mexico	3,250,000
5. Egypt	1,690,000
6. India	1,600,000
7. Iran	1,400,000
8. Brazil	1,370,000
9. Afghanistan	1,160,000
10. Nigeria	1,000,000

Source: Food and Agriculture Organization of the United Nations, 1996.

COUNTRIES—
LIVESTOCK

Most Buffaloes

India, a nation in which Hindu beliefs prohibit the consumption of beef, is, not suprisingly, where the close cousin of the domesticated cow is safe from the butcher's knife. The buffalo (not the American bi-

THE ASS is a common sight in Asia and elsewhere, though in most of Europe and North America the species has been relegated to a mere curiosity.

son, which we call the buffalo, but what we normally call the "water buffalo") remains a major source of power to draw the plow and pull the cart in most Asian nations. The top 10 countries listed here account for 93 percent of the world population of buffaloes.

Country	Buffalo Population
1. India	80,102,000
2. China	22,814,700
3. Pakistan	20,000,000
4. Thailand	4,807,150
5. Nepal	3,278,255
6. Indonesia	3,140,000
7. Vietnam	3,000,000
8. Egypt	2,800,000
9. Philippines	2,508,000
10. Myanmar	2,203,205

Source: Food and Agriculture Organization of the United Nations, 1996.

WHERE ARE THE MOST HUMPS to get over? In Somalia, the camel capital of the world.

COUNTRIES—LIVE STOCK

Most Camels, Most Humps

Camels are most prevalent, of course, in dry, desert regions, where their endurance and their ability to go for days or weeks without water make them the vehicle of choice for transportation and commerce. Indeed, because they have served so well as beasts of burden for several thousand years, these testy, mean-spirited animals have earned the name "ships of the desert."

Country	Camel Population
1. Somalia	6,200,000
2. Sudan	2,903,000
3. India	1,520,000
4. Pakistan	1,119,000
5. Mauritania	1,087,000
6. Ethiopia	1,000,000
7. Kenya	810,000
8. Chad	600,000
9. Saudi Arabia	422,000
10. Mongolia	390,000

Source: Food and Agriculture Organization of the United Nations, 1996

COUNTRIES—LIVE STOCK

Most Bull

The world bovines are primary dairy animals, and well over 200 million of them are raised to give milk. About half as many are raised for slaughter for beef purveyors. Brazil, the largest provider of the world's beef, has enjoyed a boom in production in recent years, but the cost has been great environmentally—in order to create more pasture land, Brazilian cattle ranchers have been systematically clear-cutting the Amazonian rain forests vital to the planet's overall ecological balance and to the continued survival of Amazonian Indians and many threatened species. Indeed, many consumers have begun to fight back, organizing boycotts of restaurants and grocery stores that sell beef from cattle raised on cleared rain forest land.

Country	Heads of Cattle
1. India	196,003,000
2. Brazil	165,000,000
3. China	104,450,100
4. United States	103,819,000
5. Argentina	54,000,000
6. Russian Fed.	39,700,000
7. Ethiopia	29,900,000
8. Mexico	28,141,000
9. Australia	26,952,200
10. Colombia	26,088,000

Source: Food and Agriculture Organization of the United Nations, 1996.

COUNTRIES—LIVE- STOCK

Most Chickens

A chicken in every pot? With a worldwide population of more than

10 billion chickens, a politician could almost give every person in the world *two* chickens for their pot. In the U.S., the situation is even more advantageous: with the chicken population approaching 2 billion, the proverbial politician could promise a healthy eight chickens for every proverbial pot.

Country	Chicken Population (1,000s)
1. China	2,801,838
2. United States	1,808,000
3. Indonesia	1,103,307
4. Brazil	850,000
5. India	610,000
6. Russian Fed.	482,500
7. Japan	310,000
8. Mexico	290,000
9. France	221,421
10. Iran	202,140

Source: Food and Agriculture Organization of the United Nations, 1996.

COUNTRIES— LIVESTOCK

Most Gluts of Goats

Goats, like buffaloes and camels, are not the most popular livestock animals in the U.S. (although goat cheese has made great strides recently among the culinary trend-mongers). But in other parts of the world, goats serve as a vital source of milk, as well as pretty serviceable garbage disposals. Below are the top 10 countries in the world for goat fanciers.

Country	Goats
1. China	149,908,400
2. India	120,270,000
3. Pakistan	43,767,000
4. Bangladesh	30,330,000
5. Iran	25,757,000
6. Nigeria	24,500,000
7. Ethiopia	16,700,000
8. Sudan	16,500,000
9. Indonesia	14,323,000
10. Somalia	12,500,000

Source: Food and Agriculture Organization of the United Nations, 1996.

COUNTRIES— LIVESTOCK

Horses Around

Two things played the greatest role in creating the myth of the American West: the horse and the six-shooter. A hundred years after the last badman was rounded up, and four hundred years after the Spaniards first introduced it to the New World, the horse is still popular in the United States and the rest of the Americas. Admittedly, horses are no longer as vital to agriculture, transportation and law enforcement in the New World, but the legend of the cowboy still lives on ranches across the western United States, as well as in Mexico, Brazil and the pampas of Argentina, where horse skills are more important than driver's licenses. As long as horses are still around, the legend of the cowboy will continue to thrive. Below are the top 10 countries with the biggest horse populations.

Country	Horse Population
1. China	10,038,100
2. Brazil	6,300,000
3. Mexico	6,250,000
4. United States	6,050,000
5. Argentina	3,300,000
6. Ethiopia	2,750,000
7. Colombia	2,450,452
8. Russian Fed.	2,300,000
9. Mongolia	2,150,000
10. Kazakstan	1,800,000

Source: Food and Agriculture Organization of the United Nations, 1996.

PLACES

COUNTRIES— LIVE STOCK

Hog Heavens

Just because pigs like to wallow in slop and they eat like, well ... pigs, people think they're foul creatures. Nothing could be further from the truth. Pigs, in fact, are extremely smart animals, and make wonderful pets. The tiny Vietnamese pot-bellied pig is becoming increasingly popular among lovers of exotic pets, stirring up all kinds of strife between owners of pet pigs on the one hand and condo residents and landlords on the other who still cling to the old-fashioned view of the now-noble pig. The list below represents the top 10 countries in the world in pig population.

Country	Pigs
1. China	452,198,500
2. United States	58,200,000
3. Brazil	36,600,000
4. Germany	23,736,600
5. Russian Fed.	22,600,000
6. Poland	18,758,720
7. Mexico	18,000,000
8. Spain	18,000,000
9. Vietnam	17,200,000
10. France	14,800,000

Source: Food and Agriculture Organization of the United Nations, 1996.

COUNTRIES— LIVE STOCK

Counting Sheep

Sheepishness is big in China, the world's largest producer of sheep. Even more sheep are raised there

THE BEST PLACES IN THE U.S. TO FIND WILD HORSES like those below are Nevada and Wyoming. Domestic horses, however, are most prevalent in China, where there are more than 10 million (See opposite page). Photo: Wyoming Division of Tourism.

than in Australia, the former world leader in woolly animal production. Whereas in Australia sheep outnumber people by a factor of seven to one, in China *people* outnumber sheep about 10 to one. Much as the American West was made by horsemen, the land down under was settled by sheepherders. Where Americans recall the rough and tumble way of life on the Chisolm Trail or in Dodge City, the ethos of the Australian Outback calls to mind the sweat and toil of the dusty sheep ranch and the shearing station.

Country	Sheep Population
1. China	127,260,600
2. Australia	126,350,000
3. Iran	51,499,000
4. New Zealand	48,816,000
5. India	45,390,000
6. Turkey	35,600,000
7. Pakistan	29,065,000
8. South Africa	29,000,000
9. UK	28,797,000
10. Russian Fed.	25,800,000

Source: Food and Agriculture Organization of the United Nations, 1996.

COUNTRIES—MALE POPULATION

Where the Boys Are: Most Male-Dominated Nations

With a few exceptions, the nations of the world have a majority of female citizens. Worldwide, however, males account for just slightly more than 50 percent of the population. The high concentration of males in Asia and the Middle East is the primary demographic compensation for the female majorities of the West. Indeed, in the Islamic nations of Bahrain, the United Arab Emirates and Kuwait, men outnumber women by a whopping six to four. One explanation of this fact is the large number of male workers from Palestine, Egypt, Turkey and other nearby countries who, at least until recently, have flocked to the oil-rich gulf states, while leaving their spouses and families at home.

Country	Males, 1995 (millions)
1. China	628,553
2. India	483,453
3. United States	128,557
4. Indonesia	98,553
5. Brazil	80,708
6. Pakistan	72,675
7. Russian Federation	68,947
8. Bangladesh	62,117
9. Japan	61,406
10. Nigeria	55,373

Source: United Nations, 1996; Population Division of the United Nations Secretariat, World Population Prospects, 1994.

COUNTRIES—MATH & SCIENCE SCORES

Where Future Einsteins Await Graduation

American students just don't cut the mustard compared to their international counterparts when it comes to math and science, according to the Third International Mathematics and Science Study. Researchers tested a half-million eighth graders in 41 countries and found, among other things, that American 14-year-olds scored below the world average in math—they had average scores of only 500, with the international average being 513 and the top average, among kids from Singapore, was a whopping 643. (Other Asian kids also topped the math list, with South Korea, Japan, and Hong

Kong ranked second through fourth.) What's to blame? It's not laziness, since American kids actually spend more time in math and science classes and get more math and science homework than kids in, say, Germany and Japan. Educational experts think the problem is that the U.S. curriculum is simply too easy, depending too much on rote learning and failing to challenge students to think about concepts. These two lists show the percentage of students in different countries scoring among the top 10 percent on the international math and science test. If these results are any indication, the world's future technologists seem destined to come from Singapore, South Korea, and Japan.

BEST IN MATH

Students Scoring Among Top 10%

1. Singapore	45%
2. South Korea	34%
3. Japan	32%
4. Russian Federation	10%
5. Canada	7%
England	7%
France	7%
8. Germany	6%
9. United States	5%

BEST IN SCIENCE

Students Scoring Among Top 10%

1. Singapore	31%
2. Japan	18%
South Korea	18%
4. England	17%
5. United States	13%
6. Germany	11%
Russian Federation	11%
8. Canada	9%
9. France	1%

Source: Third International Mathematics and Science Study.

COUNTRIES— MILITARY

Highest Military Expenditures, U.S. and Allies

The U.S. continues to bear the brunt of military expenses in its dealings with NATO and its other allies. In the coming years, however, with the relaxation of tensions between Eastern and Western Europe (indeed, with the disappearance of most of the West's tried and true enemies), spending on the military should be less of a burden. Europe will take on a growing fiscal share of its own defense, and regional flare-ups will require a quicker, more mobile military presence, but one which should cost less to maintain.

Country	1993 Dollars (millions)
1. United States	$297,600
2. France	$42,590
3. Japan	$41,730
4. Germany	$36,650
5. United Kingdom	$34,020
6. Italy	$20,570
7. Canada	$10,300
8. Spain	$8,289
9. Netherlands	$7,055
10. Belgium	$3,746

Source: U.S. Arms Control and Disarmament Agency, *World Military Expenditures and Arms Transfers*, Annual.

COUNTRIES— NUCLEAR POWER

Most Reactors

Until the incident at Chernobyl in 1986, we had little sense of the mounting nuclear dangers beyond our borders. Now, however, we watch the world's glowing stacks with utmost anxiety. After Chernobyl, the world began to realize that nuclear power, and its potential for hazard, is a worldwide concern. Indeed, with the opening of Eastern Europe, nuclear experts are finding a plethora of ill-designed, potentially dangerous reactors built with the Soviet technology that proved less than failsafe in the Chernobyl incident. Japan, too, has recently been suffering a spate of somewhat troubling reactor difficulties. The following list represents civil nuclear power reactors; it does not count those on board nuclear-powered vessels or those used for research purposes.

Country	Number of Reactors
1. United States	110
2. France	56
3. Japan	46
4. Great Britain	37
5. Russian Fed.	29
6. Canada	22
Germany	22
8. Ukraine	14
9. Sweden	12
10. India	9
South Korea	9
Spain	9

Source: *NY, Nucleonics Week*; SSUS 1996.

COUNTRIES—OIL RESERVES

Who Controls the Oil Supply

Gas guzzlers are back in style. The proliferation of nuclear reactors has been curbed, especially since the world has started to observe the maladies that are now surfacing more than a decade after the incident at Chernobyl in 1986. So, we and the rest of the world continue to burn oil. Certainly, our excessive consumption of and reliance on pe-

troleum is dangerous and wasteful, but until reliable alternatives can be found, access to those reserves through market channels must be preserved, or the global economic consequences are dire. Perhaps, once the euphoria of victory wears off, the dance of death in the desert will spur greater efforts to find safe, efficient, renewable energy resources—the biggest of which shines down on us every sunny day. Below are the nations that hoard the most oil.

Country	Barrels in Reserve (billions)
1. Saudi Arabia	262.5
2. Russian Fed.	191.1
3. Iraq	99.4
4. Kuwait	97.7
5. Venezuela	64.9
6. United Arab Emirates	63.4
7. Iran	58.7
8. Mexico	49.8
9. Libya	36.6
10. China	30.2

Source: Energy Information Administration; U.S. Department of Energy; *Annual Energy Review 1995*; *Oil and Gas Journal*; *World Oil*, August, 1995.

COUNTRIES— OLYMPIC TEAMS

Most Successful Over Time

The United States dominated the first Summer Olympic Games in Athens in 1896, and ever since, America has been the greatest power in the quadrennial meeting of the world's best amateur athletes. The U.S. has nearly twice as many points in our rating system—which assigns a country 10 points for each gold medal, five for each silver and three for each bronze it's won—as any other nation. It should be noted, though, that the Soviet Union did not compete in its first Summer Olympics until the Helsinki Games in 1952, but still nearly matches the performance of Germany, which had been competing for much longer. Following are the 10 most successful countries in the history of the Summer Olympics.

	Gold	Silver	Bronze	Score
1. USA				
	832	634	553	13,149
2. Germany*				
	360	375	390	6,645
3. USSR				
	395	319	296	6,433
4. Great Britain				
	169	223	218	3,459
5. France				
	175	179	206	3,263
6. Italy				
	166	135	144	2,767
7. Sweden				
	132	151	174	2,597
8. Hungary				
	142	129	155	2,530
9. Finland				
	99	80	113	1,729
10. Japan				
	92	89	97	1,656

* for purposes of our rating, medals for East Germany and West Germany were combined into the German totals

Source: *Best and Worst* original.

COUNTRIES— OLYMPIC TEAMS

Second- and Third-Place Finishers

While the the United States, Russia and Germany rack up gold after gold in the Summer Olympic Games, lesser countries are happy to pick up any medals they can. For plucky Bulgaria, second place sil-ver is just fine, thank you; nearly 42 percent of Bulgaria's medals in the Summer Olympics have been for second-place finishes. Polish medalists, on the other hand, most often have been looking on as two other competitors finish ahead of them. Nearly half the medals won by Polish athletes in the Summer Games have been bronze. Here's a look at the top five countries, among major medal-winning nations, in the percentage of medals won that have been silver or bronze.

SECOND-PLACE COUNTRIES

Country	Silver	Total	Pct.
1. Bulgaria	76	182	41.8%
2. Switzerland	69	174	39.7%
3. Denmark	60	155	38.7%
4. China	63	164	38.4%
5. Grt. Britain	223	610	36.6%

THIRD-PLACE COUNTRIES

Country	Bronze	Total	Pct.
1. Poland	110	227	48.5%
2. Holland	81	188	43.0%
3. Canada	90	216	41.7%
4. Australia	121	292	41.4%
Romania	99	239	41.4%

Source: *Best and Worst* original.

COUNTRIES—PANTS PRESSING COSTS

Most Expensive Places to Get a Crease on Your Britches

And you thought New York was expensive! Tell that to anyone who's ever spilled spaghetti sauce on his pants in Helsinki. Dry cleaning a pair of trousers in Finland costs $17.34, by far the most expensive bill in a recent survey of dry cleaning costs throughout the world. Perhaps it's just best to wear

PLACES

polyester wash-and-wear in some places—except Nepal, where dry cleaning costs only 50 cents.

Country	Cost for One Pair of Pants
1. Finland	$17.34
2. Reunion	$15.77
3. Norway	$12.33
4. Serbia	$10.85
5. Switzerland	$10.29
6. French Guiana	$9.85
7. Sweden	$9.82
8. Uganda	$9.72
9. Argentina	$9.38
10. Mauritania	$9.30

Source: *Business Traveler International*, February 1997.

COUNTRIES— POPULATION

Most Crowded

According to the latest available estimates, the world's population at the end of 1996 is 5.772 billion. Although technological miracles like satellite telecommunications have narrowed the apparent size of the world, the growth of the planet's population (and its accompanying cities, towns and other such social encampments) continues at a brisk pace. The world's two most populated nations face enormous difficulties in the coming century, as they struggle to slow their own human growth and increase their per capita standards of living.

Country	Population, 1996
1. China	1,232,083,000
2. India	944,580,000
3. United States	269,444,000
4. Indonesia	200,453,000
5. Brazil	161,087,000
6. Russian Federation	148,126,000
7. Pakistan	139,973,000

WORLD'S SMALLEST COUNTRY (the Holy See aside) is Malvinas (the Falkland Islands), which has approximately 10-times more sheep than people. (See page 140).

8. Japan	125,351,000
9. Bangladesh	120,073,000
10. Nigeria	115,020,000

Source: Population Division, Department for Economic and Social Information and Policy Analysis of the United Nations. Secretariat, *World Population Prospects: The 1996 Revision* (annex tables), United Nations, New York, 1996.

COUNTRIES— POPULATION

Smallest Nations

The two least populous places on the globe have gotten some big headlines. And there are other, previously obscure Third World wonderlands—Grenada, Rwanda, Somalia and Kuwait, to name just a few—that have made the news more than a few times in recent years. In the future, if the U.S. government needs another little guy to pick on, it might consult the following list of the countries with the smallest populations. With our declining military, they'll be easier and cheaper to blow to smithereens.

Country	Population Estimates
1. Holy See (Vatican)	1,000
2. Malvinas (Falkland Islands)	2,000
Niue	2,000
Tokelau	2,000
5. St. Helena	6,000
6. Anguilla	8,000
7. Tuvalu	10,000
8. Montserrat	11,000
Nauru	11,000
10. Turks and Caicos Islands	15,000
Wallis and Futuna Islands	15,000

Source: Population Division, Department for Economic and Social Information and Policy Analysis of the United Nations Secretariat, *World Population Prospects: The 1996 Revision* (annex tables), United Nations, New York, 1996.

COUNTRIES— POPULATION DENSITY

Elbow Room vs. Room to Roam

Population density is the kind of misleading figure that's fun to play with during cocktail parties. You can wow your friends with fascinating fictions about what it must be like to live in one of these places. But while you are fooling your friends, don't let the figures fool you. The fact is that the majority of the most densely populated countries are small nations containing large cities. And while the residents of Singapore are indeed closely packed, they are less sardine-like than the residents of Manhattan Island. Ironically, extreme crowding is a condition common to extremely destitute and extremely prosperous locales. Residents, it seems, are either too poor to get out, or too blindly anxious to get in. On the other hand, the least densely populated countries are often large countries containing large wastelands.

HIGHEST DENSITY

Country	Pop./1,000 Hectares, 1995
1. Singapore	46,689
2. Bangladesh	9,252
3. Mauritius	5,502
4. Netherlands	4,570
5. Korea, Rep.	4,557
6. Japan	3,322
7. Rwanda	3,223

8. Belgium	3,205
9. India	3,147
10. Lebanon	2,941

LOWEST DENSITY

Country	Pop./1,000 Hectares, 1995
1. Mongolia	15
2. Namibia	19
3. Australia	24
4. Botswana	26
5. Iceland	27
Surinam	27
7. Libya	31
8. Canada	32
9. Guyana	42
10. Chad	51
Gabon	51

Source: Food and Agriculture Organization of the United Nations, the United Nations Population Division.

COUNTRIES— POPULATION GROWTH

Fastest and Slowest Growth, by Percent

As recently as the beginning of the decade the slowest growing nations were in Central and Northern Europe. No more. Today's slowest growing nations are spread around Europe, as well as in Asia Minor. The real snails are those countries which have been engaged in war, namely Kuwait and the former Yugoslavian republics, as well as the former Soviet republics. The commonality among the slowest growing countries is turmoil. While the death of civilians always accompanies the gunfire, exiting refugees account for the principal declines.

SLOWEST GROWTH

Country	Annual Population Growth
1. Kuwait	-6.5%
2. Bosnia and Herzegovina	-4.4%

MONGOLIA may have the lowest population density, but there are some tight spots for the adventurous.

3. Afghanistan	-2.0%
4. Latavia, Rep	-0.9%
5. Estonia, Rep	-0.6%
6. Bulgaria	-0.5%
Hungary	-0.5%
8. Romania	-0.3%
9. Belarus, Rep.	-0.1%
Croatia	-0.1%
Lithuania	-0.1%
Russian Federation	-0.1%
Portugal	-0.1%
Ukraine	-0.1%

FASTEST GROWTH

Country	Annual Population Growth
1. Yemen	5.0%
2. Jordan	4.9%
3. Oman	4.2%
4. Gambia	3.8%
Israel	3.8%
6. Angola	3.7%
Nicaragua	3.7%

8. Kenya	3.6%
9. Cote d'Ivoire	3.5%
Malawi	3.5%

Source: United Nations Population Division and International Labour Office; *World Resources, 1996-97.*

9. United States	1,665,000
10. Vietnam	1,571,000

Source: United Nations Population Division and International Labour Office; *World Resources, 1996-97.*

COUNTRIES— POPULATION GROWTH

Fastest Sheer Population Growth

Demographers tell us that the world's population will reach over eight billion by the year 2025, from the world's present population of about 5.7 billion. It's going to be hard to feed, house and clothe all these people, not to mention getting them to buy Cokes and wear Levi's. And who knows what trouble they will cause when they find that Americans have more cable channels than they do? Of the chief governments involved, those in India and China have worked hard at population control, reducing their growth *rates* but nonetheless making litte change in the enormity of their sheer population growth. Even a tiny increase percentage-wise adds a yearly population increase roughly equivalent to the entire population of New York City, Chicago and Los Angeles *combined.* The following are the countries that add the most new citizens every year in terms of sheer numbers.

Country	Annual Population increase
1. India	17,021,000
2. China	13,231,000
3. Pakistan	3,713,000
4. Nigeria	3,113,000
5. Brazil	2,663,000
6. Bangladesh	2,463,000
7. Mexico	1,833,000
8. Iran	1,667,000

COUNTRIES— RELIGION

Most Christian

God is everywhere, of course, but those who believe in Him are a little more spread out. As the home of the Pope and the seat of the Roman Catholic church, Vatican City is the most Christian locale on earth. Among the nations of the West, bitterly divided Ireland is the most solidly religious.

Country	Percentage Christian
1. Dominican Republic	99.6%
2. Nicaragua	99.3%
3. Ireland	99.2%
4. Paraguay	98.9%
5. Grenada	98.8%
Sao Tome	98.8%
Principe	98.8%
8. Greenland	98.7%
9. Tonga	98.4%
10. El Salvador	98.2%

Source: *New Book of World Rankings*, 3rd Edition.

COUNTRIES— RELIGION

Least Chrisitian

As hard to fathom as it may be, Christmas is just another day to most people around the world. Though Christianity pervades the Western world, dominating its customs, holidays and laws, most people in the world are completely unaware of Christian traditions. Though the Muslim world is highly

PLACES

visible in its antipathy to Judeo-Christian faiths, Arab nations nonetheless harbor fairly significant Christian populations. It is in the ancient, mysterious lands of the East that one finds a truly pronounced dearth of Christians.

Country	Percentage Christian
1. China	0.1%
2. Tunisia	0.2%
Niger	0.2%
Mongolia	0.2%
5. Turkey	0.3%
6. Oman	0.4%
Morocco	0.4%
8. Cambodia	0.6%
9. Mauritania	0.7%
North Korea	0.7%

Source: *New Book of World Rankings*, 3rd Edition.

COUNTRIES— RELIGION

Smallest Jewish Population

Looking for bagels and lox in Manila? A good kosher deli in Seoul? Forget about it. According to the American Jewish Year Book, there are only 100 Jewish people in all of the Philippines and South Korea. That's .00017 percent of the Filipino and .00024 percent of the South Korean population, lower than the percentage in such places as Egypt, Iraq and Lebanon. The following are the least-Jewish countries in the world, measured by the number and percentage of the population that is Jewish.

IN SAUDI ARABIA, one of the world's ten-most repressed countries, slavery was legal well into the 20th century. Even today, adultery is punishable by death — and offenders have paid the price. (See page 144).

Country	Jewish Pop.	% Jewish
1. Philippines	100	.00017%
2. South Korea	100	.00024%
3. Egypt	200	.00039%
4. Thailand	300	.00055%
5. India	5,000	.00063%
6. Iraq	200	.00113%
7. Zaire	400	.00119%
8. Dominican Republic	100	.00146%
9. Kenya	400	.00167%
10. Lebanon	100	.00354%

Source: *American Jewish Year Book*, 1990.

COUNTRIES— REPRESSION

Most Repressive Regimes

History teaches us that the oppressed almost always rise up to overthrow their intimidaters. We have seen it happen most recently in the Balkans, Albania, Romania and again in Zaire. There are some regimes, however, that are so entrenched that they hang on, even in the age in which their citizens are increasingly becoming aware of the freedoms other nations have. Nonetheless, some dictators and royal families are so strong-armed, and their "justice" is so swift, that few dare to challenge them. For example, despite America's cozying up to Saudi Arabia, Syria and even Iran in the Persian Gulf crisis, these continue to be some of the most repressive regimes in the world, according to Freedom House, a non-profit organization that has been monitoring the state of freedom throughout the world since 1955. Despite the new-found liberty in such formerly repressive countries as Chile and the nations of Eastern Europe, Freedom House

says that nearly a third of the world's population is not free. Freedom House rates countries on a scale from 1 to 7, with 1 being the most free and 7 the least. The list below contains the countries with a rating of 7.

Country/Repressive Actions

Iraq
Invasion of Kuwait; vast secret police apparatus; widespread human rights abuses included forced relocation, arbitrary arrest, torture and summary execution.

Iran
Public executions of opponents of the regime; thousands of political prisoners; persecution of religious and ethnic minorities.

Saudi Arabia
Continued suppression of women's rights; forcibly expelled hundreds of thousands of Yemeni workers. Islamic laws are strictly and harshly enforced.

Syria
Widespread secret police system; persecution of religious and ethnic minorities.

China
Harassment and jailing of Tiananmen students and other voices of democratic reform; security forces strengthened in anticipation of further protests.

North Korea
Recalled students and officials from abroad and scattered them throughout the country, hoping to dissipate ideas of democracy from outside; only nominal economic reforms under Stalinist Kim Il-Sung.

Burma (Myanmar)
After being swamped in national elections it had called for, the military leaders refused to step down, instead arresting members of the victorious opposition.

Vietnam, Laos
Continue to affirm commitment to a one-party state.

Afghanistan
Stalemate in civil war has meant continued violence and lawlessness.
Liberia
Rival guerrilla movements and tribes engaged in bloody struggle for power after civil war that toppled Samuel K. Doe.
Somalia
Engaged in civil war to topple ruling party, which controls only the capital.
Cuba
Human rights activists jailed; in the face of communism's crumble elsewhere, Castro's grip over every aspect of Cuban society remains as strong now, or stronger, than ever.

Source: Freedom House.

COUNTRIES—ROAD SYSTEMS

Most Paved Roads

In addition to industrialization and technical advancement, a major indicator of the level of country's development is its transportation system. Not surprisingly, the United States, where the car is king, enjoys the most extensive road system in the world. And we have the Cold War to thank for it. Our interstate highway system was built, at least in part, with military preparedness in mind; passenger and commercial travel wasn't the only, or even the most important, reason for the construction of our elaborate and efficient systems of interstate roadways. But even more telling of a country's development is how much of its road network is paved: for instance, Brazil has the second longest road network, but a mere eight percent of the road system in that country is paved, whereas 90%

BRAZIL, SECOND ONLY TO THE U.S. in paved-road mileage, is approximately the same size in area, yet it has approximately 75 percent fewer roads.

of America's roads are hard-topped, as are virtually all the roads in Western Europe. Following are the 10 countries with the most roadway, in kilometers.

Country	Kilometers of Paved Roads*
1. USA	6,000,000
2. Brazil	1,600,000
USSR	1,600,000
4. Japan	1,00,000
5. Australia	900,000
6. Germany	500,500
7 United Kingdom	400,000
8. Poland	300,000
Spain	300,000
Italy	300,000

* data estimated and rounded from 1990 data

Source: World Road Statistics, International Road Federation, Geneva.

COUNTRIES—TELEVISION VIEWING

World's Biggest Couch Potatoes

The more myopic among us may believe that television is a Western phenomenon, but in truth it is an absolutely global medium. While the United States finishes a respectable third in overall sets per capita, the real leaders in world video consumption, as it turns out, are the tinyish republics of Monaco and Guam. It's comforting, perhaps, that wherever we venture in the world, we are just a few commercials from home. It's true, in most any of the far-flung reaches of the globe—from India to Brazil to Mongolia—one can flick on the set and see the reassuring visage of Columbo or J.R. Ewing.

Country	Sets per 1,000 Population
1. United States	816
2. Canada	618
Japan	618
4. Germany	559
5. Denmark	538
6. Finland	504
7. Australia	489
8. Austria	479
9. Czech Republic	476
10. Sweden	470

Source: International Telecommunications Union, World Telecom Indicators, United Nations Educational, Scientific, and Cultural Organization, *Statistical Yearbook* (SAUS, 1996).

COUNTRIES—TOURISM

Where Foreign Tourists Come From

In America's cities, especially in summer, it is not uncommon to hear British-tinged English and French spoken by hoards of people gawking at the tall buildings and store windows. These Europeans are such an odd-looking lot. Europeans? Most likely they are from Canada, where British-born transplants abound as well as French-speaking Canadians. Canada is where most foreign tourist come from. You also hear German, French and Japanese, and, of course, Spanish. Below are the countries that send the most most temporary visitors, either on business or pleasure, to the United States annually.

Country	Visitors
1. Canada	13.7 million
2. Mexico	9.6 million
3. Japan	4.4 million
4. Britain	3.0 million
5. Germany	1.8 million
6. France	.895 million
7. Brazil	.745 million
8. South Korea	.604 million
9. Italy	.546 million
10. Venezuela	.416 million

Source: U.S. Travel and Tourism.

COUNTRIES—URBANIZATION

Most Urbanized Nations

Progress is a double-edged sword. On the blunt edge, expansion, development and growth prolong and enhance living. On the sharp side, though, progress destroys natural beauty, disrupts the in-built harmonies of human existence and fosters poverty, claustrophobia and violence. In the United States, about 70 percent of the population makes its home in urban centers; in hamlet nations like Monaco, every last man makes his stand in the houses of progress.

NO HICKS HERE, NOT IN MONACO, which tied with seven other countries as the most urbanized nations in the world. Photo: Monaco Tourist and Convention Bureau.

Country	Percent Population Urban
1. Monaco	100.0%
Singapore	100.0%
Gibraltar	100.0%
Holy See	100.0%
Cayman Islands	100.0%
Guadeloupe	100.0%
Bermuda	100.0%
Nauru	100.0%
9. Macau	98.8%
10. Belgium	96.9%

Source: United Nations Population Division, Department for Economic and Social Information and Policy Analysis, 1994.

COUNTRIES— URBANIZATION

Most Rural Countries

The world's most rural countries are secluded places where Western influences seldom reach. Their citizens are insulated and completely disconnected from much of the world. Most are farmers or nomadic shephard peoples. In Bhutan, which is a tiny country at the feet of the Himalayas, barely 53,000 of the one-million inhabitants live in towns or cities. The numbers are scarcely different in any of the African nations near the top of the list.

Country	Percent Rural, 1995
1. Burundi	94%
Rwanda	94%
Bhutan	94%
4. Ethiopia	87%
Uganda	87%
Cambodia	87%
Oman	87%

8. Malawi	86%
Nepal	86%
10. Eritrea	85%

Source: Population Distribution, *World Urbanization Prospects*; *Demographic Yearbook*.

GOLF COURSES

Most Dangerous Links

Golf isn't generally thought of as a contact sport. Nor is it generally considered a dangerous pursuit, one requiring a fully-paid-up insurance policy. But if you're playing in Sun City, South Africa, you might want to consider hiring a caddy with a large-caliber rifle to protect against 15-foot alligators. Or, if you're in Singapore playing a round, you might want to trade your spiked golf shoes for a sturdy pair of Wellingtons to protect your calves from cobra bites. In Southern California, on the other hand, you might want to be accompanied on your rounds by a cordon of helmeted police. At Lost City Golf Course in Sun City, South Africa the 13th green is fronted by a stone pit filled with crocodiles, some 15 feet long. At Elephant Hills Country Club in Victoria Falls, Zimbabwe the fairways are sometimes marked by craters caused by mortar shells fired across the Zambezi River. Or, the Compton Par-3 Golf Course in Compton, California has particularly high-caliber excitement when the Crips versus Bloods trouble flares. Following are other courses you would do well to avoid if you're faint at heart.

Rank/Course

1. **Machrie Hotel Golf Course**
   Islay, Scotland
   On this old-fashioned, lay of the land links, virtually every drive and approach is blind, played over huge sand dunes.

2. **Scholl Canyon Golf Course**
   Glendale, California
   Built on a landfill, it ran into difficulties when golfers snagged clubs on buried tires and methane gas rose up from the divots. They now pump the gas to the local power company.

3. **Pelham Bay and Split Rock Golf Courses**
   Bronx, New York
   Pelham's remote location makes it ideal for dumping unfortunate souls. In a recent 10-year period, 13 bodies were said to have been found.

4. **Singapore Island Country Club**
   Singapore
   In the 1982 Singapore Open, pro Jim Stewart encountered a 10-foot cobra. He killed it, only to watch in horror as another emerged from its mouth.

5. **Beachwood Golf Course**
   Natal, South Africa
   Mrs. Molly Whitaker successfully executed a bunker shot here a few years back, but was then attacked by a monkey who leaped from the bush and tried to strangle her. An alert caddie dispatched the mischievious primate.

6. **Plantation Golf and Country Club**
   Gretna, Louisiana: With 18 holes shoved into 61 acres (less than half the norm), players must huddle against protective fencing while awaiting their turn.

7. **Lundin Links**
   Fife, Scotland
   Enjoyable links near St. Andrews, unless you're Harold Wallace, who in 1950 was hit by a train while

crossing the tracks beyond the fifth green.

Source: *Men's Health*, April, 1997.

 ## OLF COURSES

Best Private and Public Courses

What makes a golf course so exalted that its greatness will hold up over time? Well, for starters, a great course should test the skills of a scratch player from the championship tees, challenging him to play all types of shots. It should reward well-placed shots and call on the golfer to blend power and finesse. Each hole should be memorable. There should be a feeling of enticement and a sense of satisfaction in playing the course. The design should offer a balance in both length and configuration, and the course should be properly maintained. A panel of 200—which included professional and amateur golfers, administrators, local officials, journalists and golf historians—made the following selections.

BEST PRIVATE COURSES

Course/Location

1. Cypress Point Club, Pebble Beach, CA
2. Merion Golf Club, Ardmore, PA
3. Oakland Hills C.C.,Oakland, CA
4. Oakmont C.C,. Oakmont, PA
5. Olympic Club (Lake), San Francisco, CA
6. Pebble Beach Links, Pebble Beach, CA

HOLE # 7 AT PEBBLE BEACH LINKS, one of the top-ten rated private courses in the U.S. Hotel guests at the nearby Inn at Spanish Bay (See page 151) may play the 18 hole course for $245. Nonguests are required to pay $275.

7. Pine Valley G.C.,
   Clementon, NJ
8. Seminole G.C.,
   N. Palm Beach, FL
9. Southern Hills C.C.,
   Tulsa, OK
10. Winged Foot G.C.,
    Mamaroneck, NY

Not a member of the country club set? You can still find great courses to play. In fact, some public and municipal courses were conceived by the same designers as the best private courses, such as Robert Trent Jones. Other courses, such as Torrey Pines and the Edgewood Tahoe Golf Course, boast spectacular natural settings.

BEST PUBLIC COURSES

Course/Location

1. Brown Deer Park G.C.,
   Milwaukee, WI
2. Cog Hill G.C Course .#4,
   Lemont, IL
3. Edgewood Tahoe G.C.,
   Stateline, NV
4. Indian Canyon G.C.,
   Spokane, WA
5. Otter Creek G.C., Columbus, IN
6. Plumas Lake C.C., Marysville, CA
7. Tanglewood G.C., Clemmons, NC
8. Torrey Pines G.C.(South),
   La Jolla, CA
9. Wailua G.C., Kauai, HI
10. West Palm Beach C.C., FL

Source: *America's 100 Greatest Golf Courses—and Then Some*, William Davis, Golf Digest Publications.

GOLF MAGAZINE'S BEST OVERALL

Not to be confused with the previous list of its competitor *Golf Digest*, this top 10 list from *Golf Magazine* is culled from its top 100 golf course picks. Their 60-member international selection committee graded 450 nominated courses. They then gave a grade to each on a scale of A to F, and determined which courses should be in the top 10, the top 50, the top 100 or the top 200. The grades were then averaged. The courses that follow had the highest average scores.

Course/Location/Yr./Est./Yardage

1. **Pine Valley, Clementon, NJ**
   Architects: Crump/Colt, 1918
   Par-yardage: 70-6,765

2. **Cypress Point, Pebble Beach, CA**
   Architect: Mackenzie,1929
   Par-yardage: 72-6,536

3. **Pebble Beach, Pebble Beach, CA**
   Architect: Neville, 1919; Egan
   Par-yardage: 72-6,825

4. **Augusta National, Augusta, GA**
   Architects: Mackenzie/Jones, 1932
   Par-yardage: 72-6, 905

5. **Shinnecock Hill, Southampton, NY**
   Architects: Toomey/Flynn, 1931
   Par-yardage: 70-6, 912

6. **Pinehurst (no.2), Pinehurst, NC**
   Architect: D. Ross, 1903-35
   Par-yardage: 72-7

7. **Merion (east), Ardmore, PA**
   Architect: H. Wilson, 1911
   Par-yardage: 70-6,482

8. **Crystal Downs, Frankfort, MI**
   Architect: Mackenzie/Maxwell, 1932
   Par-yardage: 70-6,518

9. **Oakmont, Oakmont, PA**
   Architect: Fownes, 1903
   Par-yardage: 71-6,989

10. **Winged Foot (west), Mamaroneck, NY**
    Architect: Tillinghast, 1923
    Par-Yardage: 72-6,956

Source: *Golf Magazine*, March 1996.

PLACES

H OTELS

The Best Digs in the Whole Wide World

A hotel can be many things to many different people. To a weary family just looking for a room and a pool, it can be a budget motel chain along the interstate. To a business traveler, it can be a clean, safe, quiet place providing room service, computers, and fax machines. But to the well-heeled vacationer, a hotel can be much, much more: a luxury resort on a private, sandy beach, with exotic food and superb golfing and tennis; a castle on the English moors, with high tea served by a crackling fireplace; or a top-flight establishment in a bustling city, with fine dining and a concierge to arrange tickets to the best new plays. Which are the best hotels worldwide? *Conde Nast Traveler* conducts an annual poll to arrive at its coveted Gold List of the 500 top-rated hotels in the world, asking readers to rate such things as service, quality of rooms, restaurants, location/atmosphere, and spa programs. Following are only some of those properties, (the number one rated hotels in selected cities). The magazine, which reviews other fine hotels worthy of even a king's consideration, will be much more valuable to travelers who want the whole picture. Nonetheless, herewith "The Best in America" lists the top-rated hotel in each U.S. state (only given are those states where hotels made the Gold List). "The Best in Europe" lists the highest-rated places in each individual country. "The Best in Asia and Elsewhere" lists the most notable establishments in countries in Africa, Asia, the Pacific, and Australia.

BEST IN AMERICA

State/Hotel	Rating

ARIZONA

Canyon Ranch, Tucson   88.8
180 rooms, $1,510-$2,600 (per person, double occupancy, for 4-night package)
This 70-acre complex in the Santa Catalina foothills offers an excellent spa program with a bit of New Age conversation thrown in.

HIGHEST RATED HOTEL IN CALIFORNIA, the Inn at Spanish Bay.

CALIFORNIA

Inn at Spanish Bay, Pebble Beach   93.6
270 rooms, $255-$375
The top-ranking resort in America with some of the finest golf, the Inn at Spanish Bay features posh adobes with gaslit fireplaces and terraces overlooking the ocean.

COLORADO

Ritz-Carlton, Aspen   92.7
257 rooms, $295-$525

The highest-rated ski resort in America, the Ritz-Carlton is a huge hotel with a refined atmosphere, well-heeled clientele, and attentive staff.

LAKESIDE SUITE AT THE RITZ CARLTON, Chicago's highest-rated hotel.

DISTRICT OF COLUMBIA
Four Seasons   86.6
196 rooms, $310-$355
A sleek and sophisticated establishment in the middle of Washington's Georgetown area, the Four Seasons offers outstanding service and a great restaurant.

FLORIDA
Little Palm Island, Little Torch Key   92.2
30 rooms, $495

Little Palm Island is the ideal place for a romantic rendezvous with a Caribbean feeling, even though it's in the United States.

GEORGIA
The Cloister, Sea Island   86.9
262 rooms, $240-$290
A 1928 coastal resort (where George and Barbara Bush spent their honeymoon), the Cloister has a formal tone, and seafood is the specialty at the four restaurants.

HAWAII
Lodge at Koele, Lanai   91.8
102 rooms, $295-$450
The magisterial Lodge at Koele is in a remote site, high among the pines and eucalyptus.

IDAHO
Coeur d'Alene Resort, Coeur d'Alene   77.0
338 rooms, $59-$229
The resort boasts the world's longest floating boardwalk as well as a lakeside golf course with a unique floating green—located on an island. Some of the rooms are standard, while others are split-level suites.

ILLINOIS
Ritz-Carlton, Chicago   89.0
431 rooms, $300-$335
In a tower occupying the top 19 floors of Chicago's Water Tower Place, the classy Ritz-Carlton has opulent rooms, great food, and a wonderful piano bar.

LOUISIANA
Windsor Court Hotel, New Orleans   90.2
319 rooms, $235-$320
The Windsor Court is America's top-rated hotel located in a city. It has a courteous, quiet atmosphere, fine antiques, and excellent food.

MAINE
The Bayview, Bar Harbor   81.3
38 units, $125-$240

A formal, family establishment near the sea, the Bayview is partly a 1980s hotel, partly a 1930s inn. Nouvelle seafood is the fare of choice.

MARYLAND

Inn at Perry Cabin, St. Michaels 87.5
41 rooms, $175-$395
An 1820 hotel revived in 1990, the Inn's decor is strictly Laura Ashley, and the atmosphere is carried through by the conservatory, library, rickety floorboards, and high tea.

MASSACHUSETTS

Canyon Ranch in the Berkshires, Lenox 86.7
120 rooms, $458-$572 (7-night minimum)
The ranch is a serious and supportive spa located around a turn-of-the-century mansion.

MICHIGAN

Grand Hotel, Mackinac Is. 76.5
320 rooms, $310-$500
The Grand Hotel is located amid rolling forests and pristine lakes, but the tone is genteel, with antique-filled rooms and jacket and tie required in the evening.

MINNESOTA

Whitney Hotel, Minneapolis 71.3
96 rooms, $155-$165
A landmark hotel on the Mississippi, the Whitney was once a flour mill but now boasts an elegant interior and excellent service, with the feeling of an exclusive club.

MISSOURI

Ritz-Carlton, St. Louis 78.6
301 rooms, $165-$235
Location is important here: Located in the suburb of Clayton, the hotel—patronized by visiting dignitaries—is not near the riverfront but amid the financial district and only 15 minutes from downtown.

NEW MEXICO

Inn of the Anasazi, Santa Fe 80.7
59 rooms, $199-$345

At this elegant but laid-back Pueblo-style hotel, the rooms feature Native American culture, and the food is distinctive northern New Mexico fare.

NEW YORK

The Pierre, New York City 85.3
205 rooms, $310-$515
A warm but decidedly urban hotel with an attentive staff, the Pierre is on Fifth Avenue, overlooking Central Park.

NORTH CAROLINA

Sanderling Inn Resort, Duck 78.6
88 rooms, $114-$226
A gray-shingled inn on the Outer Banks set between the ocean and a bird sanctuary, the resort is the place for those who like biking, tennis, surf casting—and then basking in a Jacuzzi.

OREGON

Salishan Lodge, Gleneden Beach 83.5
205 rooms, $115-$210
Salishan, located in a complex overlooking the Pacific coast, offers rooms with fireplaces, Northwest cuisine, golf, tennis, and deep-sea fishing trips.

PENNSYLVANIA

Ritz-Carlton, Philadelphia 85.1
290 rooms, $205-$265
The Ritz-Carlton is a modern downtown hotel with a traditional feeling to it and a highly attentive staff.

SOUTH CAROLINA

Charleston Pl., Charleston 83.5
440 rooms, $240-$275
Charleston Place is well located in the city's historic district and boasts excellent service.

TEXAS

Mansion on Turtle Creek, Dallas 89.5
141 rooms, $310-$390
An unusual hotel incorporating the winding Turtle Creek with a 1925 mansion, this establishment has

lovely rooms, a remarkable staff, and imaginative Southwestern cuisine.

UTAH
Stein Eriksen Lodge, Deer Valley 90.4
126 rooms, $400-$525
A highly rated ski resort with 145 fireplaces, the Lodge combines rustic Norwegian decor with American hospitality.

VERMONT
Equinox Hotel, Manchester Village 81.9
181 rooms, $159-$289
Owned by Guinness, the Equinox is located in two white mansions on a great golf course.

VIRGINIA
Inn at Little Washington, Washington 86.7
12 rooms, $240-$370
The Inn began as a restaurant, then became a luxurious B&B. Located 50 miles from the District of Columbia, the restaurant is still a hot spot.

WASHINGTON
Four Seasons Olympic, Seattle 83.5
450 rooms, $230-$260
The hotel's beautiful 1934 building is on the National Registry. Plus the location is great and the staff is too.

WEST VIRGINIA
The Greenbrier, White Sulphur Springs 89.3
650 rooms, $290-$472
This is a 1910 Georgian hotel offering three golf courses, fishing, riding, tennis, a spa with sulfur-springs baths, and beautiful gardens.

WISCONSIN
American Club, Kohler 84.8
236 rooms, $155-$560
The American Club is somewhat rustic, facing the Kohler plumbing plant. It has two challenging golf courses and— expectedly—showroom-level bathrooms with Kohler fixtures.

WYOMING
Spring Creek Hotel & Conference Center, Jackson 81.3
120 rooms, $150
The views are the thing here, with balconies overlooking the Grand Tetons. The hotel is conveniently located near Jackson Hole.

BEST EUROPEAN HOTELS

Country/Hotel	Rating

AUSTRIA
Hotel Bristol, Vienna 87.7
146 rooms, $440-$590
A stylishly opulent hotel in an 1892 edifice, the Bristol faces the Opera and features the fine Korso Restaurant.

BELGIUM
Conrad International, Brussels 77.1
269 rooms, $225-$430
A very upscale and trendy new hotel, it is located in the middle of shops, expensive restaurants, embassies, and the homes of diplomats.

CZECH REPUBLIC
Hotel Place Praha, Prague 71.1
124 rooms, $352
With virtually all of Prague within walking distance, the Hotel Place Praha is in a beautifully restored Art Nouveau building and features a marvelous staff who all speak English.

ENGLAND
Cliveden, Taplow, Berkshire 96.4
37 rooms, $332-$625
Windsor Castle is downriver from this 376-acre establishment, the highest-rated resort in Europe. It has amazing grounds, an interior featuring armor and paintings by Constable and Sargent, and great French food.

FRANCE
Hotel Ritz, Paris   90.9
187 rooms, $714-$851
What more could you ask for? An 1898 palace located two blocks from the Louvre, the Ritz has stunning rooms, a pool with underwater music, and a restaurant to die for.

GERMANY
Hotel Vier Jahreszeiten, Hamburg   87.2
158 rooms, $335-$419
Conveniently located for shopping, theater, and railways, the hotel—in an 1817 property—has impeccable service, antique-filled rooms, and wonderful dining.

GREECE
Elounda Beach Hotel & Villas, Elounda, Crete   76.7
227 rooms, $85
Atmosphere is paramount here: Elounda boasts a beautiful beach, water sports, and lavish bungalows. It's also one of the least expensive places on the Gold List.

HUNGARY
Kempinski Hotel Corvinus, Budapest   73.9
369 rooms, $303-$360
Huge rooms, fine food, and an attentive staff are among the features of this contemporary hotel.

IRELAND
Adare Manor, Adare, County Limerick   82.3
64 rooms, $178-$259
A neo-Gothic stone manor is the site for this warm and friendly hotel, with nice grounds and good Irish country food.

ITALY
Four Seasons Hotel, Milan   96.9
98 rooms, $401-$476
The Four Seasons is the highest-rated hotel in the world. And no wonder: It's a former 15th-century monastery with frescoes, antique-

PRESIDENTIAL SUITE at the Four Seasons Hotel in Milan.

filled rooms, an amazing staff and restaurants, all located near Milan's fine shopping and couture houses.

MONACO
Hotel de Paris, Monte Carlo   89.6
200 rooms, $388-$449
The Hotel de Paris is a grand and regal establishment next to the Casino de Monte Carlo. Its wine cellar has more than 180,000 bottles.

NETHERLANDS
Hotel de l'Europe, Amsterdam   73.2
100 rooms, $324-$362
The hotel is in Amsterdam's historic city center, near restaurants and transportation.

PORTUGAL
Reid's Hotel, Funchal, Madeira   82.9
169 rooms, $262-$323
There's a country-estate feeling here, in an 1891 cliff-top building amid flower gardens and with a seaside pool.

PLACES

SCOTLAND
The Gleneagles Hotel,
Auchterarder   82.3
236 rooms, $309-$427
This is a remarkable resort offering famous golf courses, a riding academy, a falconry school, tennis courts, lovely views, Jacuzzis, Scottish tea, and fine dining.

SPAIN
Hotel Ritz, Madrid   82.5
156 rooms, $290-$495
The Ritz features amazing decor—antiques, handmade rugs, embroidered linens—and views of the Prado in a formal atmosphere.

SWEDEN
Grand Hotel, Stockholm   79.0
319 rooms, $368-$455
A distinguished 1874 palace across the water from the Royal Palace, the Grand is frequented by dignitaries and Nobel laureates.

SWITZERLAND
Carlton Hotel, St. Moritz   86.0
107 rooms, $272-$300
The tone is somewhat snobbish and the clientele aware of it at the Carlton, an Alpine chateau with beautiful mountain views and a glassed-in pool.

TURKEY
Cirigan Palace Hotel
Kempinski, Istanbul   86.4
334 rooms, $215-$345
Wonderfully located on the Bosphorus, the hotel has a great pool, restaurant, spa, and casino. Some rooms are in an old sultan's palace.

WALES
Llangoed Hall, Brecon   79.8
23 rooms, $269-$317
A gracious country house in the Wye Valley, Llangoed Hall is romantically decorated in Laura Ashley, plus fine art and antiques.

BEST HOTELS IN ASIA AND ELSEWHERE

Country/Hotel	Rating

AUSTRALIA
Ritz-Carlton, Sydney   95.5
106 rooms, $194-$233
A hotel geared to the business traveler, the Ritz-Carlton is right in Sydney's business district and offers excellent service and elegant dining.

CHINA
Shangri-La Hotel, Beijing   74.6
716 rooms, $160-$260
A surprisingly luxurious hotel, the Shangri-La has Hong Kong-trained chefs and a staff who speak perfect English.

EGYPT
Mena House Oberoi Hotel
& Casino, Giza   75.0
520 rooms, $140-$218
Breathtaking views of the Pyramids, the original arabesque-Islamic architecture, and good food are some of the features of this royal hunting lodge that became a hotel in 1869.

FIJI
The Regent, Fiji, Nadi   82.8
285 rooms, $179-$245
Among the attractions here are lush tropical gardens, a pool bar, stylish boutiques, and a private isle for snorkeling and sunbathing.

FRENCH POLYNESIA
Bora Bora Lagoon Resort,
Bora Bora   90.5
80 bungalows, $634-$964
A tropical island fantasy, complete with exotic birds, coconut palm trees, and thatched bungalows awaits visitors here.

FOUR SEASONS RESORT at Jimbaran Bay, Bali (Indonesia) is the highest-rated hotel in the world.

HONG KONG
The Regent   91.9
602 rooms, $285-$453
The Regent offers business travelers amazing service, plus there are great harbor views and wonderful dining.

INDIA
Inter-Continental, Bombay   74.5
650 rooms, $300-$400
The Inter-Continental combines a functional modern tower with a 1903 domed building, complete with traditional British atmosphere.

INDONESIA
**Four Seasons Resort,
Jimbaran Bay, Bali**   96.7
147 villas, $425-$2,000
The top-rated resort in the world, it features gorgeous grounds overlooking the bay, huge villas, and upscale dining.

JAPAN
Imperial Hotel, Tokyo   79.7
1,059 rooms, $364-$634
The Imperial is in Tokyo's Ginza district, across from the Imperial Palace, with excellent service for business travelers.

KENYA
**Mount Kenya Safari Club,
Nanyuki**   89.3
115 rooms, $285-$530
A secluded and beautiful establishment, among its offerings are magnificent service, good golf, a zoo with rescued animals, and strolling storks.

MALAYSIA
**Shangri-La Hotel, Kuala
Lumpur**   85.5
721 rooms, $190-$271
The hotel features glamorous decor, a convenient downtown location, and remarkable food.

MOROCCO
La Mamounia Hotel,
Marrakech 84.6
231 rooms, $290-$445
La Mamounia is a civilized hotel in an exotic locale, a 1923 palace at the edge of the desert.

NEW ZEALAND
Huka Lodge, Taupo,
North Island 83.8
17 lodges, $368-$516
What a site—near the 80-foot-high Kuka Falls, on the Waikato River with its fly-fishing. There are lush lawns, riding, tennis, and partylike barbecues.

THE PHILIPPINES
The Peninsula, Manila ♦75.0
525 rooms, $250-$305
Conveniently located in Manila, the Peninsula has a unique atmosphere, with a neoclassic exterior and sparrows in the lobby.

SINGAPORE
The Regent 93.2
441 rooms, $245-$260
Remarkable staff, large rooms, and a quiet location near the Botanical Garden make this an excellent hotel for demanding corporate executives.

SOUTH KOREA
Hotel Shilla, Seoul 75.0
565 rooms, $176-$256
Among the features here are a jogging path, exercise room, and restaurants melding Korean and Western touches.

TAIWAN
Grand Hyatt, Taipei 77.4
872 rooms, $240-$510
A modern hotel in the World Trade Center, the Grand Hyatt boasts attentive staff and six restaurants.

THAILAND
Shangri-La, Bangkok 91.7
862 rooms, $211-$279

This is a grand, modern hotel, with knowledgeable staff and excellent convention facilities.

UNITED ARAB EMIRATES
Sheraton Abu Dhabi Resort
& Towers, Abu Dhabi 75.0
260 rooms, $231-$245
Located near the financial district, this 1979 resort has spacious rooms, fine cuisine, a lively beach, and deep-sea fishing.
Source: "The Gold List," *Conde Nast Traveler,* January 1996.

IMMIGRANTS IN THE U.S.

Where Do They Come From?

Between 1880 and 1920, nearly 20 million European immigrants arrived in the United States—Scandinavians settled in the vast expanses of the Northern Plains, while Germans, Italians, and Poles found work in the mills and plants of Pittsburgh, Cleveland, Detroit and Chicago. The post-World War I period saw a sharp decline in immigration, stemming in part from growing xenophobic sentiments, and then the Depression and World War II. Immigration increased after 1960—both legal and illegal—and has continued at a high level since. The newest wave, of course, has been significantly more diverse than the one at the turn of the century: Today's immigrants—from Mexico, Cuba and Central America; from China, the Philippines and India; from Egypt and Nigeria—are literally changing the complexion of the United States. As always, immigrants to the U.S. will remain essential to the economic, social, and spiritual vitality of the country.

Following are rankings of the regions of the world and the last nations of residence from which immigrants to the United States came during various periods.

ORIGINS BY WORLD REGION, 1820-1993

Region	Total U.S.
1. Europe	37,566,702
2. North America	9,478,377
3. Asia	7,051,564
4. Caribbean	3,035,898
5. South America	1,440,413
6. Central America	1,046,963
7. Africa	417,926
8. Oceania	223,821
9. Unspecified	267,639
10. Other America	110,147

LAST NATIONS OF RESIDENCE, 1820-1993

Nation	Total U.S.
1. Germany	7,117,192
2. Italy	5,419,285
3. United Kingdom	5,178,264
4. Mexico	5,117,422
5. Ireland	4,755,172
6. Canada	4,360,955
7. Russian Fed.	3,572,281
8. Austria	1,837,232
9. Hungary	1,670,777
10. Sweden	1,288,763
11. Philippines	1,222,287
12. China	1,025,700
13. Austria-Hungary	846,076
14. Norway	803,281
15. France	800,016
16. Cuba	782,050
17. Greece	711,461
18. Korea	703,732
19. Poland	675,221
20. Dominican Republic	638,970

LAST NATIONS OF RESIDENCE, 1991-93

Region	U.S. Total
1. Mexico	1,288,693
2. Philippines	195,634
3. Dominican Republic	128,834
4. Former USSR	128,675
5. India	116,201
6. China	111,324
7. El Salvador	99,794
8. Vietnam	77,913
9. Poland	68,885
10. Haiti	67,701
11. Canada	65,370
12. Korea	61,484
13. United Kingdom	59,114
14. Jamaica	58,018
15. Hong Kong	47,723

Source, U.S. Dept. of Justice, *1993. Statistical Yearbook of the Immigration and Naturalization Service (1994)*.

THESE AMERICAN-BORN AMISH GIRLS are members of one of the smallest immigrant groups in the U.S., so small the U.S. Census does not tally them. An estimate of their number is 130,000. The original immigrants came from Switzerland in the early 1700s.

PLACES

MOUNTAINS, TALLEST IN U.S.

America is unique for its vast, flat prairie regions, and its rugged mountain ranges of the West and Pacific Northwest. Although our peaks cannot compare with the great summits of Asia, they comprise an imposing continental barrier and offer a dramatic counterpoint to our fertile lowlands. All of America's tallest peaks are in Alaska.

Mountain	Elevation (feet)
1. Mt. McKinley	20,320
2. Mt. St. Elias	18,008
3. Mt. Foraker	17,400
4. Mt. Bona	16,500
5. Mt. Blackburn	16,390
6. Mt. Sanford	16,237
7. Mt. Vancouver	15,979
8. Mt. South Buttress	15,885
9. Mt. Churchill	15,638
10. Mt. Fairweather	15,300

Source: Department of the Interior, U.S. Geological Survey.

MOUNTAINS, WORLD'S TALLEST

Denizens of Colorado and some of the U.S.'s other mountainous areas have come to regard themselves as a rugged, Alpine people. The elevations on which they encamp, however, seem dwarfish beside the great peaks of the Himalayas and other Asian chains. Indeed, oxygen is so rare on the great summits of the East that even their foothills are dizzying.

Mountain/Country	Elevation (feet)
1. Everest (Nepal)	29,108
2. K-2 (Kashmir)	29,064
3. Kanchenjunga (Nepal-Sikkim)	28,208
4. Lhotse (Nepal-Tibet)	27,890
5. Makalu (Nepal-Tibet)	27,790
6. Dhaulagiri I (Nepal)	26,810
7. Manaslu (Nepal)	26,760
8. Cho Oyu (Nepal)	26,750
9. Nanga Parbat	26,660
10. Annapurna I	26,504

BLUE RIDGE PARKWAY, the U.S.'s most popular national park (below) has many wonders just off Skyline Drive, the route that spans the summits of the Blue Ridge Mountains of Virginia.

NATIONAL PARKS

Most Visited in the U.S.

Many American families who pack up their Winnebagos for a two-week break from the hustle and bustle receive a sudden, unexpected shock when they hit their first traffic jam outside a national park seemingly in the middle of nowhere. Only then do they realize that their idea of getting away from it all has led them smack into the maelstrom. In fact, last year the National Park Service counted approximately one visit for every American. With most people vacationing sometime during the summer, it's not surprising that America's national parks fill up quickly—perhaps there's just not enough scenery to go around. The leader on this list benefits (or suffers) from its proximity to San Francisco, another big tourist attraction.

Park	Visitors
1. Blue Ridge Parkway	17,415,519
2. Golden Gate NRA	14,695,771
3. Lake Mead NRA	9,838,702
4. Great Smoky Mts. Nat. Park	9,080,420
5. George Washington Mem. Natl. Pkwy.	6,546,803
6. Gateway NRA	6,064,254
7. Natchez Trace Natl. Pkwy.	5,849,061
8. National Capital Parks	5,513,009
9. Cape Cod National Seashore	5,141,039
10. Delaware Water Gap NRA	4,726,251

Source: National Park Service, Department of the Interior.

PORTS, AMERICAN

Largest Harbors in the U.S.

In the era of the jet and the tractor-trailer, it is easy to forget the role that maritime freight lanes (and their principal ports) played in this nation's economic and social development. Our key ports were—and remain—direct and visceral links to other peoples, vessels and cultures, in a fashion which airports shall never usurp. Below are the busiest ports in the United States, in terms of the annual tonnage of shipping handled.

Port	Total Tonnage, 1994
1. South Louisiana, LA	184,855,712
2. Houston	143,662,625
3. New York City and NJ	126,100,614
4. Baton Rouge	88,245,856
5. Valdez, AK	85,096,176
6. Corpus Christi, TX	78,138,462
7. New Orleans	73,332,939
8. Plaquemine, LA	64,758,624
9. Long Beach, CA	56,520,167
10. Tampa	51,902,190

Source: Department of the Army, Corps of Engineers (SSUS, 1996).

STATES— ABORTION

Highest and Lowest Rates

Since abortion became legal with the Supreme Court's *Roe v. Wade* decision, the number of abortions grew steadily from the early 1970s until 1980; since that time, the number has remained steady. Debate has raged across the country between opponents of the practice and those who support a woman's right to choose; many states, and the federal government more recently, have attempted to limit the availability of abortions by requiring teens to notify their parents, restricting federally funded family planning clinics from offering abortion counseling, and even threatening doctors with jail terms for performing abortions. Below is a list of the states with the highest abortion rates per 1,000 women of child-

THE HIGHEST PLACE IN THE WORLD, Mount Everest (See page 160), also has the highest death toll of climbers, which has reached epidemic proportions, averaging approximately ten fatalities annually.

bearing age. Differences between states are the result of a number of factors—including the availability of abortion services, minority populations, urbanization and individual state policies on such issues as public funding for abortions for low-income services.

MOST ABORTIONS

State	Abortions/1,000 Population
1. District of Columbia	138.4
2. New York	46.2
3. Hawaii	46.0
4. Nevada	44.2
5. California	42.1
6. Delaware	35.2
7. New Jersey	31.0
8. Rhode Island	30.0
Florida	30.0
10. Massachusetts	28.4

FEWEST ABORTIONS

State	Abortions/1,000 Population
1. Wyoming	4.3
2. South Dakota	6.8
3. Idaho	7.2
4. West Virginia	7.7
5. Utah	9.3
6. North Dakota	10.7
7. Iowa	11.4
Kentucky	11.4
9. Missouri	11.6
10. Indiana	12.0

Source: *Abortion Factbook*; Readings, Guttmacher Institute; Family Planning Perspectives, 1994.

PLACES

STATES— AIDS

Childhood AIDS Cases

AIDS, of course, is not limited to the gay community. In fact, reports now suggest that Acquired Immune Deficiency Syndrome is growing most rapidly not within the gay community, where awareness and education have brought about a change in behaviors that helped spread the disease, but among intravenous drug abusers, who may be less educated about the dangers of AIDS. Sadly, the legacy of this ignorance is a growing population of children infected with the virus—since a pregnant mother who is infected is extremely likely to infect her fetus as well. Other childhood AIDS cases have resulted from blood transfusions with infected plasma. Below is a list of the states with the highest incidence of AIDS among children.

State	Pediatric Aids Cases *
1. New York	161
2. Florida	117
3. New Jersey	51
4. California	48
5. Illinois	39
6. Puerto Rico	28
7. Texas	27
8. Pennsylvania	25
Georgia	25
10. Maryland	22

* cases reported from July 1995 through June 1996

Source: HIV/AIDS Surveillance Report, 1996.

STATES— AUTOMOBILES

Highest Automobile-Related Death Rates

Whatever their practical benefits, cars too often become the engines of accidental destruction in our high-speed world. Although any road comprises a potential hazard, the long, open stretches of our sparsely populated Western and Southern states have consistently proven to be our nation's most dangerous. Yes, those in the West enjoy their freedom, but that doesn't mean they're free to cruise the roads with reckless abandon. The following are the states with the deadliest roadways, in number of deaths per 1,000 people per year, attributed to automobiles.

State	Deaths per 100,000 Population
1. Wyoming	35.42
2. Mississippi	32.18
3. New Mexico	28.78
4. Alabama	26.17
5. Arkansas	25.40
6. Montana	24.71
7. Arizona	24.44
8. South Carolina	23.99
9. Tennessee	23.95
10. Idaho	22.53

Source: Traffic Safety Facts 1995; State Traffic Data. U.S. Department of Transportation, National Highway Traffic Safety Administration.

STATES— BANKRUPTCIES

Highest Occurrence of Business Failures

The number of failed businesses in the U.S. during 1996 was almost unchanged for the third consecutive

THE BANKRUPTCY BRIDGE: On one side of the George Washington Bridge (at left) is the state with the most personal bankruptcies, New Jersey (top of photo). On the other side is the state with most business bankruptcies, New York. Photo: © New York State Department of Economic Development.

year, but dollar liabilities associated with those failures declined nine percent compared with 1995, according to The Dun & Bradstreet Corporation. Nationwide, approximately 71,800 businesses failed in 1996, which represents an increase of about 1 percent from 1995. Dollar liabilities from business failures dropped from $37.2 billion to $34 billion in the same period. Below are the states where entrepreneurs took a big beating.

State	Liabilities, 1996
1. New York	$6,048,122,288
2. California	$5,820,956,157
3. Texas	$3,594,906,772
4. Florida	$1,939,669,517
5. Colorado	$1,882,941,819
6. Pennsylvania	$1,414,131,242
7. North Carolina	$1,232,442,108
8. Indiana	$1,198,363,518
9. Ohio	$978,387,383
10. Illinois	$840,721,865

Source: Dun & Bradstreet, Business Wire, February 11, 1997.

STATES— BANKRUPTCIES

Personal Filings

Staying solvent is becoming harder and harder for Americans today. With retailers dropping their credit standards and many people carrying numerous credit cards, consumer debt is rising faster than personal incomes. The result? More people than ever before are filing for bankruptcy. In fact, bankruptcy—once shocking, shameful, and unthinkable—has become an easy way out for many consumers, allowing them to walk away from their debts while retaining their homes and many of their belongings. Some interesting factoids: More than 1 million families now file for bankruptcy each year. The average family filing for bankruptcy has an annual income of $20,500, credit card debt of $20,700, and a total debt of $51,000. The two following lists show the states with the largest average debt per bankruptcy filer and the smallest average debt per filer.

MOST SERIOUS DEADBEATS

State	Average Debt per Filer
1. New Jersey	$65,801
2. Florida	$62,029
3. Texas	$56,819
4. New Hampshire	$54,506
5. California	$53,500
6. Nevada	$46,059
7. Arizona	$43,532
8. Massachusetts	$43,421
9. Pennsylvania	$43,384
10. New Mexico	$42,954

LEAST SERIOUS DEADBEATS

State	Average Debt per Filer
1. Utah	$24,123
2. Oregon	$28,405
3. Illinois	$28,996
4. Nebraska	$28,997
5. Indiana	$29,300
6. Wisconsin	$29,846
7. Kentucky	$29,970
8. Ohio	$31,026
9. Washington	$31,953
10. South Dakota	$33,122

Source: First Chicago NBD, University of Wisconsin-Madison, American Bankruptcy Institute, CDB Infotek.

STATES— BEARS

Most Bearish States

The following figures for bear populations in the United States are estimates, since no one knows for sure how many exist. Figures pertain to the total numbers of bears on public, federally controlled lands, and include black, grizzly and brown bears. The bear has all but vanished from the wild in the East, except in specially protected areas of the Appalachians. Alaska, on the other hand, still has a fairly healthy bear population.

State	Bear Population
1. Alaska	10,000
2. Oregon	2,000
3. Colorado	1,000
4. Montana	500
Utah	500
6. Wyoming	400
7. California	100
Arizona	100

Source: Public Land Statistics, U.S. Department of the Interior.

STATES—BLACK POPULATION

Highest Percentage of Blacks

Despite their great migration northward, America's blacks have not abandoned the Southland. The highest concentrations of blacks, as a percentage of total population, still occur in the rural South. Although blacks have moved steadily toward the cities since World War II, much of that redistribution has

PLACES

been offset by differential birth-rates.

HIGHEST CONCENTRATION

State	Percent Black
1. District of Columbia	65.84%
2. Mississippi	35.56%
3. Louisiana	30.79%
4. South Carolina	29.82%
5. Georgia	26.96%
6. Alabama	25.26%
7. Maryland	24.89%
8. North Carolina	21.97%
9. Virginia	18.80%
10. Delaware	16.88%

Source: *World Almanac of the U.S.A.*, 1996.

STATES—BOMBING OF CLINICS

Most Explosive States

Each year in America hundreds of bombs go off, the most infamous and destructive of which was on April 19, 1995, in Oklahoma City, an incident that claimed 168 people. In our violent society however, there are many more bombings, most of which only scare the public rather than kill or injure them. In recent years the targets of choice have been abortion clinics. Ironically, their perpetrators bomb their fellow citizens as a protest against what they believe is worst kind of violence—violence against the unborn. Below are the states which have experienced the most bombings and arson at clinics.

State	Incidents, 1987-97*
1. California	28
2. Florida	16
3. Texas	13
4. Ohio	12
5. Oregon	11
6. Minnesota	10
7. Illinois	9

8. Virginia	7
9. Colorado	6
New York	6

* data through February 11, 1997

Source: Bureau of Alcohol, Tobacco and Firearms, February 1997.

STATES—CAPITAL PUNISHMENT

Most Recent Executions

Is there a reason why the states with the most executions are in the South and West, the areas where the population in general is moving to? The trend in capital punishment for many years was moving away from state-sanctioned executions. But about 15 years ago that changed as more and more states voted in the death penalty that they had voted out just a decade or so before. Texas has the dubious distinction of leading the pack by a three-to-one margin in number of executions during 1995. The other states were quite modest in their efforts. Of course, Texas is the largest state in the lower 48, so that might explain their large number of executions.

State	Executions, 1995
1. Texas	19
2. Missouri	6
3. Illinois	5
Virginia	5
5. Florida	3
Oklahoma	3
7. Alabama	2
Arkansas	2
Georgia	2
North Carolina	2
Pennsylvania	2

Source: Bureau of Justice Statistics Bulletin *Capital Punishment 1995*, December 1996.

PLACES

STATES—CAPITAL PUNISHMENT

Most Executions Since 1930

Texas is not the place to commit capital crimes. In the last 10 years, 78 prisoners have been executed there. Capital punishment has always been an enormously emotional issue for politically aware Americans. On one hand, most citizens acknowledge the need to establish a strong and chilling deterrent against such heinous crimes as pre-meditated murder and kidnapping. On the other, our system is based around the presumption of innocence, the apportionment of mercy and the continuing possibility of redemption. Historically, each state, through its citizens, has grappled individually with these issues. Alaska, Hawaii, Maine, Michigan, Minnesota, North Dakota, Rhode Island and Wisconsin have never seen fit to take a life. Those states that have most frequently are listed below.

State	Executions Since 1930
1. Texas	401
2. Georgia	386
3. New York	329
4. California	294
5. North Carolina	271
6. Florida	206
7. Ohio	172
8. South Carolina	167
9. Mississippi	158
10. Louisiana	155

Source: Bureau of Justice Statistics Bulletin, *Capital Punishment 1995*, December 1996.

STATES—CHILD ABUSE

States of Abuse: Most Child Abuse Fatalities

Child abuse is easy to condemn, but more difficult to curtail. In reality, child neglect and traumatization of the young is not always easy to detect. Following are the states in which the most children are victimized. Interestingly, California's rate of child-abuse fatalities is almost *three-times* the second state, New York..

State	Cases, 1994
1. California	352,059
2. New York	128,111
3. Texas	110,742
4. Florida	108,943
5. Ohio	96,747
6. Illinois	77,289
7. New Jersey	65,954
8. North Carolina	59,135
9. Michigan	57,394
10. Georgia	55,578

Source: U.S. Department of Health and Human Services; National Center on Child Abuse and Neglect; National Child Abuse and Neglect Data System, Child Maltreatment, 1994.

STATES—CHILDREN

Most Childish States

Miami Beach is world famous for its elderly population, just as Daytona Beach is famous for its youth-crazed Spring Breaks. Age, over the broad geography of this great nation, is a factor in all sorts of logistics and decisions. Size counts, weight counts, age counts—at their oldest, American retirement communities are indeed old, and at their youngest, college towns are exceedingly young. The state with the most school-age persons as a percent of the population is Utah, home of the fecund Mormons.

State	% of Pop. Under 18, 1995
1. Utah	34.6%
2. Alaska	31.4%
3. Idaho	29.9%
4. New Mexico	29.7%
5. Texas	28.8%
6. Louisiana	28.5%
7. Wyoming	28.4%
8. Arizona	28.3%
South Dakota	28.3%
10. Mississippi	28.2%

Source: U.S. Census Bureau (SAUS, 1996).

STATES— DEATH RATES

Most Accident Prone

Death is inevitable, but not on any particular occasion. Accidental death is, in principle, preventable. There are, however, regions of greater or lesser safety. If you're already accident prone, try to avoid the South and Northwest where the most accidents occur.

State	Accidental Deaths per 100,000*
1. Mississippi	59.5
2. Alaska	56.4
3. New Mexico	53.5
4. Alabama	51.1
5. Tennessee	48.1
6. Arkansas	48.0
7. Montana	47.2
8. Wyoming	46.2
9. West Virginia	46.0
10. Kentucky	45.9

* figures are for 1993

Source: U.S. National Center for Health Statistics, Monthly Vital Statistic Report and unpublished data (SAUS, 1996).

STATES— DEATH RATES

Highest Death Rates

In contemporary America, the danger to life comes more often from accident, injury and criminal victimization than the ravages of disease. While we have solved many of the most insidious medical quandaries, it remains for us to thoroughly address our social ills. The District of Columbia gets the top spot on the list in part because it has the third most murders in the U.S. Washington also has one of the most predominately black populations in the nation, a factor which also comes into play as far as its high death rates. The life expectancy for blacks in 1995 was 69.8 years; for whites, 76.5. Other factors besides murder and race play a role, such as average age, the quality of health care and environmental conditions. The following cities have the worst mix of all of those criteria and therefore the highest death rates.

States	Deaths per 100,000
1. District of Columbia	1,236.3
2. West Virginia	1,107.6
3. Missouri	1,100.8
4. Florida	1,084.6
5. Arkansas	1,073.6
6. Pennsylvania	1,061.3
7. Mississippi	1,000.7
8. Oklahoma	999.4
9. Alabama	997.3
10. Kentucky	985.7

Source: National Center of Health Statistics, Monthly Vital Statistics Report, October 1996.

TO SOME, THIS IS THE CAPITAL CITY OF THE U.S. To dentists, however, it's the capital of their profession — Washington, D.C., where there are more dentists per capita than any city or state in the U.S.

STATES —DENTISTS

Highest and Lowest Concentrations

For many, the prospect of a visit to the dentist wakes dark images of medieval dungeons and unutterable acts of torture and defilement. Nonetheless, the fast, easy availability of dental treatment is indeed a high-water mark for a community. Among our most orally conscious outposts, the data reveal, are the great Pilgrim encampments of the Eastern seaboard.

MOST DENTISTS

State	Dentists per 100,000 Pop.
1. District of Columbia	122
2. Connecticut	80
3. New York	79
4. Hawaii	78
New Jersey	78
6. Massachusetts	76
7. Colorado	71
Maryland	71
9. Oregon	69
10. Illinois	67

FEWEST DENTISTS

State	Dentist per 100,000 Pop.
1. Mississippi	38
2. New Mexico	41
Arkansas	41
4. South Carolina	42
North Carolina	42
Alabama	42
7. Nevada	43
8. West Virginia	45
South Dakota	45
Delaware	45

Source: *The World Almanac of the U.S.A.*, 1996.

STATES —DIVORCE

Highest Divorce Rates

In the second half of the twentieth century, we have witnessed the simultaneous erosion of the nuclear family, and the environment. The once iron-clad institution of marriage has retained a fraction of its earlier stability. And in our nation, it is the clean, hot states of the West which have become the largest cauldrons for marital unrest, with Nevada and Oklahoma ranking first and second in divorces per capita.

State	Divorces per 1,000, 1994
1. Nevada	9.0
2. Oklahoma	6.7
3. Tennessee	6.6
4. Wyoming	6.5
5. Alabama	6.2
Idaho	6.2
7. New Mexico	6.0
8. Florida	5.9
9. Kentucky	5.8
Arizona	5.8

Source: U.S. National Center for Health Statistics, Monthly Vital Statistics Report, 1995.

STATES—EDUCATIONAL ATTAINMENT

Most Educated

Washington, DC, is home to the highest concentration of lawyers in the United States; this, plus the preponderance of government bureaucrats and relatively low number of blue-collar jobs, helps account for its number one ranking among educated "states." When the list below appeared in the first edition of this book in 1991, the state at the top of the list had about 10% fewer people with bachelor's degrees. Following are the states that have the greatest percentage of those with bachelor's degrees.

State	Bachelor's or Better
1. District of Columbia	38.2%
2. Colorado	33.3%
3. Connecticut	32.7%
4. Massachusetts	32.6%
5. Vermont	30.3%
6. New Jersey	27.9%
Rhode Island	27.9%
8. Minnesota	26.5%
Washington	26.5%
10. Maryland	26.4%

Source: National Education Association.

STATES— ELECTRICITY COSTS

The Biggest Charge

If one senses static in the air, it is not the result of an impending storm, but of friction. The American public is beyond weariness in its struggle against mounting utility prices. All over the nation, citizens and activists are banding together to check the excesses of the quasi-public service providers, and establish a safer, more equitable system. Below are the states in which citizens pay the most for basic electrical services, measured by the cost per million BTUs.

State	Price per Million BTUs
1. New Hampshire	$31.83
2. New York	$31.43
3. Hawaii	$31.34
4. Rhode Island	$30.52
5. Connecticut	$30.07
6. Alaska	$29.72
7. New Jersey	$29.31
8. Massachusetts	$29.24

9. California $28.51
10. Maine $26.68
Source: State Energy Price and Expenditure Data System, 1993.

STATES— ELEVATION

Where to Get High . . . Legally

You don't need drugs to get high, dude. The table below lists the states with the highest *peak* elevation, which translates as the summit of the highest mountain in the state.

State	Elevation (feet)
1. Alaska	20,320
2. California	14,494
3. Colorado	14,433
4. Washington	14,410
5. Wyoming	13,804
6. Hawaii	13,796
7. Utah	13,528
8. New Mexico	13,161
9. Nevada	13,140
10. Montana	12,799

Source: National Oceanic and Atmospheric Administration; U.S. Department of Commerce; Department of the Interior, U.S. Geological Survey.

STATES—ENERGY CONSUMPTION

Biggest Turn-Ons

When most people think of "burning fuel," the context of automobiles is usually considered. However, it's in the home in which most consumers burn fuel. Be it the heat of summer or the cold of winter, it takes energy to run air conditioners and furnaces.

State	BTUs per Capita (millions)
1. Alaska	1,040.0
2. Wyoming	908.1

THE HIGHEST POINT IN THE U.S., Alaska's Mt. McKinley (See page 160).

3. Louisiana	831.4
4. Texas	560.7
5. North Dakota	516.1
6. West Virginia	439.0
7. Indiana	425.6
8. Montana	414.3
9. Kentucky	408.2
10. Oklahoma	406.2

Source: U.S. Energy Information Administration, State Energy Data Report (SAUS, 1996).

STATES— FARMING

Most Farm Acreage

Although the first Americans were quick to build lasting and expansive settlements, the early epochs of this nation were marked by their extraordinary utilization of land resources and concomitant hegemony in world agriculture. Today, a relatively tiny percentage of our nation's acreage remains under cultivation, yet our productivity remains unrivaled. This development has come apace with the introduction of highly technological means of farming (whose side effect is the displacement of the venerable citizen-farmer).

State	Acres (1,000s)
1. Texas	129,000
2. Montana	59,700
3. Kansas	47,800
4. Nebraska	47,100
5. New Mexico	44,000
South Dakota	44,000
7. North Dakota	40,300
8. Arizona	35,400
9. Wyoming	34,600
10. Oklahoma	34,000

Source: U.S. Department of Agriculture, NASS, Economics Statistics Branch, 1996.

 STATES— FARMING

Greatest Farm Income

While America's hi-tech industries garner Wall Street's attention, straightforward agricultural cultivation remains an unspoken but critical component of our economy. Although we traditionally associate farming with the rural expanses of the Great Plains region, populous, temperate states like Washington, California and Florida are also extremely important contributors to our national agricultural output.

State	Net Farm Income ($1,000s)*
1. California	$4,346,958
2. North Carolina	$2,879,856
3. Texas	$2,419,031
4. Georgia	$2,015,799
5. Iowa	$1,767,950
6. Florida	$1,704,877
7. Nebraska	$1,571,629
8. Arkansas	$1,362,642
9. Minnesota	$973,495
10. Kentucky	$952,979
* data is for 1995	

Source: Economic Indicators of the Farm Sector, USDA, ERS.

STATES—FOREIGN OWNERSHIP

Most U.S. Employees of Foreign-Based Corporations

Everyone decries the transfer of critical U.S. commercial assets into foreign hands, but few are aware of the positive contributions many foreign companies make to our economy through the establishment of domestic subsidiaries. Though the Japanese and their Asian neighbors may take American jobs as they incrementally increase the share of the domestic durable goods markets, they return many of these jobs by establishing U.S. plants to manufacture those very goods. Below are the states in which the highest percentage of workers are in the ultimate employ of a foreign corporation.

State	Total Employment (1,000s)
1. California	529.1
2. New York	350.0
3. Texas	308.9
4. Pennsylvania	235.9
5. Illinois	235.8
6. New Jersey	213.0
7. North Carolina	209.0
8. Ohio	205.6
9. Florida	201.5
10. Georgia	163.5

Source: U.S. Bureau of Economic Analysis, *Survey of Current Business; Direct Foreign Investment in the United States; Operations of U.S. Affiliates of Foreign Companies; Foreign Direct Investment in the United States; Benchmark Survey* (SAUS, 1996).

PLACES

S TATES— FORESTS

Greenest States

We don't usually think of that "little cabin in the woods" as being anywhere but in the West or the Northeast, but down south is where you're most likely to find one. This nation may be heading inevitably toward urban blight, but there are still plenty of forests that must be put asunder first. Georgia, the nation's woodiest state, boasts nearly 24 million acres of forested land. Even industrial New York still maintains almost 19 million wild acres. Here, then, are America's woodland empires.

State	Timberland Acres (1,000s)*
1. Georgia	25,000
2. Idaho	22,000
Alabama	22,000
4. Montana	21,000
Colorado	21,000
6. North Carolina	19,000
New York	19,000
New Mexico	19,000
9. Michigan	18,000
Maine	18,000

* figures rounded; ranking based on unrounded figures of 1990

Source: U.S. Forest Service.

S TATES— GASOLINE COSTS

Most Expensive Gasoline

There are uncountable injustices in the world, but few things irk the consumer more than jacked-up prices at the gas pump. Although the last decade has seen a broad roll-back in retail petroleum prices, they are on the rise again. Below are

AMERICA'S MOST FORESTED STATE, Georgia, has some of the nation's most beautiful vistas, such as the one below.

the states in which gasoline, the life-line of our country, is most costly.

State	Price per Million BTUs
1. Hawaii	$11.35
2. Connecticut	$10.35
3. Alaska	$10.24
4. Oregon	$10.24
5. New Mexico	$10.13
6. Colorado	$9.87
7. West Virginia	$9.87
8. Arizona	$9.83
9. Montana	$9.83
10. Rhode Island	$9.83

Source: State Energy Price and Expenditure Data System, 1993.

STATES— GOVERNMENT SPENDING

Highest Expenditures by State and Local Goverments

Everyone likes to be pampered. When such special treatment comes from usually menacing authority figures like government appointees and bureaucrats, we're ironically grateful. Alaskans may be the most grateful of all citizens simply because their state leads the nation in state goverment expenditures per capita. This is a function of the vast natural wealth and the small population of Alaska, where there is an unusually high cost of providing basic services.

State	Annual Expend./Capita
1. Alaska	$9,069
2. Hawaii	$4,808
3. Rhode Island	$4,176
4. New York	$4,092
5. Wyoming	$4,015
6. Connecticut	$3,815
7. New Jersey	$3,663
8. Massachusetts	$3,582

9. New Mexico	$3,465
10. Washington	$3,423

Source: *The World Almanac of the U.S.A.*, 1996.

STATES— GRADUATION RATES

Best and Worst Graduation Rates

Why do so few Alaskans quit school and so many Mississippians drop out? Could it be that there's more to do during the day in Mississippi than in Alaska, where it's already dark when the three-o'clock bell rings? Not so many years ago, a high school diploma was an invaluable possession that separated the diligent and employable from the unkempt masses. Just decades later, the value of that degree has eroded enormously, as an undergraduate university education has become the minimum prerequisite for even relatively low-level positions. This devaluation, however, has made the completion of a high school program all the more critical, because of the tremendous stigma and difficulties the high school dropout faces in the job market.

BEST GRADUATION RATES*

States	Percent with H.S. Diploma
1. Alaska	86.6%
2. Utah	85.1%
3. Colorado	84.4%
4. Washington	83.8%
5. Wyoming	83.0%
6. Minnesota	82.4%
7. Hew Hampshire	82.2%
8. Nebraska	81.8%
9. Oregon	81.5%
10. Kansas	81.3%

PLACES

WORST GRADUATION RATES*

States	Percent with H.S. Diploma
1. Mississippi	64.3%
2. Kentucky	64.6%
3. West Virginia	66.0%
4. Arkansas	66.3%
5. Alabama	66.9%
6. Tennessee	67.1%
7. Louisiana	68.3%
South Carolina	68.3%
9. North Carolina	70.0%
10. Georgia	70.9%

* percent of high school students who enroll as freshman and eventually earn a diploma

Source: *The Digest of Education Statistics*, 1996.

STATES—HAZARDOUS WASTE SITES

Has Anyone Seen My Old Syringes?

Despite the mounting awareness of environmental issues among the general public, relatively little progress has been made against the spread of toxic contaminants into our ground waters and air. The EPA is in trouble, the toxic offenders are in trouble, the victim-communities are in trouble; everyone bemoans these facts, but money is too scarce and the roots of the problem too widely spread. The following are the worst hazardous waste sites in the country, as measured by their placement on the Environmental Protection Agency list. New Jersey, New York, and Pennsylvania seem to be perpetually on their list.

State	EPA Hazard Score, 1995
1. New Jersey	107
2. Pennsylvania	103
3. California	96
4. New York	80
5. Michigan	78
6. Florida	55
7. Washington	52
8. Wisconsin	41
9. Illinois	38
Ohio	38

Source: Environmental Protection Agency, Supplementary Materials: National Priorities List, Proposed Rule, November 1995 (SAUS, 1996).

STATES—HEALTH CARE

Cost of Hospital Care

Medical mishaps are invariably traumatic, but for the uninsured, even the smallest health crisis represents a financial nightmare. Simply put, the cost of contemporary health care has become completely daunting and unman- ageable for most, and actually out of reach for the less than well-off. The latter part of the 1990s may well witness a popular referendum for the creation of some sort national health insurance collective. Following are the states which have the highest hospital-care costs.

State	Average Cost per Day
1. District of Columbia	$1,304
2. California	$1,301
3. Alaska	$1,263
4. Washington	$1,206
5. Massachusetts	$1,131
6. Connecticut	$1,121
7. Utah	$1,115
8. Arizona	$1,091
9. Oregon	$1,077
10. Texas	$1,055

Source: American Hospital Association, 1996.

PLACES

STATES— HEALTH INSURANCE

Persons Without Health Insurance

While the southern and western states are at the forefront of many continental trends, here's one they shouldn't be proud of: the percent of the population in their states without health insurance. This has been an issue with Hillary Rodham Clinton. The states in the west and south have the highest percentage of insurance-deprived residents, with New Mexico having almost one-quarter of its population so deprived. Is this a reason for some kind of national health care?

State	% with No Coverage, 1995
1. New Mexico	25.6%
2. Texas	24.5%
3. California	20.6%
4. Louisiana	20.5%
5. Arizona	20.4%
6. Mississippi	19.7%
7. Oklahoma	19.2%
8. Nevada	18.7%
9. Florida	18.3%
10. Arkansas	17.9%
Georgia	17.9%

Source: U.S. Census Bureau, Current Population Survey, February 1996.

STATES— HIGH SCHOOL

Most Public High School Graduates

The number of public high school graduates continues to rise, even though more and more families are opting to send their children to private schools. But since our population in general continues to grow, so do the number of high school gradu-ates. A closer look at the numbers, though, reveals interesting trends. California is the most populous state, so you would expect it to have the highest number of public high school graduates, but in second place is Texas, followed by New York, both of them quite a distance from the leader. Does this mean the public education system in California is that much better than in Texas or New York? Is it the proximity to *Beverly Hills 90210* that inspires their teenagers? Check it out.

State	Graduates, 1995 (1,000s)
1. California	262.0
2. Texas	162.4
3. New York	135.5
4. Ohio	110.1
5. Pennsylvania	107.2
6. Illinois	105.8
7. Florida	90.3
8. Michigan	88.5
9. New Jersey	65.8
10. North Carolina	59.7

Source: U.S. National Center for Education Statistics, *Digest of Education Statistics*.

STATES— HOUSING

Most Crowded Housing Units

Two's company, but is three a crowd? Not when it comes to our housing units. In this entry a crowd is defined as more than one resident per room. In 1990, a bit less than 5 percent of American homes were crowded. That figure represents a very small rise since 1980, the only year a rise has been recorded since the first census of housing in 1940. But there's been an interesting switch. In 1940, crowded homes were generally found in the rural south. Today, only about one-third

CALIFORNIA (view from Golden Gate Park in San Francisco) is the most international U.S. state, in that it absorbs more immigrants than any U.S. state and more people work for foreign-owned corporations than any other state.

are found there, supplanted by the urban metropolitan areas. By 1990, over one-fourth of all crowded units nationally were located in four metro areas—Houston, Los Angeles, Miami and New York. A comparison of two areas over the decades will serve to illustrate. In 1940, the rate of crowded housing in Alabama was at about 40 percent (twice the national rate), while in California it was only 13 percent. By the 1990s, the two states had almost switched. California's rate had dropped a little, to over 12 percent, while Alabama's was below the national average. Following are the top-ten states in which the percentage of housing units have more than one person per room.

State	% "Crowded" Housing Units
1. Hawaii	15.9%
2. California	12.3%
3. Alaska	8.6%
4. District of Columbia	8.2%
5. Texas	8.1%
6. New Mexico	7.9%
7. Arizona	7.4%
8. New York	6.5%
9. Nevada	6.4%
10. Louisiana	6.0%

Source: U.S. Census Bureau, Department of Commerce; October, 1996.

STATES—IMMIGRANT ABSORPTION

Between 1995 and the year 2025, the U.S. will absorb 24.7 million immigrants. Many will settle in the

PLACES

West. California's total population is projected to leap by 18 million over this period. This is by far the nation's largest gain. Even though California boasts a sizable out-of-state migration, this loss is more than offset by the 14 million it will add via natural increase (births minus deaths) and the almost nine million it should accrue through international migration. Such a gain will boost California's share of the nation's population from 12 percent in 1995 to 15 percent in 2025.

State	Projected Immigrants (1,000s)
1. California	8,725
2. New York	3,886
3. Florida	1,856
4. New Jersey	1,201
5. Illinois	1,037
6. Texas	1,008
7. Massachusetts	831
8. Virginia	605

CASINOS, like the one below in Las Vegas, are one of the chief reasons that Nevada citizens enjoy some of the highest incomes in the U.S. Photo: Las Vegas News Bureau.

9. Maryland	593
10. Pennsylvania	405

Source: U.S. Census Bureau, Department of Commerce, *Census and You*, October 1996.

STATES— INCOME

Highest and Lowest Per Capita Incomes

Per capita income varies greatly across the United States. As the table below shows, people in Connecticut enjoy almost twice the personal income of their counterparts in Mississippi. Cost of living alone cannot explain the differential. The high income levels in Connecticut and New Jersey no doubt are helped by their vicinity to the financial and legal centers in New York. The rural South and the Great Plains, on the other hand, suffer from their reliance on lower-intensity economies.

HIGHEST INCOMES

State	Per Capita Income, 1995
1. Connecticut	$30,303
2. New Jersey	$28,858
3. Massachusetts	$26,994
4. New York	$26,782
5. Maryland	$25,927
6. New Hampshire	$25,151
7. Nevada	$25,013
8. Illinois	$24,763
9. Hawaii	$24,738
10. Alaska	$24,182

LOWEST INCOMES

State	Per Capita Income, 1995
1. Mississippi	$16,531
2. Arkansas	$17,429
3. West Virginia	$17,915
4. New Mexico	$18,055
5. Oklahoma	$18,152
6. Utah	$18,223

7. Montana	$18,482
8. Kentucky	$18,612
9. North Dakota	$18,663
10. Alabama	$18,781

Source: U.S. Census Bureau, Department of Commerce (SSUS, 1996.)

STATES— INFANT MORTALITY

Highest Rates

Though the South's relatively high infant mortality rate is tragic, it pales by comparison with some foreign countries. In Africa, for example, many nations have infant mortality rates that are almost *15 times* higher! The loss of a child is the most terrible of familial tragedies. Despite advances in medicine, the possibility of miscarriage, deformity or stillbirth is very real in our society. Most disturbing are the disproportionately higher rates of infant mortality among disadvantaged populations. The following states suffer the highest infant mortality rates in the nation.

State	Deaths/1,000 Live Births, 1994
1. Mississippi	11.0
2. Louisiana	10.6
3. Georgia	10.2
4. Alabama	10.1
5. North Carolina	10.0
6. South Dakota	9.6
7. Illinois	9.3
South Carolina	9.3
9. Arkansas	9.2
10. Maryland	9.0

Source: U.S. National Center for Health Statistics (SSUS, 1996).

STATES— JURY PAY

At his criminal trial, O.J. Simpson was judged by a jury "of his peers," in accordance with traditions of American Jurisprudence. Were they really his peers? Some say that today's juries are more likely to be civil servants, rather than ordinary citizens. Why? Most government employees get full pay when they serve on juries, whereas those employed by private companies usually do not. That means nongovernment employees (the majority of the U.S.) are more likely to avoid jury duty if they can. Jury pay throughout the country ranges from $5 to $50 a day, and if company policy is to cut off one's salary while he or she serves in a lengthy trial, exemption is asked for and most often given, leaving the selections from among government workers, the elderly and the unemployed. Five states pay $50 a day: New York, Colorado, Wyoming, Connecticut and Indiana. Alaska pays $25 for half a day of service. Two states pay the low of $5, New Jersey and California. One state, New Mexico, pays $4.25 an hour. All federal courts pay $40 a day. Alabama and Nebraska are among the few states that require a company to continue paying full-salary to an employee on jury duty, which rarely lasts longer than 10 days. Some companies pay the difference between jury pay and salary; companies that continue full-salary payments generally limit them to 10 to 30 days of jury duty. While 27 states have eliminated occupational exemptions, and seven put limits on them, hardship exemptions are generally freely given. Federal and state laws forbid employers from firing workers chosen for jury duty. The following list details jurors'

PERHAPS THE GREATEST TREASURE IN ALASKA is the vast expanse of federally owned land, the most public acreage in all 50 states.

daily pay in the best and worst paying states.

BEST PAYING STATES

State	Daily Pay
1. Alaska*	$50.00
Colorado	$50.00
Connecticut	$50.00
Indiana	$50.00
New York	$50.00
Wyoming	$50.00
7. South Dakota	$40.00
8. New Mexico**	$34.00
9. District of Columbia	$30.00

* $25.00 per half-day (figure calculated as full day)
** $4.25 per hour (figure calculated as 8-hour day)

WORST PAYING STATES

State	Daily Pay
1. California	$5.00
New Jersey	$5.00
3. Missouri	$6.00
4. Idaho	$10.00
Iowa	$10.00
Kansas	$10.00
Maine	$10.00
Ohio	$10.00
Oregon	$10.00
South Carolina	$10.00

Source: National Center for State Courts, 1995.

STATES—LAND OWNERSHIP

Most and Least Land Owned by the Federal Government

Of the more than 2 billion acres in the United States, the federal government owns a whopping 30 percent, making it by far the biggest landowner in the country. More than four-fifths of the land in

PLACES

Alaska is under federal control, compared to less than one percent of the land in Iowa. The vast majority of federally owned land is used for national parks, forests and wilderness areas, as well as for military purposes. The government even makes money in some unexpected ways from its land—for instance, many of the ski resorts in Colorado are located in national forests and are leased from the government by the resort owners. Below are the states where Uncle Sam is the biggest landlord, and, contrarily, where his presence is least felt.

MOST FED-OWNED LAND

States	Percent Owned by U.S.
1. Alaska	81%
2. Nevada	79%
3. Idaho	61%
4. Utah	60%
5. Oregon	52%
6. Wyoming	47%
7. Arizona	45%
8. California	44%
9. New Mexico	33%
10. Colorado	30%

LEAST FED-OWNED LAND

States	Percent Owned by U.S.
1. Iowa	0.4%
2. Rhode Island	0.6%
3. Maine	0.7%
New York	0.7%
5. Nebraska	1.1%
6. Ohio	1.3%
Kansas	1.3%
8. Illinois	1.4%
Connecticut	1.4%
10. Texas	1.6%

Source: Public Land Statistics, U.S. Department of the Interior.

STATES— LOTTERY PAYOUTS

Show Me the Money!

Wasn't too long ago that gambling was considered a major sin. Now all but 14 states have lotteries. Critics often point to the fact that lotteries and other forms of sanctioned gambling attract the very people who can least afford it—the poor. However, more and more states over the past two decades, have looked to gambling as an easy fix for their financial woes. In many states, officials promised that money made off gambling would go directly to help out schools, but instead the money often disappeared into the general municipal fund. However people feel about making money off of taking money, the fact is that in 1994, states paid out $15.3 billion to lottery winners, with Massachusetts (the home of the Salem witch hunts 200 years ago) leading the way with a payout of almost $1.7 billion.

State	Payouts, 1994 ($1,000s)
1. Massachusetts	$1,659,338
2. Texas	$1,523,407
3. Ohio	$1,115,020
4. New York	$1,107,476
5. Florida	$1,071,087
6. California	$966,351
7. Illinois	$794,716
8. Pennsylvania	$782,974
9. New Jersey	$708,722
10. Michigan	$683,995

Source: U.S. Census Bureau, *Census and You*, June 1996.

PLACES

STATES—LOTTERY SPENDING

Do You Feel Lucky?

People don't just like to gamble, they like to win. Ask a casino manager in Vegas. They know that the casinos that have the best odds, at-

FACTORY JOBS still bring myriad new residents to Illinois, the nation's second-largest state for manufacturing jobs. Pictured above is Chicago's Lake Shore Drive.

tract the biggest crowds. The same is true when it comes to state lotteries. In general, the states with the best odds for winning have the most action at lottery sales outlets. Mas-

sachusetts, for example, pays about 60 cents in winnings for every dollar of ticket sales. It's first on the state lottery spending list. Rhode Island and Delaware, also on the following list, have the overall first and third-highest odds of winning in their state lotteries. Following are the states where residents apparently feel the luckiest.

State	Lotto Spending per Capita
1. Massachusetts	$382
2. Oregon	$228
3. Maryland	$186
4. New Jersey	$171
5. Rhode Island	$168
6. Ohio	$162
7. Connecticut	$160
8. Florida	$146
9. Georgia	$143
10. Delaware	$136

Source: U.S. Census Bureau, *Forecast* newsletter, November 1996.

STATES— MANUFACTURING

Highest Concentrations of Manufacturing Jobs

The presence of industry in the modern era in a mixed blessing. Few communities can resist the lure of ready jobs for their restless populations, but fewer still can gracefully absorb the impact of environmental contamination and resource depletion. In America, unsurprisingly, the bulk of manufacturing jobs are centralized in regions of high population.

State	% Manufacturing Employment*
1. North Carolina	24.9%
2. Illinois	24.6%
3. Arkansas	24.2%
4. Mississippi	24.0%
5. Wisconsin	23.5%
6. Michigan	22.9%

South Carolina	22.9%
8. Alabama	21.7%
Tennessee	21.7%
10. Ohio	21.0%

* figures are for 1995

Source: U.S. Bureau of Labor Statistics (SSUA, 1996).

STATES—MARIJUANA, SOFTEST PENALTIES

Where to Go to Pot

If you absolutely insist on smoking marijuana, there are some places you should consider doing it over others. Even though some states still have overbearing penalties on the books, many don't enforce them strictly. The states listed below are those with the most lenient *laws*, though a few states with stricter laws are just as soft on marijuana offenders. The penalties in the states with the softest laws are listed below. They apply to first-offense convictions only. Most states have increased penalties for subsequent offenses. Beware, however, that some states have additional or enhanced penalties for certain offenses, such as selling within a specified distance of a school. When "possession" is indicated, it generally implies that it is intended for personal consumption. Possession of large amounts of marijuana will, in most cases, lead to charges of "possession with intent to distribute." Units of weight vary from state to state.

For comparative purposes: one ounce (oz.) = 28.35 grams (g); one pound (lb.) = 16 ounces = 453.59 grams and one kilogram (kg.) = 1,000 grams = 2.2 pounds.

Key to Abbreviations: Immediately following the name of the state, the letter D or C may appear. These designations mean the following:

D: The state has "decriminalized" marijuana to some degree. In general, this means that there is no possible prison time or criminal record for first-time possession of a specified amount for personal consumption. Instead, it is treated like a minor traffic violation.

C: State allows for the conditional release or alternative/diversion sentencing of first-time possession offenders. In general, this means that an individual can be put on probation instead of on trial. Upon successful completion of the program, the individual is spared any of the stated penalties and accompanying criminal record.

1. Alaska
For Possession:
Up to 8 oz. — up to 90 days; $1,000
Greater than 8 oz. — up to 1 year; $5,000
Greater than 1 lb. — up to 5 years; $50,000

2. Minnesota (C, D)
For Possession:
"Small amount" (Up to 42.5 g.) — $200 + drug education
Less than 10 kg. — up to 5 years; $10,000
Up to 10 kg. — up to 20 years; $250,000
50 kg. or more — up to 25 years; $500,000
Greater than 100 kg. — up to 30 years; $1,000,000

3. New Mexico (C)
For Possession:
Up to 1 oz. — 0-15 days; $100 (lst offense); 0-1 years; $1,000 (subsequent offenses)
Greater than 1 oz. — 0-1 years; $1,000
Greater than 8 oz. — 0-2 years ; $6,667 (1st offense): 0-4 years; $6,667 (subsequent offenses)

4. New York (C, D)
For Possession:
Up to 25 g. — $100
Greater than 25 g. — 0-3 months; $500
Greater than 2 oz. — 0-1 years; $1,000
Greater than 8 oz. — 0-4 years; $5,000
Greater than 1 lb. — 0-7 years; $5,000
Greater than 10 lbs. — 0-15 years; $5,000

5. North Carolina (C, D)
For Possession:
Less than .5 oz. — 0-30 days; $100 (time sentence must be suspended)
Up to .5 oz. — 1-120 days, community service or intermediate/active probation
Greater than 1.5 oz. — 8-13 months
Greater than 50 lbs. — 25-30 months; $5,000
Greater than 100 lbs. — 35-42 months; $25,000
Greater than 2,000 lbs. — 70-84 months; $50,000
10,000 lbs. or more — 175-219 months mandatory minimum; minimum fine $200,000

6. Ohio (C, D)
For Cultivation and Possession:
Less than 100 g. — Minor Misdemeanor
100-200 g. — 0 to .08 years in prison (against prison)
200-1000 g. — .25 to 1 years in prison (against prison)
1-5 kg. — 1 to 5 years in prison (no presumption)
5-20 kg. — 1 to 5 yrs in prison (for prison)
20 kg. or more — 24 months Mandatory; up to 8 years
For Possession of paraphernalia — 0-30 days; $250

7. South Carolina
For Possession:
Less than 1 oz. — 0-30 days; $100-$200

Possession of paraphernalia — $500

8. Mississippi (D)
For Possession:
Up to 1 oz. — $100-$250
Greater than 1 oz. — 0-1 years; $1,000
1 kg. or more — up to 20 years; $1,000-$I,000,000
Possession of paraphernalia — up to 6 months; $500

Source: National Organization for the Reform of Marijuana Laws (NORML), 1996, 1997.

STATES— MILITARY PERSONNEL

Highest Concentrations of Soldiery

The minions of our peacetime Army—and of its somewhat civilized sub-chapters, the National Guard and the Coast Guard—are scattered equitably. In greatest numbers, they have followed the sun—to populous, land-rich states like California and Texas, and to sun-bleached U.S. utopias like Hawaii, Virginia and Florida, though most grunts rarely get the chance to sample the luxuries of their exotic, paradise-like surroundings.

State	Military Personnel, 1994
1. California	230,566
2. Virginia	173,032
3. Texas	133,847
4. North Carolina	104,793
5. Florida	86,161
6. Georgia	73,470
7. Hawaii	56,720
8. Washington	48,550
9. Maryland	41,343
10. South Carolina	36,718

Source: Army Times *Guide to Military Installations in the U.S.* (SAUS, 1996).

PLACES

STATES— MINORITIES

Minority College Enrollment

Minority Americans have made substantial educational strides through the good offices such as the United Negro College Fund and through minority scholarship and assistance programs offered by federal and state governments. Whether such assistance will be permitted to continue, however, is in question, as conservative factions continue to challenge affirmative action. Below are the states where minorities make up the highest percentage of college students.

State	Enrollment per 1,000 Students*
1.California	810
2. Texas	326
3. New York	303
4. Illinois	192
5. Florida	182
6. Michigan	90
7. New Jersey	89
8. North Carolina	88
9. Georgia	87
10. Virginia	82

* data is for 1994

Source: U.S. National Center for Education Statistics, *Digest of Education Statistics* (SAUS, 1996).

STATES— PAROLEES

Thy Brothers' Keepers No More

As jails become more and more overcrowded, many states have no other recourse than to ease the process of parole, freeing criminals before their full sentence in order to free up prison space for new batches of convicts. This can create problems of recidivism; in addition, re-

THE DISTRICT OF COLUMBIA is a city of mosts, including the most parolees per capita.

spect for the criminal justice system is lessened on the part of both the convict and the public in general; finally, many in the public wonder if the courts and the prison systems are taking their roles seriously. Following are the states where the door spins the fastest—those with the most parolees per 100,000 members of the population.

MOST PAROLEES

State	Parolees per 100,000 Pop.*
1. District of Columbia	1,523
2. Pennsylvania	799
3. New Jersey	793
4. Texas	774
5. Oregon	641
6. Louisiana	613
7. Maryland	418
8. New York	409
9. California	403
10. Georgia	368

LEAST PAROLEES

State	Parolees per 100,000 Pop.*
1. Maine	4
2. Washington	22
3. North Dakota	24
4. Connecticut	50
5. Nebraska	55
6. Minnesota	63
7. Mississippi	78
8. Rhode Island	79
Ohio	79
West Virginia	79

* Data is as of January 1, 1996
Source: Department of Justice, 1996.

STATES— POPULATION

Largest Households

Could it be the snow-capped mountains? The "big sky"? The "don't fence me in" philosophy? What accounts for the fact that the Mountain Division (which includes Arizona, Colorado, Idaho, Montana, Nevada, New Mexico, Utah and Wyoming) is the fastest growing region in number and size of households? Probably nothing more than a reflection of the country's general movement west. In any case, the number of households in the Mountain Division leaped 14 percent between 1990 and 1995, nearly twice the rate of any other division. A household, according to the Census Bureau, comprises everyone living in a housing unit (either a house, apartment or a single room that constitutes separate living quarters). Of the 11 states where the number of households climbed 10 percent or more, six of them were in the Mountain Division. Following are the states with the biggest households. By comparison, the U.S average is 2.64 persons per household.

State	Persons per Household, 1995
1. Utah	3.12
2. Hawaii	2.98
3. California	2.82
4. Alaska	2.81
5. Idaho	2.75
New Mexico	2.75
7. Texas	2.74
8. Mississippi	2.73
9. New Jersey	2.72
10. Louisiana	2.71

Source: U.S. Census Bureau; Department of Commerce.

STATES— POPULATION

Largest Population and Most Seats in U.S. House

The U.S. population's shift away from the Northeast and Midwest—and toward the South and West—means a shift in political power as

PLACES

well. Representation in the U.S. House of Representatives is determined by the official census numbers, taken every 10 years. The 1990 census confirms that shift of population and power. In all, a total of 19 seats in the U.S. House of Representatives was shifted as a result of the 1990 census. Eight states increased their representation in Congress; all of those states are in the South or West. California gained seven seats for a total of 52, Florida gained four seats to 23, and Texas gained three seats for a total of 30. Arizona (6), Georgia (11), North Carolina (12), Virginia (11), and Washington (9) each gained one seat. On the other hand, 13 states have less representation than they did in the previous Congress which was based on the 1980 census. New York (31) lost three seats. Illinois (20), Michigan (16), Ohio (19), and Pennsylvania (21) lost two seats. Iowa (5), Kansas (4), Kentucky (6), Louisiana (7), Massachusetts (10), Montana (1), New Jersey (13), and West Virginia (3) lost one seat. The following table below lists the official census by states and the number of representatives each state was entitled to elect to the House of Representatives in the 1996 elections.

State	Population, 1996
1. California	31,878,234
2. Texas	19,128,261
3. New York	18,184,774
4. Florida	14,399,985
5. Pennsylvania	12,056,112
6. Illinois	11,846,544
7. Ohio	11,172,782
8. Michigan	9,594,350
9. New Jersey	7,987,933
10. Georgia	7,353,225

Source: Population Estimates Program, Population Division, U.S. Census Bureau, 1996.

STATES—POPULATION DENSITY

Most and Least Elbow Room

While there are more people on the Eastern Seaboard than there are bears, there are places in the Northwest where bears outnumber humans. Just more proof that there truly is a place for for everyone. Despite the general shift of the population westward and southward, the states that are densest (with people) are still primarily located in the Northeast and Mid-Atlantic areas. The following list represents the states with the most- and least-dense populations in 1990.

MOST DENSELY POPULATED

State	Population per Square Mile
1. New Jersey	1,042.0
2. Rhode Island	960.3
3. Massachusetts	767.6
4. Connecticut	678.4
5. Maryland	489.2
6. New York	381.0
7. Delaware	340.8
8. Pennsylvania	265.1
9. Ohio	264.9
10. Florida	239.6

LEAST DENSELY POPULATED

State	Population per Square Mile
1. Alaska	1.0
2. Wyoming	4.7
3. Montana	5.5
4. South Dakota	9.2
5. North Dakota	9.3
6. Nevada	10.9
7. Idaho	12.2
8. New Mexico	12.5

9. Nebraska   20.5
10. Utah   21.0
Source: U.S. Census Bureau, 1990.

STATES—POPULATION PROJECTIONS

Most Peopled States in the Year 2025

Want to see an American trend in progress? Take a look at the Census Bureau's population projections by state in the year 2025. We've been moving west and south since the pilgrims landed at Plymouth Rock and the trend is still continuing. By the year 2025, California, Texas and Florida will lead the pack, and

CALIFORNIA, with its vast natural beauty and unspoiled coastline, attracted what is now the nation's largest state population. Despite prolific growth elsewhere, the state will still have the nation's largest population in 2025.

even Georgia makes it into the list of top-10 most populous states. As recently as 1994, Georgia was ranked 12th, behind North Carolina. Both states are projected to grow the first part of the next century.

State	Population, Year 2025 (1,000s)
1. California	49,285
2. Texas	27,183
3. Florida	20,710
4. New York	19,830
5. Illinois	13,440
6. Pennsylvania	12,683
7. Ohio	11,744
8. Michigan	10,078
9. Georgia	9,869
10. New Jersey	9,558

Source: U.S. Census Bureau, 1996.

STATES— POVERTY RATES

Where America's Poor Are Concentrated

About 15 percent of families in the U.S. are officially designated as being below the poverty level. Though the official floor to qualify for federal programs "for the poor" is adjusted annually for inflation, it hovers around $15,000 for a family of four. Among children in the nation, a depressing 22 percent are poor and the numbers are growing. Following are the states with the highest percentage of persons in poverty.

State	% Population in Poverty
1. New Mexico	25.3%
2. Mississippi	23.5%
3. District of Columbia	22.2%
4. Alabama	20.1%
5. South Carolina	19.9%
6. Louisiana	19.7%
7. Texas	17.4%

8. Oklahoma	17.1%
9. California	16.7%
West Virginia	16.7%

Source: U.S. Census Bureau, *Poverty in the United States*, October 1996.

STATES— PRISON POPULATION

Largest Inmate Populations

Serious crime in this nation is an epic problem in itself, but the handling, supervision and rehabilitation of the perpetrators of these crimes creates a second, multi-dimensional crisis. Our courts and prisons are crowded to the bursting point. Simplistic quick fixes are not available. Resolution can only come through substantive social reform. The following are the states where the prison population is the largest.

State	Prison Population
1. California	134,718
2. Texas	126,123
3. New York	68,889
4. Florida	64,076
5. Ohio	44,365
6. Michigan	38,964
7. Illinois	37,881
8. Pennsylvania	31,062
9. North Carolina	28,724
10. Virginia	23,785

Source: *Sourcebook of Criminal Justice*, 1995.

STATES— PRISON POPULATION

Most Prisoners on Death Row

Capital punishment has always presented an agonizing dilemma in society. In our era, the decision to take a life is vested in the governments of the individual states. In all, thousands of men await the final dispen-sation of their God and their governor, in the nation's gas chambers and lethal-injection rooms.

State	Prisoners on Death Row*
1. California	444
2. Texas	394
3. Florida	351
4. Pennsylvania	200
5. Illinois	164
6. North Carolina	154
7. Ohio	150
8. Alabama	144
9. Arizona	121
10. Oklahoma	119

* as of April 30, 1996

Source: *Sourcebook of Criminal Justice, 1995*; NAACP Legal Defense and Educational Fund, Inc.

STATES— PRISONS

Most Suicides in Jail

Society, perhaps mistakenly, believes that rehabilitation is the core of our criminal judicial system. As an abstract institution and collection of individualism, we wish to see criminal elements pay for their misdeeds, yet the abortive loss of life through prison suicide is an inarguably tragic and fatal end to an already misspent existence. Below are the numbers that spell out this tragedy, measured in the number of suicides among institutionalized people in a single year.

State	Inmate Suicides, 1995
1. California	22
2. Texas	19
3. Pennsylvania	15
4. Florida	9
Michigan	9
6. New York	8
Ohio	8
8. Illinois	7

9. New Jersey   5
   Oklahoma   5

Source: *Corrective Compendium*, June 1996.

STATES— PUBLIC ASSISTANCE

Highest Concentration of Citizens on Public Aid

It is a commonly held misconception that the majority of Americans receiving welfare and other public assistance are denizens of the inner city. In actuality, public aid is very much a rural phenomena, with nearly one person in five receiving some form of assistance in the troubled, agrarian South. Below are the states with the highest percentage of their populations receiving public assistance.

State	Percent Receiving Aid
1. California	11.7%
2. Mississippi	10.9%
3. New York	10.0%
4. Louisiana	9.7%
5. West Virginia	9.6%
6. Kentucky	9.3%

WHERE'S THE MOST LIKELY PLACE to be stationed in the military? California, the state with the most military personnel (See page 184).

7. Michigan   9.1%
8. Tennessee   9.0%
9. New Mexico   8.7%
10. Rhode Island   8.6%

Source: U.S. Census Bureau (SAUS, 1996).

STATES— PUBLIC SCHOOLS

Highest Expenditures per Pupil

Those who assure their legislaters that spending money on education is a sure way to increase academic performance would do well to check out Washington, DC. Though more is spent per student on education in the nation's capitol than in any other state, academic performance is among the country's lowest. Although the mere expenditure of dollars cannot assure an improvement in the average quality of American public education, adequate funding is a prerequisite for the overall recovery of our teaching institutions. Wealthy, populous, highly industrialized states have traditionally led the nation in their financial commitment to education, but in this era, smaller, progressive states have often achieved per capita parity with their wealthier neighbors. The following are the states that spend the most money on their students.

State	Expenditure per Pupil*
1. District of Columbia	$10,180
2. New Jersey	$9,677
3. New York	$9,175
4. Alaska	$8,882
5. Connecticut	$8,473
6. Rhode Island	$7,333
7. Pennsylvania	$6,983
8. Massachusetts	$6,959
9. Maryland	$6,958

10. Wisconsin $6,717
  * expenditures for 1993-94
  academic year

Source: *Digest of Education Statistics*, 1996.

STATES— PUBLIC SCHOOLS

Best and Worst Teacher Salaries

The American educational system is in a state of crisis. As a nation, we must come to grips with creeping illiteracy, overcrowding in the classroom and drugs and violence in our once-hallowed institutional halls. Although solutions in this crisis are difficult to craft, it is clear that the apportionment of more money for our chronically underpaid educators is a national priority. Below are the states that best polish the apple for their beleaguered teachers, as well as those for which the apple's skin is most dull.

BEST TEACHER SALARIES

State	Salary*
1. Connecticut	$50,598
2. Alaska	$47,864
3. New York	$47,612
4. New Jersey	$47,038
5. Michigan	$46,575
6. Pennsylvania	$44,510
7. District of Columbia	$43,142
8. Massachusetts	$40,976
9. Rhode Island	$40,729
10. California	$40,667

WORST TEACHER SALARIES

State	Salary*
1. South Dakota	$26,037
2. North Dakota	$26,317
3. Louisiana	$26,811
4. Mississippi	$26,818
5. New Mexico	$28,394

6. Oklahoma	$28,745
7. Montana	$28,785
8. Utah	$28,919
9. Arkansas	$28,950
10. Idaho	$29,784

  * salaries for 1994-95 academic year

Source: *Digest of Education Statistics*, 1996.

STATES— PUBLIC SCHOOLS

Student/Teacher Ratios

Student/teacher ratios—the number of students for every teacher—have been growing in recent years. The figure serves as a good measurement of the amount of individual attention each student enjoys in school. In the best "state," Washington, D.C., there is one teacher for about every 13 students in the classroom; in Utah, the average class contains about 24 students.

BEST STUDENT/TEACHER RATIOS

State	Ratio,
1. District of Columbia	13.2
2. Maine	13.8
New Jersey	13.8
Vermont	13.8
5. Connecticut	14.4
South Dakota	14.4
7. Nebraska	14.5
8. Virginia	14.6
9. Rhode Island	14.7
10. Massachusetts	14.8

WORST STUDENT/TEACHER RATIOS

State	Ratio,
1. Utah	24.3
2. California	24.0
3. Washington	20.2
4. Michigan	20.1
5. Oregon	19.9

CASINOS IN LAS VEGAS AND RENO provide a tax base that makes low tuitions possible at public universities in Nevada, one of the top-ten states for bargains in higher education. Photo: Las Vegas News Bureau.

6. Arizona	19.3
7. Florida	19.1
Idaho	19.1
9. Nevada	18.7
10. Tennessee	18.6

    * ratios for 1994-95 academic year

Source: *The Digest of Education Statistics*, 1996.

S TATES—PUBLIC UNIVERSITIES & COLLEGES

Education Bargains

The cost of attending four-year private college has gotten out of hand. Although we think of ourselves as egalitarian, Americans must realize that educational privileges, de

facto, are being doled out with elitist favoritism, as tuition and other expenses at the top private institutions soar beyond the reach of a large portion of the populace. As a saving grace, however, America has maintained its battle-worn system of public universities, the last great bargains in higher education. Below are the states in which college expenses at land-grant universities are most affordable.

State	Average Tuition, 1995-96
1. District of Columbia	$1,118
2. Hawaii	$1,576
3. North Carolina	$1,639
4. Idaho	$1,682
5. Nevada	$1,684
6. Florida	$1,767
7. Texas	$1,820
8. Oklahoma	$1,839
9. Tennessee	$1,920
10. New Mexico	$1,940

Source: *Digest of Education Statistics*, 1996.

S TATES— RELIGION

Jewish Population

Alas, the once-largest Jewish state in the world, New York, is losing its Jewry. So are New Jersey and Illinois. Elsewhere, other bastions of Judaism are gaining, mainly due to migration. Nonetheless, New York leads the nation both in overall Jewish population and in the percent of the population that is Jewish: almost 10 percent of New York's populace is Jewish. There's a reason: European Jews, like other ethnic groups who came to America, tended to settle first in the metropolitan areas on the East Coast for several reasons: their proximity to

Ellis Island, their ability to find work easily, and, eventually, the presence of a well-established Jewish community. For reasons of practicality—and because of real and perceived persecution—areas of the South and the Great Plains contain the fewest Jewish people, both in total numbers and in percentage. So good luck finding a *latke* in Idaho.

MOST JEWS

State	Jewish Population
1. New York	1,645,000
2. California	922,000
3. Florida	638,000
4. New Jersey	436,000
5. Pennsylvania	331,000
6. Massachusetts	268,000
Illinois	268,000
8. Maryland	212,000
9. Ohio	128,000
10. Texas	109,000

FEWEST JEWS

State	Jewish Population*
1. South Dakota	less than 500
Idaho	less than 500
Wyoming	less than 500
4. North Dakota	1,000
Mississippi	1,000
Montana	1,000
7. West Virginia	2,000
Arkansas	2,000
9. Utah	3,000
Alaska	3,000

* data does not include populations under 500; figures rounded

MOST JEWS, BY PERCENT

State	Percent Pop. Jewish
1. New York	9.0%
2. New Jersey	5.5%
3. Florida	4.7%
4. Massachusetts	4.5%
5. District of Columbia	4.4%
6. Maryland	4.3%
7. California	3.0%
Connecticut	3.0%
9. Pennsylvania	2.7%
10. Illinois	2.3%

Source: U.S. Census Bureau (SSUS, 1996).

STATES—RELOCATION

States Most People Leave To Go To College

When thinking about going to school, many people consider leaving their home state to pursue an education in an entirely different environment. Some people leave to explore, some people flee from oppressive local surroundings, and others simply believe that life will be better in new surroundings. The state that leads the way numerically is New York; however, a comparable number of students come from other states to balance that number, so there is not too much net change.

States	Students Who Leave
1. New York	25,989
2. New Jersey	24,152
3. California	18,569
4. Illinois	17,933
5. Pennsylvania	14,742
6. Massachusetts	12,828
7. Ohio	11,063
8. Connecticut	10,962
9. Maryland	10,510
10. Florida	10,505

Source: *Digest of Education Statistics*, 1996.

STATES—RELOCATION

Most Popular Locales for Attending College Out-of-State

When people decide that an out-of-state school would be better or more

PLACES

IS IT THE CITY ITSELF, or its many fine universities that attract out-of-state students? New York City is the number-one choice for students who leave their home state to get a college education.

State	Out-of-State Students
1. New York	24,801
2. Massachusetts	22,876
3. Pennsylvania	21,156
4. California	19,452
5. Florida	12,896
6. Ohio	12,714
7. Virginia	12,260
8. Texas	12,239
9. North Carolina	12,090
10. Indiana	11,036

Source: *Digest of Education Statistics*, 1996.

STATES— SALARIES

Best and Worst Salaries

Dreaming of better days? Want to go where the money is good? You'll make the most in Washington, DC, but you'll spend it quickly— our capitol is one of the most expensive places to live in America. The same is true for Alaska, not too mention freezing temperatures and a dearth of daylight in the winter. Below are the best- and worst-paying states in the U.S.

HIGHEST SALARIES

State	Average Salary*
1. District of Columbia	$40,919
2. Connecticut	$33,811
3. New Jersey	$33,439
New York	$33,439
4. Alaska	$32,657
5. Massachusetts	$31,024
6. California	$29,878
7. Michigan	$29,541
8. Illinois	$29,107
9. Maryland	$28,416
10. Delaware	$27,952
* salaries for 1994	

interesting than the in-state offerings, what attracts them? It could be the prestige of the schools available (strongly suspected as the number one reason in the second through fifth listings here) or the environment the school can provide (a heavy factor in the number one rating). Whatever the reasons, a lot of people come from out of state to attend college. The following rating shows the most attractive states for prospective college students.

While some big corporations chase cheap labor in the Sunbelt, the states with the lowest average annual pay languish in the obscurity from which they have always suffered. A large number of the lowest-paid live in states in the northern plains, with huge amounts of land and few people.

LOWEST SALARIES

State	Average Salary*
1. South Dakota	$19,255
2. North Dakota	$19,893
3. Montana	$20,218
4. Mississippi	$20,382
5. Arkansas	$20,898
6. Nebraska	$21,500
7. Idaho	$21,938
8. Wyoming	$22,054
9. Iowa	$22,189
10. Oklahoma	$22,293

* salaries for 1994

Source: U.S. Bureau of Labor Statistics (SAUS, 1996).

STATES—
SENIOR CITIZENS

Most Growth in Seniors through year 2020

One thing you can't escape, besides death and taxes, is growing old. Where we decide to grow old is another matter. More and more of us are choosing to spend our golden years in the West. In 1993, nine of the largest states had more than one million elderly. But by the year 2020, according to Census Bureau projections, 19 states will have more than one million elderly. Who cares? Well, the states with high projections should. The truth is that a burgeoning elderly population can strain a state's resources if suffi-

cient counter-balancing plans aren't in place. Not that the scenario is a nightmare. One myth put to rest in the numbers is that most elderly are poor and/or sick. Not until most of us reach the mid-80s will we become infirm. But even that isn't as bad as it sounds. The numbers bear out that only one in four of this age group (85+) live in a nursing home, and of them only half need help with everyday activities.

State	Growth in Seniors by 2020
1. Nevada	115.6%
2. Arizona	111.9%
3. Colorado	108.0%
4. Georgia	104.0%
5. Washington	103.5%
6. Alaska	103.3%
7. Utah	102.4%
8. California	100.5%

* data is for population age 65 or older

Source: U.S. Census Bureau, Department of Commerce, 65+ in the United States Series, June 1996.

STATES—
SENIOR CITIZENS

Senior Centers: Greatest Concentrations of the Elderly

When time comes to hang up the work gear and settle down to enjoy the golden years, a good number of Americans pack up and head to Florida. There, soothed by the temperate climate and the gentle Gulf breeze, seniors can soak up the sun without a pang of guilt. Indeed, Florida leads the nation in senior citizens, with nearly a fifth of its population past retirement age. But despite the growing popularity of the desert Southwest, many seniors choose to stay at home to luxuriate in the time they've earned. Florida is followed, not by Arizona, Nevada or California as one might expect, but by less exotic commonwealths as Pennsylvania, Rhode Island and West Virginia. Here, then, are the retired states of the Union, measured by percentage the population 65 years and older.

State	Percent Seniors, 1995
1. Florida	18.6%
2. Pennsylvania	15.9%
3. Rhode Island	15.7%
4. West Virginia	15.3%
5. Iowa	15.2%
6. Arkansas	14.5%
North Dakota	14.5%
8. South Dakota	14.4%
9. Connecticut	14.3%
10. Massachusetts	14.2%

Source: U.S. Census Bureau (SAUS, 1996).

STATES— SIZE

Biggest Land Mass

The vast, wild area of Alaska makes up fully 16 percent of the total land mass of the United States. That's twice as much as Texas, where the inhabitants boast that everything is bigger. America's last great frontier contains some of the most pristine—and some of the most valuable—land in the Union. In fact, one could fit 539 Rhode Islands inside Alaska. Fascinating food for thought.

BIGGEST STATES

State	Total Acreage
1. Alaska	365,481,600
2. Texas	168,217,600
3. California	100,206,720
4. Montana	93,271,040
5. New Mexico	77,766,400
6. Arizona	72,688,000

7. Nevada	70,264,320
8. Colorado	66,485,760
9. Wyoming	62,343,040
10. Oregon	61,598,720

SMALLEST STATES

State	Total Acreage
1. District of Columbia	39,040
2. Rhode Island	677,120
3. Delaware	1,265,920
4. Connecticut	3,135,360
5. Hawaii	4,105,600
6. New Jersey	4,813,440
7. Massachusetts	5,034,880
8. New Hampshire	5,768,960
9. Vermont	5,936,640
10. Maryland	6,319,360

Source: Public Land Statistics, U.S. Department of the Interior.

STATES— TAXES

Highest & Lowest Tax Burdens

It probably comes as no surprise that the states with the highest per capita tax burden are mostly in the Northeast, while the states with the lowest tax burden are in the south and west. This reflects the generally more liberal attitude in the Northeast, where social programs and the expense they incur have always been supported by tax dollars. Logic dictates that states with higher populations, and populations concentrated in urban areas, will be asked to provide more services to those populations, while states with more sparse and rural populations will see less demand.

MOST TAXING STATES

State	Per Capita Taxes, 1996
1. Connecticut	$8,096
2. District of Columbia	$7,518
3. New Jersey	$7,159

4. Massachusetts	$6,409
5. New York	$6,352
6. Delaware	$6,179
7. Illinois	$6,046
8. Nevada	$5,965
9. Maryland	$5,958
10. Alaska	$5,939

LEAST TAXING STATES

State	State Taxes Paid, 1996
1. Mississippi	$3,413
2. West Virginia	$3,702
3. Utah	$3,823
4. New Mexico	$3,904
5. Oklahoma	$4,000
South Carolina	$4,000
7. Arkansas	$4,007
8. Kentucky	$4,028
9. Louisiana	$4,104
10. Alabama	$4,105

Source: Tax Foundation.

STATES— TAXES

Highest and Lowest Gasoline Tax

Ever notice that gas can be so much cheaper over the state line? It's because the next state over has a lower gasoline tax and your state government has jacked the price up by pennies, nickels or even dimes per gallon. Perhaps your state government sees gas as a good means of raising revenue, or maybe the gas tax is intended as a piece of social engineering, preventing drivers from clogging over-used roads. Whatever the reason, the trend is definitely toward higher and higher gas taxes. The federal government recently added more gasoline tax to the total, and even further taxes are on the horizon.

LOWEST GASOLINE TAX

State	Gas Tax, 1995 (Cents)
1. Georgia	7.5
2. Alaska	8.0
3. Wyoming	9.0
4. New Jersey	10.5
5. Florida	12.5
6. Indiana	15.0
Michigan	15.0
8. Hawaii	16.0
South Carolina	16.0
Vermont	16.0

HIGHEST GASOLINE TAX

State	Gas Tax, 1995 (Cents)
1. Connecticut	37.0
2. Rhode Island	29.0
3. Montana	27.0
4. Nebraska	26.0
5. West Virginia	25.4
6. Idaho	25.0
7. Nevada	24.0
Oregon	24.0
9. Wisconsin	23.7
10. Maryland	23.5

Ssource: U.S. Federal Highway Administration, *Highway Statistics Annual*, 1996.

STATES— TAXES

Highest and Lowest Sales Tax

Don't let the state sales-tax tables below fool you. As high as the tax rates may seem, you may pay even more sales tax, depending on the *city* in the state you make your purchases in. Many major U.S. cities like New York and Chicago have city sales tax on top of state sales tax. That means you can pay near 10% in some cities and it can be even higher, depending on *what* you buy. There are luxury taxes, hotel taxes, service taxes, use taxes and taxes on leases, just to name a few. What's next? Taxes on taxes? Anything is possible when it can be legislated.

THE DISTRICT OF COLUMBIA, the nation's leader in sales taxation, has used the proceeds well. The District's subway is one of the most efficient and pleasant to ride in the world. It has also eased some traffic conjestion.

HIGHEST SALES TAX

State	State Tax
1. District of Columbia	7.50%
2. Mississippi	7.00%
Rhode Island	7.00%
4. Minnesota	6.50%
Nevada	6.50%
Washington	6.50%
7. Illinois	6.25%

Texas	6.25%
9. California	6.00%
Connecticut	6.00%
Florida	6.00%
Kentucky	6.00%
Maine	6.00%
Michigan	6.00%
New Jersey	6.00%
Pennsylvania	6.00%
Tennessee	6.00%
West Virginia	6.00%

LOWEST SALES TAX

State	State Tax
1. Alaska	0.0%
Delaware	0.0%
Montana	0.0%
New Hampshire	0.0%
Oregon	0.0%
6. Colorado	3.0%
7. Virginia	3.5%
8. Alabama	4.0%
Georgia	4.0%
Hawaii	4.0%
Louisiana	4.0%
New York	4.0%
North Carolina	4.0%
South Dakota	4.0%
West Virginia	4.0%

Source: *Places Rated Almanac*, 1997.

STATES— TAXES

Tax Freedom Day

The people at the Tax Foundation invented Tax Freedom Day to illustrate how long Americans have to work to pay their taxes. If, for instance, you lived in Connecticut, you would slave almost five months for the state and federal governments before you could keep anything you had earned. Conversely, if you lived in Alabama, you would work only a little more than three and a half months before you could start keeping your money. It's a little like summer vacation—kids in the next town over always seemed to get out of school a week or two earlier, romping on the beach or at the playground. That's how the folks in Connecticut must feel about their compatriots in Alabama or Mississippi, for whom Tax Freedom Day comes earliest. Now, if you really want to get depressed, factor in city, county and who-knows-what other taxes. Fortunately—and probably for your sanity—the Tax Foundation kept it simple by just taking into account state and federal taxes.

EARLIEST "LIBERATION"

State	Freedom Day
1. Alabama	April 23rd
2. Mississippi	April 24th
Missouri	April 24th
4. Louisiana	April 25th
Delaware	April 25th
South Dakota	April 25th
7. West Virginia	April 26th
8. South Carolina	April 27th
9. Tennessee	April 28th
Utah	April 28th

LATEST "LIBERATION"

State	Freedom Day
1. Connecticut	May 31st
2. New York	May 26th
3. District of Columbia	May 22nd
4. New Jersey	May 18th
5. Minnesota	May 13th
6. New Mexico	May 12th
Rhode Island	May 12th
8. Hawaii	May 11th
Vermont	May 11th
10. Washington	May 10th
New Hampshire	May 10th

Source: Tax Foundation, Washington, DC, 1996.

STATES— TEEN POPULATION

Highest Concentration of Teenagers

The phone lines are jammed, the radios are blaring and the streets are packed. All this can only mean one thing: teenagers. Some say that adolescence is a very difficult time; for Mom and Pop, at least, that is certainly true. On the other hand, George Bernard Shaw said youth is wasted on the young. Following are the states with the highest concentration of teenagers.

State	Percent Under Age 18, 1995
1. Utah	34.6%
2. Alaska	31.4%
3. Idaho	29.9%
4. New Mexico	29.7%
5. Louisiana	28.5%
6. Wyoming	28.4%
7. Arizona	28.3%
South Dakota	28.3%
9. Mississippi	28.2%
10. District of Columbia	20.7%

Source: U.S. Census Bureau (SAUS, 1996).

STATES— TEENS

Teen Pregnancy

Maybe it's those hot, sultry nights down south, or the other cliches of southern living—gin and tonics, southern belles and mint juleps—but whatever the reason, it appears that the teen pregnancy rate is highest down in Dixie. It's worst in Mississippi, followed by other states in the "deep South"; and nearby New Mexico and Oklahoma don't fare so well either. The figures that follow represent the percentage of total pregnancies which occured among teenagers.

State	% Teen Pregnancies, 1995
1. Mississippi	22.2%
2. Arkansas	19.6%
3. Louisiana	19.2%
4. Alabama	18.5%
5. New Mexico	18.4%
6. South Carolina	17.3%
7. West Virginia	17.2%
8. Kentucky	17.1%
9. Oklahoma	17.0%
10.Tennessee	16.9%

Source: National Center For Health Statistics, October 4, 1996.

STATES— UNEMPLOYMENT

Best Benefits

Despite the cries of those who say technology takes away jobs, unemployment is at an almost 30-year low. Not since 1970 have fewer Americans been out of work. It was then that unemployment dropped to 4.9 percent. It hasn't been below five percent since. Nonetheless, with a glut of unfilled jobs, some choose the unemployment line instead of getting on the bus and heading to work. Below are the states with the highest average unemployment payments. In some states, an unemployed individual can draw well above the averages shown below if his or her situation calls for it. Reports of weekly benefits approach $400 for some individuals. Tough life when one considers how humiliated they must be when their checks arrive at midday when all the neighbors are at work.

State	Average Benefits per Week
1. Hawaii	$270.03
2. New Jersey	$252.63
3. Massachusetts	$244.40
4. District of Columbia	$231.75
5. Minnesota	$228.22
6. Rhode Island	$225.73
7. Michigan	$221.04
8. Pennsylvania	$219.48
9. Connecticut	$214.29
10. New York	$207.71

Source: Bureau of Labor Statistics (SAUS, 1996).

STATES— URBANIZATION

Most Urbanized Populations

The oft-maligned Washington, DC, is the epitome of contemporary urban America, with virtually 100 percent of its people making their homes within a city. (Of course it is the only such "city/state" of its kind in America.) Although most city dwellers occasionally entertain fantasies of idyllic escapes to pastoral wonderlands, a sizable majority of the American public makes its full-time home in or around an urban setting. The most urbanized states in the nation are as follows.

State	Percent Urban Population
1. District of Columbia	100.0%
2. California	92.6%
3. New Jersey	89.4%
4. Hawaii	89.0%
5. Nevada	88.3%
6. Arizona	87.5%
7. Utah	87.0%
8. Rhode Island	86.0%
9. Florida	84.8%
10. Illinois	84.6%

Source: U.S. Census Bureau (SAUS, 1996).

STATES—VACATION DESTINATIONS

American vacationers must like warmth and sunshine. Forty-eight percent of us prefer Florida as a domestic vacation site, putting it in first place as a U.S. vacation wonderland. California is second, with 34. Hawaii, despite being out-of-the-way and quite pricey, rates third. The following list is based on a readership survey regarding favorite vacation spots and the percentage of individuals who vacation at various destinations.

State	Percent
1. Florida	48%
2. California	34%
3. Hawaii	26%
4. Nevada	14%
5. Colorado	11%
6. Arizona	9%
Texas	9%
8. New York	8%
9. District of Columbia	5%
Louisiana	5%

Source: *Chicago Tribune*, January 15, 1995.

STATES—VOTER CONCIENTIOUSNESS

Greatest Turnout in Most Recent Presidential Election

In a presidential election, overall, only about half of the eligible voters go to the polls, and the turnout can be even lower in some elections. Hence, most presidents aren't elected by the "majority of the American people," as we so idealistically like to assume. The newly freed people of Asia and Eastern Europe look to the United States as their democratic ideal. But, truth be told, voters are at times apathetic. One never knows what, if anything, will move them. Sometimes they are penetrating in their analysis and their desire to grapple with central issues. At other times, they vote to follow fashion, on an impulse or out

of habit. Still other times, they don't vote at all. Following are the most conscientious Americans in terms of exercising their franchise.

WITH ALL THE DEVELOPMENT IN THE SUN BELT, the West and the Southwest, Florida (above) still remains the most popular vacation destination.
Photo: Greater Miami Convention and Visitors Bureau.

State	% Registered Who Voted*
1. Maine	71.90%
2. Minnesota	64.07%
3. Montana	62.06%
4. South Dakota	60.53%
5. Wyoming	59.43%
6. Vermont	58.08%
7. Iowa	57.72%
8. Wisconsin	57.43%
9. New Hampshire	57.30%
10. Oregon	57.14%

* figures are for 1996 presidential election.

Source: Federal Election Committee, State Election Offices; Congressional Research Service; Election Data Services Inc., 1996.

PLACES

STATES—WOMEN IN CITY GOVERNMENT

Highest Percentage of Female Mayors

As of 1995, 18 of the 100 largest U.S. cities had women mayors. Of the 971 mayors of cities with populations over 30,000, 174, or 17.9 percent, are women. Following is a list of the top states for female mayors of cities with populations of 10,000 or more.

State	Percent Female Mayors
1. California	24.7%
2. Missouri	24.5%
3. Connecticut	23.5%
4. Massachusetts	20.8%
5. Florida	19.3%
6. Texas	17.2%
7. New York	15.9%
8. Ohio	14.6%
9. Illinois	12.9%
10. Pennsylvania	11.6%

Source: National League of Cities, 1995.

STATES—WOMEN IN STATE GOVERNMENT

Highest Percentage of Women in State Legislature

Women have certainly come a long way, baby. It is no longer unusual to see a female state governor, national senator or congressperson. Women like Olympia Snowe, Pat Schroeder and Ann Richardson have paved the way, certainly. But it is taking time. Although women make up a bit more than half the population, in no state do they make up half the legislative body. The most progressive region seems to be New England, half of which is on the top-10 list in percentage of female legislators. Even in those states, however, the percentage is far below their equivalent percentage in the general population.

HIGHEST PERCENTAGE

State	% Women in Legislature, 1995
1. Washington	39.5%
2. Nevada	34.9%
3. Colorado	32.0%
4. Arizona	30.0%
5. New Hampshire	29.9%
6. Vermont	29.4%
7. Maryland	28.7%
8. Idaho	28.6%
9. Maine	27.4%
10. Kansas	27.3%

LOWEST PERCENTAGE

State	% Women in Legislature, 1995
1. Arkansas	12.6%
2. South Carolina	12.4%
3. New Jersey	11.7%
4. Mississippi	11.5%
Pennsylvania	11.5%
6. Virginia	11.4%
7. Oklahoma	10.7%
8. Louisiana	9.7%
9. Kentucky	8.0%
10. Alabama	4.3%

Source: Center for the American Woman and Politics.

THINGS

ADVERTISING IN THE GAY PRESS

Businesses are forever looking for new marketplaces in which to sell their wares, and it's never been a secret that the gay and lesbian community has a good chunk of disposable income on its hands. However, many businesses were reluctant to invest in this potentially controversial area. That appears to be changing. Total advertising spent in the gay and lesbian press in 1996 was over 20 percent above what it was in 1995. Currently there are 138 gay-oriented newspapers, magazines and arts/entertainment guides published throughout the country, but mostly in urban areas with large populations of gays and lesbians. What kind of businesses are spending money to reach this audience? The following are the businesses that spend the most.

Category	Percent of Ad Budget
1. Bars, clubs	14.3%
2. Phone services	13.5%
3. Classified ads	9.1%
4. Gay events, meetings	5.4%
5. General retail	5.0%
6. Travel, out-of-town gay events	4.6%

Source: *Mulryan/Nash's Gay Press Report, 1996.*

AIDS

AIDS and the Generations

AIDS cuts across age barriers, jumps the generation gap and stalks us all. Even fetuses are not immune—for they often pay for the ignorance and excesses of their progenitors. Two things must be learned: that age and experience provide no insulation, and that we all must band together to warn of and destroy this virus. The most stricken groups are those in the age brackets from 25 to 44: three-quarters of all known HIV infections are among people in that age span. But even the elderly are not immune— among males, fully six percent of all AIDS cases are recorded to have stricken those above the age of 55. The following list gives the break-

THE FASTEST AMERICAN...land animal, that is, the pronghorn antelope. (See page 210). Photo: Wyoming Travel Commission.

down of the AIDS epidemic by age of the victims.

MALES: MOST INFECTED

Age Group	Percent of AIDS Cases
1. 30-34	23%
35-39	23%
3. 40-44	16%
4. 25-29	14%
5. 45-49	9%
6. 50-54	5%
7. 20-24	3%
55-59	3%
9. 60-64	2%
10. 65+	1%

FEMALES: MOST INFECTED

Age Group	Percent of AIDS Cases
1. 30-34	23%
2. 35-39	21%
3. 25-29	16%
4. 40-44	13%
5. 45-49	6%
20-24	6%
7. 50-54	3%
8. 55-59	2%
65+	2%
10. 60-64	1%

Source: *HIV/AIDS Surveillance Report*, 1996.

AIDS

Most Common Ways to Transmit AIDS

Though AIDS transmission as a percent of infections is declining among homosexuals, it is rising among heterosexuals. It's an alarming trend, considering the vast majority of sexual partners conform to the latter. According to most experts, AIDS can only be transmitted from an infected individual to one who is uninfected. The following list reveals the most frequent means by which the HIV virus is transmitted from one person to another, as recorded among those testing positive for the virus. Sexual intercourse and the sharing of hypodermic needles are the most common means of transmission. The list below reveals that although homosexual contacts make up the majority of transmissions, the epidemic is by no means confined to the gay community. In fact, as that community becomes more educated and continues taking more precautions to prevent transmission, the acceleration at which the virus spreads has slightly quelled; unfortunately, intravenous drug users often lack education about the dangers of shared needles, and attempts among AIDS activist groups to distribute free needles to drug users has met with intense opposition.

Transmission Method	% Cases*
1. Male homosexual	51%
2. Intravenous drug use	25%

3. Heterosexual contact   8%
4. Male homosexual/IV drugs   7%
    Other undetermined factors   7%
6. Hemophilia/coagulation
     disorder   1%
    Blood transfusion,
     components or tissue   1%
    * reported July 1994-June 1995;
     July 1995-June 1996

Source: *HIV/AIDS Surveillance Report*, 1996.

AIRLINE DISASTERS

Greatest Passenger Losses

Though the crash of Flight 800 and the downing of a crowded Valu Jet airliner over Florida, are tragic, the fatalities pale by comparison with some of the biggest of all time on the following list. Despite constant reassurances from the airline industry and from statisticians that commercial airline travel is the safest means of transport available, most of us still feel at least a little trepidation when stepping onboard a plane. To some, the whole idea of heavier-than-air flight still seems preposterous—what could possibly get such a huge craft off the ground? Psychologists have even taken to forming therapy groups for those afflicted with a fear of flying, and several self-help books have recently been published to assist airwary travelers in overcoming their hesitance about setting themselves aloft. However, no matter how much psychotherapy and baby-sitting, certain events give one cause for concern, like the anonymous pilots who talk about the "black-dot," or most dangerous, airports; the Northwest pilots convicted of pilot-

ing an early morning flight after a night of heavy drinking; news reports of the ease with which reporters pass through detection devices with weapons or drive directly out onto the tarmac through supposedly tight security; and, of course, media images of wreckage and destruction on the occasion of a great air disaster. Below we have compiled the most deadly of those air tragedies. It's interesting to note that two of the 10 greatest air tragedies were military shoot-downs of commercial jet-liners; another two were the result of terrorism. Six of the top 10 have been deemed accidental.

Date/Description	Fatalities
1. March 27, 1977	**582**
A Pan Am 747 collides with a KLM Royal Dutch Airlines 747 on the runway in Tenerife in the Canary Islands.	
2. August 12, 1985	**520**
Japan Airlines 747 crashes into a mountain in Japan.	
3. December 11, 1996	**350**
Saudia Airlines 747-100 collides with a Kazakstan Airlines Ilyushin 76TD in Dedri, India. The Kazakstan Airlines had 37 fatalities.	
4. March 3, 1974	**346**
Turkish Airlines DC-10 crashes near Paris.	
5. June 23, 1985	
Air India Boeing 747 crashed in the Atlantic Ocean.	
6. August 19, 1980	**301**
Saudi Arabian L-1011 crashes during emergency landing in Riyadh.	
7. August 8, 1996	**298**
An African Air Antonov crashes in Kinshasa after takeoff.	
8. July 3, 1988	**290**
Iranian A300 Airbus is mistaken for an attacking jet and shot out of the sky by the U.S.S. Vincennes in the Persian Gulf.	

9. May 26, 1979   **275**
An American Airlines DC-10 plunges to earth shortly after take-off from Chicago O'Hare Airport.

10. December 21, 1988   **270**
Pan Am Flight 103 is blown up by a terrorist bomb over Lockerbie, Scotland; all 259 on board are killed, along with 11 on the ground.

Source: NTSB Aviation Accident Statistics (Aviation Safety Web Pages, Aircraft Accident Database).

AIRLINES

Most Popular Airlines

Despite cheaper gasoline prices as the 1990s progress, air travel is up. The economy also adds to this trend: it has has been humming along, and vacationers are opting to spend a little more to get in the air rather than on the road. Below are the greatest beneficiaries of the trend, ranked by the number of passengers they have carried.

Airline	Passengers, 1995 (1,000s)
1. Delta	86,909
2. American	79,511
3. United	78,664
4. USAir	56,674
5. Southwest	50,039
6. Northwest	49,313
7. Continental	35,013
8. Trans World	21,551
9. America West	16,802
10. Alaska	10,084

Source: Air Transport Association of America.

AIRLINES

Overall Quality

Everyone complains about flying. The flights are late, the food stinks, the tickets get messed up. You might get bumped, and your luggage will probably get lost. And then there are more important concerns, like flight safety. At least some airlines are considered better than others overall at providing passengers with quality service. Best of all is Southwest Airlines, according to an annual independent ranking of the nation's nine largest airlines. For 1996, carriers were rated on 19 criteria, including on-time arrivals and departures, mishandled baggage, denied boardings, age of aircraft, number of accidents, fares, overall financial stability, pilot deviations, and customer complaints. The rankings are trustworthy since they are based on objective data, in large part drawn from reports filed by each airline with the Department of Transportation. Dallas-based Southwest—known for its low-cost, no-frills approach and quick resolution of customers' complaints—topped the list in 1996 for the second year in a row. Also noteworthy is the performance of Continental, which moved up from last place in 1995 to fifth place in 1996. TWA, which has run into financial trouble of late, brings up the rear.

Rank/Airline
1. Southwest
2. American
3. United
4. Delta
5. Continental
6. Northwest
7. USAir
8. America West
9. TWA

Source: National Institute of Aviation Research.

THINGS

A IRLINES

On-Time Performance

Gotta make a connection? Check with your travel agent. Nowadays, the Department of Transportation keeps detailed records of on-time performance for the major domestic carriers, not only overall, but for specific flights. This information is available to travel agents on their computerized booking systems. Each flight gets a score based on its past average on-time performance. Knowing this information will allow travelers to avoid chronically late flights when time is pressing. Following is a list of overall on-time performance for the major carriers, by percentage of flights arriving within 15 minutes of their scheduled arrival time in an average month in 1996.

Airline	% flights on-time
1. Southwest Airlines	86.8%
2. ContinentalAairlines	76.6%
3. Northwest Airlines	76.6%
4. US Airways	75.7%
5. United Airlines	73.8%
6. American Airlines	72.2%
7. Delta Airlines	71.2%
8. America West Airlines	70.8%
9. Alaska airlines	68.6%
10. Trans World Airlines	68.5%

Source: U.S Department of Transportation, 1996.

A LBUMS

Greatest Rock Guitar Albums

The editors of *Guitar World* took it upon themselves to determine the greatest guitar albums in the history of rock and roll. Not an easy task, considering that "greatness" means different things to different people. Do you judge an album's greatest on the sheer technical prowess its player displays? On originality? On influence? In the end, *GW's* editors decided that the ideal rock guitar album would combine all three elements. Below is their list of the 10 greatest rock guitar albums of all time.

THE GREATEST ROCK GUITAR ALBUM ever, *Are You Experienced*; Jimi Hendrix, Artist.

Album/Artist/Guitar Player(s)

1. *Are You Experienced?* Jimi Hendrix, Jimi Hendrix
2. *Van Halen* Van Halen, Eddie Van Halen
3. *Layla*, Derek and the Dominos Eric Clapton, Duane Allman

4. **The Chess Box**, Chuck Berry
   Chuck Berry
5. **Led Zeppelin IV**, Led Zeppelin
   Jimmy Page
6. **Band of Gypsys,** Jimi Hendrix
   Jimi Hendrix
7. **At Fillmore East**, The Allman
   Brothers
   Duane Allman, Dickey Betts
8. **The Sun Sessions**, Elvis Presley
   Scotty Moore
9. **Blow by Blow**, Jeff Beck
   Jeff Beck
10. **Passion and Warfare**, Steve
    Vai, Steve Vai

Source: *Guitar World*, June 1991.

LBUMS

Longest Winning Streak at Billboard's #1

Only *one* of the great rock 'n rollers, believe it or not, has had monster albums that have dominated the Billboard charts for long stretches of time. That's Elvis, of course. Even the Beatles and the Rolling Stones have not made such a distinction. Surprisingly, the most popular albums in history are predominantly soundtracks. What accounts for this? Undoubtedly, a movie's popularity will contribute to the sale of its soundtrack album—people normally not interested in buying a pop album may be more inclined to if they liked the film. In addition, soundtracks such as *Saturday Night Fever* feature a number of different artists, and may even contain music from different genres, such as rock, disco, jazz and Motown, thus appealing to a wider range of fans.

BIGGEST CHART-BUSTER in the history of recorded music.

Record/Year Released	Weeks at #1
1. **West Side Story** Soundtrack, 1962	54
2. **Thriller** Michael Jackson, 1983	37
3. **South Pacific** Soundtrack, 1958	31
4. **Calypso** Harry Belafonte, 1956	31
5. **Rumours** Fleetwood Mac, 1977	31
6. **Saturday Night Fever** Soundtrack/The Bee Gees/Various Artists, 1978	24
7. **Purple Rain** Prince, 1984	24
8. **Please Hammer Don't Hurt 'Em** M.C. Hammer, 1990	21
9. **Blue Hawaii** Elvis Presley, 1961	20
10. **The Bodyguard** Whitney Houston/Various Artists, 1992	20

Source: *Entertainment Weekly*, 1996.

THINGS

AMUSEMENT PARKS

Most Popular Theme and Amusement Parks

Disney and Orlando, Florida, those are proper names vacationers must have etched on their itineraries. Big fun is big business, and the customer is always right, so long as he spends, spends, spends. So come early, come often, to these best known pleasure spots, judged by 1996 attendance.

Park	Attendance, 1996
1. Disneyland Anaheim, CA	**15,000,000**
2. The Magic Kingdom at Walt Disney World Lake Buena Vista, FL	**13,803,000**
3. EPCOT at Walt Disney World Lake Buena Vista, FL	**11,235,000**
4. Disney-MGM Studios at Walt Disney World Lake Buena Vista, FL	**9,975,000**
5. Universal Studios, Florida, Orlando, FL	**8,400,000**
6. Universal Studios, Hollywood Universal City, CA	**5,400,000**
7. Sea World of Florida, Orlando, FL	**5,100,000**
8. Busch Gardens Tampa	**4,170,000**
9. Six Flags Great Adventure Jackson, NJ	**4,000,000**
10. Sea World of California, San Diego	**3,890,000**

Source: *Amusement Business*, December 16, 1996.

ANIMAL PELTS

Number of Skins Per Fur Coat

Any fur larger than a simple stole is a rag-tag agglomeration of the flattened skins of numerous slaughtered small animals. The average mink coat is composed of some 60 pelts—that's *60* animals killed for each coat. Fifteen dam-builders make one beaver coat; while 16 threatened coyotes make a fairsized cloak. Next time you don that luxurious pelt, take time to think how much blood has been spilt so you can preen in front of your fellow fur-wearers. What, indeed, is the attraction?

Fur	Pelts per Coat
1. Mink	60
2. Sable	50
Muskrat	50
4. Opossum	45
5. Red Fox	42
6. Raccoon	40

THE LIST ABOVE SPEAKS VOLUMES about why these people are protesting.

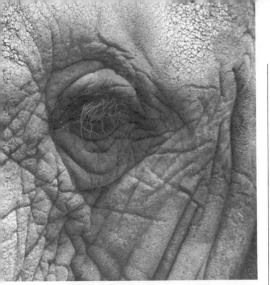

QUITE A WEIGHT! Almost two years, the longest gestation period of all animals.

7. Otter	20
8. Lynx	18
9. Coyote	16
10. Beaver	15

Source: People for the Ethical Treatment of Animals.

A NIMALS—
GESTATION PERIODS

One thing a female African elephant can never forget is her pregnancy, a nearly *two-year* vigil. By contrast, the human female takes roughly 270 days to bring her infant from conception to normal live birth. All in all, that is a respectable gestation period for a sizable mammal, but it cannot compare with the 645 the average Asian Elephant puts into the process, or the 480 days the also portly White Rhino puts in. Animal psychologists are yet to determine whether post-partum depression lasts a comparable time for these beasts.

Species	Gestation Period (days)
1. African Elephant	660
2. Asian Elephant	645
3. White Rhinoceros	480
4. Black Rhinoceros	450
5. Giraffe	425
6. Bactrian Camel	406
7. Ass	365
Grant's Zebra	365
9. California Sea Lion	350
10. Horse	330

Source: *Walker's Mammals of the World*, 5th Edition.

A NIMALS—
RATES OF SPEED

The Fastest and Slowest

Even the fastest man alive cannot compete with many common animals of the jungle. In the age of the jet and the sports car, we tend to take great speeds for granted. Just one tick of the geological clock earlier, however, man relied exclusively on the fleetness of his feet, and those of the animals he harnessed. Herewith, then, are the highest speeds ever recorded for the tortoise, the hare and a host of God's other creatures.

SPEEDSTERS

Species	Top Speed (mph)
1. Cheetah	70
2. Pronghorn Antelope	61
3. Wildebeest	50
Lion	50
Thomson's Gazelle	50
6. Quarter Horse	48
7. Elk	45
Cape Hunting Dog	45
9. Coyote	43
10. Rabbit (domestic)	35

SLOW POKES

Species	Top Speed (mph)
1. Human	27
2. Black Mamba	20
3. Six-lined Race Runner	18
4. Squirrel	12
5. Pig	11

6. Chicken	9
7. Spider	1.17
8. Giant Tortoise	0.17
9. Three-toed Sloth	0.15
10. Garden Snail	0.03

Source: *Natural History Magazine*.

ART ACTIVITIES

As the arts struggle against television, the Internet and family financial pressures, many artistic leisure activities in the American landscape are reeling from low rates of public participation. However, some arts activities are holding their own or increasing in popularity. Art museums and galleries made the largest strides in attendance: from 1982 to 1992 the percentage of adults visiting museums and galleries increased four percent—from 22.1 percent of respondents to 26.7 percent, an increase of more than 12 million visitors a year. Attendance at arts and crafts fairs was second, with a gain of almost two percent, from 39 percent to 40.7 percent, or seven million new participants. Drama was third in percent gain, almost 1.6 percent more people attend legitimate stage plays, from 11.9 percent to 13.5 percent. These gains were offset by losses in visitors to U.S. historical sites, attendance at operettas and musicals, and in readers of fiction and poetry. Historic park sites were hardest hit, with a decline of 4.5 percent in the proportion of adults who visit them at least once a year. Overall, 41 percent of American adults attended an arts event in 1992, compared to 39 percent in surveys taken in 1985 and 1992. The survey found that in general blacks attend fewer art events than do whites or Asians—notably opera and ballet—but jazz was more popular among blacks than among those other groups. While 10.1 percent of whites attended at least one jazz event in 1992, the figure for blacks was 16.2; for other racial and cultural groups, the rate was 4.9 percent. Blacks showed greater gains in attendance at live performances than did whites—perhaps, the NEA says, because of the growing black middle-class. Following are the percentage of adults attending major arts activities.

Activity	Percent Who Attend
1. Arts and crafts fairs	40.7%
2. Historic parks	34.5%
3. Art museums	26.7%
4. Musicals	17.4%
5. Plays	13.5%
6. Classical music	12.5%
7. Jazz	10.6%
8. Ballet	4.7%
9. Opera	3.3%
10. Other arts events	3.0%

Source: *The Peoplepedia*, 1996.

ASSETS—HOLDINGS OF BABY BOOMERS

You Are What You Own

The single-family home is still the main asset of middle-aged Americans, according to a Census Bureau study. It also concluded that 21 percent of boomers own stocks or mutual-fund shares with a median value of $4,563. Since the Dow Jones Industrial Average rose to over 8,000 in 1997, the figure is substantially higher. About 23 percent own U.S. savings bonds, valued at only $600. IRA and KEOGH

THINGS

accounts attract 25.8 percent of the boomers, their median value being $8,634. Seven percent have interest-earning asset in bonds, funds, or government securities valued at more than $9,000. The Employee Benefit Research Institute finds that 45 percent of Americans expect to live 11 to 20 years after the retirement age of 65. One-fourth expect one to 10 years of retirement, although the average number of years remaining at age 65 is 17.2 years, according to EBRI, which says that many boomers will live many years beyond even that, and will have to stretch their savings nest-egg from 10 years to 20. Following are the median value of assets held by baby boomers age 35 to 44, and percent of householders owning them.

Asset	Value%	Who Own
1. Home (equity)	$31,082	67.4%
2. Rental property (equity)	$30,114	9.3%
3. Other real estate	$18,284	10.8%
4. IRA/KEOGH accounts	$8,634	25.8%
5. Equity in business	$9,703	16.0%
6. Other interest earning accounts	$9,311	7.4%
7. Stocks/mutual funds	$4,563	21.3
8. Bank interest earnings	$2,325	75.0%
9. U.S. savings bonds	$600	23.2%
10. Checking accounts	$481	48.8%

Source: U.S. Census Bureau, 1991.

ATTORNEY'S FEES

Highest Paid Law Specialties

With lawyers, it seems to be a matter of "show them the money." Pro bono work notwithstanding, America's lawyers charge exceedingly high rates. In fact, in 1996, partners in the nation's law firms billed their clients a median hourly rate of $183—a 4.5 percent increase over 1995. This list shows the highest paid legal specialties. Note that new law associates—just out of law school, with hefty loans to pay off—charge substantially less than their older, more experienced, and more well-heeled colleagues. They get away with charging an average of only $95 an hour.

Specialty	Median Hourly Rate
1. Intellectual-Property	$207.00
2. Taxation	$201.00
3. Bankruptcy	$197.50
4. Corporate	$187.50
5. Estate Planning and Probate	$178.50
6. General Practice (partners)	$160.00

Source: *Law Office Management and Administrative Report,* Anderson-Boyer Group.

AUTOMOBILES— ASIAN

Most Popular Manufacturers

Though they are continually urged to buy American, some people in the United States still prefer imports, at least when it comes to automobiles. And the imports they favor are Asian—mostly Japanese and also Korean. This list shows U.S. auto sales by Asian car manufacturers in 1996. Toyota—maker of the ever-popular Camry and Corolla—and Honda—maker of the Accord and Civic—are clearly dominant. But Nissan, with its Sentra, is running a strong third.

Manufacturer	Units Sold
1. Toyota	793,529
2. Honda	786,154
3. Nissan	500,377
4. Mazda	180,975
5. Mitsubishi	172,186
6. Subaru	120,748
7. Hyundai	108,468
8. Acura	105,443
9. Lexus	74,001
10. Suzuki	10,388

Source: Industry sales statistics.

AUTOMOBILES— COLORS

The colors Americans choose for their automobiles are almost always a sign of the times. During the Great Depression, black was the most popular color. Green, the color of renewal, was in vogue after World War II. In the 1960s and '70s, white dominated. In the late 1980s and early '90s, high-tech, cool colors reigned, with various shades of blue dominating. In the mid-'90s, green once again dominated, perhaps a function of Americans being once again renewed, after a disastrous recession in the early part of the decade. Green and white are among the top two colors Americans pick for all types of vehicles, ranging from luxury cars to light trucks and vans. Below are the most popular colors and the corresponding percentage of colors of all full size and intermediate cars, the most popular types of vehicles in the U.S.

FAST ENOUGH TO GET A SPEEDING TICKET on the Interstate, the cheetah, world's fastest land animal, can reach speeds of 70 mph (See page 210).

Color	Percent of Registrations
1. Green	19.4%
2. White	18.1%
3. Light brown	11.8%
4. Medium red	10.0%
5. Black	5.7%
6. Teal/aqua	5.5%
7. Silver	4.6%
8. Bright red	4.2%
9. Dark red	3.3%
10. Medium blue	3.0%

Source: American Automobile Association

AUTOMOBILES— CUSTOMER SATISFACTION

The traditional favorites in terms of consumer satisfaction, the Acura and Mercedes, have fallen a few notches in recent years. The relative newcomers, Infiniti and Lexus, are the cars Americans seem to be the most satisfied with. While foreigners may be leading the way to perfection, consumers can take comfort in the fact that surveys like this are forcing all car makers to improve the quality of their products.

Make	Satisfaction Index
1. Infiniti	168
2. Lexus	166
3. Acura	159
4. Mercedes-Benz	158
Saturn	158
6. Honda	154
7. Cadillac	151
8. Lincoln	150
9. Audi	149
10. Volvo	148

Source: J.D. Power and Associates, 1996 Customer Satisfaction Study, July 9, 1996.

A UTOMOBILES— DEPENDABILITY

For three years in a row Lexus has been been the highest-ranked make in the J.D. Power and Associates Vehicle Dependability Study. Cadillac ranks second based on another solid year of improvement, their third in the last four years. Audi ranks third based on the tremendous improvement of its 100 Series model. The study was conducted among original owners of 1992 model-year vehicles. Owners were asked to rate their vehicle across 89 problem categories based on the last year of ownership. The industry average was 393 problems per 100 autos.

Model	Problems per 100 Autos
1. Lexus	217
2. Cadillac	240
3. Audi	242
4. Infiniti	261
5. Lincoln	269
6. Acura	278
7. Mercedes-Benz	282
8. Honda	290
9. Buick	299
10. Toyota	301

Source: J.D. Power and Associates, March 25, 1997.

A UTOMOBILES— DEADLIEST/SAFEST

The idea that a large car is safer than a small one seems logical, and that logic holds true, except that a large car also is safer than a small truck. Only the heavier cars and minivans made the list of safest vehicles, as measured by driver fatalities. This list, taken from a study conducted by the Insurance Institute for Highway Safety, counts driver deaths per 100,000 registered vehicles for each of 184 cars, minivans and trucks. Covering the years 1989-93 for 1988-92 models, the top spot is held by a Volvo, with no driver deaths recorded. Helping maintain the Swedish auto maker's reputation for safety, Volvo took the number two spot, as well.

FEWEST FATALITIES

Make/Model	Deaths per 100,000 Cars
1. Volvo 240—4-Door midsize car	0
2. Volvo 740/760—4-door midsize luxury car	1.85
3. Plymouth Voyager large passenger van	2.23
4. Mercedes 190D/E midsize luxury car	3.06
5. Lexus LS 400 large luxury car	3.55
6. Dodge Caravan large passenger van	3.79
7. Buick Riviera midsize luxury car	3.96
8. Ford Aerostar large passenger van	4.06
9. Jaguar XJ6—large luxury car	4.08
10. Mazda MPV large passenger van	4.13

The power and thrill of the great American muscle cars make for an unmatched driving experience. Unfortunately, letting that Corvette or Camaro go flat-out on a winding country road can be more than just exhilarating—it can be deadly. So it isn't surprising that these two models head the list of the most deadly automobiles. They are owned predominantly by young males—the most accident prone of all drivers. Also among the top 10 are a number of models with less muscle but also less size—subcompacts like the Chevy Chevette and Sprint and the Honda Civic. It remains to be seen whether the addition of airbags will have a dramatic effect on the death rates in either muscle cars or sub-compacts.

MOST FATALITIES

Make/Model	Deaths per 100,000 Cars
1. Chevrolet Corvette	5.2
2. Chevrolet Camaro	4.9
3. Dodge Charger/Shelby	4.5
4. Ford Mustang	4.4
5. Nissan 300ZX	4.2
6. Chevrolet Chevette 4-door	4.1
Chevrolet Sprint 2-door	4.1
8. Honda Civic CRX	3.9
9. Pontiac Firebird	3.8
10. Plymouth Turismo	3.6
Pontiac Fiero	3.6

Source: Insurance Institute for Highway Safety.

AUTOMOBILES— EUROPEAN

Most Popular Manufacturers

European imports are not nearly as popular as their Asian counterparts. In the following list of U.S. auto sales by European car manufacturers in 1996, only Volkswagen and BMW scored more than 100,000 in sales—quite low compared with Japan's Toyota, Honda and Nissan. Still, some European carmakers are showing relative strength. It was the first time Mercedes topped the 90,000 mark in U.S. sales, and the first time BMW sold over 100,000 cars.

IS IT THE CAR OR THE DRIVER? Irresponsible drivers can be deadly in the safest cars and vice versa; however, the one above is the automobile that has the most fatalities per car, the Chevy Corvette.

Manufacturer	Units Sold
1. Volkswagen	162,291
2. BMW	105,761
3. Mercedes	90,844
4. Volvo	88,580
5. Saab	28,440
6. Audi	27,379
7. Jaguar	17,878
8. Porsche	7,151

Source: Industry sales statistics.

AUTOMOBILES— QUALITY

Best and Worst Initial Quality

When it comes to quality, some cars are just better than others, and it's especially upsetting when you stumble upon one of those problem vehicles soon after purchasing it. To chart the problems many buyers experience with new cars, the respected firm of J. D. Power and Associates conducts an annual Initial Quality Survey of models, ranking them by problems per 100 vehicles during the first 90 days of ownership. Here are the 1997 makers with the least and most problems during those early days. Among the top five are luxury brands—Infiniti, Lexus and Mercedes-Benz. As a point of reference, the industry average for the '97 model year was 86 problems per 100. That may sound high, but it's a big improvement: In 1996, there were 110 problems per 100 new vehicles.

FEWEST PROBLEMS

Manufacturer	Problems per 100 Cars
1. Infiniti	55
2. Lexus	57
3. Honda	60
4. Toyota	64
5. Mercedes-Benz	66
6. Volvo	69
7. Saturn	73
8. Nissan	78
9. Acura	79
Audi	79

MOST PROBLEMS

Manufacturer	Problems per 100 Cars
1. Kia	275
2. Land Rover	143
3. Pontiac	130
Suzuki	130
4. Hyundai	125
5. Mitsubishi	124
6. Eagle	121
7. Porsche	111
8. Cadillac	110
Saab	110

Source: J. D. Power and Associates.

AUTOMOBILES— SALES

Top-Selling Passenger Cars

Alas, or at last—the most appropriate exclamation, of course, depends on what nationality you are—half the cars on the best- seller list are American. Ford, with its Taurus model at the top, dominates all makes as well as the the big three American manufacturers as far as total sales in the U.S. Nonetheless, Japanese cars are still selling well.

Model	Units Sold, 1996
1. Taurus	378,144
2. Accord	367,137
3. Camry	354,035
4. Escort	292,900
5. Civic	290,843
6. Saturn	286,155
7. Cavalier	277,352
8. Lumina	246,824
9. Grand Am	224,530
10. Corolla	216, 167

Source: Automuseum, 1997.

AUTOMOBILES— TIRES

Top Tires

Consumer Reports evaluated all-season tires used on the most commonly purchased automobiles such as sedans, station wagons and minivans. Most of the tires in the testing were in the $50 to $70 price range. The criteria for their rankings included the test results of each tire set's braking, emergency handling, and impressions of routine handling and comfort. The testers scored these factors on a scale of 0 to 100. Their interpretation of the resultant scores is: 81 to 100 is "excellent," 61 to 80 is "very good," 41 to 60 is "good," 21 to 40 is "fair," and 0 to 20 is "poor."

Brand/Model	Score
1. Pirelli P400 Touring	85
2. Dunlop SP40 A/S	66
3. Goodyear Regatta	65
4. Cooper Lifeliner Classic II	64
5. Kelly-Springfield Navigator 800S	55
6. Firestone FR680	52
General Ameri G4S	52
8. Michelin XW4	51
9. Goodyear WeatherHandler	50
BF Goodrich The Advantage	50

Source: *Consumer Reports*, February, 1997.

BANKS— AMERICAN

Largest American Commercial Banks

One mark of a great nation is its ability to foster financial institutions whose influence extends beyond its physical borders. Although the swollen coffers of America's largest commercial banking institutions represent equal parts prosperity and risk, it is indisputable that the agglomeration of large, central stores of wealth provides the nation with the ability to undertake sweeping projects, and to weather short-term shifts in the winds of international finance. While many American banks have seen tough times in the last five years, few doubt their long-term health. Below are the largest commercial banks with headquarters in the U.S., in terms of total assets.

Bank	Assets (millions)
1. Chase Manhattan Bank	$317,579
2. Citibank	$256,853
3. Bank of America	$232,446
4. NationsBank	$187,297
5. J.P. Morgan & Co.	$184,879
6. First Union	$131,879
7. First Chicago NBD	$122,002
8. Wells Fargo Bank	$104,135
9. Bankers Trust Co.	$104,002
10. Banc One	$90,453

Source: Corporate Finance Network, 1997.

BASKETBALL, COLLEGE TEAMS

Greatest College Teams of All Time

UCLA is the most successful program in the history of college basketball, but not until the Bruins won the national championship in 1995 under coach Jim Harrick could that honor be truly attributed to more than just the genius of longtime coach John Wooden, who led the Bruins to victory in 10 national championship games. The roll-call of great basketball programs proceeds through the biggest names in college hoops history: Kentucky, Indiana, North Carolina, Kansas... Our rating adds all-time winning percentage (times 1000) plus number of national championships (times 100) to yield a final score that rewards both long-term success in the regular season and the ability to reach the ultimate goal: the national title. Here are the top 10.

School /Yr.	%	Titles	Score
1. UCLA, 1977	.698	11	1778
2. Kentucky, 1993	.760	6	1360
3. Indiana, 1996	.651	5	1151
4. N. Carolina, 1986	.737	3	1037

5. Kansas 1998

| | .693 | 2 | 893 |

6. Duke, '91

| | .669 | 2 | 869 |

7. Louisville 1982

| | .654 | 2 | 854 |

8. UNLV, 1938

| | .735 | 1 | 835 |

9. Arkansas, 1973

| | .659 | 1 | 759 |

10. St. John's, 1989

| | .690 | 0 | 690 |

* scores based on data up to 1995-1996 season

Source: *Best and Worst* original.

BASKETBALL TEAMS

Greatest NBA Teams of All Time

Our analysis of the greatest NBA championship teams gives the heaviest weight to winning percentage, but also takes into account a team's talent relative to other clubs, both past and present. The rating formula takes regular-season winning percentage as a base, then adds

CHICAGO BULLS ®

THE 1996 TEAM is the best that ever played, thanks in part to Michael Jordan, the fourth best basketball player of all time, (See page 20) and Phil Jackson, the coach with the best NBA winning percentage (See page 18).

10 percentage points each for the number of Hall of Famers on the roster (for teams with active players or those not yet eligible for the Hall, informed estimations were made), the number of league leaders in various statistical categories, and if the team carried the season's Most Valuable Player. For instance, the top-rated 1996 Chicago Bulls won a record 72 games for a winning percentage of .878. In our estimation the team earned 30 bonus points for three future Hall of Famers in Michael Jordan, Scottie Pippen and Dennis Rodman (yes, he'll be elected someday). In addition, Jordan and Rodman led the league in scoring and rebounding, respectively (20 bonus points); and Jordan earned the MVP (10 bonus points). These are the top 10 NBA teams of all time.

%/HF'ers/Ld'rs/MVP/Bonus/Score*					
1. 1996 Chicago Bulls					**.938**
	.878	3	2	1	.06
2. 1972 Los Angeles Lakers					**.901**
	.841	3	3	0	.06
3. 1967 Philadelphia 76ers					**.900**
	.840	3	2	1	.06
4. 1960 Boston Celtics					**.877**
	.787	8	1	0	.09
5. 1986 Boston Celtics					**.877**
	.817	4	1	1	.06
6. 1992 Chicago Bulls					**.857**
	.817	2	1	1	.04
7. 1971 Milwaukee Bucks					**.845**
	.805	2	1	1	.04
8. 1965 Boston Celtics					**.845**
	.775	5	1	1	.07
9. 1983 Philadelphia 76ers					**.843**
	.793	3	1	1	.05
1987 Los Angeles Lakers					**.843**
	.793	3	1	1	.05

* scores based on data up to 1996

Source: *Best and Worst* original.

BATTLES, BLOODIEST

The twentieth century has yielded many extraordinary advances in military technology. We can now kill more, better and faster than ever before. Of the battles that follow, only two are not from either WWI or WWII. They include one from the Korean conflict and the other from the worst retreat in history, Napoleon's march from Russia. The World Wars, which galvanized so much of humanity in the struggle to kill each other, make up the bulk of this record, including the grimmest statistic of all, the bloodiest battle. In World War I, near the town of Ypres in southwest Belgium, the massed Allies slugged it out with the massed Central powers in the bloodiest single battle of history. Over 380,000 men were killed on each side, with wounded and missing running at 600,000 for the Allies and slightly less for the Central powers. The British commander Haig visited the battlefield only once, and had to be taken away in incredulity at what he was ordering his men into. Madly, in the First World War, the European powers fought not once, but time and again for the same shell-pocked, devastated, bloody ground; the Italians and the Austrians fought a stupefying *eleven* Battles of the Isonzo in the course of three years, with no clear-cut decision on either side on that front (Caporetto, the Austrian breakthrough, came further north). The sheer horror of the battles on the Western front in the First World War should have convinced the world of war's futility, but sure enough, World War II erupted any-way. There is a certain numbness that settles on the mind upon reading these ratings, but here are the numbers anyway. Casualties include dead, wounded and missing from both sides.

Battle/War	Total Casualties
1. Ypres I World War I	1,800,000
2. Somme River I World War I	1,265,000
3. Po Valley World War II	740,000
4. Moscow World War II	700,000
5. Gallipoli World War I	500,000
6. Artois-Loos World War I	428,000
7. Berezina River War of 1812	400,000
8. Stalingrad World War II	350,000
9. 38th Parallel Korean War	320,000
10. Somme River II World War I	300,000

Source: *Encyclopedia of Battles.*

BEER— AMERICAN

Most Popular Domestic Brews

America seems to have cooled its affections for foreign quaffs, and renewed its interest in home-based hop houses. The rise of the "micro-breweries"—small, local brewers that turn out a premium product in relatively small numbers for avid fans— heralds a turn in taste back toward home. The new "domestic-ity" is everywhere: at the ball park, in the living room, even at the yacht club. Our heads may not always be completely clear when we drink, but we do know enough to buy American. Bud still runs way ahead of the pack, with a firm grip on America's malted taste buds. Bud and its parent company, Anheuser-Busch of St. Louis, maintain a firm grip on the American beer market—A-B products account for four of the top-10-selling brews.

Brand	Barrels Sold, 1995 (millions)
1. Budweiser	37.2
2. Bud Light	17.9
3. Miller Lite	15.8
4. Coors Light	12.9
5. Busch	8.1
6. Natural Light	7.1
7. Miller Genuine Draft	5.8
8. Milwaukee's Best	4.7
9. Miller High Life	4.4
10. Busch Light Draft	4.2

Source: Impact U.S. Beer Market Study, 1996.

HE MAKES IT, you drink it. Augie Busch (below) owns and operates the brewery that makes America's favorite, "Bud."

BEER—BRITISH

Best "Gourmet" Brews

The advent of American microbreweries has given American beer drinkers hearty, full-bodied alternatives to traditional, watered-down American beers and flavorful imports. But microbreweries are local; their products seldom find their way beyond their home turf. So lovers of strong brews still look overseas for satisfaction. German beer is the sentimental favorite, but for real flavor, the choice is British. They drink their beer warm in Britain, therefore brewers don't have the masking effects of cold temperatures to hide off any tastes or shortcuts in the brewing process, and the British can be quite unforgiving of inferior products. *Bon Appetit* magazine convened a panel of beer experts to choose the 10 best British beers available here. The selections represent styles and prices (in Chicago, IL) with enough variety to please any domestic palate or budget.

Rank/Beer/Origin

1. **Bass Pale Ale, England**
   Well-balanced, malty flavor with clean aftertaste—$1.50/12 oz.
2. **MacAndrew's Scotch Ale, Scotland**
   An ale with a smokey and spicy taste—$3.00/17 oz.

3. **McEwan's Scotch Ale, Scotland**
Dense and sweet, with a whiff of molasses—$1.50/12 oz.

4. **Newcastle Brown Ale, England**
Strong flavor of spicy malt, with a crisp finish—$1.30/12 oz.

5. **Samuel Smith Nut Brown Ale, England**
Smoky, loaded with flavor—$2.50/16 oz.

6. **Theakston Old Peculiar Yorkshire Ale, England**
A great finisher with a lush flavor—$1.50/12 oz.

7. **Thomas Hardy's Ale, England**
Dark and porter-like; bottled with natural yeast to improve with age—$3.00/33 oz.

8. **Traquair House Ale, Scotland**
Worth the expense with a flavor rich in hops—$5.00/12 oz.

9. **Welsh Ale, Wales**
Thick flavor, bitter finish. A favorite of Welsh poet Dylan Thomas—$2.50/16 oz.

10. **Whitbred Traditional Pale Ale England**
Fresh tasting with very good balance—$1.00/12 oz.

Source: *Bon Appetit* magazine.

OOKS

Best-Selling Children's Books of All Time

The children's paperback-book market is dominated by a handful of extremely popular and successful authors—Judy Blume, S.E. Hinton and Laura Ingalls Wilder, with the latter's *Little House* books accounting for six of the 10 best-selling children's paperbacks of all time. Hinton and Blume especially address modern problems kids face growing up. The list of best-selling hardcover children's books, on the

THE BEST BREW of the Brits.

other hand, is dominated by classics such as *Peter Rabbit* and *Mother Goose* and, of course, Dr. Seuss.

PAPERBACKS

Book/Author/(Yr. Pub'd)	Copies Sold
1. *The Poky Little Puppy* Janette S. Lowrey (Golden, 1942)	14,000,000
2. *The Tale of Peter Rabbit* Beatrix Potter (Frederick Warne, 1902)	9,331,266
3. *Tootle* Gertrude Crampton (Golden, 1945)	8,055,500
4. *Saggy Baggy Elephant* Kathryn and Byron Jackson (Golden, 1947)	7,098,000
5. *Scuffy the Tugboat* Gertrude Crampton (Golden, 1955)	7,065,000

6. *Pat the Bunny*   6,146,543
Dorothy Kunhardt
(Golden, 1940)

7. *Green Eggs and Ham*   6,065,197
Dr. *Seuss* (Random
House, 1960)

8. *The Cat in the Hat*   5,643,731
Dr. *Seuss* (Random
House, 1957)

9. *The Littlest Angel*   5,424,709
Charles Tazewell (Children's
Press/Ideals, 1946)

10. *One Fish, Two Fish, Red Fish,
Blue Fish*   4,822,331
Dr. Seuss (Random House, 1960)

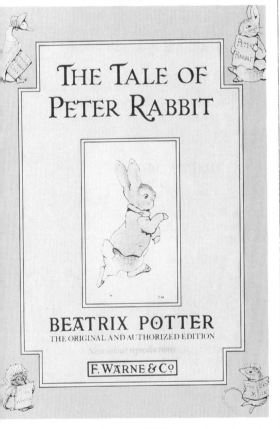

STAYING POWER! In print for almost a century, the book above still sells over 50,000 copies each year.

HARDCOVER

Book/Author/(Yr. Pub'd)   Copies Sold

1. *Charlotte's Web*   7,894,103
E.B. White, illustra-
tions by Garth Williams
(HarperCollins,1974)

2. *The Outsiders*   7,798,000
S.E. Hinton (Dell, 1968)

3. *Tales of a Fourth Grade
Nothing*   6,371,000
Judy Blume
(Dell, 1976)

4. *Shane*   6,161,000
Jack Schaefer
(Bantam, 1983)

5. *Are You There, God?
It's Me, Margaret*   6,015,000
Judy Blume (Dell, 1972)

6. *Where the Red
Fern Grows*   5,625,000
Wilson Rawls
(Dell, 1974)

7. *A Wrinkle In Time*   5,617,000
Madeleine L'Engle
(Dell, 1973)

8. *Island of the Blue
Dolphins*   5,513,000
Scott O'Dell
(Dell, 1971)

9. *Little House on the
Prairie*   5,291,059
Laura Ingalls
Wilder, illustrations
by Garth Williams
(HarperCollins, 1971)

10. *Little House In the
Big Woods*   5,227,120
Laura Ingalls Wilder,
illustrations by
Garth Williams
(HarperCollins, 1971)
* figures are through the end of
1995

Source: *Publishers Weekly* Web
Page, April 21, 1997.

THINGS

BOOKS— HARDCOVER

Longest-Running Bestsellers

Editors at major publishing houses are paid handsomely for the ability to predict a book's chances at bestsellerdom. Yet no one has figured it out to the point where it happens predictably. The number one bestseller for 1996, for example, was *The Celestine Prophecy*, a fictional account of a spiritual search. Right behind it, in the number two position, was the story of a presidential couple very much like the Clintons, with an anonymous author who was eventually discovered to be Joe Klein of *Newsweek*. Given the difference between the content of the two books—as well as most books on bestseller lists—how's an editor to know what to look for? Following are the best-selling hardcover books for 1996.

FICTION

Book/Author/Publisher	Weeks on List
1. *The Celestine Prophecy*, James Redfield, Warner	48
2. *Primary Colors*, "Anonymous"/Joe Klein, Random House	31
3. *The Horse Whisperer*, Nicholas Evans, Delacorte	25
The Tenth Night, James Redfield, Warner	25
5. *The Runaway Jury*, John Grisham, Doubleday	23
6. *How Stella Got Her Groove Back,* Terry McMillian, Viking	21
7. *Executive Orders*, Tom Clancy, Putnam	18
8. *Absolute Power*, David Balducci, Warner	17
9. *Moonlight Becomes You*, Mary Higgins Clark, Simon & Schuster	16
10. *Gods and Generals*, Jeff Shaara, Ballantine	15
The Deep End of the Ocean, Jacquelyn Mitchard, Viking	15

NONFICTION

Book/Author/Publisher	Weeks on List
1. *Men Are From Mars, Women Are From Venus*, John Gray, HarperCollins	52
2. *The Zone*, Barry Sears with Bill Lawren, Regan Books	41
3. *The Seven Spiritual Laws of Success*, Deepak Chopra, New World Library	39
Simple Abundance, Sarah Ban Breathnach, Warner	39
5. *Emotional Intelligence*, Daniel Goldman, Bantam	38
6. *Midnight in the Garden of Good and Evil*, John Berendt, Random House	37
7. *Undaunted Courage*, Stephen E. Ambrose, Simon & Schuster	36
8. *The Dilbert Principle*, Scott Adams, HarperBusiness	35
9. *Rush Limbaugh is a Big Fat Idiot*, Al Franken, Delacorte	24
10. *In Contempt*, Christopher A. Darden with Jess Walter, ReganBooks	20

Source: *Publishers Weekly*, January 6, 1997.

BOOKS

Most Influential

There's been a lot of debate recently about the Great Books— whether such a "canon" should remain part of the educational curriculum, or, indeed, whether one can even judge a work's "greatness." The original concept behind the Great Books series, developed by Robert M. Hutchins and Mortimer Adler, was to bring together the works that were most fundamental in forming and espousing the driving ideas of our society and our culture—from philosophy and political science to mathematics and even fiction. The debate now raging is over the "Euro-centric" nature of the traditional canon of great books—the fact that these works were overwhelmingly the creations of dead white European men, and that alternate views of the world— female, ethnic, modern, African, Latin American, Asian—are slighted. Be that as it may, there are quantitative methods of establishing just what the most influential works in the world are. One of these methods is citation analysis, which measures the number of times a particular work is mentioned in academic writing. An analysis performed by the editors of the Arts and Humanities Citation Index yielded this list of the most- cited works published in the twentieth century, in a seven-year period from 1976 to 1983. The most cited work in that period was *The Structure of Scientific Revolutions*, a work by Thomas S. Kuhn that explored the ways in which scientific ideas are formulated and sci-entific theories developed from those ideas. Second on the list, surprisingly, is a work of fiction, James Joyce's *Ulysses*. Philosophy is well-represented in the top ten, with Ludwig Wittgenstein's *Philosophical Investigations*, as well as the works by the French thinkers Jacques Derrida, Roland Barthes and Michel Foucault and German phenomenologist Martin Heidegger. These great books, it seems, represent a wide variety of viewpoints.

Book/Author	Citations
1. *Structure of Scientific Revolutions* Thomas S. Kuhn	855
2. *Ulysses* James Joyce	710
3. *Anatomy of Criticism* Northrop Frye	699
4. *Philosophical Investigations* Ludwig Wittgenstein	668
5. *Aspects of the Theory of Syntax* Noam Chomsky	640
6. *The Order of Things* Michel Foucault	488
7. *Of Grammatology* Jacques Derrida	475
8. *S/Z* Roland Barthes	454
9. *Being and Time* Martin Heidegger	450
10. *European Literature and the Latin Middle Ages* Ernst R. Curtius	434

Source: Current Contents, April 1987.

BOOKS— PAPERBACK

Longest-Running Bestsellers

Not many people are aware that paperback books did not originate in the United States. And most young people probably don't realize that there was a time when a "respectable" book meant a hardcover book, one which is full size, with stiff covers and heavy pages. Then, in June of 1939, Dutch publisher Robert Fair de Graff created a new publishing company called Pocket Books, with the objective of publishing exclusively "softcover" books, "complete and unabridged" versions of popular hardcover books. Publishing has never been the same since. Today's paperback industry is just as "respectable" as its older cousin, and includes "mass market" books, which are those sold in bookstores, supermarkets, drug stores and airports, most of which measure approximately 4" x 7". The larger size softcover books, "trade paperbacks," are approximately 5" x 8" and upwards, the most common size being 6" x 9". Regardless of which type of paperback you choose, they're still less expensive than hardcover books. Now almost every hardcover publishing house has a paperback counterpart, and deals between publishers and writers of hardcover books often include arrangements for paperback rights after the hardcover edition is published. Following are the longest-running paperback bestsellers of 1996.

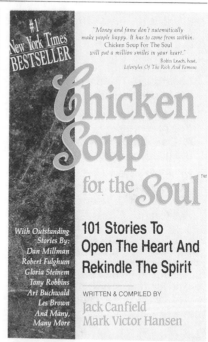

"Money and fame don't automatically make people happy. It has to come from within. Chicken Soup For The Soul will put a million smiles in your heart."
Robin Leach, host,
Lifestyles Of The Rich And Famous

#1 New York Times BESTSELLER

Chicken Soup for the Soul™

With Outstanding Stories By:
Dan Millman
Robert Fulghum
Gloria Steinem
Tony Robbins
Art Buchwald
Les Brown
And Many,
Many More

101 Stories To Open The Heart And Rekindle The Spirit

WRITTEN & COMPILED BY
Jack Canfield
Mark Victor Hansen

REJECTED by virtually every major New York publisher, the book set records for sales as well as sequels.

4. *The Mouse on the Mile (Green Mile #2),*
   Stephen King, Signet   17
5. *Sleepers,*
   Lorenzo Carcaterra,
   Ballantine   15
   The Lost World,
   Michael Crichton,
   Ballantine   15

MASS MARKET PAPERBACKS

Book/Author/Publisher   Weeks on List

1. *The Rainmaker,*
   John Grisham, Island/Dell   35
2. *The Two Dead Girls (Green Mile #1),*
   Stephen King, Signet   26
3. *Beach Music,*
   Pat Conroy, Bantam   18

TRADE PAPERBACKS

Book/Author/Publisher   Weeks on Lilst

1. *Chicken Soup for the Soul,*
   Jack Canfield and Mark Victor Hansen, eds., Health Communications   52
   Snow Falling on Cedars,
   David Guterson, Vintage   52
   Reviving Ophelia,
   Mary Pipher, Ballantine   52

THINGS

Source: *Publishers Weekly,* January 6, 1997.

WANT TO SEE A SHOW BUSINESS RECORD as it actually takes place? Every night you'll find one here at the Winter Garden in New York City, as *Cats* sets a new record for the longest run on Broadway. Production is now underway for a full-length animated feature version of *Cats,* based on a screenplay by Tony Award-winning playwright Tom Stoppard. The production will eventually be released by Universal Pictures and will feature a new song written for the film.

THINGS

BOXING

Biggest Heavyweight Upsets

By the time heavyweight champion Mike Tyson signed on to fight the relative unknown Buster Douglas in Tokyo on February 10, 1990, the sporting media was treating Tyson bouts as routine, almost boring affairs, which, of course, was before he bit a chunk out of Evander Holyfield's ear on June 28, 1997. The Vegas oddsmakers had given Douglas only a 45-to-1 chance to wrest the title from "Iron Mike" Tyson, known for his vicious punches and his violent character, both in and out of the ring. But when the smoke cleared from that ring in Tokyo, Tyson had tumbled from boxing's firmament with a stunning fall in the 10th round, and folks had to stand up and take notice. The shine was off the Tyson myth, and a new folk hero had emerged in the rotund Douglas. Although Douglas turned out to be a one-punch wonder—after bulking up to a full-figured 246 pounds, he was easily dispatched by Evander Holyfield in his first title defense—the unlikely hero from Ohio had scored the biggest upset in boxing history. Here are other top upsets, with their pre-fight odds:

Winner/Loser	Odds Against
1. Buster Douglas/Mike Tyson	45-1
2. Muhammad Ali/G. Foreman	10-1
3. James Braddock/Max Baer	10-1
4. Cassius Clay/Sonny Liston	7-1
5. Leon Spinks/Muhammad Ali	6-1
6. Jersey Joe Walcott/ Ezred Charles	6-1
7. Evander Holyfield/Mike Tyson	6-1
8. Ingemar Johansson/ Floyd Patterson	4-1
9. James Corbett/ John L. Sullivan	4-1
10. George Foreman/Joe Frazier	3-1

Source: *National Sports Review*, 1991; HBO, 1997.

BROADWAY

Longest-Running Plays

High prices keep many from the Great White Way. But rationale aside, Broadway is still very much Broadway, and the spark has not dimmed. Though *Chorus Line* shut down its hugely successful run of 6,137 shows in 1991,there a star shinningis just as bright, *Cats.* The fabulously successful musical opened at the Winter Garden in New York on October 7, 1992. Since then it has won seven Tony Awards, including Best Musical. More than 8,250,000 people have seen the show on Braodway. "Now and Forever," the production' slogan, has lived up to its name. It has played in more than 20 theaters worldwide in as many nations, and 47 million people have enjoyed a live performance some where in the world. Today, as of this writing, it is still at the Winter Garden setting records each time the lights dim.

Play	Performances*
1. *Cats*	6,173
2. *Chorus Line*	6,137
3. *Oh! Calcutta* (revival)	5,959
4. *Les Miserables*	3,845
5. *Phantom of the Opera*	3,542
6. *42nd Street*	3,486
7. *Grease*	3,388
8. *Fiddler on the Roof*	3,242
9. *Life with Father*	3,224
10. *Tobacco Road*	3,182

* through July 21, 1997

Source: *Variety*

WORLD'S TALLEST BUILDING, Sears Tower, dominates the skyline of Chicago, the city that possesses the "Best Architecture in America" (See page 80).

BUILDINGS

America's Tallest Buildings

One tick back on the geological timescale, the American skyline was defined by trees, mountain tops and eagles' nests. Today, much of our land lies in the shadows of the great steel and concrete shelters we have erected. Of our tallest structures, the top two are of recent vintage; but the venerable Empire State Building still holds its own.

Building/(City)	Height (feet)
1. Sears Tower (Chicago)	1,454
2. One World Trade Center (NYC)	1,368
3. Two World Trade Center (NYC)	1,362
4. Empire State Bldg. (NYC)	1,250
5. Amoco Building (Chicago)	1,136
6. John Hancock Center (Chicago)	1,127
7. Chrysler Building (NYC)	1,04
8. NationsBank Plaza (Atlanta)	1,023
9. First Interstate World Center (Los Angeles)	1,018
10. Texas Commerce Tower (Houston)	1,002

Source: *The World's Tallest Building Page*, World Wide Web. February 15, 1997.

CANCER

Most Prevalent New Cases

While cancer in general has no gender preference, there are certain types that men are prone to, and others that are more likely to affect women. Breast cancer, though not unknown in men, is the most common cancer type in women. Cancer of the prostrate gland cannot affect women, however, due to the fact that females have no such organ. Below are the most common new cases that are diagnosed in the U.S.

FEMALE CANCER CASES

Cancer Type	New Cases
1. Breast	180,200
2. Lung	79,800
3. Colon and rectal	64,800
4. Uterine	34,900
5. Ovarian	26,800
6. Non-Hodgkin's lymphoma	23,300
7. Skin (excluding basal & squamous)	19,400
8. Bladder	15,000
9. Cervical	14,500
10. Pancreatic	14,200

MALE CANCER CASES

Cancer Type	New Cases
1. Prostate	334,500
2. Lung	98,300
3. Colon and rectal	66,400
4. Bladder	39,500
5. Skin (excluding basal & squamous)	34,900
6. Non-Hodgkin's lymphoma	30,300
7. Oral cavity and pharynx	20,900
8. Kidney	17,100
9. Leukemia	15,900
10. Stomach	14,000

Source: American Cancer Society, 1997

CANDY BARS AND PACKAGED SWEETS

Most and Least Fattening

In the last decade Americans have become aware that calories are not the only measure of how fattening a treat actually is. Candy is always a threat to the waistline, especially when you count fat grams along with calories. Some American candies, however, are worse than others. Researchers examined the nutritional content of some of America's favorite treats. Following are their findings ranked in order of percent of calories from fat.

MOST FATTENING OVERALL

Candy/Weight/Fat	Total Calories
1. Mr. Goodbar	240
1.65 ounces, 15 grams fat	
2. Reese's Peanut Butter Cup	250
1.6 ounces, 15 grams fat	
3. Hershey's Milk Chocolate	240
1.55 ounces, 14 grams fat	
4. Almond Joy	250
1.76 ounces, grams fat	
5. Kit Kat	250
1.5 ounces, 12 grams fat	
6. M&M's Peanut	250
1.74 ounces, 13 grams fat	

LEAST FATTENING OVERALL

Candy/Weight/Fat	Total Calories
1. Good & Plenty	191
1.8 ounces, 0 grams fat	
2. Life Savers	88
0.9 ounces, 0 grams fat	
3. Sugar Daddy	218
2 ounces, 1 gram fat	
4. York Peppermint Pattie	180
1.5 ounces, 4 grams fat	
5. Tootsie Roll	252
2.25 ounces, 6 grams fat	
6. Junior Mints	192
1.6 ounces, 5 grams fat	

Source: Tufts University's Diet & Nutrition Center

CEREALS

Most Popular Breakfast Cereals

Though Kellogg's Corn Flakes and Rice Crispies are still main staples in cereals, America's tastes in breakfast grains are shifting. Cheerios, once number one, has fallen to the number two spot. Sales of Total, once the number four selling cereal in America, is not even on the top-ten list. Nonetheless, the realitively low cholesterol levels and fat content keep cereals on America's breakfast tables. Newer, more natural products, however, have been seriously competing with the processed grain products of cereal giants like Kellogg's and General Mills (though they have yet to make the list). Granolas, natural wheat and oat bran cereals have become increasingly popular. Following are the top 10 cereal brands of late.

Brand	Market Share, 1995
1. Kellogg's Frosted Flakes	4.24%
2. General Mills Cheerios	3.66%
3. Kellogg's Corn Flakes	3.03%
4. Kellogg's Rice Krispies	2.77%
5. General Mills Honey Nut Cheerios	2.76%
6. Kellogg's Raisin Bran	2.68%
7. Kellogg's Froot Loops	2.43%
8. Kellogg's Special K	2.11%
9. Kellogg's Corn Pops	2.10%
10. Gen. Mills Lucky Charms	1.99%

Source: *Advertising Age*, Ad Age Dataplace, 1996.

CHOCOLATES, MOST POPULAR

They Still Melt in Your Mouth

Despite the growing popularity of elite, foreign chocolate makers like Tobler, Lindt, and Cadbury, the U.S. market is still dominated by the old stand-by chocolate treats. Because the U.S.'s candy companies are primarily privately held, their exact sales figures are not publicly announced, however a range based on estimates by a snack industry periodical is provided in the table that follows.

Candy	Total Sales (millions)
1. M&M's	over $800
2. Snickers	$500-799
3. Reese's Peanut Butter Cup	$400-499
4. Hershey's Kisses	$200-299
Milky Way Bar	$200-299
Kit Kat	$200-299
7. Hershey's Milk Chocolate with Almonds	$100-199
Hershey's Milk Chocolate	$100-199
Butterfingers	$100-199
Three Musketeers	$100-199
Nestle's Crunch	$100-199
Twix Cookie Bars	$100-199

Source: *Confectioner Magazine*, May/June, 1997.

CIGARETTES

Most Popular Cigarette Brands

Despite setbacks, cigarettes still do a "healthy" business, with stalwart Marlboro still very much alive (although the Marlboro man—at least the actor who portrayed him—is dead, from, guess what?—lung cancer). But lately, the American tobacco industry has been running scared. In the wake of a cigarette backlash, the tobacco companies have taken on a new strategy: capitulating under the threat of class action suits, lead by Liggett and Myers, which consented to pay over $200 billion to suffers who contend their health has suffered from cigarette smoking. And now, after years of constant warnings about the dangers of cigarette smoke from the nation's most respected health experts, the American public is finally

THE NINETEENTH-CENTURY MINER at right is wearing Levi's 501 jeans, the world's first, and still best-selling, blue jeans. It would surely knock his jeans off to know that today the best-selling article of clothing is panty hose.

getting the message, and cigarette smoking is on the decline. Smokers are outcasts, relegated to dark, dreary corners of restaurants, airports, offices and other public spaces.

Brand	Market Share, 1995
1. Marlboro	30.1%
2. GPC	5.8%
Winston	5.8%
4. Doral	5.7%
5. Newport	5.6%
6. Basic	4.7%
7. Camel	4.4%
8. Salem	3.7%
9. Kool	3.6%
10. Virginia Slims	2.4%

Source: *Brandweek*, Superbrands '97, October 7, 1996.

CLOTHING

Most Popular Apparel Manufacturers

Alas, America's top-selling garment is no longer the venerable blue jean, with its slow fade, long life and comfort. Perhaps to the chagrin of the truly macho, America's top-seller is *pantyhose*. Even so, the blue jean has so pervaded our culture that they've even broken the formal dress code of many normally stodgy American restaurants and business offices. In many companies, the low-tech, jeans-and-sneakers look has replaced the suit and tie as the fashionable businessman's statement. The following are the top American apparel manufacturers.

Brand	Total Sales (billions)
1. Hanes, Champion, L'eggs	$7.1
2. Levi's Dockers	$6.7
3. Lee, Wrangler, Vanity Fair	$5.0
4. Fruit of the Loom, Gitano	$2.4
5. Liz Clairborne, Dana Buchman	$2.0
6. Melrose, Prophecy, Sag Harbor	$1.3
7. Russell	$1.1
8. Warner's, Olga, Calvin Klein Lingerie	$0.9
9. Nike	$0.8
10. Jones, New York	$0.7

Source: *Brandweek*, Superbrands '97, October 7, 1996.

C OFFEE

Most Popular Coffee Brands

The new "McDonald's" of the 1990s is surely the aromatic Starbucks. More and more, Americans are getting strung out on java. But the medical community is unsure just what this addiction means in terms of the nation's health. Just as one research team publishes a paper decrying the harmful effects of caffeine, another group somewhere else purports to show its beneficial, medicinal qualities. In the face of such conflicting opinion, we go chugging mass quantities of the dark brew, from double-decaf capuccino in trendy urban cafes to the stalwart regular coffee served up at truckstops across the land. The leading U.S. brand, Folgers, sells more than $1 billion in caffeine-crusted java each year alone. The following are the top 10 coffee brands in America. These figures do not take into account the massive quantities of consumers at coffee shops such as Starbucks and SBC.

Brand	Market Share, 1995
1. Folgers	27.4%
2. Maxwell House	19.2%
3. Private Label	7.6%
4. General Foods Coffee	4.7%
5. Hills Bros.	4.1%
6. Maxwell House Master Blend	4.1%
7. Tasters Choice	4.0%
8. Chock Full O Nuts	2.2%
9. Folgers Singles	2.0%
10. Yuban	1.9%

Source: *Advertising Age*, Ad Age Dataplace, 1996.

C OLLEGES— BIG TEN

Ph.D. Production in Big Ten Schools

The schools of the Big Ten offer a diverse curriculum that caters to the needs of their very large student bodies. Still, these schools, most of which are public and state-sponsored, produce a fair number of eventual Ph.D.'s from among their undergraduates.

The numbers are not as great in terms of the percentage of the undergraduate student body that eventually earns Ph.D's, but that is understandable, given the public mandate of these schools, and their somewhat more open admissions policies. Given these considerations, we present here the Ph.D. productivity of the Big Ten schools, ranked from first to last by the number of baccalaureate earners who go on to get a doctoral degree.

School	Ph.D.'s Conferred*
1. Univerity of Wisconsin	783
2. Ohio State University	710

3. Univeristy of Minnesota	707
4. University of Illinois	666
5. University of Michigan	649
6. Purdue University	493
7. Michigan State University	429
8. Indiana University	348
9. University of Iowa	307
10. Northwestern University	305

* 1993-94 academic year

Source: U.S. Department of Education, National Center for Education Statistics; Higher Education General Information Survey; Integrated Postsecondary Education Data System, Completions Survey, May 1996.

COLLEGES—BUSINESS PROGRAMS

Best Business Schools in the U.S.

Business degrees have never been more popular. The bad news is that it is harder than ever to get into the schools listed here. Applications at the top 25 schools have risen by 33 percent since 1994, while at the same time, the schools are admitting even smaller percentages of candidates. Stanford is the most selective: in 1996 they accepted just one out of every 14 applicants. The good news is that if you do get in to one of these schools, the rewards are big. Average job offers jumped by 30 percent, to three per graduate. The median starting pay for an MBA from a top-25 school is a whopping $81,569, up 16 percent in two years.

Rank/School

1. University of Pennsylvania (Wharton School of Business)
2. University of Michigan
3. Northwestern University (Kellogg School of Business)
4. Harvard University
5. University of Virginia (Darden School of Business)
6. Columbia University
7. Stanford University
8. University of Chicago
9. MIT (Sloan School of Business)
10. Dartmouth University (Tuck School of Business)

Source: *Business Week*, November 25, 1996.

THE GRADUATES below at Columbia University, one of the top-ten business schools in the U.S., waive their meal tickets.

COLLEGES— CONTRIBUTIONS

The Rich Get Richer: Most Generous Alumni

Alumni and other individuals are responsible for nearly half of all voluntary support—contributions—for American colleges and universities—a total of over $4 billion annually. Other entities involved in such support include corporations, foundations and religious organizations. Most colleges in recent years have realized the great financial resources represented by alumni and have intensified fundraising efforts to tap that resource. The following are the institutions that reap the biggest windfall from those tax-deductible contributions, measured by total 1989 voluntary support.

University	Alumni Support, 1993-94
1. Harvard University	$111,118,392
2. Yale University	$105,363,162
3. Stanford University	$85,847,503
4. Cornell University	$83,103,358
5. University of Michigan	$48,024,024
6. University of Illinois	$45,603,919
7. Columbia University	$44,723,895
8. University of Pennsylvania	$38,516,406
9. Princeton University	$37,670,803
10. Texas A&M University	$33,059,868

Source: *Chronicle of Higher Education*, 1995.

COLLEGES— COSTS

Most Expensive Colleges

The cost of the *average* college education for a student beginning college work in 1997 is $47,507, according to *Moneywise* magazine. For a child who is one-year old in 1997, the same education will cost $140,250 assuming seven percent inflation, according to the same magazine. American higher education has reached a dangerous pass. Tuition and fees at private colleges have climbed into the high monopoly-money stratosphere, while government loans, grants and subsidies have fallen to discouragingly low levels. The "education" president, George Bush, has done little to address the financial aid shortfall which confronts this country. If the problem is not taken under rapid advisement, many of our most promising students will miss the opportunity to maintain competitiveness with their foreign counterparts. "You get what you pay for," so the expression goes, but at the following prices you better be getting a whole bunch. The most expensive schools offer name recognition, a great network of alumni to help find employment after graduation, the best professors and courses, etc., not to mention the fact that the educational environment is superior: diverse student body, plenty of activities, excellent facilities and other opportunities to learn. But are those the prices that the market itself establishes? The courts recently found the Ivy League schools guilty of fixing their prices so that no school within the group set tuition prices that varied widely with any other. The schools argued that this practice made the prospective student's choice one based on the school itself, and not on cost; the courts decided that lack of competition made the tuition prices artificially high. Measured by tuition costs alone (skipping over room and board, which tacks on at least $5,000 more per school year), here are the most expensive schools you can attend.

School	Tuition*
1. Middlebury College, NH	$28,240
2. Bates College, ME	$27,415
3. Connecticut College, CT	$27,375
4. Franklin and Marshall College, PA	$26,400
5. Bennington College, VT	$25,800
6. Hampshire College, MA	$22,900
7. Brown University, RI	$22,280
8. Colby College, ME	$22,190
9. Kenyon College, OH	$22,010
10. Amherst College, MA	$22,007

* figures are for 1995-96 academic year

Source: *College Information Handbook*; College Board Online, 1997.

COLLEGES—DEGREES AWARDED

Most Bachelor's Degrees Awarded

Which schools account for the most degrees awarded to a single class? Naturally, the larger numbers come from the largest schools, but after attrition and people who don't make the four- year trek, the graduating class is always less than what it started out to be. Graduation is still the goal of most, and the people who do make it can feel justifiably proud. The following schools have awarded the most bachelor's degrees to a given class in a single year.

School	Bachelor's Awarded, 1993-94
1. Pennsylvania State University	8,040
2. University of Texas, Austin	7,497
3. Ohio State University	7,182
4. Texas A&M University	6,933
5. Michigan State University	6,664
6. Brigham Young University	6,249
7. University of Washington	6,103
8. University of Illinois, Urbana-Champaign	6,026
9. University of Wisconsin, Madison	5,827
10. Arizona State University	5,766

Source: *Digest of Education Statistics, 1996.*

COLLEGES—DEGREES AWARDED

Most Master's Degrees Awarded

When a master's-level student looks for a school, prestige is a factor, as indicated by the results of this ranking. In fact, most of the master's degrees come from "name" schools, private institutions rather than public. Location is also important—a large number of master's degrees are earned by those who are currently in the workforce or returning to school after some time spent working; these students tend to gravitate toward schools in large metropolitan areas, such as New York, Los Angeles and Boston. The two schools at the top of the list are, not surprisingly, both located in New York City, the center of the American financial and corporate community. The leading bestowers of master's degrees are as follows:

School	Master's Awarded, 1993-94
1. New York University	4,553
2. Columbia University	4,385
3. University of Michigan	2,858
4. Boston University	2,725
5. Harvard/Radcliffe University	2,630
6. University of Texas, Austin	2,619
7. University of Southern California	2,589
8. University of Illinois, Urbana-Champaign	2,583

9. Ohio State University   2,408
10. George Washington
University   2,304

Source: *Digest of Education Statistics*, 1996.

COLLEGES—DEGREES AWARDED

Most Ph.D.s Awarded

Where do academicians come from? Specifically, Ph.D. recipients? It seems that those interested in pursuing the doctoral degree want one of two conditions as far as educational environment. On one hand, there are the relaxing, comfortable climates of California and Texas, apparently fertile grounds for nurturing scholarly work. On the other, there are darker, colder and perhaps more introspective environments of the northeast or upper-midwest. With this in mind, the most Ph.D.s come from the following institutions:

School   Ph.D.'s Awarded, 1993-94

1. University of California, Berkeley   896
2. University of Wisconsin, Madison   783
3. University of Texas, Austin   714
4. Ohio State University, Main Campus   710
5. University of Minnesota, Twin Cities   707
6. University of Illinois, Urbana-Champaign   666
7. University of Michigan, Ann Arbor   649
8. Columbia University   644
9. University of California Los Angeles   620
10. Stanford University   560

Source: U.S. Department Of Education; National Center For Education Statistics; Higher Education General Information Survey; Degrees And Other Formal Awards Conferred Survey; Integrated Postsecondary Education Data System Completions Survey, 1996; *The Digest of Education Statistics*, 1996

COLLEGES—FIELDS OF STUDY

Most Popular Undergraduate Degrees

A few decades ago, the American higher education system saw a renaissance of Liberal Arts study. In these pragmatic, economically troubled times, though, it is not surprising that these sublime but financially unrewarding pursuits have once again declined in popularity. With spiraling tuition costs, today's average student is asking for an education which will bring immediate, tangible results. But are we trading long-term cultural, political and, yes, economic health for immediate gain? Is anybody worried that three times as many undergraduates want to study business management rather than engineering? Or that this country grants twice as many bachelor's degrees in the visual and performing arts as it does in the physical sciences? As the list following demonstrates, we've become much better at managing, advertising and selling products than we are at actually developing and building them, much better at dancing and acting than at discovering and inventing.

Field   Bachelor's Awarded, 1993-94

1. Business Management/ Marketing   246,654
2. Social Sciences   133,680
3. Education   107,600
4. Engineering   78,225

5. Health Professions 74,421
6. Psychology 69,259
7. English/Literature 53,924
8. Communications 51,827
9. Biological/Life Sciences 51,383
10. Visual/Performing Arts 49,053
Source: *Digest of Education Statistics*, 1996

COLLEGES—FIELDS OF STUDY

Most Popular Master's Degree Subjects

Going on to pursue an advanced degree is an interesting decision. Master's degree study is more intense and focused than undergraduate study, and the numbers receiving master's degrees are considerably less than the plethora of undergraduate awards. The choice to pursue such an advanced degree is dictated by the needs of the profession you are going into, and whether such a degree is required (or imperative) for credibility in the profession. The top two subject areas fit these requirements respectively. The number one subject, education, requires a master's in order to attain rank in the teaching profession. In the number two subject, business and management, the M.B.A. has become the standard that many businesses require for today's marketplace. Following are the most popular master's degree subjects rated by the number bestowed annually.

Field	Master's Awarded, 1993-94
1. Education	98,938
2. Business Management/ Marketing	93,437
3. Engineering	29,754
4. Health Professions	28,025

THE UNIVERSITY OF CALIFORNIA at Berkeley (above) produces the most Ph.D.s of all educational institutions in the U.S.
Photo: Jane Scherr.

5. Public Administration	21,833
6. Social Sciences	14,561
7. Psychology	12,181
8. Computer/Information Sciences	10,416
9. Visual/Performing Arts	9,925
10. English/Literature	7,885

Source: *Digest of Education Statistics*, 1996.

COLLEGES—FIELDS OF STUDY

Most Popular Ph.D. Degree Subjects

The Ph.D. is the highest level of educational achievement. It is also the most difficult to actually attain because of the amount of time in school required—the wait for many doctoral students can last more than 10 years! As can be expected, the most Ph.D.s are found in the field of education, because it is the logical extension of the field itself. The numbers of Ph.D.s awarded is quite small—the total from the list below does not add up to the 10th-ranked baccalaureate subject area. In a wry comment on wisdom through increasing education, the Ph.D. in business management is ranked 5th, dropping from the one and two spots it occupies for the B.A. and M.B.A. The following are the top 10 areas of study in which doctorate degrees are awarded annually.

Field	Ph.D.'s Awarded, 1993-94
1. Engineering	6,908
2. Health Professions	5,979
3. Agriculture	4,650
4. Visual/Performing Arts	4,534
5. Business Management/ Marketing	3,627
6. Social Sciences	3,563
7. Public Administration	1,902
8. Protective Services	1,448
9. Education	1,364
10. Psychology	1,344

Source: *Digest of Education Statistics*, 1996.

COLLEGES—FIELDS OF STUDY

Strangest Majors

If you want to major in Swahili, where do you look for a program of study? Surprisingly, according to *Lovejoy's College Guide*, there are more than 10 institutions that offer Swahili as a major. If you really want a "different" established major program of study (many institu-

tions offer the option of creating your own major, but that does not enter into this rating), the following colleges are worth a look. The schools below have programs of study that are offered at four or fewer colleges or universites; the list does not include the engineering sub-disciplines, which are legion and of which Rensselaer and M.I.T. have many.

Institution/Rare Major(s)

1. **Rensselaer Polytechnical Institute, NY**
   Strategic Studies
   Nuclear Metallurgy
   Quantum Mechanics
   Radio Biology
   Radio Isotope Technology
   Endocrinology
   Medical Physicist
2. **Massachusetts Institute of Technology, MA**
   Bio-Mechanics
   Cryogenics
   Holographics
   Nuclear Metallurgy
   Quantum Mechanics
3. **Hampshire College, MA**
   Brazilian
   Finnish
   Conflict-War Studies
4. **Stetson University, FL**
   Orthoptics
   Ornithology
   Endocrinology
   Icthyology (fish studies)
5. **University of California, Davis, CA**
   Enology (winemaking)
   Pomology (fruit growing)
   Endocrinology
6. **University of Rhode Island, RI**
   Commercial Fishing
   Aquaculture
7. **Rochester Institute of Technology, NY**
   Glass Science
   Gunsmithing

8. **SUNY College of Environment & Forestry**
   Ornithology
   Icthyology
9. **University of New Haven, CT**
   Arson Investigation
   Biomedical Computing
10. **Nicholls State University, LA**
    Sugar Cane Technology
    Northern Studies
    Maine Maritime Academy, ME
    Craft/Boat Design
    Slippery Rock University, PA
    Cruise Marketing
    High Point College, NC
    Fur Design/Marketing

Source: *Lovejoy's Guide*, 19th Edition.

COLLEGES— MERIT SCHOLARS

Where the Brains Are

The National Merit Scholarship Corporation provides scholarships to the best and brightest students in the country, based on college board scores. Harvard/Radcliffe not only has the most merit scholars in the freshman class, but also a very high *percentage* of National Merit Scholars in its entering class, compared with larger schools such as the University of Texas at Austin. The following is a list of the colleges with the most freshman National Merit Scholars enrolled.

School Freshman Merit Scholars, 1996	
1. Harvard/Radcliffe	391
2. University of Texas, Austin	299
3. Rice University	204
4. Stanford University	184
5. Texas A&M University	183
6. University of Florida	177
7. Yale University	165
8. Iowa State University	154
9. University of Oklahoma	153
10. University of California, Berkeley	131

Source: *Chronicle of Higher Education*, 1996.

COLLEGES— INTERNET ACCESSABILITY

Most "Connected" Schools

So you think a college student's future career success lies in his or her connections? It depends what kind of connections you mean. If it's being hooked up to the Internet and making wide and varied use of computers, then the students at MIT have a definite edge, since the Cambridge, Massachusetts-based school tops the list of the nation's 100 most wired campuses. Today's college students are amazingly computer-savvy and Net-friendly—critical skills for any future career success in an increasingly technological world. And a large number of colleges are providing their students with numerous opportunities to take advantage of on-campus technology. Some 4,000 schools were polled on their use of computers and the Internet for academics, social life, and student services, resulting in a list of the top 100 most wired schools. All of the 100 offer on-line access to library catalogs, and most also provide students with unlimited access to the Web, with Web space for their own home pages, and with ports in every dormitory room. A large number also let students see their transcripts on-line, register for classes on-line, and add or drop classes on-line. Interestingly, only two members of the Ivy League—Dartmouth and Princeton—made it to the top 25. So much for the storied connections made at Harvard.

Following are the ten most wired schools.

Rank/ School

1. Massachusetts Institute of Technology
2. Northwestern University
3. Emerson College
4. Rensselaer Polytechnic Institute
5. Dartmouth College
6. University of Oregon
7. New Jersey Institute of Technology
8. Indiana University-Bloomington
9. Middlebury College
10. Carnegie Mellon University

Source: *Yahoo!, Internet Life,* May 1997.

COLLEGES— R&D

Top Research and Development Universities

Below we have listed the top 10 universities in the United States in terms of expenditures on research and development. Johns Hopkins is the leader in medical research among American universities. The rating does not include spending on arts, education, humanities, law or physical education and is expressed in terms of annual expenditures on scientific and engineering research and development.

University	Fiscal 1993
1. Johns Hopkins University	$745,515,000
2. University of Michigan	$425,868,000
3. University of Wisconsin, Madison	$372,362,000
4. Massachusetts Institute of Technology	$365,553,000
5. University of Washington	$335,329,000
6. University of Minnesota	$332,033,000
7. Texas A&M University	$322,691,000
8. University of California, San Francisco	$314,599,000
9. Cornell University	$310,949,000
10. University of California, San Diego	$307,051,000

Source: *Chronicle of Higher Education,* 1995.

COLLEGES— SELECTIVITY

The Other Reason to Dread April 15: The Most Selective Schools in the Country

The Ides of April aren't feared merely by those who owe big bucks in taxes to Uncle Sam. April 15 is the traditional date that prospective college students hear whether they've been admitted to the school of their choice. The hardest universities to get into are, understandably, in the most highly competitive category of *Barron's Profiles of American Colleges.* Ivy league schools and military academies top the list as the most selective of the crop. Considering the instant name recognition, the network of contacts established and the strength of the educational experience, it is no wonder that so many apply to these places, thereby forcing a rather brutal selection process to narrow the field.

Institution	Percent Accepted
1. Harvard University, MA	12%
2. Cooper Union, NY	13%
U.S. Military Academy, NY	13%
4. Princeton University, NJ	14%

U.S. Naval Academy, MD   14%
6. Amherst College, MA   19%
   Stanford University, CA   19%
   U.S. Coast Guard
   Academy, CT   19%
9. Yale University, CT   20%
10. Brown University, RI   21%

Source: *Barron's Profile of American Colleges, 21st Edition, 1997.*

COLLEGES—STUDENT BODY

Largest Enrollment—Campus

Would you like to be a little fish in a big pond? At the Universities of Minnesota and Texas, Ohio State University and other huge campuses, students need not fear falling asleep in a lecture—there's very little chance the professor will notice among the hundreds of bodies in the lecture hall. Of course, many of the largest classes are freshman lectures, and the teacher/student ratio decreases as students sort out their majors and take more courses specific to their field of study. So don't be too daunted by these huge campus numbers.

School/Campus	Enrollment, 1994
1. University of Minnesota, Twin Cities	51,478
2. Ohio State University, Main Campus	49,542
3. University of Texas, Austin	47,957
4. Miami-Dade Community College	47,069
5. Houston Community College System	45,893
6. Arizona State University	42,189
7. Texas A&M University	42,018
8. Michigan State University	40,254
9. University of Wisconsin, Madison	39,361

10. University of Illinois, Urbana-Champaign   **38,545**

Source: U.S. Department of Education; National Center for Education Statistics; Integrated Postsecondary Education Data System, Fall 1994 Enrollment Survey, 1996.

COLLEGES—STUDENT BODY

Largest Undergraduate Enrollment

Choosing a college to go to is one of the most difficult decisions a high-schooler makes. Should you pick a tough college? A religious school? A college you can most likely be accepted at? And the questions continue: What will the teachers be like? The students? The following rating ranks the colleges by undergraduate population. If you wish to become one of the faceless masses in an undergraduate population, or if you just like crowds, these are the places to go. As you may surmise, state schools are the largest, with immense undergraduate populations. For schools within a state system, figures given are for the main branches.

School	Undergraduate Population
1. Ohio State University	35,475
2. University of Texas	35,086
3. Texas A & M University	34,371
4. Pennsylvania State University	32,790
5. Michigan State University	31,329
6. Arizona State University	31,212
7. University of Florida	30,522
8. Purdue University	27,982
9. Brigham Young	27,625
10. University of Illinois	26,673

Source: *Barron's Profiles of American Colleges*, 21st Edition, 1997.

THINGS

COLLEGES—STUDENT BODY

Most Foreign Students

Around the world, the value of an education at an American institution is taken for granted. International students come to the U.S. to learn expertise in science, mathematics, medicine, management and a wide range of other fields, and take that knowledge back to their own countries for public and private gain. The American school that welcomes the most foreign students is Miami-Dade, the largest community college in the country, and one of the finest. One of the reasons for the large foreign enrollment is that, as a community college, the school has less strict admission standards, so foreign students don't need to master the intricacies of placement tests and admissions policies. Following are the four-year schools at which you're most likely to meet (or even room with) a foreign student. Figures for large schools are for the main campuses.

School	Foreign Student Pop., 1994-95
1. Boston University	4,734
2. University of Southern California	4,259
3. University of Wisconsin	3,964
4. New York University	3,832
5. Ohio State University	3,760
6. University of Texas	3,753
7. Columbia University	3,644
8. Harvard University	3,410
9. University of Pennsylvania	3,168
10. University of Illinois	3,064

Source: *Chronicle of Higher Education*; Information Bank.

COMPUTERS

Most Popular Personal Computers

Compaq is now the top seller of PCs, at least in the fourth quarter of 1996, when total PC sales volume was 7.7 million units. This represents an increase of slightly more than 15 percent over the same period in 1995. However, data indicates that sales performance has become increasingly tied to the particular segments PC vendors have chosen as their focus. Vendors whose focus was first-time consumer PC buyers had particular difficulty. Apple's sales declined on a year-to-year basis. Following are the top-selling computer brands.

Vendor	Unit Sales*	Mkt. Share
1. Compaq	1,080,000	14.0%
2. IBM	740,000	9.6%
3. Packard Bell	655,000	8.5%
4. Dell	617,000	8.0%
5. Gateway 2000	547,000	7.1%
6. Toshiba	530,000	6.9%
7. Hewlett Packard	521,000	6.7%
8. Apple	400,000	5.2%
9. Acer	325,000	4.2%
10. NEC	290,000	3.8%

* fourth quarter, 1996

Source: *Computer Intelligence*, January 1997.

COMPUTERS—SOFTWARE

Most Popular Software Programs

In the computer world, hardware niches and knock-offs abound, but the real creativity is definitely a software affair. The computer age has introduced many new terms to the American lexicon, but none as ubiquitous as "Windows," the leading environment in which users operate a PC. Following are America's bestsellers, the software giants through which the eponymous information of the Information Age continues to flow.

WINDOWS 95 SOFTWARE

Rank/Title/Manufacturer

1. **Microsoft Windows 95**
   (Upgrade)
   Microsoft
2. **Microsoft Flight Simulator**
   Microsoft
3. **Command & Conquer Red Alert**
   Virgin
4. **Madden NFL T97**
   Electronic Arts
5. **Print Shop Deluxe III**
   Broderbund
6. **NASCAR II**
   Sierra On-Line
7. **Where in the World is Carmen Sandiego**
   Broderbund
8. **Print Shop Ensemble III**
   Broderbund
9. **NHL Hockey T97**
   Electronic Arts
10. **Goosebumps**
    Dreamworks Interactive

CD-ROMS

Rank/Title/Manufacturer

1. **Myst**
   Broderbund
2. **Microsoft Flight Simulator**
   Microsoft
3. **Command & Conquer Red Alert**
   Virgin
4. **101 Dalmatians Storybook**
   Disney
5. **Microsoft Windows 95**
   (Upgrade)
   Microsoft

6. **Madden Football T97**
   Electronic Arts
7. **Toy Story Activity Center**
   Disney
8. **Print Shop Deluxe III**
   Broderbund
9. **Barbie Fashion Designer**
   Mattel
10. **Quake**
    Id Software

THE BEST-SELLING COMPUTER GAME of all.

PC GAMES (DOS/WINDOWS)

Rank/Title/Manufacturer

1. **Myst**
   Broderbund
2. **Microsoft Flight Simulator**
   Microsoft
3. **Command & Conquer Red Alert**
   Virgin
4. **Madden Football T97**
   Electronic Arts
5. **Barbie Fashion Designer**
   Mattel
6. **Quake**
   Id Software

7. **NASCAR II**
Sierra On-Line
8. **Duke Nukem 3d**
Formgen
9. **NHL Hockey T97**
Electronic Arts
10. **Monopoly Multimedia**
Hasbro

MACINTOSH GAMES

Rank/Title/Manufacturer

1. **Myst**
Broderbund
2. **Warcraft II**
Davidson
3. **X-Wing**
LucasArts
4. **Links Pro**
Access
5. **Commanche**
Nova Logic
6. **Doom II**
GT Interactive
7. **Monopoly**
Virgin
8. **Command & Conquer**
Virgin
9. **Mac Attack Pack**
Aztech New Media
10. **Top Ten Pack II**
Electronic Arts

BUSINESS SOFTWARE (WINDOWS/WINDOWS 95/NT)

Rank/Title/Manufacturer

1. **Microsoft Windows 95 (Upgrade)**
Microsoft
2. **Norton Antivirus**
Symantec
3. **Viruscan**
McAfee
4. **First Aide Deluxe**
Cybermedia
5. **Corel Word Perfect Suite (Upgrade)**
Corel
6. **Microsoft Plus**
Microsoft
7. **Oil Change**
Cybermedia
8. **Norton Utilities**
Symantec
9. **UnInstaller**
MicroHelp
10. **Netscape Navigator**
Netscape

BUSINESS SOFTWARE (MACINTOSH)

Rank/Title/Manufacturer

1. **Ram Doubler**
Connectix
2. **System 7.x**
Apple
3. **Norton Utilities**
Symantec
4. **Symantec SAM**
Symantec
5. **Netscape Navigator Personal l Edition**
Netscape
6. **Adobe Photoshop (Upgrade)**
Adobe
7. **Dogz**
Virgin
8. **Speed Doubler**
Connectix
9. **Catz**
Virgin
10. **Art Explosion 40,000 Images**
Nova Development

Source: *PC Data*, December 1996.

CONDOMS

The Least Likely to Leak

The condom is not only the oldest artificial form of birth control, but wearing one is also a proven method for preventing sexually transmitted diseases. It's no surprise, then, that today's health concerns have increased their use tremendously. Marketers have taken advantage of this new popularity with offerings that fill the wall of the local pharmacy, but not all are equally effective. A study sought to determine reliability of condoms and tested the leading brands for both the potential for viral leakage and their overall reliability. While nothing is perfect, as shown by the fact that no brand scored 100 points out of the 100 used in the study's weighted scale, the top seven brands showed no HIV leakage.

Make	Score
1. Ramses Sensitol	91.3
Ramses Non-Lube	91.3
3 Gold Circle Coin	85.2
4. Gold Circle	83.7
Sheik Elite	83.7
6. Durex Nuform	81.7
7. Pleaser	80.2
8. Ramses Extra	78.7
9. Embrace Her	77.3
10. Hot Rubber (Switzerland)	77.2

Source: Mariposa Foundation; University of California, Los Angeles; University of Southern California.

CONSUMER SATISFACTION

According to a survey of 50,000 Americans, as a whole they are satisfied with many of the products turned out by workers and management in the electronic, appliance, clothing and prepared food products industries. Dissatisfaction is evident, however, with those in the service sector, the fastest-growing area of the economy. Nondurable manufacturing showed a satisfaction index of 81.6 in a 1994 survey that rated 200 companies in about 40 industries on a scale of zero to

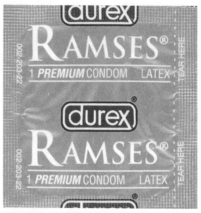

THE TOP-RATED CONDOM, Ramses Sensitol.

100. Durable goods earned a rating of 79.2. Express delivery scored 81 and long-distance phone service 82, the highest in the service sector. Other services, such as hospitals, rated poorly, at a below-average 74.4. The U.S. Postal Service, included in the category of transportation, utilities and communications, rated a score of only 60, lowest in that category. The Internal Revenue Service, included in the public administration group, scored lowest of all in the survey at 55. Second to the service sector was manufacturers of durables such as autos, appliances and computers, which scored 79.2, with appliances receiving the highest score in the sector, at 85. Restaurants and fast-food establishments rated only a 69, compared to 77 for department and discount stores in the retail sector. U.S. companies overall scored a satisfaction rating of 74.5, which survey organizers said was too low to protect U.S. business from foreign competition. Following are index scores of various other products and services rated from zero to 100.

THINGS

NONDURABLES, MOST SATISFYING

Items	Index Score
1. Canned foods	87
Chocolate, confectionaries	87
3. Milk, ice cream	86
4. Baked goods, bread, etc.	84
5. Cereal	83
Beer	83
7. Cold meats, cheese	82
Apparel	82
9. Cigarettes	80
10. Athletic shoes	79

DURABLES, MOST SATISFYING

Items	Index Score
1. Household appliances	85
2. Consumer electronics	83
3. Express delivery	81
4. Local phone service	80
5. Automobiles	79
6. PCs/printers	78
7. Broadcasting/TV	77
8. Electric service	75
Transportation, communications, utilities	75
10. Airlines	72

Source: University of Michigan; the American Society for Quality Control, 1994.

CONTRACEPTIVES

What Works . . . Most of The Time

Just like children, things that prevent conception are not perfect either. Using at least *something* to prevent pregancy, however, can be up to 94 percent effective. Following is an estimate of how confident you can be that the contraceptive of choice will work. The table indicates the type of contraceptive that proved ineffective, as well as the percentage of women who experienced an unintended pregnancy as a result.

Method	Average Use
1. No method (chance)	85.0%
2. Spermicides	30.0%
3. Sponge	24.0%
Withdrawal	24.0%
5. Periodic abstinence	19.0%
6. Cervical cap	18.0%
Diaphragm	18.0%
8. Condom	16.0%
9. Pill	6.0%

And the good news is that there are millions of people who can thank various items in the preceding table for their very existence. Had the contraceptives been more effective, they wouldn't have had the privilege of drawing a breath.

Source: *Facts in Brief*, Alan Guttmacher Institute, 1996.

CONTRACEPTIVES

Most Popular

Sterilization is a drastic step in contraception. Non-reversible, it means the end of the ability to procreate for those who go through with it. Yet voluntary contraceptive sterilization is the most widespread method of birth control among Americans who use contraceptives. The decline of IUD use also contributes to the higher number of women relying on sterilization. Use of the pill, which had declined in the late 1970s for health concerns, has also become more popular, due to its high rate of effectiveness and convenience. Condom use has increased rapidly among teenagers and single women and is the method of choice for the younger set.

Method	Percent Who Use
1. Sterilization	42.1%
2. Pill	28.5%
3. Condom	17.7%
4. Other methods	4.8%
5. Diaphragm	2.8%
6. Periodic abstinence	2.7%
7. IUD	1.4%

Source: *Facts in Brief,* Allan Guttmacher Institute, 1996

CORPORATIONS

Most and Least Admired

What's there to admire about corporations? According to *Fortune* magazine's Corporate Reputations Survey, plenty. Corporate reputations are made by the old standbys: hard work, resourcefulness and tight budgeting. This year, Coca-Cola was the Most Admired corporation, a position they've held for two years running. Some newcomers to the Most Admired list were United Parcel Service, Pfizer and Berkshire Hathaway. Notably absent, however, from this year's list were such bedrock corporations as AT&T and Viacom. With AT&T, the problem is all the new competition due to deregulation. Viacom suffered from some upper level musical chairs. At the bottom, on the Least Admired list were four newcomers: Cal Fed Bancorp, Beverly Enterprises (a health care provider), Flagstar (food service) and Canandaigua Wine. TWA achieved a rather dubious distinction of making the Least Admired list three years straight. Following is the list of Most Admired and Least Admired corporations and their scores.

MOST ADMIRED

Company	Score
1. Coca-Cola	8.87
2. Mirage Resorts	8.44
3. Merck	8.34
4. UPS	8.31
5. Microsoft	8.29
6. Johnson & Johnson	8.27
Intel	8.27
8. Pfizer	8.23
9. Procter & Gamble	8.18
10. Berkshire Hathaway	8.18

LEAST ADMIRED

Company	Score
1. Cal Fed Bancorp	4.44
Amerco	4.44
3. Beverly Enterprises	4.31
4. USAir Group	4.13
5. Flagstar	4.07
6. Morrison Knudsen	4.05
Canandaigua Wine	4.03
8. Kmart	3.82
9. Standard Commercial	3.76
10. TWA	3.42

Source: *Fortune* magazine, March 3, 1997.

CORPORATIONS—ADVERTISING

Top-Spending Advertisers

So you say you change the channel whenever an ad comes on TV? Or maybe you get up to see what's in the refrigerator. If that's true and we're *all* not watching the commercials, then how come so many people can recite ad dialogue verbatim and we find ourselves absent-mindedly humming TV commercial jingles? Face it: Ads are a part of our lives, from yesterday's "Where's the beef?" to Nike's ubiquitous "Just do it" today. Like the Energizer bunny, they just keep coming.

The following are the ten top corporate advertisers today, each of which spent more than $1 billion in 1995. Of the top two, Procter & Gamble produces brands like Ivory, Crest, Cheer, Crisco, and Pampers, while Philip Morris is the tobacco giant that also owns Kraft Foods and Miller Brewing.

Co.	1995 Ad Expenditures (millions)
1. Procter & Gamble	$2,777
2. Philip Morris	$2,577
3. General Motors	$2,047
4. Time Warner	$1,307
5. Walt Disney	$1,296
6. Sears, Roebuck	$1,226
7. Chrysler	$1,222
8. PepsiCo	$1,197
9. Johnson & Johnson	$1,173
10. Ford Motors	$1,149

Source: *Advertising Age.*

CORPORATIONS—BLACK-OWNED

Largest Black-Owned Corporations

Equal opportunity is a stated goal and policy in the business world, and prejudice has been noticed, if not remedied, in our age. But beyond the general economic malaise, black enterprise has still not achieved the economic vigor that a truly equitable social climate would create. The achievement and vision of the most-successful black-owned companies are hardly at issue; what must be addressed is the inability of enough others to emulate their successes. The following are the largest companies in the U.S. with blacks at the helm.

Company	Revenues, 1995 (millions)
1. TLC Beatric International	$2,100.0
2. Johnson Publishing Co.	$316.2
3. Philadelphia Coca Cola Bottling Co.	$315.0
4. H.J. Russell & Co.	$172.8
5. Pulsar Data Systems	$165.1
6. Uniworld Group NY	$133.7
7. Burrell Communications Group	$127.9
8. The Anderson-Dubose Co.	$119.5
Granite Broadcasting Co.	$119.5
10. BET Holdings	$115.0

Source: *Black Enterprise*, June 1996.

CORPORATIONS—DEFENSE CONTRACTORS

Largest U.S. Defense Contractors

With the remarkable potency and efficiency demonstrated by the U.S.'s so-called "smart weapons" in the Gulf War, the public has begun to reassess and forgive the capitalistic excesses of these industrial superpowers. These are the companies that make the missiles, tanks, guns and planes for the Department of Defense which so proved themselves in the sands and skies of Kuwait and Iraq.

Company	D.O.D. Contracts (1,000s)*
1. Lockheed Martin	$10,482,787
2. McDonnell Douglas	$8,020,868
3. Tenneco	$3,709,810
4. General Motors	$2,992,929
5. Northrop-Grumman	$2,913,072
6. Raytheon	$2,890,409
7. General Electric	$2,103,657
8. Loral	$1,967,305
9. Boeing	$1,780,287
10. United Technologies	$1,774,835

* figures are for 1995

Source: Department of Defense.

THINGS

C ORPORATIONS— INDUSTRIAL

Largest American Industrial Enterprises

No single event or resource catapulted America to its current hegemony in world affairs, but it is obvious that our nation's industrial might was fundamental in our emergence from colonial obscurity. The shape of American business grows and recedes in staggered response to the movement of the world and the economic health of the nation, but in the end, few players have entered or left the high stakes industrial game since the resolution of the first World War. The biggest disappearing act has occurred among meat-packing companies, such as Swift and Armour, who used to hold several of the top 10 spots as late as the 1950s, before yielding to the oil, automotive and conglomerate monoliths that dominate the American business scene today.

Largest American Industrial Enterprises

Company	Sales, 1996 (millions)
1. General Motors	$164,069
2. Ford	$146,991
3. Exxon	$134,357
4. Wal-Mart	$93,627
5. Mobil	$80,782
6. General Electric	$79,179
7. IBM	$75,947
8. Philip Morris	$69,204
9. Chrysler	$61,400
10. AT&T	$52,184

Source: Hoover Business Resources, 1997.

C ORPORATIONS— MARKET VALUE

Most Valuable Companies in U.S.

The market value of a company is the product of the share price of its stock multiplied by the number of outstanding shares. As recently as 1990, IBM was the nation's most valuable company, worth almost $75 billion. Years later, not only has its value fallen, its rank slipped to fifth. General Electric, which had a value of $58 billion in 1990, soared to number one and increased in value more than two-fold. Following is the list of the top 10 most valuable companies, a veritable stable of the warhorses of American business.

Company	Market Value (millions)
1. General Electric	$126,523
2. Coca-Cola	$101,280
3. AT&T	$98,122
4. Exxon	$98,093
5. Philip Morris	$76,613
6. Merck	$76,496
7. IBM	$68,257
8. Johnson & Johnson	$62,629
9. Microsoft	$60,811
10. Procter & Gamble	$57,058

Source: *Fortune* magazine, 1997.

C ORPORATIONS— MEDIA COMPANIES

Is Biggest Best?

One of the most alarming trends in recent years is the merger of the giant media conglomerates. Many observers contend that the fewer companies that get us our information, the less reliable it will be. They argue that competition motivates reporters or news directors to get scoops. With the consolidation of

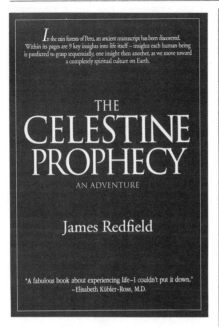

In the rain forests of Peru, an ancient manuscript has been discovered. Within its pages are 9 key insights into life itself – insights each human being is predicted to grasp sequentially, one insight then another, as we move toward a completely spiritual culture on Earth.

THE

CELESTINE PROPHECY

AN ADVENTURE

James Redfield

"A fabulous book about experiencing life–I couldn't put it down."
–Elisabeth Kübler-Ross, M.D.

JAMES REDFIELD'S BOOK (see page 223) is no ordinary bestseller. Its run of 48 weeks on *Publisher's Weekly*'s Bestseller List makes it the longest-running bestseller of all time.

the media, it's likely there will fewer incentives to get to the underlying truth. Time, Inc. and Warner Cable Company started the consolidation of major U.S. media in the early 1990s. The trend escalated in 1995 when two blockbuster announcements were made within a few months of each other. First, Disney announced it was buying the ABC Television Network for $19 billion. Shortly afterward, Westinghouse announced it was buying the troubled CBS Network. Hence, within a three month period, two of the three major television networks were swallowed by larger corporate scavengers. The remaining broadcast network, NBC, had already been taken over by General Electric

years before. Following are the largest media companies in the U.S.

Company	Revenue, 1995 (millions)
1. Time Warner	$9,884.7
2. Disney Capital Cities/ABC	$7,391.5
3. Tele-Communications Inc.	$5,118.0
4. CBS	$4,318.3
5. Gannett Co.	$3,998.7
6. NBC TV	$3,919.0
7. Advance Publications	$3,217.0
8. News Corp.	$2,945.0
9. Cox Enterprises	$2,749.8
10. Hearst Corp.	$2,513.0

Source: *Advertising Age*, Ad Age Dataplace, 1996.

CORPORATIONS— PRIVATE

Largest Privately-held Companies in the U.S.

The American dream is fueled in large part by the stock market— its ups and downs are followed assiduously by rapt investors both big and small, watching the fortunes of their stocks wax and wane with every flutter of the economy or of world politics. But some business people prefer not to place the fortunes of their enterprises at risk in this arena. The stories of the largest privately held companies—those which do not trade their stocks on the open market—run the gamut. Following are the most lucrative companies in the pantheon of private ownership.

Company	Sales, 1995 (millions)*
1. Cargill	$51,200
2. Koch Industries	$25,200
3. United Parcel Service	$19,576
4. Continental Grain	$13,500
5. Mars	$13,000
6. Goldman Sachs Group	$10,910
7. Publix Super Markets	$8,665

8. Arthur Andersen & Co. $8,134
9. Ingram Industries $8,000
10. Bechtel Group $7,885

* figures for 1996

Source: *Forbes*, 1996.

CORPORATIONS— RESEARCH AND DEVELOPMENT

Most Spent on R&D

Chemical and pharmaceutical companies lead the world in spending on research and development. Less than a decade ago, automobile manufacturers and high-tech companies took the honor. The change is a result of drug research costs going up, and digital technology expenses going down.

Company	1997 (millions)*
1. DuPont	$990
2. Dow Chemical	$770
3. Bayer Corp.	$600
4. PPG Industries	$265
5. Dow Corning	$206
6. Rohm and Haas	$200
7. Eastman Chemical	$185
8. Hoechst Celanese	$179
9. Union Carbide	$168
10. BOC Group	$150

* funds budgeted

Source: *Chemical Week*, March 27, 1996.

CORPORATIONS— RESEARCH AND DEVELOPMENT

Spending on R&D as a Percent of Sales

The commitment to research and development should not be measured solely, or even primarily, by sheer dollar amounts spent. Indeed, a better measure of a company's efforts in the R&D arena is by the percentage of sales it pours into development of new products and ideas. The following measure of R&D commitment takes R&D spending as a percentage of sales.

Company	R&D Percent of Sales
1. Dow Corning	7.9%
2. Bayer Corp	6.9%
3. Rohm and Haas	5.0%
4. Dow Chemical	3.9%
5. Eastman Chemical	3.4%
6. Hoechst Celanese	2.5%
BOC Group	2.5%
8. DuPont	NA
PPG Industries	NA
Union Carbide	NA

NA: Not Available

Source: *Chemical Week*, March 27, 1996.

CORPORATIONS— RESEARCH AND DEVELOPMENT

Top European R&D Spenders

The big drive to unify Europe economically is creating a behemoth America and Japan cannot take lightly. In addition, the new political structure of Eastern Europe has opened up additional resources, from scientific research down to raw materials and manpower for the continental powerhouse. In France, for example, the government has stated a commitment to raise R&D spending to three percent of the GNP; in Scandinavia, companies are teaming up with others from foreign countries to perform joint research and development of all kinds. All over Europe, a new confidence in the business climate is sparking renewed interest in high-tech research and newfangled products, the better to compete with the established leaders, the U.S. and Japan. The following are the European companies with the biggest spending on research and development.

Company	R&D Spending (millions)
1. Hoechst*	$2,349
2. Bayer**	$2,206
3. BASF	$1,478
4. Rhone-Poulenc**	$1,398
5. ICI	$375
6. Elf Atochem	$294
7. Henkel	$250
8. Montell Technology	$100
9. Degussa	$71
10. Borealis	$61

* 57 percent of spending is on pharmaceuticals and health R&D
** includes pharmaceutical R&D

Source: *Chemical Week*, March, 1996.

CORPORATIONS— SOCIAL RESPONSIBILITY

Who's Good for Humankind?

Someone is keeping tabs on how good the nation's corporations are at being socially responsibile. Almost 200 companies were rated by various criteria for possible inclusion in the "consumer honor roll," an unofficial designation of the Council on Economic Priorities. The eight major areas of social responsibility that were rated were: corporate stewardship of the environment, opportunities for minorities, opportunities for women, workplace issues, family benefits, community outreach, charitable giving and corporate disclosure. Below is an alphabetical listing of the top-20 rated companies.

Company
Adolph Coors
Anheuser-Busch
Aveda Corp.
Avon Products
Ben & Jerry's
Colgate-Palmolive
General Mills
Giant Food
Grand-Metropolitan PLC
Hewlett-Packard
Johnson & Johnson
S.C. Johnson & Son
Kellogg Co.
Levi Strauss & Co.
Nordstrom, Inc.
Rhino Records
Tom's of Maine
Warner-Lambert

Source: *Shopping for a Better Environment* (Sierra Club Books).

CREDIT CARDS

Most Popular Credit Cards

Americans love their credit cards. The amount of our indebtedness has been steadily increasing since World War II, and really speeding up since the late 1970s. Our total indebtedness has gone from $302 billion in 1980 to $925 billion in 1994. Much of this is due to the credit card. These handy pieces of plastic have been a boon to the banks who issue them. If you put your money in a bank to hold, they'll give you maybe five or six percent interest. But if you borrow money from that same bank's credit card, they'll charge you about nine percent over prime. Back in the early 1980s, when interest rates were high, credit card rates were over 20 percent. In medieval times that was considered usury.

Card	% Population with Card, 1995
1. VISA	35.5%
2. MasterCard	23.2%
3. Gasoline credit card	23.0%

4. VISA Gold	20.6%
5. Discover	17.5%
6. MasterCard Gold	16.4%
7. ATT Universal card	11.2%
8. American Express Green	7.3%
9. American Express Gold/ Platinum	4.5%
10. Optima	2.3%

Source: USA DATA, 1995.

CRIMES

Most Frequent in U.S.

There is, it is said, nothing new under the sun, and that adage applies particularly to criminal misdeeds. One may invent many things, but very few of us, it seems, have dreamt up new vices. Thus, it is not surprising that the most commonly perpetrated crimes are those which involve a direct monetary motive, i.e., larceny and burglary. We've left minor transgressions off the list, such as speeding and pulling the tags off of pillows and mattresses.

Offense	Rate of Incidence, 1995
1. Larceny-Theft	every 4 seconds
2. Burglary	every 12 seconds
3. Motor Vehicle Theft	every 21 seconds
4. Aggravated Assault	every 29 seconds
5. Robbery	every 54 seconds
6. Forcible Rape	every 5 minutes
7. Murder	every 24 minutes

Source: FBI Uniform Crime Reports, 1996.

CRIMES

Costliest Criminal Acts

For every loss there's a gain. Here, the criminal wins, you lose. Beside the obvious loss of property, money or life, there is always an unquanti-

fiable emotional cost to any serious criminal misdeed. As we move into another era of recession and deprivation, we can expect that the magnitude and frequency of money-motivated criminal acts will increase. We can only hope that the cost of these misdeeds does not extend further to human health and happiness. The resurgence of the concept of "victims' rights" may do something to redress some of the loss, both economic and psychological, involved in the perpetration of crimes. We all know that crime doesn't pay, but here are the highest-paying crimes, in any case.

Crime	Average Associated Loss
1. Motor vehicle theft	$5,129
2. Robbery-bank	$4,015
3. Misc. nonresidence burglary	$1,546
4. Daytime nonresidence burglary	$1,515
5. Robbery-commercial house	$1,351
6. Daytime residence burglary	$1,314
7. Larceny-Theft, over $200	$1,307
8. Misc. residence burglary	$1,275
9. Burglary-nonresidence	$1,257
10. Burglary-residence (dwelling)	$1,211

Source: FBI, *Crime in the United States*, 1996; Offense Analysis, 1995.

CRIMES

Most Popular Infractions

In high school, there are popular girls and popular boys; so too, there are popular crimes among felons. Although the property-related crimes of theft and larceny are still the most common felonious offenses, criminal acts involving substance abuse (and its resultant diminished states) are becoming increasingly common. D.U.I., drug possession, drunkenness and disorderly conduct are all among the nation's 10 most frequent violations.

Offense	Arrests, 1995
1. Larceny-theft	1,530,200
2. Drug abuse violations	1,476,100
3. Driving under the influence	1,436,000
4. Other assaults	1,290,400
5. Disorderly conduct	748,600
6. Drunkenness	708,100
7. Liquor laws	594,900
8. Aggravated assault	568,480
9. Fraud	436,400
10. Burglary	386,500

Source: FBI Uniform Crime Reports, 1996.

CRIMES

Most Popular White-Collar Infractions

In the wake of Whitewater, America has become a nation obsessed—some even say infatuated—with whitecollar criminals. The clever machinations of the three-piece-suit set seldom fail to titillate and provoke. The McDougals, Boeskys and Milkens of this world are at once admired and despised for the sheer size of the dollar amounts involved in their crimes. The results of such ambivalence, more often than not, are spells in some of the more luxurious of federal facilities. Of the white-collar offenses tried in our federal courts, acts of common fraud are most frequent. Forgery and embezzlement, too, are perennial favorites, collectively resulting in almost 4,000 convictions each

year. These, then, are the most popular white-collar crimes in the country.

Federal Offense	Convictions per Year
1. Bank fraud and embezzlement	2,511
2. Other fraud	1,105
3. Tax fraud	977
4. Federal program fraud	781
5. Against business institutions	601
6. Insurance fraud	328
7. Health care fraud	254
8. Consumer fraud	234
9. Advance fee scheme	170
10. Federal procurement fraud	166

Source: U.S. Department of Justice, Executive Office for U.S. State's Attorneys, United States Attorneys' Offices Statistical Report: Fiscal Year 1995.

CRIMES

Average Prison Sentences

Despite the fact that most convicted drug traffickers are small-time criminals, not higher-ups in the Colombian drug cartel, they are surprisingly high in the rankings of prison sentences, a reflection, perhaps, of society's growing intolerance of narcotics. In this era of pragmatically necessitated leniency (through parole, dismissal, probation and work-release), judge and jury are forced to hand down almost comically severe, lengthy terms, in order to ensure that a truly desperate offender is not rotated back into the community. America's will to punish the hardened criminal is increasing, but the concomitant funds for newer, bigger prisons and workers to service those institutions are not forthcoming. Following are average prison sentences for various crimes.

Offense	Average Sentence (months)
1. Murder	253.2
2. Kidnapping, hostage-taking	183.3
3. Robbery	108.5
4. Drug trafficking	89.7
5. Racketeering, extortion	83.6
6. Sexual abuse	81.4
7. Firearms	80.3
8. Arson	58.7
9. Assault	55.2
10. Manslaughter	45.7

Source: U.S. Sentencing Commission, Annual Report, 1995.

EATH

Most Common Causes

If danger is measured by the number of mortal occurrences, hospitals must certainly be the centers of peril. As late as 1960, most people died at home; in these days of over-institutionalization, 80 percent of all deaths occur in a medical facility or nursing home. The message, unenforceable though it may be, remains, DON'T GET SICK. Diet and exercise can seriously lessen the chances of succumbing to heart disease, the number-one killer in the U.S. Malignant neoplasms—cancer—are the number two killer, and life-style changes can also mitigate the threats from this scourge.

Cause	Deaths per 100,000 Pop., 1995
1. Heart diseases	738,781
2. Malignant neoplasms	537,969
3. Cerebrovascular diseases	158,061
4. Chronic Obstructive Pulmonary disease	104,756
5. Accidents and adverse effects	89,703

ALMOST TEN-TIMES MORE TRAFFIC DEATHS are related to cars than motorcycles, but vehicle-for-vehicle, the motorcycle is the most dangerous mode of transportation on the road.

6. Pneumonia and Influenza	83,528
7. Diabetes Mellitus	59,085
8. Human Immunodeficiency Virus infection	42,506
9. Suicide	30,893
10. Chronic liver disease and cirrhosis	24,848

Source: National Center for Health Statistics, 1995.

DEATH

Transportation-Related Calamities

Transportation-related deaths are on the rise. In 1996 there were two major plane crashes, killing over 300 people, and there is an epidemic of rail crashes that killed pedestrians, motorists and passengers. Those who want to play it safe may opt to take the bus. According to the book *What the Odds Are*, the probability of getting killed on your next bus trip is an incredible one in 500 million. Following are figures on transportation fatalities.

THINGS

Type	Fatalities, 1993
1. Passenger cars	21,494
2. Light trucks, vans	8,487
3. Pedestrians (by cars)	5,638
4. Motorcycles	2,444
5. Pedalcycles	814
6. Recreational boating	800
7. Medium, heavy trucks	610
8. Private planes	715
9. Pedestrians (by trains)	610
10. Passengers (rail)	58

Source. National Transportation Safety Board.

DICKENS NOVELS

The Greatest of Them All

If you don't know what the word "Dickensian" means, check out this rating. According to our ranking of novelists (see "WRITERS" on page 64), Charles Dickens is the fourth greatest of all time. He was also one of the most prolific writers of his generation. So, if you haven't yet enjoyed the pleasures of a Dickens novel, here are the most important ones, rated by the amount of scholarly research that has been

WORLD'S DUMBEST DOG? If basset hounds could read, they'd probably think so.

done on each one, as indicated in the MLA International database.

Novel	Score
1. *Bleak House*	140
2. *Great Expectations*	83
3. *David Copperfield*	81
4. *Our Mutual Friend*	48
5. *Oliver Twist*	43
6. *Little Dorritt*	42
7. *A Tale of Two Cities*	41
8. *The Pickwick Papers*	38
9. *Hard Times*	36
10. *The Mystery of Edwin Drood*	34

Source: "Best and Worst" original.

DOGS

The Smartest and Dumbest Breeds

Dog trainer and psychology professor Stanley Coren polled 100 dog obedience judges for their opinions of the intelligence of specific breeds. The list does give a good indication of the relative intelligence of dogs, but it's a better measure of how well a dog can please its owner based on its work or obedience. Simply put, it's a rating of what you can teach a dog to do to make you happy. But purebred dogs are bred for specific, sometimes single qualities, where intelligence is secondary, if it matters at all. The Afghan Hound, for example, is the super model of canines, but finished dead last in the rankings. Then there's the question of just what work you want the dog to do. The Bloodhound finished number 74 out of 79, but its ability to track scents is legendary. Greyhounds, ranked at 46, run like the wind. But neither breed, according to this list, would seem good for much else.

Still, if it's overall trainability you're looking for, you can't go wrong using these rankings as your guide. Following is a ranking of Coren's pertaining to the intelligence of dog breeds.

SMARTEST DOGS

Rank/Breed

1. Border Collie
2. Poodle
3. German Shepherd
4. Golden Retriever
5. Doberman Pinscher
6. Shetland Sheepdog
7. Labrador Retriever
8. Papillon
9. Rottweiler
10. Australian Cattle Dog

DUMBEST DOGS*

Rank/Breed

1. Basset Hound
2. Mastiff
3. Beagle
4. Pekingese
5. Bloodhound
6. Borzoi
7. Chow Chow
8. Bulldog
9. Basenji
10. Afghan Hound

> * list is in order of "lack of intelligence" (Afghan is the "dumbest" breed); overall 122 breeds were measured; above are the bottom 10 of all 122

Source: *The Intelligence of Dogs*, by Stanley Coren, 1994.

DOGS

Most Popular Pure-Bred Dogs

Mutts are cute, cuddlesome and lovable, but pure breeds are where it's

THESE BORDER COLLIE PUPS aren't yet smart enough to know they're not allowed on the couch. Once full-grown, however, border collies are the smartest among all breeds.

at for today's credibility-conscious canine customer. In recent years, the affable Cocker Spaniel, at number one, has been a particular favorite, while the oft-underfoot poodle has held its furry-own in the number-three spot. The following are the most popular pure-bred dogs, as measured by the number of dogs registered with the American Kennel Club.

Breed	Dogs Registered, 1995
1. Labrador Retriever	132,051
2. Rottweiler	103,656
3. German Shepherd	78,088
4. Golden Retriever	64,107
5. Beagle	57,063
6. Poodle	54,784
7. Cocker Spaniel	48,065
8. Dachshund	44,680
9. Pomeranian	37,894
10. Yorkshire Terrier	36,881

Source: American Kennel Club.

THINGS

DRUGS— LEGAL

Most Popular Over-the-Counter Drugs

Pain-relief medications are big business, and number one at the cash register is Tylenol, which made an astonishingly quick comeback into the nation's medicine chest after the product-tampering incident of a few years back. Americans, it seems, are prone to headaches. Perhaps it is the anxiety of our lives, or the unacceptably high noise levels in our cities. Whatever the cause, we want relief, and we find it, most often, at the counter of the local mart, pharmacy or convenience store. Americans plunked down more than half a billion dollars for Tylenol, a Johnson & Johnson brand of the pain-reliever acetomeniphen. Added evidence of our nation's stressed-out, gluttonous tendencies can be found in the non-pain relief medications on the list such as Pepcid AC and Tums.

Product	Total Sales (millions)
1. Tylenol (analgesics)	$808.0
2. Private label (analgesics)	$600.5
3. Private label (cough/cold, allergy, sinus medication)	$519.8
4. Advil	$340.3
5. Pepcid AC	$254.1
6. Tylenol (cough/cold, allergy, sinus)	$243.3
7. Robitussin	$225.6
8. Excedrin	$179.6
9. Tums	$159.6
10. Benadryl	$158.6

Source: *Brandweek*, Superbrands '97, October 7, 1996.

DRUGS— RECREATIONAL

Most Popular Among High School Seniors

Although the 1980s were marked by the re-emergence of traditional (even conservative) values among our youth, abuse of legal and illegal recreational drugs remains a problem of monumental proportions. Nearly eight out of 10 American high school seniors reported use of alcohol. Nearly one in two has consumed marijuana or hashish. The following are the drugs of preference for "high" schoolers, in the percentage of seniors who have admitted consuming particular substances within the two months prior to the survey.

Substance	Percent Who Have Used
1. Alcohol	79.2%
2. Cigarettes	63.5%
3. Any illicit drug	50.8%
4. Marijuana/hashish	44.9%
5. Smokeless tobacco	29.8%
6. Any illicit drug other than marijuana	28.5%
7. Inhalants	16.6%
8. Stimulants	15.3%
9. Hallucinogens	14.0%
10. LSD	12.6%

Source: University of Michigan, Monitoring The Future, a 1996 study.

EMERGENCY ROOM VISITS

Most Ailments Treated

At one time, automobile crashes, fires or natural catastrophes would be the events that would bring the crowds into the emergency rooms of local hospitals. But for the past

15 years or so, more and more people are forced to use emergency room services as their primary means of health care. Without insurance, or a relationship with a local doctor, they are forced to turn to the emergency room as a first line of defense. But no matter what the reason, emergency room visits are quite intense—and democratic. Below is a list of the most common reasons for seeking help. By far, the winner is the bane of most children facing a tough exam—the stomach ache. That's followed by the bane of most middle-aged men—chest pain.

Aliment	Number Treated (1,000s)
1. Stomach and abdominal pain cramps and spasms	5,256
2. Chest pain and related symptoms	4,435
3. Fever	4,281
4. Headache, pain in head	2,530
5. Injury in upper-extremity	2,380
6. Back symptoms	2,205
7. Symptoms referable to throat	2,038
8. Vomiting	1,903
9. Earache or ear infection	1,845
10. Pain not referable to a specific body system	1,827

Source: National Center for Health Statistics; U.S. Department of Health and Human Services, 1996.

ENCYCLOPEDIAS

Wordiest Encyclopedias

The heyday of the door-to-door encyclopedia salesman is well- past, but the days of hard sell in that field are not. Each publication offers a dizzying array of premiums, alternative configurations and nebulous claims. On the theory that the best value is the biggest book, here are the word counts for the fattest of the shelf hogs. Tops on the list is the Encyclopedia Britannica, with an amazing 44 million words spread among its three dozen volumes.

Encyc.	Length in Words (millions)
1. New Encyclopedia Britannica	44.0
2. Encyclopedia Americana	30.8
3. Colliers Encyclopedia	21.0
4. World Book Encyclopedia	10.0
5. Academic American Encyclopedia	9.1
6. Funk and Wagnall's New Encyclopedia	9.0
Compton's Encyclopedia	9.0
8. Standard Encyclopedia	8.0

Source: *Kister's Best Encyclopedias*.

ENTERTAINMENT

Most Popular Events

What we will buy tickets for says a lot about our times. For example, boxing has diminished from its heyday, when Gillette brought a slate of boxing matches directly into the living room every Friday night, via the old black-and-white television. Times have changed. We are more aware of the brutal nature of a sport whose primary aim is to hurt and maim the opponent. Perhaps that's why boxing matches no longer appear weekly—or for free— on network television during prime time. Today they are now dressed-up and hyped up so that a boxing match bears little resemblance to the simple free event seen on television 40 years ago. Perhaps because of their relative rarity, boxing matches can be expensive. Three out of the top 10 grossing events of 1996 were boxing matches. And they featured

THINGS

the same boxer, Mike Tyson, who was making his comeback after serving a stretch in prison for rape. From prison to a $7 million paycheck for a one-night stand isn't exactly typical of how cons emerge from the slammer.

Event/Venue Gross Ticket Sales, 1996

1. **Radio City Christmas Spectacular**   **41,190,039**
Radio City Music Hall, New York City, November 18, 1995-January 7, 1996.

2. **Beauty and the Beast**   **14,669,529**
Opera House, John F. Kennedy Center, Washington DC, June 1—September 29, 1996.

3. **Tyson vs. Holyfield Boxing Event**   **14,150,700**
MGM Grand Garden, Las Vegas, November 1996.

4. **Tyson vs. Bruno Boxing Event**   **10,238,680**
MGM Grand Garden, Las Vegas, March 16, 1996.

5. **Riverdance**   **7,289,125**
Radio City Music Hall, New York City, October 2- 20, 1996.

6. **Phantom of the Opera**   **6,415,592**
Chrysler Hall, Norfolk, VA, November 23, 1995-January 6, 1996.

7. **Seldon vs. Tyson Boxing Event**   **6,305,900**
MGM Grand Garden, Las Vegas, September 6, 1996.

8. **Miss Saigon**   **6,113,863**
Festival Hall, Tampa Bay Performing Arts Center, Tampa, January 11—February,24, 1996.

9. **Beauty & the Beast**   **5,680,184**
Fox Theatre, Atlanta, October 4-November 10, 1996.

MOST POPULAR ENTERTAINMENT EVENT OF ALL, the Radio City Christmas Spectacular at Radio City Musical Hall in New York City.

10. National Finals Rodeo   **4,400,000**
Thomas & Mack Center, University of Nevada, Las Vegas, December 1-10, 1995.
Source: *Amusement Business*, December 16, 1996.

FAST FOODS

Healthiest

The typical fast-food meal of which Americans are so fond— burgers, fries, a soft drink—ranks extremely low in overall nutritional value, primarily because of the fat, cholesterol and salt content. Of course, the convenience of such meals, not their nutritional value, is what makes them popular. But even if you're on the run, there are some healthy alternatives to the burgers-and-soda staple. Most fast-food joints now offer salads and other healthy options. The rankings of nutritional value here are based on the nutripoint system developed by Dr. Roy Vartebedian and Kathy Matthews. For a complete description of their methodology, see the source.

The Top 10 Foods	Nutripoints
1. Wendy's Chef Salad	6.0
2. McDonald's Salad Oriental	5.0
3. Wendy's Hot Stuffed Potato	4.5
4. Roy Rogers Hot-topped Potato	4.0
5. Pizza Hut Supreme Pizza	3.5
6. P.H. Cheese Thin 'n' Crispy	3.0
Pizza Hut Pepperoni Pan	3.0
8. Pizza Hut Cheese Pan	2.5
9. Various Pizza Hut Pizzas	2.0

Source: *Nutripoints: The Breakthrough Point System for Optimum Nutrition*, Roy E. Vartabedian & Kathy Matthews (Harper & Row, 1990).

FAST FOODS

Most Fat in Fast Food Breakfasts

Fast food is not the unmixed bag of chemicals and bio-toxins that some suspect. Nor, however, is it the on-balance best nutritional alternative open to most of us. One of the biggest culprits in the American diet is fat, which, in fast foods, is almost everywhere. The thorns in the nutritional forest are many; tread softly over these morning munchables.

Breakfast	Gram of Fat per Serving
1. Burger King Croisan'wich w/Sausage	40
2. McDonald's Biscuit w/Sausage and Egg	35
3. Hardee's Sausage and Egg Biscuit	35
4. Burger King French Toast Sticks	29
5. Roy Rogers Crescent with Sausage	29
6. Jack in the Box Pancake Platter	22
7. McDonald's Egg McMuffin	12
8. Roy Rogers Apple Danish	12
9. McDonald's Hot Cakes with butter and syrup	9
10. McDonald's English Muffin with butter	5

Source: Mayo Clinic Nutrition Letter.

FAST FOOD CHAINS

Top Burger Joints

For every burger Burger King sells, McDonald's sells almost two. American chopped beef transcends socio-economic structures; it crosses ethnic borders and traverses

SZECHUAN SHRIMP, the Chinese dish with lowest percent of calories from fat.

geographic boundaries. More than pizza, chop suey or apple pie, the hamburger binds this great country together. Iowa farm boys chomp on burgers while driving in their pick-ups. Sophisticated New Yorkers lunch over burgers. Hollywood movie executives eat burgers with avocados. Following are the top places Americans get their burgers.

Chain	U.S. Sales, 1995 (millions)
1. McDonald's	$15,905.0
2. Burger King	$8,400.0
3. Wendy's	$4,600.0
4. Jack in the Box	$1,123.6
5. Sonic Drive-In	$880.5
6. Carl's Jr.	$569.2
7. Checker Drive-In	$373.6
8. Whataburger	$362.3
9. Rally's Hamburgers	$360.0
10. White Castle	$325.7

Source: *Nation's Restaurants.*

FAST FOOD CHAINS

Where Chickens Rule

We may be the "home of the brave," but Americans love a good chicken. We take it on picnics and bring it to ball games. We eat it at family gatherings and meetings. As the Colonel says, "It's finger lickin' good." Following is where you'll find more chickens than almost anywhere.

Chain	U.S. Sales, 1995 (millions)
1. Kentucky Fried Chicken	$3,700.0
2. Boston Market	$792.0
3. Popeye's Famous Fried Chicken	$656.0
4. Chick-fil-A	$501.6
5. Church's Chicken	$501.0
6. Kenny Rogers Roasters	$275.0

Source: *Nation's Restaurant News*, April 29, 1996.

FOOD

Chinese Foods, Most and Least Fattening

Just when you thought it was safe, that seemingly "healthiest of fast food," Chinese, is under scrutiny. The following dishes were ordered from Chinese take-out restaurants in Washington, DC, Chicago and San Francisco, sent to an independent lab and analyzed under the auspices of the Center for Science in the Public Interest. The Center suggests: If you're not very hungry, you'll do fine with 1 cup of soup or a single egg roll; however, going for a filling meal, such as Kung Pao Chicken, will give you more fat than you should consume during a whole day! According to the Center, a suggestion for the health conscious is to add lots of rice to each meal (increasing the amount of food consumed while reducing the fat percentage) and go for anything "steamed" rather than fried! Following are some of the most popular Chinese dishes ranked by fat content, from least to most.

FAT CONTENT

Dish/(Number of cups)	Grams of Fat
1. Hot & sour soup (1)	4
2. Egg roll (1)	11
3. Szechuan Shrimp (4)	19
4. Stir-fried vegetables (4)	19
5. Shrimp w/garlic sauce (3)	27
6. Hunan tofu (4)	28
7. Chicken Chow Mein (5)	32
8. House Lo Mein (5)	36
9. Beef w/broccoli (4)	46
10. House fried rice (4)	50
11. Gen. Tso's Chicken (5)	59
12. Moo Shu Pork (4)	64
13. Orange (Crispy) beef (4)	66
14. Sweet & sour pork (4)	71
15. Kung Pao Chicken (5)	76

For the "calorie counter," here is another assessment of the calories you add from consuming the following dishes. The calories were calculated based on one cup of the named dish combined with one cup of steamed rice.

CALORIES/FAT CONTENT

Following is a ranking by percent of calories from fat, from the least to most:

Dish (2 Cups)	Cal's	% from Fat
1. Szechuan Shrimp	509	14%
2. Stir-fried vegetables	400	14%
3. House Lo Mein	497	15%
4. House fried rice	605	18%
5. Chicken Chow Mein	450	18%
6. Hunan tofu	454	19%
7. Shrimp w/garlic sauce	552	21%
8. General Tso's Chicken	657	25%
9. Beef w/broccoli	563	26%
10. Orange (Crispy) beef	724	27%
11. Kung Pao Chicken	653	32%
12. Sweet & sour pork	827	34%
13. Moo Shu Pork	574	35%

Source: Nutrition Action Healthletter, September 1994.

FOOD

Highest in Fiber

Long before advertising firms began capitalizing on a renewed interest in what was once called roughage, people recognized the contributions of fruit, vegetables and grains for promoting healthy digestion. Hence, the salad. Nutritionists have only recently begun to study the effects of this "non-nutritive substance," and the results are preliminary. However, studies indicate that a fiber-rich diet may help to ameliorate afflictions ranging from constipation, hemorrhoids and irritable bowel syndrome to colon cancer, gallstones and diabetes. On the other hand, some high-fiber diets (like those found among villagers in Uganda) have been found coincident with zinc deficiency, sigmoid volvulus and esophageal cancer. It is estimated that the average American consumes no more than 20 grams of fiber per day; for a strict vegetarian, that number approaches 60. At this time, there is no daily recommended allowance, but the National Cancer Insitute has suggested 25 to 35 grams daily. The figures cited below have been adjusted to reflect a single serving.

Food	Fiber (grams per serving)
1. Pumpkin/squash seeds	25.5
2. Elderberries (raw)	25.2
3. Walnuts (black, dried)	20.2

4. Peanuts (oil-roasted)   19.2
5. Chia seeds (dried)   18.0
6. Chirimoya   15.3
7. Winged bean tuber (raw)   14.8
8. Kellogg's All-Bran,
   Extra Fiber   13.0
9. Winged beans (raw)   12.5
10. Arrowhead Mills Bran
    cereal   12.2

Source: *Food Values: Fiber* (Harper & Row).

NEED POTASSIUM? Here's the best source. Need calories? The potato, even a plain, undressed one, is the highest of all vegetables in caloric content (See page 316).

(See page 316).

FOOD

Highest in Potassium

The Food and Drug Administration has not set a recommended daily allowance for potassium, although it is recognized as an essential part of a diet. Dr. Roy Vartebedian and Kathy Matthews, in their book *Nutripoints*, have used guidelines from the National Research Council to establish a level of about 5,600 milligrams of potassium daily in a healthy diet. One of the best places to get that nutrient is the potato, which has about twice as much dietary potassium as the banana, a common source of potassium. Below we have listed the amount of potassium, in milligrams, for the top 10 foods in this category. Amounts are based on a normal serving.

Food	Potassium (mg per serving)
1. Potato	844
2. Cantaloupe	825
3. Prune juice	706
4. Avocado	602
5. Watermelon	559
6. Raisins	545
7. Dates	541
8. Tomato juice	536
9. Apricots	482
10. Orange juice	473

Source: Human Nutritional Information Service, U.S. Department of Agriculture.

FOOD

Most and Least Nutritious

The nation's increased health-consciousness means more people are checking the nutritional value of the foods they eat. Food companies have begun advertising their fiber content, cholesterol levels and other important nutritional information. But until recently, no one had ranked the *overall* nutritional value of various foods. In *Nutripoints*, Dr. Roy E. Vartebedian and Kathy Matthews do just that. The Nutripoints food ratings assign a point for a comparable, standard portion of each of over 3,000 foods. Positive points are awarded for Essentials—complex carbohydrates, protein, dietary fiber (weighted twice), vitamins and minerals. Negative points are assigned for Excessives: total fat, saturated fat, calories, sodium, sugar, caffeine, cholesterol and alcohol, with the latter two weighted three times negatively. (For the exact formula, see the source). The most nutritious foods overall are leafy green vegetables and fortified breakfast cereals. Seafood rated higher than meats and poultry. Junk foods, it turns out, are just that: most snack foods earned negative nutripoints. So dig into your turnip greens, but for heaven's sake, stay away from those sweetbreads!

HEALTHIEST

Food Item	Nutripoints
1. Turnip greens	79.0
2. Raw chopped spinach	75.0
3. Bok choy	72.5
4. Total whole wheat cereal	64.5
5. Cooked mustard greens	62.0
6. Total corn flakes cereal	57.5
7. Cooked beet greens	56.5
8. Product 19 cereal	56.0
9. Parsley (fresh)	54.5
10. Raw broccoli	53.0

UNHEALTHIEST

Food Item	Nutripoints
1. Sweetbreads	-52.0
2. Scrambled eggs	-13.5
3. Caviar	-11.5
4. Little Debbie Snack Cake	-8.5
5. Gatorade	-8.0
6. Lipton Iced Tea	-7.5
7. Salted butter	-7.5
8. Coconut oil	-7.0
9. Heavy cream	-7.0
10. Soft drink, w/caffeine	-7.0

Source: *Nutripoints*, Dr. Roy E. Vartebedian and Kathy Matthews.

FOOTBALL— COLLEGE TEAMS

Greatest College Football Teams of All Time

The vagaries of the national championship system in college football are many. Over the years the method for determining the champion has changed numerous times, and even today there are two separate polls, each purporting to name the year's best team. Because of the debatable way they are determined, national championships are not the most important factor when devising a rating of the best college football programs of all time. For our purposes, we find that winning percentage over time offers the best means of judging the success of a college football team. Not surprisingly, the top football program by this measure (as it would be by most others) is Notre Dame, the school that brought us Knute Rockne, the Gipper and Joe Montana, among others. These are the 10 most successful college football programs in history.

School	Years	Percent*
1. Notre Dame	107	.760%
2. Michigan	116	.743%
3. Alabama	101	.736%
4. Oklahoma	101	.715%
5. Texas	103	.709%
6. Ohio State	106	.703%
7. USC	103	.703%
8. Nebraska	106	.698%
9. Penn State	109	.695%
10. Tennessee	99	.689%

* scores based on data up to 1996

Source: *Best and Worst* original.

FRANCHISES

Fastest-Growing

Franchises continue to be a popular way for many people to get a business of their own. The advantages of owning a franchise are obvious—your business has instant brand recognition, you get help setting it up, and success, while not guaranteed, is given a better chance than a business started from scratch. McDonald's is still the fastest growing franchise in the world. The average cost to start up a McDonald's is a hefty $400,000, not including the franchise fee, which varies. But despite the high cost, the returns still make the franchise popular among budding entrepreneurs. Next to food, commercial cleaning franchises are growing as the country's work force continues to have difficulty finding time for housecleaning. Minimum start-up costs for a Jani-King franchise is a modest $2,400.

Franchise	New Units, 1995-96
1. McDonald's	2,665
2. Yogen Fruz Worldwide	1,699
3. Subway	1,343
4. Jani King	985
5. 7-Eleven Convenience	833
6. Snap-On Tools	718
7. Novus Windshield Repair	692
8. Coverall Cleaning Concepts	452
9. Coldwell Banker Residential Affiliates, Inc.	412
10. Blimpie International, Inc.	386

Source: *Entrepreneur* magazine, February 1997.

FRUIT

Highest in Calories

Fruit is a decidedly refreshing alternative to the all-too-usual bevy of junk food pseudo-sweets, but the over-anxious fruit eater must be cautioned. If you think you can munch nature's sweet bounty with utter impunity, your waistline will quickly suffer. Here are the fruits with the highest calorie content—eat them with caution and in moderation.

Fruit	Serving Size	Calories
1. Figs	5	238
2. Raisins	1/2 cup	218
3. Watermelon	slice	155
4. Mango	1 average	135
5. Apple	1 large	125
6. D'Anjou Pear	1	120
7. Prunes	5 large	115
8. Dates	5	115
9. Banana	1	105
10. Cantaloupe	1/2	95

Source: Human Nutrition Information Service.

GIFT PREFERENCES

Whatcha Wanna Get for. . . ?

Whether it's a birthday, a wedding or even Christmas, money is the preferred gift of 66 percent of American adults age 18 and over. The desire for monetary gifts runs through nearly every age group, educational attainment and income status. According to a recent survey on gift-giving, on a scale of 1 to 5 among 16 gift categories, money scored a high 5 for 66 percent of affluent people with household incomes of $75,000 or more annually.

Overall, the average among survey respondents was a scale value of 4.2 in favor of money, the highest ranking for all categories of gifts. Eighty-six percent of affluent Americans ranked travel 4.6 on the scale. At the low end of the income group—those earning less than $20,000 annually—gifts of travel appealed to 75 percent of the respondants. Gifts of jewelry please young women the most, according to the survey, especially 18-to-24-year-olds, almost 80 percent of whom value it as a gift, though it was only ranked 3.4 on their preference list. Following are selected gifts ranked by their average preference scores, one being least preferred and five most preferred, according to Discovery Research Group/Present Perfect Survey:

Gift	Total
1. Money	4.20
2. Travel	3.80
3. Clothing	3.42
4. Audio/video	3.27
5. Books	3.17
6. Photographs	2.99
7. Home accessories	2.98
8. Jewelry	2.94
9. Flowers/plants	2.77
10.Kitchen gadgets/ appliances	2.73

Source: *The Peoplepedia*, 1996.

GROCERY ITEMS

"Store Brands" Most Purchased

Highly advertised brand-name consumer products face a growing challenge from cheaper store-brand products at the supermarket in the 1990s, according to surveys of the buying habits of Americans, with

COINS FOR THE KITTY, sawbucks or C-notes, it's what people really want when it comes to a gift—MONEY!

milk, bread and juices the favorite choices of consumers trying to save money. Some store-brand products already outsell national brands, according to the Private Label Manufacturers Association. A $30 billion market in 1993, private-label purchasing represented seven percent of supermarket, drugstore, and retail outlet spending, up two percent from 1992. Biggest buyers of store-brands—which a national survey dubbed "heavy buyers"—are most likely to be blue-collar workers who live in the South on a $20,000 to $40,000 annual income, typically age 35 to 44. Heavy buyers spend an average of $660 a year on store-brand goods, compared to $5,400 for all consumer packaged items, according to a 1992-93 survey by A.C. Nielsen Consumer Information Services. The survey found that heavy buyers make up 17 percent of all shoppers in the nation but account for 42 percent of store-brand spending. Following are the top 10 private-label items, in descending

THINGS

order of purchases by the heavy buyers.

Rank/Store-brand Item

1. Milk
2. Bread/baked goods
3. Cheese
4. Vegetables (canned)
5. Vegetables (frozen)
6. Juices/drinks (shelf stable)
7. Packaged meat
8. Paper napkins
9. Eggs (fresh)
10. Cereal

A second segment of the store-brand market that the survey termed "occasional buyers," spends an average of $260 annually on private-label products, out of $3,800 on all packaged goods. The annual household income of this group ranges from $30,000 to $60,000, with the household head 45 to 64, high-school educated, working part-time, or retired. The largest numbers of occasional buyers are in the East or West. Forty-four percent of all shoppers fall into the "occasional" category; they account for 44 percent of spending on private-label products. "Infrequent buyers," the third survey segment, are both low and high-income, earning between $20,000 and $60,000 annually, and most likely to be under age 35 or over age 65 and living in the Midwest, according to the survey. Infrequent buyers make up 39 percent of all shoppers in the country. They spend less than $90 on private-label products, out of $2,800 on all items, and account for only 14 percent of spending on store-brand products.

Source: *American Demographics*, February 1995.

HEALTH CARE EXPENDITURES

Who's Getting all the Money?

It's no revelation that it costs a bundle to get sick, but who's getting all the money? And it does cost money! But though the costs are escalating, they are being contained a bit. Part of the containment is due to low inflation. As recently as 1990, health care costs went up almost 10 percent annually. By 1994 costs went up more modestly: a 3.5 percent increase for drugs, 5.3 percent for doctors and 7.9 percent for hospital stays. While that's better, costs are still too high in most people's opinion. Following is a breakdown of the main expenditures for health care in the U.S.

Payee	Annual Expenditure, 1993
1. Hospitals	$359 billion
2. Physicians	$167 billion
3. Nursing homes	$74 billion
4. Drugs	$71 billion
5. Administration/ Insurance	$48 billion
6. Other services	$45 billion
7. Dental services	$41 billion
8. Public health	$24 billion
9. Other personal health care	$20 billion
10. Research and development	$16 billion

Source: Bureau of Labor Statistics, Health Care Financing Administration.

HIGHWAYS

Most Crowded

The flow of traffic in and out of urban areas presents significant challenges for city planners, especially since the exodus to the suburbs during the 1950s and '60s. As

America's love affair with the automobile continued to thrive—and our highway system was forced to cope with ever increasing usage—our culture developed a new malady: traffic-induced stress headaches. The mostly likely places to acquire such an affliction are in the following locations.

Route/City	Average Daily Traffic*
1. **I-5, I-10, S.R. 60 & S.R. 101**/Los Angeles	560,000
2. **U.S. Route 59 at I-610/ Houston**	330,000
3. **I-35 and I-30/Dallas** East L.A. Interchange	200,000
4. **I-93/Boston** North and South Lanes	190,000
5. **I-278/ New York** Gowanus Expressway	175,000
6. **I-10 & I-610/ New Orleans** East-West Freeway	174,000
7. **I-495 & I-95/ Washington, DC** Woodrow Wilson Bridge	172,000
8. **I-35 West/Minneapolis** Northbound lanes of I-35 West at Minnehaha Creek in South Minneapolis.	100,000
9. **I-94/Milwaukee**	80,000
10. **I-290/Chicago and I-88/Chicago** Eisenhower Expressway—Traffic from these two highways merge daily.	77,000

*figures are for two-way traffic

Source: American Automobile Association; *USA Today*, October 31, 1996.

HORMONE-REPLACEMENT SYMPTOMS

The Worst Side Effects

Hormone replacement therapy is a new way to try to cure an old problem: menopause. Thirty-nine percent of menopausal women have

NUTS! If you're fond of fiber, but not of pumpkin seeds or raw elderberries, they'll provide the roughage you need. All the aforementioned are among the foods highest in fiber (See page 263).

reportedly tried it, usually prompted by the experience of hot flashes and other symptoms. Forty percent of younger women nearing menopause tried the treatment for as long as a year before they entered the stage, which is defined as the stoppage of the menstrual flow for at least one year. Sixty-nine percent of the younger women and 70 percent of women at the closing stage of menopause who had tried the therapy were still on it at the time of the survey. Sixty-five percent of those in the therapy reported side effects, and 76 percent of those reported two or more effects. The chief effect was weight gain, reported by 60 percent of the women, with 46 percent of those who took hormones for more than a year gaining 16 or more pounds. Excessive bleeding was the second-biggest side effect, at 46 percent; breast tenderness and water retention followed at 42 percent and 41 percent, respectively. Following are the side effects reported by those who underwent hormone-replacement therapy.

Side Effect	Percent Who Suffer
1. Weight gain	60%
2. Excessive bleeding	46%
3. Breast tenderness	42%
4. Water retention	41%
5. Headaches	22%
6. Anxiety	19%
7. Cramps	18%
8. Nausea	14%

Source: *The Peoplepedia*, 1996.

OTELS

Largest Hotel Chains

Establishing a national or international hotel chain is a hugely capital-intensive undertaking, so it is not surprising that this recessionary era has seen the birth of very few. The hotel game is dominated by a handful of traditional players, whose individual images have changed little in modern times. The biggest noise in travel accommodations, in the last few years, has been made by stripped-down, economy chains like Motel 6, which promise clean, basic rooms at a fraction of most competitors' luxurious prices; and, at the other end of the scale, is the rise of the "all-suite" hotel, which plays on the upscale traveler's desire for more space. These are the largest chains in hotel-happy America.

Chain	Rooms*
1. Hospitality Franchise Systems	472,416
2. Holiday Inns	395,917
3. Choice Hotels	303,535
4. Best Western International	281,789
5. Marriott International	195,685
6. Hilton Hotels	144,279
7. Sheraton Hotels/Inns/ Resorts/Suites	128,753
8. Motel 6	91,794
9. The Promus Companies	85,166
10. Carlson Hospitality Worldwide	84,891

* figures as of December 1995

Source: America Hotel/Motel Association.

OTELS

Most Lucrative Hotel Chains, Worldwide

Home is where you hang your hat, and most often, travelers have made themselves at home at tried-and-tested hotels like Holiday Inn, Marriott or Ramada. In fact, the top international hotel chains all are American-born. Well-heeled travelers worldwide prefer to park it at the Holiday Inn over other luxury locations.

Chain	Sales, 1995 (billions)
1. Holiday Inn	$5.8
2. Marriott, Courtyard	$5.3
3. Best Western	$4.9
4. ITT Sheraton	$4.1
5. Ramada	$4.0
Howard Johnson	$4.0
Days Inn	$4.0
8. Radisson	$2.9
9. Hyatt	$2.7
10. Comfort Inn, Clarion	$2.2
11. Westin	$2.2
12. Inter-Continental	$1.8

Source: Business Travel News; *Brandweek*, Superbrands '97, October 7, 1996.

INDUSTRIES— SAFETY

Highest Occupational Injury and Illness Rates

Those who think nursing homes are sedate, docile workplaces are badly mistaken. Nursing homes, scheduled airlines and air courier services led all other industries in overexertion incidents, the most common way in which lost-worktime injuries occur. Other common work hazards include being struck by objects. Logging and wood container manufacturing topped the list of industries in this category. The roofing and water supply industries registered the highest rates for falls on the same level. Following are tabulations of industries with the highest incidence rate per 10,000 workers.

Industry	Rate per 10,000 Employees
1. Nursing Homes	318
2. Air Transport	307
3. Logging	241
4. Wood Containers	227
5. Roofing	121
6. Water Supply	118
7. Taxicabs	114
8. Hats/millinery	104
9. School Buses	102
10. Men's Suits	89

Source: Bureau of Labor Statistics, May 8, 1996.

INDUSTRIES— SIZE

Largest U.S. Industries

As Mark Twain would have said, reports of the death of American manufacturing have been greatly exaggerated. Despite the talk, American industries still make things. True, the production lines are not as crowded as they once were. And while today's manufacturers do, in fact, often have plants outside the U.S., many foreign-based manufacturers have U.S. factories. In sum, Americans still make things. Following are the industries in which the most Americans are employed.

Industry	Employees (1,000s)
1. Durable Goods Manufacturing	10,735
2. Health Services	9,722
3. Eating and Drinking places	7,568
4. Nondurable Goods Manufacturing	7,549
5. Business Services	7,406
6. Wholesale Trade	6,683
7. Transportation	4,106
8. Hospitals	3,887
9. Special Trade Contractors	3,585
10. Food Stores	3,482

Source: Bureau of Labor Statistics, March 1997.

INDUSTRIES— UNEMPLOYMENT

Highest Unemployment

Unemployment is as low as it's been in the last several decades. Not since 1970 has it fallen below five percent. Notwithstanding, some industries are suffering. The high unemployment in the agriculture and construction industries is evidence of their susceptibility to forces they have little control over, from floods that affect agriculture to interest-rate fluctuations that affect construction. Or, a particularly dry growing season can be the straw that breaks the back of the small farmers, many of whom are already

CONSTRUCTION WORKERS like the one above are the most likely of all occupational groups to be unemployed. One in 11 recently have been.

overextended financially, and eventually forced into bankruptcy. In the construction industry, a slow housing market, bad weather and the seasonal and project-oriented nature of the work make for high unemployment. Following are the industries which suffer the worst unemployment.

Industry	Percent Unemployed
1. Construction	9.0%
2. Agriculture	8.8%
3. Wholesale and Retail Trade	6.5%
4. Nondurable Goods Manufacturing	5.3%
5. Services	5.0%
6. Transportation 4.3%	
Public Utilities	4.3%
8. Mining	4.2%
9. Durable Goods Manufacturing	4.0%
10. Finance	3.0%
Insurance	3.0%
Real Estate	3.0%
13. Government	2.9%

Source: Bureau of Labor Statistics, March 1997.

INFLATION, CONSUMER ITEMS

Most Inflated

In the early 1980s, the U.S. began to feel like a corner of the encroaching third world, with inflation gone runaway, and crises mounting in our schools and on our streets. Fortunately, the interceding years have brought some relief from the double-digit inflation of those sorry times. For a nation that claims to be committed to equal educational opportunity for all, educational services and equipment are the expenses that have seen the most inflation. It's good to see, at least, that the market works the way it's supposed to—as demand goes up, so do prices. The following rating is based on the Consumer Price Index as a measure of inflation from 1982 to March, 1997.

Item	CPI Score
1. Personal and educational services	256.7
2. Personal and educational expenses	255.0
3. Tobacco and smoking products	237.4
4. Medical care services	237.1
5. School books and supplies	235.3
6. Medical care	232.7
7. Other renter's cost	226.4
8. Medical care commodities	213.9
9. Professional medical services	213.2
10. Private transportation services	194.1

Source: Bureau of Labor Statistics, March, 1997.

THINGS

INFLATION
CONSUMER ITEMS

Least Inflated

Ah, value! While it may seem that nothing is cheap, in these ultra-pricey times, certain things, at least, have remained less-outrageously priced than others. First among these is fuel. In the last two decades, we geared ourselves to embargo mentalities, gas shortages and price escalation. But for the brief Gulf War, the nineties look to be—and already have been—an era of relatively steady fuel cost. The following measure of inflation takes 1982 prices as a base of 100, hence the items of the list hardly went up at all in the last 15 years.

Item	CPI Score
1. Private transportation commodities	105.4
2. Gasoline	107.4
3. Motor fuel	108.1
4. Fuel oil/other household fuel commodities	109.6
5. House furnishings	111.2
6. Fuels	119.2
7. Household furnishings and operations	125.2
8. Gas (piped) & electricity (energy services)	125.3
9. Female apparel	126.1
10. Footwear	126.3

Source: Bureau of Labor Statistics, March, 1997.

JOBS

Best and Worst

What is the best job in America? Perhaps the question has no valid answer; but more likely it has many. For most people, the very best job is the one they most enjoy doing. A painter for whom art is both a love and a means of making a living may believe that not only is his or her job the best one possible, but also the only one possible. Certain professionals, such as clergymen, do not feel a need to choose a vocation, believing themselves called to their occupations. But for those of us who must pick careers without the aid of divine guidance, it would be blessing enough to find a sensible, consistent system for ranking the thousands of possibilities. The Jobs Rated Almanac analyzed more than 90 job-related factors that contribute to the quality of 250 careers in six primary areas: income, stress, physical demands, work environment, outlook and security. The overall ranking of best and worst jobs is based on the sum of the rankings in those six areas. The best job overall was found to be an actuary—the person who calculates risks for insurance companies. Actuaries work in extremely comfortable surroundings, are well-paid, have few physical demands, relatively low stress and extremely good security and job outlook. Compare that to the migrant farmworker, who toils for long hours in the field, is poorly compensated and enjoys very little job security.

BEST JOBS OVERALL

Occupation	Score
1. Actuary	118
2. Software Engineer	124
3. Computer Systems Analyst	131
4. Accountant	218
5. Paralegal Assistant	222
6. Mathematician	223
7. Medical Secretary	230
8. Computer Programmer	263
9. Parole Officer	279
10. Medical Records Technician	294

CAN A JOB IN THE GREAT OUTDOORS, a lumberjack's, be that bad—the worst job there is? The outdoors isn't so great when the temperature is ten below or 100 above. And what's a lumberjack to do then? Go to work, just like he has to do when it's raining, or snowing, or when his back is sore, or when his hands are so raw he can barely grab an ax.

WORST JOBS OVERALL*

Occupation	Score
1. Lumberjack	1440
2. Dancer	1357
3. Construction Worker (Laborer)	1342
4. Cowboy	1329
5. Roustabout	1319
6. Taxi Driver	1301
7. Fisherman	1297
8. Roofer	1280
9. Automobile Painter	1262
10. Seaman	1252

* list in descending order (lumberjack is the worst job)

Source: *Jobs Rated Almanac*, 1995.

JOBS, CLAUSTROPHOBIC

The Most Confining Occupations

Like to get out and move around at work? Don't be an astronaut. In training and on space flights, astronauts are confined to extremely cramped quarters for long periods of time, sometimes by themselves or with one or two others. Of course, astronauts undergo rigorous testing to ensure that they can cope with the mental stress from such environments, so any claustrophobics are presumably weeded out. A stressful, tense or competitive atmosphere, such as you'll find in a hospital operating room, on a theatrical stage or in a lab, also contributes to a poor work environment. Confined spaces, heavy responsibility and tight schedules detract from one's ability to "blow off steam" when pressure mounts. The following are the jobs in which one is confined the most, be it in a vehicle or elsewhere in which there is little freedom to roam.

Rank/Occupation

1. Astronaut
2. Surgeon
3. Dancer
4. Fashion Model
5. Psychiatrist
6. Dr. of Osteopathy
7. Photojournalist
   Actor
8. Wholesale Sales Rep.
   Auto Salesperson
9. Basketball Player
10. Attorney

Source: Jobs Rated Almanac, 1992.

JOBS—FATALITIES AT WORK

Who's Dying to Go to Work

For some people, work is a chore. But for others, it's dangerous, and potentially deadly. During the past few decades the workplace has generally been a safer place, thanks to programs instituted by OSHA, not to mention the fear of liability that many corporations have. Nevertheless, for many people, a day on the job is a day of danger. Following are the occupations at which the most workers die on the job.

Fatalities per 100,000 Workers	
1. Sailors and deckhands	115
2. Fishermen	104
3. Lumberjacks	101
4. Airplane pilots and navigators	97
5. Mining machine operators	78
6. Structural metal workers	64
7. Garbage collectors	60
8. Construction laborers	39
9. Grader, dozer and scraper operators	3
Farm workers, including supervisors	3

Source: Bureau of Labor Statistics, 1995.

JOBS— GROWTH

Fastest Growing and Declining Jobs

Occupations that already have a large quantity of workers will be the fastest growing, according to the latest projections. Possible exceptions will be in the health care and educational fields. Other characteristics of the fastest growing job fields are that they will require the least education and training, and, consequently, will be some of the lowest paying jobs. Occupations that are declining are the ones hit by technological advances and organizational change. For example, bank tellers are losing jobs due to the proliferation of ATM machines. Automation will effect other jobs, particularly for typists and word processors. A mitigating factor in this scenario is that the commonplace software has become so easy and simple to master that professionals and managers are doing their own typing and word processing.

FASTEST GROWING

Occupation	New Openings
1. Cashiers	562,000
2. Janitors	559,000
3. Retail salespersons	532,000
4. Waiters and waitresses	479,000
5. Registered nurses	473,000
6. General managers and top executives	466,000
7. Systems analysts	445,000
8. Home health aides	428,000
9. Guards	415,000
10. Nursing aides and orderlies	387,000

FASTEST DECLINING

Occupation	Jobs Gone
1. Farmers	273,000
2. Typists and word processors	212,000
3. Bookkeeping and accounting clerks	178,000
4. Bank tellers	152,000
5. Sewing machine operators	140,000
6. Private household servants	108,000
7. Computer operators	98,000
8. Billing, posting machine operators	64,000
9. Office machine operators	56,000

THINGS

10. Textile machine
   operators   47,000

Source: Source: U.S. Department of Labor, *Monthly Labor Review*, November 1995.

JOBS, OFFICE

Cushiest Work Environment

The office can be a prison for some, but a palace for others. Highly compensated lawyers enjoy the best overall office environments—indeed, the greatest sign of success for a lawyer in many a firm is the coveted corner office. Senior partners at big law firms lounge in spacious surroundings with superb views, serviced by fully stocked bars, cable television hook-ups and even showers for those late-night legal sessions. Your noble representatives in Congress also enjoy some office amenities to make-up for the slave wages they bicker about so frequently. In general, the higher one goes on the corporate-governmental ladder, the more comfortable one becomes.

Rank/Occupation

1. Attorney
2. Senator/Congressman
3. Bank Officer
4. Advertising Account Executive
5. Public Relations Specialist
6. Insurance Agent
7. Stockbroker
8. Architect
9. Engineer
10. Reporter

Source: *Jobs Rated Almanac*, 1995

JOBS—NO DEGREE REQUIRED

Best and Worst Jobs Requiring No College Diploma

In many occupations requiring no formal education, professional advancement depends to a large extent on a person's job per-formance, the building up of a clientele and a reputation for quality service. Most of the top 10 jobs in this category are oriented toward personal service and require some training, though not at the college level. The losers in job outlook for non-degreed workers are predominantly unskilled-labor jobs, which are traditionally unstable, because they are to some extent seasonal and hiring levels are closely tied to fluctuations in the economy.

BEST JOBS

Rank/Occupation

1. Paralegal Assistant
2. Astrologer
3. Tax Examiner/Collector
4. Computer Service Technician
5. Personnel Recruiter
6. Cosmetologist
7. Teacher's Aide
8. Cashier
9. Architectural Drafter
10. Electrical Technician

WORST JOBS *

Rank/Occupation

1. Lumberjack
2. Dancer
3. Construction Laborer
4. Cowboy
5. Roustabout
6. Taxi Driver
7. Fisherman

THINGS

8. Roofer
9. Automobile Painter
10. Seaman

* the lowest scoring jobs are atop the list (Seaman is the "best" of the worst jobs)

Source: *Jobs Rated Almanac*, 1995.

OBS—
PAY

Best-Paying Jobs With No College

Who says you've got to go to college to make it in this world? There are a number of good positions for those with less than four years of college that still offer substantial potential for income. Here we are talking about fields that employ a large number of workers—not limited professions such as movie star, professional actor or news anchor—that are high-paying but may not require a college degree. Unionization certainly helps when it comes to blue-collar salaries, and some of the highest-paying fields in which a college degree is not essential are supervisory positions in heavily unionized fields such as transportation and manufacturing. Other blue-collar jobs that command high pay are those that also require specialized training or expertise. So just because you don't have a degree, don't fret. There are still a number of good opportunities available. Following are the top paying careers which do not require four years of college.

Occupation	Average Salary*
1. Baseball Player (Major League)	$1,188,000

In his "office" or even a step away in "the great outdoors" where there's plenty of space, this worker has the most claustrophobic job of all (See page 275).

2. Race Car Driver (Indy Class)	$420,000
3. Baseball Umpire (Major League)	$140,000
4. Congressperson	$134,000
5. Choreographer	$83,000
6. Fashion Model	$76,000
7. Sheet Metal Worker	$58,000
8. Musician	$53,000
9. Singer	$53,000
10. Glazier	$52,000

* salaries are for 1995, and rounded to nearest 1,000

Source: *Jobs Rated Almanac*, 1995

JOBS— PAY

Best-Paying Professional Careers

Here we define profession as an occupation that, in addition to requiring a specialized college degree, requires specific certification, usually by a state board. The top eight professional occupations ranked by income are all in the field of health care. This reflects a willingness in the market to compensate health care professionals for the pressures they are saddled with and the responsibilities that we entrust to them, namely, our well-being. However, registered nurses are near the bottom on the pay scale for professionals—earning a mere $37,000 annually. The sacrifices in time and money for proper training and licensing, not to mention the long hours once that license is earned, do not pay off for registered nurses the way they do for most other health care professionals. Surprisingly, lawyers rank below the middle of the pack in professional income, although the law is considered a very lucrative field. Better to

have clients who are sick, then, rather than afoul of the law.

Occupation	Average Salary*
1. Surgeon	$194,000
2. Orthodontist	$193,000
3. Dentist	$111,000
4. Psychiatrist	$110,000
5. Physician (General Practice)	$104,000
Podiatrist	$104,000
7. Attorney	$86,000
8. Financial Planner	$82,000
9. Osteopath	$81,000
10. Optometrist	$80,000

* salaries are for 1995, and rounded to nearest thousand

Source: *Jobs Rated Almanac*, 1995.

JOBS— PAY

Best-Paying Outdoor Jobs

Always remember that no matter how much you love the great outdoors, it's not so great when it's below zero or 95 degrees in the shade. Nevertheless, when most people think of outdoor jobs they imagine a lifeguard on a sunny beach or lumberjack standing amid a green forest enjoying a cool summer breeze. A few may think of professional baseball players, who enjoy some of the most glamorous and highest paying of all jobs, while scampering about on the field of dreams under the summer afternoon sun or on lazy mid-summer evenings. For those with more earthbound talents, lucrative outdoor occupations include professional and research positions in such areas as geology, oceanography and construction. Those who love the outdoors or are looking to escape an oppressive office environment need not resign themselves to low pay or overly strenuous work.

Occupation	Average Salary*
1. Baseball Player (Major League)	$1,188,000
2. Football Player (NFL)	$655,000
3. Race Car Driver (Indy Class)	$420,000
4. Baseball Umpire (Major League)	$140,000
5. Oceanographer	$56,000
6. Geologist	$56,000
7. Zoologist	$55,000
8. Archeologist	$52,000
Anthropologist	$52,000
10. Construction Foreman	$37,000

* salaries are for 1995, and rounded to nearest thousand

Source: *Jobs Rated Almanac*, 1995.

JOBS— SAFETY

Most Dangerous Occupation

Just as certain industries are relatively hazardous, so are certain occupations. In measuring their relative risk, case shares are compared with employment shares for the same occupation. The following list presents the 10 occupations with the most injuries and illnesses involving days away from work. Together, these 10 occupations accounted for about one-third of the approximately 2.25 million cases reported in 1994, double their share of employed workers. Eight of the 10 had case shares exceeding employment shares, with nonconstruction laborers, nursing aides and construction laborers having the greatest disparity. In contrast, cooks and cashiers faced a lower injury risk than their employment shares would indicate; the large number of

injuries and illnesses in these jobs reflected the workforce size of the occupations.

Occupation	Injuries and Illnesses*
1. Truckdrivers	163.8
2. Laborers, nonconstruction	147.3
3. Nursing aides, orderlies	101.8
4. Janitors and cleaners	60.6
5. Laborers, construction	55.7
6. Assemblers	53.0
7. Carpenters	37.4
8. Stock handlers and baggers	37.2
9. Cooks	36.3
10. Cashiers	35.6

* missed work days, per 100 workers

Source: Bureau of Labor Statistics, Survey of Occupational Injuries and Illnesses, 1994.

JOBS— SAFETY

Most Common Causes of Death on the Job

For those stuck in a humdrum office job, the 9-to-5 regimen may be a deadly bore. But for many, work is just plain deadly. These are the most common causes of deaths on the job, ranked by the percentage of all worker deaths attributed to each cause. As the list indicates, automobile accidents account for the highest percentage of deaths among the work force—more than one-quarter of all employee fatalities are auto-related. The second-leading on-the-job killer is heart attacks, dropping from its top ranking in overall causes of death. Those who work outdoors with heavy machinery and dangerous equipment are at a much greater risk of dying on the job than the average office drone.

Cause	Percent of Worker Deaths
1. Highway accidents	21%
2. Homicides	16%
3. Contact with objects and equipment	15%
4. Shooting	12%
5. Collision between vehicles	10%
6. Struck by object	9%
Fall to lower level	9%
8. Noncollision of vehicle	6%
Nonhighway (farm, industrial premises)	6%
Electrocutions	6%

Source: Bureau of Labor Statistics, August 8, 1996.

JOBS— SECURITY

Most and Least Secure

What, exactly, is job security? For some, it's the freedom to choose your job location. For others, it's the ability to stand up to a pushy or obnoxious boss, knowing you're indispensable to the company. For all, security means financial stability and emotional tranquillity. But security, in some regard, often requires sacrifice in another. The *Jobs Rated Almanac* measured jobs on a variety of factors, including outlook, unionization, job classification, physical hazards, competitiveness and high unemployment rates. On this system, even zero unemployment is no guarantee of security—the military, for instance, is all-volunteer, and one can only be dismissed on disciplinary grounds; but soldiers face life-threatening situations, and thus military jobs do not top the list. But even negative job growth does not necessarily hamper job security— although philosophers, anthropologists and other academics may see a decline in the overall number of jobs in their fields in the coming years, tenured college professors enjoy relative immunity from layoffs and dismissals. So once you're in, you're in for life. The following are the most and least secure jobs in the work force.

MOST SECURE

Occupation	Score
1. Computer Systems Analyst	150
2. Physical Therapist	48
3. Paralegal Assistant	44
4. Audiologist	15
5. Medical Secretary	1
6. Parole Officer	-10
7. Occupational Therapist	-15
8. Software Engineer	28
9. Speech Pathologist	-35
10. Medical Records Technician	-37

LEAST SECURE

Occupation	Score
1. Farmer	-447
2. Football Player (NFL)	-439
Basketball Player (NBA)	-439
Baseball Player (Major League)	-439
5. Roustabout	-424
6. Lumberjack	-416
7. Shoe Maker/Repairer	-395
8. Bricklayer	-391
9. Communications Equipment Mechanic	-386
10. Drill-Press Operator	-377

Source: *Jobs Rated Almanac*, 1995.

JOBS— STRESS

Most and Least Stressful Occupations

"Job-related stress" became buzzwords in the 1980s. Declining economic fortunes abroad and hard times at home have increased the pressures on the American worker to produce more in less time. The pace of economic life has quickened, work tools have become more complicated and harder to use, competition more threatening to security, financial deals bigger. All of this takes its toll on the psychological well-being of the worker. Yet, despite the fact that the increased pace of the office wears down office workers, very few of them face the possibility of death because of their performance. No more stressful situation can arise of the job than the responsibility for the safety of oneself or others. This, then, is the most telling criterion in judging a job's stressfulness. The following ratings of job stress are from the *Jobs Rated Almanac*, which assigned overall scores to 250 jobs based on 22 weighted factors involved in contributing to job stress. Factors most heavily weighted included lives being at risk, physical demands, competitiveness, deadlines, environmental conditions, and public scrutiny or contact. Firefighters and most others in the top 10 scored near the top for each of the most heavily weighted categories— those involving physical, as opposed to psychological, well-being. So the next time you feel stressed out staring at a computer screen all day, just be thankful you're not leaping out the window of a flaming building with a baby in your hands.

NEXT TO THE PRESIDENT, the man above has the most stressful job there is.

MOST STRESSFUL

Occupation	Score
1. President (U.S.)	176.550
2. Firefighter	110.936
3. Corporate Executive (Senior)	108.625
4. Race Car Driver (Indy Class)	101.775
5. Taxi Driver	100.491
6. Surgeon	99.463
7. Astronaut	99.349
8. Police Officer	99.893
9. Football Player (NFL)	92.799
10. Air Traffic Controller	83.138

LEAST STRESSFUL

Occupation	Score
1. Medical Records Technician	15.480
2. Janitor	16.320
3. Forklift Operator	18.180
4. Musical Instrument Repairer	18.776
5. Florist	18.806
6. Actuary	20.187
7. Appliance Repairer	21.123
8. Medical Secretary	21.147
9. Librarian	21.400
10. Bookkeeper	21.462

Source: *Jobs Rated Almanac*, 1995.

THINGS

JOBS— TRAVEL

See the World: Occupations With the Most Free Travel Opportunities

Most of us cherish the occasional chance to take off on a trip, even if only on business. But ask the true frequent business flyer what he thinks of his twice-weekly jaunts to Milwaukee, Huntsville or Topeka, and one gets a truer perspective on the supposed glamour of business travel—stomach-churning taxi rides through rush-hour traffic to make a flight, only to face long delays at unfamiliar airports, waking up in a strange bed every other morning, eating unfamiliar food, seeing little of one's family until the weekend, only to have the cycle repeat itself on Monday morning. Yes, America's business is conducted more and more on the fly these days, but for the frequent flyer, the lure of travel wears thin after a while. On the other hand, some jobs are implicitly flight-oriented—i.e. flight attendant and pilot—so if you don't like the jet-set life, better consider another field. These are the careers with the most travel opportunities annually.

Occupation	Trips per Year
1. Flight Attendant	240
2. Pilot	192
3. Senator/Congressman	100
4. Baseball Player (Maj. Lea.)	80
5. Wholesale Sales Representative*	60
6. Nuclear Plant Decontamination Technician	50
7. Basketball Player (NBA)	41
8. Astronaut	34
9. Baseball Umpire (Maj. Lea.)	30
10. Basketball Coach (NBA)	25

* some workers are required to pay their own travel expenses

Source: *Jobs Rated Almanac*, 1995.

JOBS— WORK WEEK

Occupations with the Longest Work Weeks

People used to talk about "banker's hours" in reference to those who had short work weeks. But perhaps the phrase should be recast as "baseball players' hours." According to research performed by the editors of the *Jobs Rated Almanac*, baseball players and umpires, as well as basketball players, enjoy the shortest work weeks of any workers in their survey of 250 jobs, clocking in just 30 hours a week. Bank officers, on the other hand, worked an average of 42.5 hours, and bank tellers 40 hours. The President of the United States logs the most hours on the job. Because workers hours are hard to ascertain exactly—the existing data is generally inconsistent— estimates are used in the following rankings.

Work Week/Occupation

1 65-hour Work Week
President of the U.S.
2. 55-hour Work Weeks
Firefighter
Corporate Executive (Senior)
Osteopath
Physician (General Practice)
Psychiatrist
Rabbi
Surgeon
3. 52.5-hour Work Weeks
Catholic Priest
Dairy Farmer
Farmer
Protestant Minister

4. 50-hour Work Weeks
- Agency Director (Nonprofit)
- Attorney
- Chiropractor
- Judge, Federal
- Optometrist
- Personnel Recruiter
- Pharmacist
- Podiatrist
- Railroad Conductor
- Roustabout
- Seaman
- Software Engineer
- Undertaker
- Veterinarian

Source: *Jobs Rated Almanac*, 1995.

JURY AWARDS

Biggest Payouts

Has the court system become nothing more than another lotto game, where any injury offers the chance at mega-bucks, or are these awards merely the jury's way of righting a wrong inflicted upon an innocent victim by an faceless, uncaring and unrepentent corporate society? Unless one wants to argue for the elimination of the jury system in such cases, it seems the monetary awards in personal injury and other civil cases will only continue to rise. Nonetheless, there is a movement under way in this country, headed up in large part by large corporations and insurance companies, called tort reform. The movement is meant to limit the amount of damages a defendant is liable for and the discretion of juries in setting that amount in a civil or personal injury lawsuit. But who really pays? In the main, those same corporations and insurance companies do. The movement has made strides in the past several years, influencing some state legislatures to pass laws capping monetary awards, but the list below of the top 10 jury awards in civil or personal injury suits shows that the tort reform movement is failing.

Case/Description	Award
1. Wrongful Death	**$500 million**

Wrongful death suit for boy killed after opening trash container illegally filled with chemicals.

2. Product Liability	**$350 million**

Awarded in Missouri in death from crash of helicopter made by Turbomeca S.A.

3. Medical Malpractice	**$98.5 million**

Awarded for baby left quadriplegic due to oxygen deprivation during birth in Long Beach, CA.

4. Product Liability	**$90 million**

Awarded to woman who broke her neck when Suzuki Samurai rolled over.

5. Product Liability	**$70 million**

Awarded in Missouri in death from crash of helicopter made by Turbomeca S.A.

6. Sexual Harassment	**$50.4 million**

Awarded to a Wal-Mart worker for abuse by supervisor at a St. Louis Store.

7. Medical Malpractice	**$45.3 million**

Awarded for baby who developed cerebral palsy after lack of oxygen during birth at New York hospital.

8. Malpractice	**$42 million**

For malpractice by interns at New York hospital in delivery of girl now 17 and deaf, retarded and speech-impaired.

9. Medical	**$40 million**

To a family of boy sent to distant hospital by HMO who later lost hands and arms due to delayed treatment of rare disease.

10. Medical	**$40 million**

To woman who lost a hand due to improper use of needle during lung surgery at a Long Island, NY, hospital.

Source: *Lawyers Weekly; Business Insurance*, January 22, 1996.

THINGS

JUVENILE DELINQUENCY

Most Common Acts

In adulthood, we often review our childhoods and middle years through rather darkly tinted glasses. Horseplay, mischief—even petty criminality—are tokens of those liminal times of life. The security and decency of our society depends on the eventual recognition and repentance of these then-minor missteps. Listed below are the most common acts of juvenile delinquency, measured by the percentage of the total adolescent population that has at one time or another participated in the act.

Offense	Arrests, 1994
1. Aggravated Assault	70,108
2. Marijuana Possession	61,003
3. Weapon law violations	52,278
4. Robbery	47,046
5. Heroin/cocaine possession	21,004
6. Heroin/cocaine sale	20,327
7. Dangerous mfg./nonnarcotic drug possession	8,951
8. Marijuana sales/mfg.	8,112
9. Forcible rape	4,873
10. Dangerous nonnarcotic drug sales/mfg.	3,142

Source: U.S. Federal Bureau of Investigation, *Crime in the United States* (SAUS, 1996).

LAKES

Largest Natural Lakes

Amid its other extraordinary geological distinctions, it is often forgotten that North America embodies the world's most mag-

IT LOOKS LIKE THE OCEAN, it's called a sea, but it's actually a lake—the world's largest one, the Caspian Sea.

nificent concentration of inland seas. Of the planet's 10 principal natural lakes, North America is home to three. Such is our great aquatic heritage.

Lake/Country	Area in Sq. Miles
1. Caspian Sea, USSR-Iran	152,239
2. Superior, US-Canada	31,820
3. Victoria, Tanzania-Uganda	26,828
4. Aral, USSR	25,659
5. Huron, US-Canada	23,010
6. Michigan, US	22,400
7. Tanganyika, Tanzania-Zaire	12,700
8. Baikal, USSR	12,162
9. Great Bear, Canada	12,000
10. Nyasa, Tanzania-Mozambique	11,600

Source: Department of the Interior.

LANGUAGES

America's Most and Least Common Foreign Tongues

Not since World War II have so many Americans spoken a foreign language at home. Today, one in seven U.S. residents speaks a language other than English. Spanish is the leading tongue, spoken by 17 million Americans—54 percent of whom do not use English at home. All told, 31.8 million American residents speak 329 foreign languages in their households. This represents an increase of 34 percent in foreign language usage in American households since 1980. Asian languages are spoken by 14 percent of the foreign language speakers, reflecting the new wave of immigration from that region of the globe. The use of European languages has declined the most, as the descendants of the old immigrants abandon such languages as German, Yiddish, Polish and Italian, and as immigration from Europe is superseded by that from Latin America, Asia and Africa. The following list indicates the most common foreign languages in use in more than 150,000 U.S. households.

MOST COMMONLY SPOKEN

Language	Households
1. Spanish	7,339,172
2. French	1,702,176
3. German	1,547,099
4. Italian	1,308,648
5. Chinese	1,249,213
6. Tagalog	843,251
7. Polish	723,483
8. Korean	626,478
9. Vietnamese	507,069
10. Portuguese	429,860

LEAST COMMONLY SPOKEN*

Language	Households
1. Japanese	427,657
2. Greek	388,260
3. Arabic	355,150
4. Hindi	331,484
5. Russian	241,798
6. Yiddish	213,064
7. Thai/Lao	206,266
8. Persian	201,865
9. Creole	187,658
10. Armenian	150,000

* rankings are in descending order (Amenian is the least spoken)

Other languages spoken by more than 100,000 American residents, and the states in which they are chiefly used are: Navajo (New Mexico), Hungarian (New Jersey), Hebrew (New York), Dutch (Utah), Mon-Khmer (Rhode Island) and Gujarathi (New Jersey).

Below are the five states with the most and the fewest foreign language speakers by percentage in the home.

MOST FOREIGN LANGUAGE SPEAKERS

State	Percent of Foreign Speakers
1. New Mexico	35.5%
2. California	31.5%
3. Texas	25.4%
4. Hawaii	24.8%
5. New York	23.3%

FEWEST FOREIGN LANGUAGE SPEAKERS

1. Kentucky	2.5%
2. West Virginia	2.6%
3. Arkansas	2.8%
4. Alabama	2.9%
Tennessee	2.9%

Most of those who speak foreign languages at home—94.2 percent—speak some English. More than half of foreign-language users—56.1 percent—speak English "very well," 23 percent speak it "well," and 15.2 percent speak it "not very well." Only 5.8 percent speak no English at all.

Source: U.S. Census Bureau.

L IBRARIES

Best University Research Libraries, U.S.

This rating is based on an index developed by the Association of Research Libraries to measure the relative size of university libraries. The factors in creating the index include the number of volumes held, number of volumes added during the previous fiscal year, number of current serials, total expenditures and size of staff. It does not measure a library's services, the quality of its collections or its success in meeting the needs of users.

University Library	No. of Volumes
1. Harvard	13,143,330
2. University of California, Berkeley	8,242,196
3. UCLA	6,606,361
4. Yale	9,599,371
5. University of Illinois, Urbana-Champaign	8,665,814
6. University of Toronto	6,713,029
7. Columbia University	6,664,748
8. University of Michigan	6,774,515
9. Stanford University	6,549,725
10. University of Texas	7,176,889

Source: *Chronicle of Higher Education*, Information Bank, 1996

L IQUORS

Most Popular Liquour Brands

Tastes in booze are fickle. In a year where volume levels were uniformly flat, Absolut excelled, jumping up two spots under Seagram's stewardship, while Jose Cuervo fell off the list with Gallo's brandy taking its former slot. Although many of us cannot stand the straight tastes of the hard liquors we consume, most often we are quite specific and insistent about the brands we order. Drinking "premium" liquors like Stolichnaya or Absolut may do little for our taste buds, but, apparently, it does much for the respect that we are accorded by other, more-bargain conscious drinkers.

Brand	Total Depletions (1,000s)
1. Bacardi	6,120
2. Smirnoff Vodka	5,800
3. Seagram's Gin	3,840
4. Jim Beam	3,260
5. Absolut	3,165
6. Seagram & Crown	3,050

7. Popov Vodka	3,000
Jack Daniel's Black	3,000
9. Canadian Mist	2,960
10. E & J Brandy	2,525

Source: Impact Study of Distilled Spirits, 1996.

MAGAZINES— AD REVENUE

Who Sells the Most Advertising

Even at $2.95 a copy and up, odds are that your favorite upscale magazine is a bargain. Newsstand sales and subscription fees often counterbalance only a fraction of the actual price of producing a slick fashion rag or design magazine. The real bucks? Advertising. Ad revenue is the make-or-break factor for most periodicals. Up-scale readership can often offset relatively low readership—magazines targeting specific readership groups are the current trend, and glossies that target the well-to-do merely have to show advertisers the figures for their readers to have them flocking to the ad pages. But, despite continued refinement of the target audiences, the magazines with the highest ad revenue continue to be those with the widest appeal among the population in general.

Publication	Ad Rev., 1995 (millions)
1. *Parade*	$515.6
2. *People*	$437.7
3. *Sports Illustrated*	$435.7
4. *TV Guide*	$406.9
5. *Time*	$404.5
6. *Newsweek*	$331.9
7. *Better Homes*	$274.4
8. *Business Week*	$267.6
9. *Good Housekeeping*	$238.7
10. *USA Weekend*	$229.6

Source: *Advertising Age*, August 26, 1996.

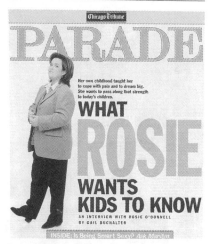

Her own childhood taught her to cope with pain and to dream big. She wants to pass along that strength to today's children.

WHAT ROSIE WANTS KIDS TO KNOW

AN INTERVIEW WITH ROSIE O'DONNELL BY GAIL BUCHALTER

INSIDE: Is Being Smart Sexy? Ask Marilyn

THE PICTURE HAS NEVER BEEN ROSIER at Parade, where more dollars are spent by advertisers than in any other magazine in print.

MAGAZINES— CIRCULATION

Largest Circulation Periodicals

The magazine with the widest circulation in the country, *Modern Maturity*, is an organ of the largest association in the country, the American Association of Retired Persons. Armed with this mouthpiece, AARP has in recent years become a strong political lobbying force for the rights of the elderly and against cuts in benefits. Women, the list below shows, are the strong magazine readers—five of the 10 top magazines in circulation are specifically targeted at women, and homemakers in particular.

Magazine	Total Circulation*
1. *Modern Maturity*	20,528,786
2. *Reader's Digest*	15,072,260
3. *TV Guide*	13,013,938
4. *National Geographic*	9,025,003
5. *Better Homes & Gardens*	7,605,325

IT'S NOT FOUND ON NEWSTANDS, so many haven't even heard of it, *Modern Maturity*, the largest-circulation publication in the English Language.

6. *The Cable Guide*	5,260,421
7. *Family Circle*	5,239,074
8. *Good Housekeeping*	4,951,240
9. *Ladies' Home Journal*	4,544,416
10. *Woman's Day*	4,290,216

* second half of 1996

Source: Audit Bureau of Circulations; Business Publisher's Association.

MENOPAUSE

Most Common Symptoms

Troublesome symptoms commonly suffered by women at the onset, during and after menopause can be eased by diet and exercise, according to a wide-ranging study of 15,000 women reporting on their experiences. Of those who found menopause "not bothersome," 64 percent exercised three or more times a week, compared with 39 percent who exercised two or fewer times a week. The benefits of three-times-a-week exercise did not stop there. Of the 15 most common symptoms of a menopause, those who regularly worked out were nearly 50 percent more likely to report five or fewer symptoms than those who did not. Fifty-eight percent of women in the survey of those just reaching menopause, in menopause and just after menopause described the phases as "somewhat bothersome," or no more than annoying, according to the pollsters. More than 50 percent said for the most part the symptoms were mild. Hardest hit were respondents between the ages of 40 to 44, almost 33 percent of whom found the experience "very bothersome," compared to 21 percent of women 45 to 49 and 18 percent of women 50 to 54. Six percent of women who reached menopause at age 55 or older also found it "very bothersome." Hot flashes were found not to be inevitable—17 percent of the respondents experienced them in the stage before menopause began, at an average age of 48.7. On the other hand, 40 percent of the respondents overall and 46 percent of the women on the brink of menopause felt flashes, along with the other top troublesome symptoms: weight gain and sleep loss. Sixty percent of the women reported taking on 10 pounds. Sixty-two percent of the women who reported hot flashes said the flashes awakened them at night. Following are the most commonly reported symptoms during menopause, in percent of menopausal women who report the symptom.

Symptons	Percent
1. Weight gain	42%
2. Sleep problems	41%
3. Hot flashes	40%
4. Fatigue	37%
5. Lost sexual desire	36%
6. Forgetfulness	35%
7. Joint pain	34%
8. Mood swings	33%
9. Water retention	31%
Vaginal dryness	31%

Source: *The Peoplepedia*, 1996.

MERGERS AND ACQUISITIONS

Biggest Corporate Marriages and Buyouts

Just as the eighties was the decade of the deal, the nineties is the decade of the deal and the downsize. Whether the deals were friendly and mutually beneficial, no one had ever seen anything like it before. It seems unlikely that we will ever get back to the time when businesses grew from the ground up, rather than by proxies, buyout and mergers. Whatever happened to the Horatio Algers and Sam Waltons? Following are the biggest deals ever—so far.

Company/Acquirer/Year	Price*
1. RJR Nabisco	$30.6 billion
Kohlberg Kravis Roberts, 1988	
2. Electronic Data	
Systems	$28.0 billion
Shareholders, 1995	
3. Lucent Tech.	$24.1 billion
Shareholders, 1995	
4. NYNEX	$21.3 billion
Bell Atlantic, 1996	
5. McCaw Cellular	
Communications	$18.9 billion
AT&T, 1993	
. Capital Cities/ABC	$18.9 billion
Walt Disney, 1995	
7. Pacific Telesis	
Group	$16.5 billion
SBC Communications, 1996	
8. Warner	
Communications	$14.1 billion
Time, 1989	
9. Kraft	$13.4 billion
Philip Morris, 1988	
. Gulf Oil	$13.4 billion
Standard Oil of Califonia, 1984	

* data as of October 1996
Source: Securities Data Co.

MOVIES— ACCLAIM

Top Movies, 1980-90

The top movies were rated according to three factors: (1) Academy Awards (including Best Picture, Best Director, Actor or Actress); (2) box office and video rental grosses; and (3) critical response. In the first category, 25 points each were awarded for best picture, best director and best actor/actress, and 10 points for best supporting actor/actress. In category two, high box office gross was awarded 25 points, high video rental 10 points. In category three, each movie critic's vote counted for seven points, with six critics' assessments being used. *E.T. The Extra-Terrestrial* is the all-time top money making movie, with *Batman* running a close second. However, *Rain Man* made it to the top of list because not only was it a box office and video rental smash, but it also received 1988 Academy Awards for Best Director and Best Actor categories, along with numerous kudos from the critics.

Movie	Total Score
1. *Rain Man*	121
2. *Tootsie*	77

HOLD IT HIGH, for that's a diploma's cost—so high, in fact, that the costs associated with an education are the most inflated consumer items (See page 272). However, with the disparity in income of those with no education and those with one, the educational expenses are recouped many-fold.
Photo: Harvey Mudd College.

3. *The Last Emperor*	71
4. *Raging Bull*	67
5. *Hannah and Her Sisters*	62
6. *Indiana Jones and the Last Crusade*	42
7. *Batman*	35
Lethal Weapon 2	35
9. *E.T. The Extra-Terrestrial*	32

Source: *Best and Worst* original.

MOVIES— COSTS

Fattest Flicks Ever Financed

Want to see someone drowning in debt? Kevin Costner and his flop, *Waterworld*, did it to the tune of an estimated $100 million. But at least he planned to spend a lot of money. Most films lose because their pro-

duction costs get out of line, inadvertently. There are many things that contribute to a film's going over budget—long production delays, problems with shooting on locations, stars' salaries that jump through the roof with each new sequel and, perhaps most noticeably, the ego of the director. The classic case of the over-budget movie was Michael Cimino's *Heaven's Gate*. After winning critical acclaim, including the Best Picture and Best Director Oscars for *The Deer Hunter*, Cimino's studio, United Artists, gave him free reign to achieve his artistic vision. The resulting $40 million mega-flop led to the dissolution of the once-proud UA studios, which had been founded by Charlie Chaplin and Mary Pickford in the days of the silent movies. A mere 10 years after the *Heaven's Gate* fiasco, Cimino's $40 million seems like a mere drop in the bucket when such flops as *Days of Thunder, Tango and Cash, Ishtar* and *Santa Claus*(?!), which previously would have broken most studios, simply get passed over in silence. In Hollywood more than most places, money doesn't buy quality, not to mention success. The preponderance of dogs and pointless sequels on the list of most expensive movies proves that point, as does such recent, low- budget successes as *Metropolitan* and *The Terminator*.

Movie	Production Cost (millions)
1. *Water world*	$100
2. *Die Hard 2*	$70
Who Framed Roger Rabbit?	$70
3. *Total Recall*	$65
The Godfather, Part III	$65
4. *Rambo III*	$58

THINGS

5. Days of Thunder	$55	
Tango and Cash	$55	
Ishtar	$55	
Superman	$55	
9. Superman II	$54	
10. The Adventures of		
Baron Munchausen	$52	
11. Annie	$52	
12. The Cotton Club	$51	
Hudson Hawk	$51	
14. Another 48 Hours	$50	
Batman	$50	
Coming to America	$50	
Santa Claus	$50	

Source: *The New York Times*, 1997.

3. Jurassic Park	$357	1993
4. Forrest Gump	$327	1994
5. The Lion King	$313	1994
6. Independence		
Day	$306	1996
7. Home Alone	$285	1990
8. Return of the		
Jedi	$264	1983
9. Jaws	$260	1975
10. Batman	$251	1989

* re-released in 1997

Source: MovieWeb, February 4, 1997.

MOVIES— GROSS

Top Grossing Films of All Time

Although a host of halogen-hot stars and directors overtly fuel the glow in and around Tinseltown, two names dominate any discussion of celluloid super-success: Steven Spielberg and George Lucas. These genial gents are responsible for some of the most profitable films of all time. The incredible worldwide popularity of Lucas's *Star Wars* trilogy and Spielberg's lovable *E.T.* demonstrate most clearly the fact that the movies are a place we go to escape from reality, rather than confront it. In fact, most of the 10 top-grossing films of all time deal with fantasies—though one is more reality-based, dealing with an oversized, murderous shark who can't stop snacking. And that's about as realistic as it gets when the big Hollywood investors pick their movies.

Film	Gross (millions)	Yr. Released
1. E.T.	$407	1982
2. Star Wars*	$358	1977

MOVIES— LENGTH

When's Intermission? Longest Films Ever Released

Some movies are long; others just *seem* to be. The list below details the top-10 longest movies ever made for commercial release. The appropriately named *The Cure for Insomnia*, shown only once, consisted entirely of footage of a person asleep. The Hollywood productions below, *Cleopatra* and *Heaven's Gate*, cost exorbitant amounts of money and were commercial and critical flops, the latter even resulting in the eventual financial ruin of its studio, United Artists. On the other hand, *Berlin Alexanderplatz*, the German director Werner Fassbinder's adaptation of Alfred Döblin's novel of Weimar Germany; *Little Dorritt*, a two-part adaptation of the Dickens novel; and *Shoah*, a documentary about the Holocaust, met with extreme critical and some financial success, despite their lengths. The following are the longest commercially released movies ever made.

Movie	Length
1. *The Cure for Insomnia*	85 hours
2. *Mondo Teeth*	50 hours
3. *Berlin Alexander Platz*	15 hours, 21 min.
4. *Shoah*	9 hours, 21 min.
5. *Empire*	8 hours
6. *Little Dorritt*	5 hours, 57 min.
7. *Les Miserables*	5 hour,s 5 min.
8. *Greatest Story Ever Told*	4 hours, 20 min.
9. *Cleopatra*	4 hours, 3 min.
10. *Heaven's Gate*	4 hours
11. *Gone With the Wind*	3 hours, 42 min.

Source: *The Guinness Book of Movie Facts*.

M OVIE STUDIOS

The Biggest Box: The Movie Biggies By Market Share

In these disparate days, the economics of risk and reward have dictated that Hollywood commit its redoubtable resources to a relatively few films per year. These few products, in turn, are concentrated in even fewer, well-accessorized hands. Herewith, the nation's largest distributors, producers and refiners of prime celluloid. With the encroachment of cable television, video and other media into Hollywood's once unique entertainment domain, many of the studios are either diversifying or being bought-up by foreign interests.

Studio Distributor	Market Share, 1995
1. Buena Vista *	18.7%
2. Warner Bros.	16.2%
3. Universal	12.7%
4. Sony **	12.6%
5. Paramount	10.1%
6. Fox	7.6%
7. New Line	6.8%
8. MGM/UA	6.2%

A GREAT WAY TO GO and the number-one choice of murderers in the U.S. (See table on opposite page).

9. Miramax	3.6%
10. Savoy	1.3%

* includes Walt Disney, Hollywood and Touchstone
** includes Columbia and TriStar

Source: *Advertising Age*, Age Dataplace, 1996.

M URDER

Most Popular Methods

Somewhere out there someone is out to get somebody and it could be you. According to the book *What the Odds Are*, one out of every 1,000 random strangers you meet has murdered someone. Think about that next time you're at a crowded airport or flowing with the crowd leaving a sports event. The odds of getting murdered in the U.S., in fact, is a gut-wrenching one in 99. That translates to about one percent of Americans dying at the hands of a murderer. And exactly what is it this good fellow—the vast majority are males—has in his hand. The following table lists the weapons of choice of the nation's murders.

Method	Victims, 1995
1. Firearms	13,673
2. Knives or cutting instrument	2,538
3. Personal weapons (hands, fists, etc.)	1,182
4. Other weapons	989
5. Blunt objects	904
6. Strangulation	232
7. Explosives	190
8. Fire	166
9. Asphyxiation	135
10. Narcotics	22

Source: FBI Uniform Crime Reports, 1996.

M URDER

Most Likely To Kill

If the information in the previous entry scared you—the bit about there being so many murderous strangers—there's more bad news. Strangers are not among the most likely to kill you. The people with whom you are acquainted are much more likely to shoot you or stick you than strangers ever are. The facts also reveal that our chances of getting it from a friend or wife are almost one in 20. So choose your acquaintances carefully, and make friends with them quickly. Following are the relationships of victims to their killers.

Relationship to Victim	% Homicides
1. Unknown relationship	39.4%
2. Acquaintance	26.7%
3. Stranger	15.1%
4. Wife	3.7%
5. Friend	2.9%
6. Girlfriend	2.4%
7. Other family	1.9%
8. Son	1.4%
9. Husband	1.3%
10. Daughter	1.1%

*figures are for 1995

Source: FBI Uniform Crime Reports, 1996.

M USICAL INSTRUMENTS

Since 1980, very few instrumentalists have made the popular music charts. Many who grew up during the 1960s and 1970s, however, cut their musical teeth on the music of greats as disparate as Al Hirt, Chet Atkins and Liberace. Music lessons were a regular after-school activity for almost a quarter of all American kids. More than 57 million adults play at least one instrument; half of them play two or more. Three-quarters of these musicians play music regularly. This list shows the various instruments Americans play and the numbers involved.

Instrument	Number Who Play*
1. Piano	21.0 million
2. Guitar	19.0 million
3. Organ	6.0 million
4. Flute	4.0 million
Clarinet	4.0 million
6. Drums	3.0 million
Trumpet	3.0 million
8. Violin	2.0 million
9. Harmonica	1.7 million
10. Saxophone	1.0 million

* figures are for

Source: *The Peoplepedia*, 1996.

M USICAL TASTES

Best- and Least-Loved Music

It might rock you, but rock and roll is not the number one best-loved music in America. Fifty-one percent of Americans like country music, which makes it the number-one

best-loved music. Musical tastes vary significantly within various demographic stratas. For example, opera was liked by only 13 percent of those who responded to a poll conducted by the National Endowment for the Arts. However, opera's highest proportion of likeability, 26 percent, came from persons with a graduate school education; the next, 21 percent, from persons aged 65 to 74. Seventeen percent of opera fans had an annual family income of $50,000. Rap drew a 12 percent likeability rating, but the survey did not include the genre in its breakdown. Men and women were equally divided, at 52 percent, in their liking of bluegrass. The genre was liked by 57 of whites, but just 19 percent of blacks; 61 percent of persons aged 45 to 54; 59 percent of those with some high school; and 57 percent from fans with an annual salary of $15,000 to $24,999. Seven in 10 younger adults aged 18 to 24 liked rock, and more than a third liked country, easy listening, and blues/R&B. Only 10 percent of the group expressed an affinity for folk music, and only five percent for opera. Men liked rock more than women—48 percent to 39 percent—as did the better educated and more affluent. Between 53 percent and 55 percent of collegians and persons earning $50,000 or more annually said they like rock. Black listening tastes ran to blues/R&B (59 percent), jazz (54 percent), and easy listening (39 percent). African Americans showed the least affinity for opera (eight percent), folk and percent), folk and show tunes (15 percent), classical (18 percent), and bluegrass (19 percent). Following is the percent of adults who favor a specific type of music.

BEST-LOVED MUSIC

Music	Percent
1. Country	51.7%
2. Mood/easy listening	48.8%
3. Rock	43.5%
4. Blues/R&B	40.4%
5. Hymns/gospel	39.8%
6. Big band	35.0%
7. Jazz	34.2%
8. Classical	33.6%
9. Bluegrass	30.0%
10. Show Tunes/operettas/ musicals	27.8%

LEAST-LOVED MUSIC*

1. Soul	25.0%
2. Contemporary folk	23.1%
3. Ethnic	21.5%
4. Latin/salsa	20.0%
5. Reggae	20.0%
6. Parade/marching band	18.0%
7. New Age	16.0%
8. Choral/glee club	15.5%
9. Opera	13.0%
10. Rap	12.0%

* list is in descending order.
Source: *The Peoplepedia*, 1996.

NEWSPAPERS— CIRCULATION

Top Daily Newspapers in Circulation

The American newspaper is fighting a bitter war with magazines for attention of readers who want "infotainment"; that is, news that entertains while it informs. More and more, the nation's daily newspapers are running feature stories, replete with color pictures, elaborate graphics, easy-to-read charts, bold headlines and, most of all, shorter stories that don't tax the attention spans of readers. If circulation is a measure of how well it's done, *USA Today* is the leader. Still, the most popular daily in the U.S. remains the staid *Wall Street Journal*, which doesn't even use black-and-white pictures, much less color. The paper still employs those strange pointillist drawings in place of photography. Following are the largest newspapers in the U.S.

Paper	Circulation
1. *Wall Street Journal*	1,763,140
2. *USA Today*	1,523,610
3. *New York Times*	1,081,541
4. *Los Angeles Times*	1,012,189
5. *Washington Post*	793,660
6. *New York Daily News*	738,091
7. *Chicago Tribune*	684,366
8. *Newsday*	634,627
9. *Houston Chronicle*	541,478
10. *Detroit Free Press*	531,825

Source: *Editor & Publisher International Yearbook*, 1996.

NOVELS— AMERICAN

Greatest American Novels of All Time

Every writer dreams of creating the Great American Novel. But it's already been done. The top two novels on our list are the undisputed masterpieces of American fiction—at least they are now. Mark Twain's *Huck Finn* has had to fight being banned from school libraries for whatever reason as recently as 10 years ago. Melville's *Moby Dick* went unrecognized upon its publication—its greatness only gradually became recognized. We rated novels in the same way as writers—

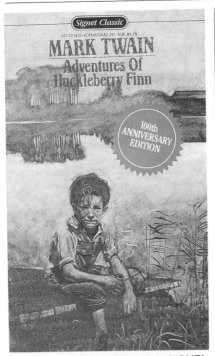

Signet Classic

451-CE1912-(CANADA $2.25)-U.S. $1.75

MARK TWAIN
Adventures Of
Huckleberry Finn

100th ANNIVERSARY EDITION

THE GREATEST AMERICAN NOVEL OF ALL TIME.

by the total number of citations in the MLA International Bibliography of literary and linguistic scholarship. Interestingly, these novels are not the highest scoring literary works by an American. That spot is reserved for Ezra Pound's *Cantos*, a cycle of poetry written over the course of thirty-five years. The *Cantos* notched 244 mentions in the MLA index. The top American play of all time is Eugene O'Neill's *Long Day's Journey Into Night*, with an overall score of 47. The highest scoring novel by a woman writer was Kate Chopin's 1899 work *The Awakening*, with 81 points. The book was harshly criticized upon publication for its frank discussion of female sexuality, and it took sixty years for *The Awaken-*

ing to be rediscovered. Also scoring highly on the list were *The Sun Also Rises* by Ernest Hemingway, with a score of 83, Melville's *Billy Budd* (75) and two more novels by Henry James, *The Turn of the Screw* (74) and *The Ambassadors* (71).

Novel/Author	Score
1. Adventures of Huckleberry Finn Mark Twain	240
2. Moby Dick Herman Melville	225
3. Gravity's Rainbow Thomas Pynchon	177
4. The Scarlet Letter Nathaniel Hawthorne	168
5. Absalom, Absalom William Faulkner	139
6. The Great Gatsby F. Scott Fitzgerald	122
7. The Sound and The Fury William Faulkner	111
8. Portrait of a Lady Henry James	95
9. As I Lay Dying William Faulkner	89
10. Light in August William Faulkner	87

Source: *Best and Worst* original.

ODDS

Biggest Poker Longshots

It is always important to know where one stands. The merits of this precaution are especially obvious in connection with quicksand and toxic waste seepage, but even in the wacky world of wagering, it is nice to know what foundations our feet are planted on. So next time you draw a card, idly wondering, "What are the chances?" please be advised. These are the odds for being dealt various hands on the opening deal in regular five-card poker, with no wild cards. We haven't calculated odds when "Deuces, Jacks and the King with the Ax" are wild. For you poker faces out there, here are your odds:

Hand	Odds Against
1. Royal Flush	649,739 to 1
2. Other Straight Flush	72,192 to 1
3. Four of a Kind	4,164 to 1
4. Full House	693 to 1
5. Flush	508 to 1
6. Straight	254 to 1
7. Three of a kind	46 to 1
8. Two Pairs	20 to 1
9. One Pair	4 to 3
10. No matches	1 in 1

Source: *What the Odds Are.*

PIZZA PALATES

Most Popular Pizza Places

Is there a more popular food among kids than pizza, that great product of the imaginative Italians? Rumor has it that the flat, pie-shaped dish was named after the city where it originated, Pisa. But the food's popularity is due more to American taste than Italian entrepreneurship. Pizza became a staple here in the new world, and has subsequently been re-exported back to Italy. Naturally, this dictates that there is some debate as to whether pizza holds an Italian or American passport. Whatever its true heritage, pizza gets a generally favorable press among nutritionists. Of all the fast foods available, pizza is generally considered the healthiest. A cheese pizza has less fat and cholesterol than most burgers, beef or chicken. But its not totally safe. Physics comes to play here. Tomato sauce cools slower than melting

cheese, which is why so many of us burn the roof of our mouth.

Chain	Sales, 1995*
1. Pizza Hut	$5,440.0
2. Domino's Pizza	$2,100.0
3. Little Caesars Pizza	$2,050.0
4. Papa John's Pizza	$458.7
5. Sbarro, the Italian Eatery	$416.0
6. Round Table Pizza	$373.8
7. Chuck E. Cheese's	$262.0
8. Godfather's Pizza	$260.0

* U.S. systemwide foodservice sales in millions

Source: *Nation's Restaurant News,* April 29, 1996.

POLITICAL ACTION COMMITTEES

Freest Spending P.A.C. Groups

The American social and political systems are based around the free competition of disparate ideas. These days, such ideas don't get far without the support of self-interested groups. Political Action Committees—the PAC's—exist to lobby for the interests of one group or another at the pantheon of U.S. policy, the Capitol. Some are innocuous and impartial, others only sound so.

PAC	Disbursements*
1. Emily's List	$9,190,660
2. Dem. Rep. Independent Voter Education Committee	$6,214,520
3. Assoc. of Trial Lawyers of Amer.	$3,322,980
4. NRA Political Victory Fund	$2,950,770
5. Campaign America	$2,921,813
6. Natl. Education Assoc.	$2,562,574
7. Amer. Federation of State County & Municipal Employees	$2,418,440
8. AT&T PAC	$2,207.903

9. Intl. Brotherhood of
   Elec. Workers $2,132,304
10. VOTE/COPE of
    NYSUT $2,056,875

   * figures are for January 1, 1995
   to June 30, 1996

Source: Federal Election Committee, 1996.

POLITICAL ACTION COMMITTEES—

Largest Labor PACs in Washington

PACs work for us and against us. They are, in fact, simultaneously "us" and "them." PACs work for and against abortion, for the Democrats and the Republicans, to sell weapons and to ban them. A number of PACs look out for the concerns of the working class. These, then, are the top 10 labor-related political action committees laboring on Capitol Hill, for the interests of unionists nationwide.

PAC	Dollar Receipts*
1. Emily's List	$9,388,631
2. Democratic Representative Independent Voter Education Committee	$6,900,158
3. Amer. Fed. of State County & Municipal Employees— People, Qualified	$4,998,227
4. Amer. Medical Assoc.	$3,577,743
5. UAW-V-CAP (UAW Voluntary Community Action Program)	$3,573,858
6. NEA	$3,455,672
7. NRA Political Victory Fund	$3,271,300
8. Assoc. of Trial Lawyers of Amer.	$3,260,235

9. Dealers Election
   Action Committee of
   the Natl. Auto Dealers
   Assoc. (NADA) $2,639,029
10. Machinists Non-
    partisan Political
    League $2,549,778

   * January 1, 1995 though June 30, 1996

Source: Federal Election Committee, 1996.

PLASTIC SURGERY

Most Popular Procedures

Tens of thousands of Americans turn to the surgeon's scalpel (or, more and more these days, laser) to improve their appearances. Modern technology, through the magic of computer imagery, allows a plastic surgeon to individualize many procedures, particularly the nose- job, giving the patient a wider bridge, a stronger, fuller nose, a gently refined tip. Other elective procedures that are growing in popularity include mentoplasty, or chin implants (often in conjunction with a face-lift and rhinoplasty to improve the profile); blepharoplasty, or eyelid surgery, which eliminates fat and excess skin around the eye to remove bags and pouches; and dermabrasion, or face sanding, in which wire brushes or diamond fraizes gently scrape the face, removing the outer layer of skin, smoothing its texture and removing superficial scars and age lines. Procedures that have declined in popularity over the past several years include eyebrow surgery, hair transplants and surgery on birthmarks.

THINGS

MOST POPULAR FOR WOMEN

Procedure	Annual Cases, U.S.
1. Liposuction	44,000
2. Eyelid Surgery	42,000
3. Breast Enlargement	39,000
4. Facelift	30,000
5. Breast Implant Removal	29,000

MOST POPULAR FOR MEN

Procedure	Annual Cases, U.S.
1. Nose Reshaping	10,000
2. Eyelid Surgery	8,600
3. Liposuction	6,600
4. Breast Reduction	4,400
5. Facelift	2,600

Source: American Society of Plastic and Reconstructive Surgeons.

 OEMS

Most Anthologized Poems in English

Poetry has always been one of the more esoteric of linguistic arts, which is why anthologies, rather than works by individual poets, are popular. The anthology allows the reader to sample the styles of a number of different poets from different eras and different places. Still, most anthologies of poetry in English feel the need to include a number of "greatest hits," some of which are familiar to the general reader, while others may be more obscure. The following are the 10 most anthologized poems in the English language, as registered by *The Concise Columbia Book of Modern Poetry: The Top 100 Poems*. The list is replete with pre-20th century poems; topping the list is English Romantic poet William Blake's "The Tyger." Only one American, Robert Frost, has a poem in the top ten; his is also the only 20th-century poem to make the list.

Poem/Poet
1. *The Tyger*   William Blake
2. *Sir Patrick Spens*   Anonymous
3. *To Autumn*   John Keats
4. *That Time of Year Thou Mayst in Me Behold*   William Shakespeare
5. *Pied Beauty*   Gerard Manly Hopkins
6. *Stopping by Woods on a Snowy Evening*   Robert Frost
7. *Kubla Khan*   Samuel Taylor Coleridge
8. *Dover Beach*   Matthew Arnold
9. *La Belle Dame sans Merci*   John Keats
10. *To the Virgins, to Make Much of Time*   Robert Herrick

Source: *The Concise Columbia Book of Poetry.*

 ADIO GROUPS

Largest Station Owners

The lyrics to an old rock and roll song went "Video killed the radio star," and sometimes that seemed to be true. Still, despite the fact that most people watch TV, radio continues to be part of all our lives, whether we listen to it while driving, working, or as background noise. Radio doesn't seem likely to be in danger of fading away, either. Increasingly, just like TV, radio has become big business, with a fairly small number of companies owning many local stations. This has led to concentrated ownership in some markets, with one company owning several stations in a specific city— and that in turn has led to fears on the part of advertisers of rising ad rates. The trend has also attracted the attention of the Justice Department, which has challenged some radio station deals in the interest of maintaining competition and upholding the antitrust laws. But the trend seems to be continuing. Here are the ten largest radio groups in the nation, based on 1995 revenues.

Company	Revenues (millions)
1. CBS Radio Station Group	$961.0
2. Evergreen Media Corp.	$362.7
3. Jacor Communications	$359.2
4. American Radio Systems License Corp.	$344.1
5. ABC	$269.8
6. Chancellor Broadcasting	$262.2
7. Clear Channel Communications	$255.2
8. SFX Broadcasting	$213.7
9. Cox Enterprises	$181.2
10. Bonneville International	$123.9

Source: BIA Publishers, Inc.

RADIO FORMATS

Most Popular Radio Formats

Tastes in American music must not have changed much. When it comes to the musical format of radio stations, the rankings are almost the same as they were in 1990, in the first edition of this book. Music aside, one significant difference in radio programing is the enormous growth of the talk shows. In 1990, there were only 405 stations in the U.S. at which news and talk were the principle formats. Today, it has more than tripled to over 1,200. Despite widespread popularity of rap and alternative among the young, radio programming goes where the American mindset goes. The O.J. Simpson trial was one of those places. With the trial sprang renewed interest in radio talk shows, hence the news/talk format is now the third most popular format in radio. And Rush Limbaugh, the fat, frank and forthright conservative who people love to cheer for or laugh at may have helped popularized the format as well.

Format	Stations, 1996
1. Country	2,558
2. Adult Contemporary	1,592
3. News, Talk, Business, Sports	1,262
4. Top-40	824
5. Religion	745
6. Oldies	659
7. Rock	419
8. Spanish and Ethnic	342
9. Adult Standards	383
10. Urban, Black, Urban AC	294

Source: M Street Corporation, 1996.

RESTAURANT CHAINS

Largest Franchised Restaurant Chains

Fast food is everywhere—there is no escape. On the strength of crispy fries, greasy burgers and unfailing fast pitches, chains like McDonald's and Burger King have established themselves as credible forces in the international economic arena. At those airy heights, competition is fierce, and the chains compete savagely for market share and public awareness, all the while counting up the billions of burgers, drumsticks and pizzas dished out to a hungry world. These are the biggest of the

THINGS

fast-food franchisers, in total annual sales—led, of course, by the ubiquitous Golden Arches. We've also listed the number of franchises for each chain.

Restaurant	Sales	Stores
1. McDonald's	$15,905	11,368
2. Burger King	$8,400	6,492
3. Pizza Hut	$5,440	8,883
4. Taco Bell	$4,500	6,490
5. Wendy's	$4,600	4,197
6. Kentucky Fried Chicken	$3,700	5,152
7. Hardee's	$3,325	3,395
8. Subway	$2,600	10,003
9. Domino's	$2,100	4,242
10. Dairy Queen	$1,200	5,000

Source: *Nation's Restaurant News*, April 29, 1996.

RETAIL STORES

The Biggest Apparel Retailers

In the last decade, large department stores, upscale cosmopolitan clothiers and other traditional retail leaders have faced major slumps and cutbacks. At the same time, aggressive, streamlined, discount merchandisers like Wal-Mart have made enormous economic inroads by playing to a younger, more fashion- and price-conscious crowd. The result has been the displacement of those stalwart department stores in the retail apparel business by these stores.

Store	Sales, 1995 (Billions)
1. Wal-Mart	$93.6
2. Sears	$34.9
3. Kmart	$34.4

THE STEEL PHANTOM at Kennywood Park, near Pittsburgh, has the longest drop of all roller coasters (22 stories) and reaches a speed of 80 mph, making it the world's fastest (See page 304).

4. Kroger	$24.0
5. Mervyn's, Target	$23.5
6. J.C. Penney	$21.4
7. American Stores	$18.3
8. Price/Costco	$17.9
9. Safeway	$16.4
10. Home Depot	$15.5

Source: *Brandweek,* Superbrands '97, October 7, 1996.

RETAIL STORES

The Largest Pharmacy Chains in the U.S.

Is there a connection between America's drug problem and the ubiquitous drug store? Past generations grew up, not at the shopping mall, but at the *drug* store. That's where millions of youths of the fifties and sixties "hung." On the busiest corner of most neighborhoods the spot to meet was marked by a neon sign that proclaimed "DRUGS." The corner drug store, owned by Mom and Pop America, was always well-stocked with Hershey Kisses and cherry Cokes at the soda fountain. It was a fundamental part of our national mythos, a herald of bygone, more innocent times. Today, however, chains predominate in today's pharmaceutical retail climate, and size and service mean all. With the loss of innocence, though, comes better service in the form of wider selection, more diverse product lines and computerized prescription systems. You may not be able to hop up to the counter and get a Coke at your local pharmacy any more, but you can get your film developed, buy a six-pack and pick up a Sony Walkman. Such is the march of progress. The following are the largest pharmacy chains in the country, measured by number of stores nationwide.

Chain	Stores
1. Rite Aid	3,653
2. Eckerd	2,638
3. Revco D.S.	2,553
4. Walgreen's	2,193
5. CVS	1,366
6. Medicine Shoppe	1,122
7. Shoppers Drug Mart	850
8. American Drug Stores	832
9. Jean Coutu	469
10. Long's Drug Stores	328

Source: *Chain Drug Review,* December 16, 1996.

ROADS, SCENIC

Best Drives in the U.S.

Scenic America, a national conservation organization, has released its annual list of America's Most Important Scenic Byways. They were chosen not only because of their distinctive scenic qualities, but also because they possess cultural, historic or natural significance. They are, alphabetically:

Road/Location

1. **Black Hawk Trail, Dixon-Rockford, IL**
   Illinois 2, 40 miles

2. **Buccaneer Trail, Fernandina Beach-St. Augustine, FL**
   Florida A1A, 52 miles

3. **Cascades Lake Highway, Bend, OR**
   Oregon 372, 68-mile loop

4. **Delaware 9, New Castle-Little Creek, DE**
   73 miles

THINGS

5. **Delaware River Scenic Drive, Easton-Morrisville, PA**
   Delaware 32 and 611, 60 miles

6. **Highway 12 Scenic Byway, Bryce Canyon Natl. Park-Capitol Reef Natl. Park, UT**
   Utah 12, 120 miles

7. **Leon County's 5 "Canopy Roads," Tallahassee, FL**
   Centerville Road, Meridian Road, Miccosukee Road, Old Bainbridge Road and Old St. Augustine Road, 65 miles

8. **San Mateo One Scenic Byway, Pescadero-Half Moon Bay, CA**
   California 1, 26 miles

9. **Richmond-Terre Haute, IN**
   U.S. 40, 140 miles

10. **Central-Copper Harbor, Keweenaw, Peninsula, MI**
    U.S. 41, 18 miles

Source: *Los Angeles Times*, March 24, 1996.

ROLLER COASTERS

Most Ups and Downs In the Fast Lane

Roller coasters—those dropping, climbing, twisting, speeding thrill rides—have been delighting Americans since 1870, when an abandoned mine train in Pennsylvania was used to carry passengers down a slight mountain grade. They have, of course, become increasingly sophisticated, fast, and exciting since that time, some featuring speeds of 80 miles per hour and drops of more than 20 stories. Today, according to the American Coaster Enthusiasts Worldwide, or ACE, there are 92 operating wood coasters in North America and 181

BLACK HAWK TRAIL, now paved and designated as Illinois Route 2, runs from Dixon to Rockford, Ill. Once the hunting ground of the Blackhawk Indians, it's where Abraham Lincoln served in the U.S. Army during the Indian Wars.

operating steel coasters. But that's nothing compared with the 1920s, the golden age of coasters, when there were about 1,500 in the United States. The first list below is of "Coaster Classics," a designation given out by ACE to traditional coasters around the world that meet strict criteria designed to ensure that riders have wild, uninhibited rides just like in the golden olden days. To be a Coaster Classic, a ride must have wooden trains, use traditional lap bars (not individual ratcheting lap bars), and let riders view the upcoming drops and thrills (so there are no headrests). In addition, they must let riders sit wherever they want and not use bucket seats or seat dividers (so riders can slide from side-to-side). The location of the rides is given, along with the official name of the coaster (which sometimes is simply Roller Coaster). The second list details the "mostest" in coasters; that is, the rides that can lay claim to some sort of superlative any coaster enthusiasts would kill to get a ride on.

COASTER CLASSICS

Location/Coaster Name/Park Name

British Columbia—Vancouver
 Roller Coaster—Playland
Colorado—Denver
 Cyclone—Lakeside
Illinois—Lemont
 Little Dipper—Hillcrest
Illinois—Melrose
 Little Dipper—Kiddieland
Kansas—Wichita
 Roller Coaster—Joyland
Kent—Margate (United Kingdom)
 Scenic Railway—Dreamland
Lancashire—Blackpool (United Kingdom)
 Roller Coaster—Blackpool Pleasure Beach
Lancashire—Blackpool (United Kingdom)
 Zipper Dipper—Blackpool Pleasure Beach
Merseyside—Southport (United Kingdom)
 Cyclone—Pleasureland
New York—Brooklyn
 Cyclone—Astroland
New York—Rye
 Kiddy Coaster—Playland
Norfolk—Great Yarmouth (United Kingdom)
 Roller Coaster—Pleasure Beach
Ohio—Aurora
 Big Dipper—Geauga Lake
Ohio—Powell
 Sea Dragon—Wyandot Lake
Oklahoma—Oklahoma City
 Wildcat—Frontier City
Pennsylvania—Altoona
 Skyliner—Lakemont
Pennsylvania—Conneaut Lake
 Blue Streak—Conneaut Lake Park
Pennsylvania—Ligonier
 RolloCoaster—Idlewild Park
Pennsylvania—West Mifflin
 Jack Rabbit—Kennywood
Pennsylvania—West Mifflin
 Thunderbolt—Kennywood
Pennsylvania—Williams Grove
 Cyclone—Williams Grove
Washington—Puyallup
 Roller Coaster—Western Washington Fair
West Virginia—Huntington
 Big Dipper—Camden
West Virginia—Huntington
 Lil Dipper—Camden

"MOSTEST" IN COASTERS

The Fastest: the Steel Phantom West Mifflin, Pa.—80 mph.
The Roughest Ride: the Riverside Cyclone, Agawam, Mass.—first drop from 0 to 60 mph in 3 seconds

The Smoothest Ride: the Yankee Cannonball. Salem, N.H.—2,000 feet long, 35 mph, 2-minute ride

The Longest Drop: the Steel Phantom West Mifflin, Pa.—22 stories (also the fastest–see above)

The Most Terrifying: the Twister. Denver—twisting ride that includes a 65 mph plunge into a tunnel along a high-banked curve

The Most Bizarre: the Dragon Coaster, Rye, N.Y.—a 2-minute ride through the mouth of a dragon

Source: American Coaster Enthusiasts Worldwide, Inc.; America By the Numbers.

SHAKESPEAREAN PLAYS

Greatest and Most Ignored

In another rating, we saw that Shakespeare rates as the greatest writer of all time (see "People" chapter). And in this rating, we note the greatest works of that greatest of writers. Topping the list is the tragedy *Hamlet*, the tale of the tragic Prince of Denmark, which contains, among innumerable other great quotations that have become part of the Bard's cultural legacy, the immortal soliloquy "To be or not to be." From the list below, which rates the plays according to the number of citations for each work in the MLA International Bibliography, Shakespeare's most lasting and important plays turn out to be primarily his tragedies—after *Hamlet*, the next greatest Shakespearean plays are *King Lear*, *Macbeth* and *Othello*. Comedies also appear in the top 10 list; absent from the list of bests are the historical dramas. If Shakespeare's sonnets

were included in this list, they would rank seventh, with an overall score of 173. However, his other poetry does not fare so well. "The Rape of Lucrece" scored a measly 24, while "Venus And Adonis" tallied 21, "The Phoenix and the Turtle," 8, and "The Lover's Complaint" a meager 4. The rating does not include plays of doubtful or composite authorship, such as *Edward III* or *The Two Noble Kinsmen*.

GREATEST PLAYS

Play	Score
1. *Hamlet*	724
2. *King Lear*	423
3. *Macbeth*	271
4. *Othello*	265
5. *The Tempest*	210
6. *The Merchant of Venice*	181
7. *A Midsummer Night's Dream*	166
8. *Measure for Measure*	153
9. *Romeo and Juliet*	151
10. *The Winter's Tale*	132

MOST IGNORED PLAYS

Play	Scores
1. *Henry VI, Part I*	18
2. *Henry VI, Part III*	20
3. *Henry VI, Part II*	23
4. *The Comedy of Errors*	24
5. *The Two Gentlemen of Verona*	26
6. *Henry VIII*	28
7. *Timon of Athens*	35
8. *Much Ado About Nothing*	38
9. *Pericles*	39
10. *The Merry Wives of Windsor*	42

Source: *Best and Worst* original.

SNAKES, POISONOUS

The Most Venomous of Vermin

Most people have a built-in horror of snakes, and that fear is more justified than not. Snakes attack in one of two extremely unpleasant ways: either they coil around the victim, crushing it to death before ingesting it, or they bite, injecting a paralyzing or death-dealing poison through the fangs. No wonder the snake is the symbol of evil in the Judeo-Christian heritage. Most venomous snakes are relatively small, but just because a snake is shockingly big does not mean that it isn't also appallingly toxic: the Black Mamba grows to 14 feet, but the venom will get you right off the bat. These, then, are the most venomous members of the serpent world.

Rank/Species

1. Coral Snake
3. Rattlesnake
4. Cottonmouth Water Moccasin
5. Copperhead
6. Bushmaster
7. Fer-de-Lance
8. Asian Pit Viper
9. Sharp-Nosed Pit Viper
10. Puff Adder

SOFT DRINKS

Most Popular Soft Drinks

Coca-Cola is not merely a soda, it is an unshakable American icon. In fact, these days, Coke is the most recognizable brand name in the world. Pepsi has nipped at the giant's heels for decades, but somehow, Coke has always managed to stay on top— this despite some enormous strategic and marketing gaffes in the past decade. First and foremost was changing the tried-and-true formula to create the brief, unpopular "New Coke." Then there was the Magic Cans promotion fiasco, in which consumers could win money inside of cans of Coke. The winning cans were filled with a non-potable water so that you couldn't tell which were winners just by feel, but some winners consumed the water anyway, making them sick; the campaign also violated one of the great rules of marketing—people who paid money for a Coke didn't get a Coke. And then there was the pompous 1991 Super Bowl spot that replaced the culmination of a lengthy customer contest with a stark announcement that the Persian Gulf war was too serious an issue for the Coke contest to continue. What better forum for making such a pronouncement than the Super Bowl? Pepsi, on the other hand, used the same forum to introduce a popular new ad campaign. Yes, Coke has stumbled of late, but never yet has the giant fallen. These days, indeed, "Coca-Cola" is no one single thing. Classic, Cherry, Diet, decaf—all are valid options in today's bubbly market.

Brand	Case Sales (millions)
1. Coca-Cola	1,827.0
2. Pepsi-Cola	1,404.5
3. Diet Coke	793.0
4. Dr. Pepper	548.4
5. Diet Pepsi	511.2
6. Mountain Dew	503.2
7. Sprite	439.3
8. 7-UP	250.7
9. Caffeine Free Diet Coke	202.3
10. Caffeine Free Diet Dr. Pepper	101.6

Source: *Brandweek*, Superbrands '97, October 7, 1996)

SNACK FOOD

Each year Americans spend approximately $8 billion on snack food, much of it fried, high in fat, covered with gooey cheese and absolutely delicious! Without a doubt, snack foods are the favorites when Mom and Dad are not around to police the voracious appetites that are part of youth. But adults crave treats too, especially when the scale isn't around to police *their* appetites. What are the favorites of our nutritionally misspent youth? Following are their picks for snacks, with the percentages of those who eat them regularly:

Snack Food	Percent Who Consume
1. Pizza	82%
2. Chicken nuggets	51%
3. Hot dogs	45%
4. Cheeseburgers	42%
Macaroni and Cheese	42%
6. Hamburgers	38%
7. Spaghetti and meatballs	37%
Fried chicken	37%
9. Tacos	32%
10.Grilled cheese sandwiches	22%

Source: Gallup Poll, 1995.

SPORTS— PARTICIPATION

Most Popular

In our exercise-conscious culture, non-competitive pastimes like swimming, exercise walking and bicycling garner far more participants than classic, highly organized team activities like baseball, basketball and football. Perhaps because one can do them alone. As we age, it just seems to be more and more difficult to gather up the req-

AMERICANS LOVE TO PLAY THE GAME, one of the top-ten participation sports.
Photo: The Flames at the University of Illinois.

uisite numbers to engage in such team sports.

Activity	Participants (1,000s)
1. Exercise walking	70,794
2. Swimming	60,277
3. Bicycle riding	49,818
4. Exercise with equipment	43,784
5. Camping	42,932
6. Fishing—fresh water	40,477
7. Bowling	37,356
8. Basketball	28,191
9. Hiking	25,301
10. Golf	24,551

Source: National Sporting Goods Association, *Sports Participation in 1994: Series I* (SAUS, 1996).

SPORTS FRANCHISES

Greatest Sports Teams of All Time

Certain sports teams are synonymous with success. While other franchises content themselves with a championship once every few decades, others expect nothing less than victory, and achieve it season after season. Though every team goes through periods of mediocrity, the top franchises on our list—the Yankees, Canadiens, Celtics and Lakers—are never down for very long, evidence of savvy front offices and of a tradition of winning that infuses new players when they don these teams' uniforms. We rated the success of professional sports franchises in football, basketball, baseball and hockey as the sum of franchise winning-percentage (times 1000) and total number of championships won (times 100). These are the winningest teams in North American sports history:

EVEN IN A SO-SO YEAR, it's the number-one sports franchise of all time.

Franchise / %	Titles	Score*
1. New York Yankees		
.562	23	2862
2. Montreal Canadiens		
.607	21	2707
3. Boston Celtics		
.623	16	2223
4. Los Angeles Lakers		
.607	11	1707
5. Toronto Maple Leafs		
.502	11	1602
6. Green Bay Packers		
.541	9	1441
7. St. Louis Cardinals		
.516	9	1416
8. Chicago Bears		
.599	8	1399
9. Dallas Cowboys		
.602	5	1102
10. Edmonton Oilers		
.568	5	1068

* scores based on data up to 1996
Source: *Best and Worst* original.

STRESS

Most Stressful Events

In 1967, Doctors Thomas Holmes and Richard Rahe published their findings about how stress can effect your health in an article called "The Social Readjustment Scale," printed in *The Journal of Psychosomatic Research.* Drs. Holmes and Rahe gave stressful events point values and found that any combination of points totaling 300 or more would in all probability lead to a major illness. Holmes' and Rahe's findings have stood the test of time and are now widely regarded and reprinted. If your point total seems to be getting up there, perhaps you ought to consider taking a vacation—that is, if you can afford the 13 stress points it will cost you.

Event	Point Value
1. Death of a spouse	100
2. Divorce	73
3. Marital separation	65
4. Jail or other institution	63
Death of close family member	63
6. Major injury or illness	53
7. Marriage	50
8. Being fired at work	47
9. Marital reconciliation	45
Retirement	45

Source: *The Social Readjustment Scale*, by T. Holmes and R. Rahe.

SUPERBOWL SPONSORS

Most Commercial Minutes Purchased on the Super Bowl

Oh, the Super Bowl—January's annual communal ritual, when viewers attending innumerable parties gather in front of the TV to watch the winner of the AFC battle the winner of the NFC to decide the National Football League champion. It doesn't seem to matter that the game is often a blowout—in 1995, for example, the 49ers beat the Chargers by a score of 49-26. What matters is that it's Super Bowl Sunday! Half the fun, in fact, is the halftime show—and the other half may well be the ads that have their premiere during the game. Advertisers have engineered the game— and the ads—into an Event, taking full advantage of the fact that over the years, the Super Bowl has continued to attract huge numbers of viewers in every demographic group. Super Bowl advertisers pay dearly for the chance to air their wares before those viewers: For the 1997 game, a 30-second segment cost an average of $1.2 million. This list shows the advertisers that purchased the most minutes for the 1997 game.

Company	Minutes Purchased
1. Anheuser-Busch	4.0
2. Pepsi	3.0
3. Oscar Meyer	1.5
Porsche	2.5
4. Coca-Cola	1.0
Fox Film Studio	1.0
Honda	1.0
Nike	1.0
Nissan	1.0
Paramount	1.0

Source: *Advertising Age.*

SUPER BOWLS

Top 10 Televised Super Bowls

Among all professional sporting events, Super Bowls are without question the most watched games in broadcast history. Of the top 10 most-watched television programs of all time, according to A.C. Nielsen figures, Super Bowls account for most of the programs on the list. Super Bowl games traditionally draw more than 100 million viewers. Our list ranks the top 10 according to shares and ratings, the standard measures for determining audiences for a given program. A share is the percentage of all households watching television generally when the program is on, and ratings reflect the percentage of people who are watching the specific program.

Game/Date/Matchup	Share/Rating
1. XVI 1/24/82 San Francisco/Cincinnati	**73/49.1**
2. XVII 1/30/83 Washington/Miami	**69/48.6**
3. XX 1/26/86 Chicago/New England	**70/48.3**
4. XII 1/15/78 Dallas/Denver	**67/47.2**
5. XIII 1/21/79 Pittsburgh/Dallas	**74/47.1**
6. XVIII L.A. Raiders/Washington	**71/46.4**
7. XIX 1/20/85 San Francisco/Miami	**63/46.4**
8. XIV 1/20/80 Pittsburgh/L.A. Rams	**67/46.3**
9. XXI 1/25/87 N.Y. Giants/Denver	**65/45.8**
10. XXVIII 1/29/94 San Diego/San Francisco	**64/45.5**

Source: Nielsen Media Research.

TELEVISION, CABLE

Largest Cable Operators

The Big Three—NBC, CBS and ABC—have been watching their shares of the television market dwindle over the past two decades. The Fox Network is on the scene now, stealing a lot of network thunder (and viewers). And from humble origins, such cable networks as the all-sports ESPN and the all-news CNN have achieved true network parity, particulary in the wake of the latter's non-stop coverage of the O.J. Simpson Trial. Perhaps the single most important moment in cable's history—the moment that legitimized CNN, and all of cable TV, for that matter—was when the Iraqi authorities cut the three news networks' lines out of Baghdad, while CNN remained on the air from the stricken city. From that point forward, television would never be the same. The following are the top cable stations in the country, in terms of total number of subscribers.

Network	Subscribers (millions)
1. ESPN	67.9
2. CNN	67.8
3. TBS	67.6
4. USA Network	67.2
5. The Discovery Channel	67.0
6. TNT	66.6
7. C-Span	66.1
8. MTV: Music Television	65.9
9. Arts & Entertainment Network	65.0
10. TNN (The Nashville Network)	64.8

Source: National Cable Television Association, January-March, 1996

TELEVISION, EPISODES

The Greatest Episodes of All Time

In these post-modern times, our gathering place is often in front of the TV. Nothing has captivated the nation in the last 50 years more than the tube. On its screen, we have witnessed the world go by as it happened, as well as how television writers imagined it could happen. We've seen bikini-clad crime fighters, live assassinations, and hilarious comedy. Certain of these episodes have left an indelible impression on us via a particular favorite episode that rang especially true, shockingly bizarre, or particularly funny. Here we go back to some of them, at least the ones the gurus of television point to as the best ever. Following are the top ten television episodes of all time, as determined by the staff of *TV Guide* and Nickelodeon Television.

TV Show/Date Aired/Synopses

1. The Mary Tyler Moore Show
October 25, 1975
Death is made hilarious in this taboo-shattering episode, which featured characters at the fictional WJM-TV, all trying to cope with the freak death of Chuckles the Clown, the station's kiddy-show host. Dressed as a peanut to lead a circus parade, Chuckles met his maker when a "rogue elephant tried to shell him." Mary Tyler Moore takes her character through the emotional gamut, while Ed Asner and Ted Knight worked both the comic and the tragic to make this the most memorable episode of all time.

2. I Love Lucy
May 5, 1952
Lucille Ball's genius for physical comedy is brought front and center in her portrayal of the "Vitameatavegamin Girl" for a TV variety show. She's supposedly promoting the health benefits of the wonder potion, but ends up getting sloppy drunk on it instead. Mayhem ensues, with Lucy giving her final endorsement of the "bittle lottle" by calling it "this stuff."

3. ER
March 9, 1995
You think you've had bad days at the office? Anthony Edwards depicts Dr. Mark Greene— the normally steady- handed emergency room maestro—unraveling toward disaster with harrowing accuracy. Hampered by problems at home and work, Greene misdiagnoses a pregnant woman and continues a series of missteps that sends the whole "ER" into pandemonium.

4. Seinfeld
February 12, 1992
No show has ever portrayed the mundane, trivial events of everyday life with such dead-on hilarity. This episode typically featured numerous "non-plots" in its telling of Jerry "dating" and then "losing" pro baseball player Keith Hernandez to Elaine; George concocting various ploys to extend his unemployment benefits; and Kramer bungling one of them by his failure to answer the phone: "Vandelay Industries."

5. The Odd Couple
January 28, 1956
The pair that wrote the book on incompatibility. Through some cosmic screw-up, Felix and Oscar (Tony Randall and Jack Klugman, respectively) ended up as roommates in New York City. In this episode, the mismatched Manhattanites attempt to team-up to win a game show, but a communication breakdown results. Answers get botched and tempers flare as only Felix and Oscar could do it.

6. The Honeymooners
January 28, 1956
Ralph Kramden was always the dreamer, hatching one money-making scheme after another, each to no avail. In this episode, Ralph (Jackie Gleason) gets a shot as a contestant on a popular music game show, and prepares intensely for the big day. Ed (Art Carney) his accompanist, warms up for each practice session with a chorus of "Swanee River." Naturally, Ralph is getting annoyed, hearing it time-and-time-again. Of course, fate deals Ralph the Joker when, finally on the contestant's stand during the broadcast, he is asked to name the composer of "Swanee River." Ralph stutters and does his classic "humminahumminas" a good long time before incorrectly blurting out his answer, "Ed Norton."

7. Cheers
November 27, 1986
One of the best-written, best-acted series ever, Cheers hit a high water mark during a Thanksgiving episode. The gang at the bar has no plans for Turkey Day, so they all head over to Carla's for dinner— but first Norm's (George Wendt) "birdzilla" has to finish cooking. The hungry guests start getting restless, and it isn't long before the side-dishes start flying, in one of the greatest on-screen food fights ever. In this episode, Norm's never-seen wife, Vera, joins the shindig too, but the instant she walks in the door, she is hit in the face with a pie.

8. The Dick Van Dyke Show
September 15, 1965
Mess with the boss, and you're asking for trouble. Reveal the fact that he has a toupee, and . . . who

knows what will happen? Boisterous mirth, that's what. When Laura (Mary Tyler Moore) reveals on a game-show that her husband's boss (who happens to be a national TV star) dons a rug, it's not a question as to "what" the boss (Carl Reiner) will do, but "how" he'll do it. TV Guide called this episode a "caustic meditation on male vanity and office etiquette." And it's funny!

9. The Bob Newhart Show
November 22, 1975
Poker-face Bob Newhart, better than anyone, can elicit laughs with his blood-hound eyes. And doubly so with his blood shot eyes. In this madcap, inebriated whirl, his character, a psychotherapist, can't accompany his wife on a Thanksgiving holiday because he wants to be available to Mr. Carlin, one of his wacko patients. Carlin, hating to be alone, comes over to watch football with Bob and his pals. Pretty soon, the whole gang is swigging copious amounts of grain alcohol. By the time the delivery guy drops off their enormous order of Chinese food, the boys are loaded. Then Bob's wife arrives.

10. The X-Files
October 13, 1995
In this stellar, mind-blowing episode, Peter Boyle plays Bruckman, a life insurance salesman who can predict people's deaths. This particular skill puts him in danger, and puts the X-Files gang to work. Scully (Gillian Anderson), one of the show's stars, asks Bruckman when she will die. "You don't," he tells her. And with that tantalizing clue, the mystery marches on.

Source: *TV Guide*, June 28-July 4, 1997.

TELEVISION PROGRAMS

Top-Rated TV Series of the 1950s

Today's TV generation is, in fact, made up of the children of yesterday's TV generation. So, in the name of mutual understanding—and in attempt to bridge the generation gap with a single span—here are the golden hits of Ma and Pa's couch potato past. The list is notable for its preponderance of the now-extinct variety show, as well as the prime-time quiz show.

Program	Average Rating
1. *Arthur Godfrey's Talent Scouts*	32.9
2. *I Love Lucy*	31.6
3. *You Bet Your Life*	30.1
4. *Dragnet*	24.6
5. *The Jack Benny Show*	22.3
6. *Arthur Godfrey and Friends*	19.5
7. *Gunsmoke*	15.6
8. *The Red Skelton Show*	15.2
9. *December Bride*	13.8
10. *I've Got a Secret*	12.9

Source: A.C. Nielsen.

TELEVISION PROGRAMS

Top-Rated TV Series of the 1970s

The Seventies are back!!! Run away!!! On the music scene there are neo-psychedelic, seventies-flashback culture kids. Across the country, bell-bottoms, leisure suits, long sideburns and, worst of all, disco, are re-emerging from well-earned hibernation. All this hubbub has awoken a parallel interest in that era's questionable-classics of the small screen. From *The Brady*

Bunch to Batman, the re-runs are rolling back the years, shifting gears and transporting us the era of Convoy and Convy (Bert). Indeed, a Chicago theater group has been packing them in with weekly performances of *Brady Bunch* episodes, word for word from the original scripts. Next year, watch out for the Sonny and Cher reunion tour.

Program	Average Rating
1. *All In The Family*	23.0
2. *M*A*S*H*	17.6
3. *Hawaii Five-O*	16.6
4. *Happy Days*	15.9
5. *The Waltons*	14.0
6. *Mary Tyler Moore Show*	13.7
7. *Sanford and Son*	13.4
8. *One Day at a Time*	11.4
9. *Three's Company*	10.8
10. *60 Minutes*	10.0

Source: A.C. Nielsen.

TELEVISION PROGRAMS

Top-Rated TV Series of the 1980s

The top television shows were rated according to three factors: (1) Emmy Awards; (2) Nielsen ratings; and (3) television critic's evaluations. In the first category, 15 points were awarded for each Emmy Award. In category two, 10 points were awarded for each year the show was in the top 10 in Nielsen's annual year-end ratings. In category three, each television critic's vote counted for four points—six critics's judgments were used. Although *The Cosby Show* consistently had the highest Nielsen ratings from 1986 through 1989, it garnered only one Emmy for Best Series. *Nightline's* ratings,

on the other hand, were not as high, but it is considered by critics as one of the best news shows on the air. What began as a response to the 1979 Iranian hostage crisis has turned out to be an intelligent and much-needed alternative to Johnny Carson's monologues.

Show	Total Score
1. *Cheers*	131
2. *Hill Street Blues*	119
3. *The Golden Girls*	108
4. *Cagney & Lacey*	78
5. *The Cosby Show*	73
6. *L.A. Law*	71
7. *thirtysomething*	69
8. *The Wonder Years*	43
9. *Nightline*	24
Lonesome Dove	24

Source: *Best and Worst* original.

TELEVISION PROGRAMS

Highest-Rated Syndicated Programs

Though we often watch them on network stations like NBC, CBS or ABC, they are not "network" shows. They are "syndicated shows," produced independently, by smaller creative studios who sell the rights to broadcast them to stations on the airwaves, cable and satellite. Among these programs are America's favorite game shows. Inexpensive to produce but highly lucrative in the long-run, the games shows *Wheel of Fortune* and *Jeopardy!* are estimated to be worth several hundred million dollars in syndication rights. That has made Merv Griffin, the man who has controlled those rights, a rich man. Syndicated programs often develop their own highly devoted following, those folks who slip through the

FOR MANY YEARS—and probably for many more— she's still the most popular toy, Barbie. And she's still going with Ken, but is likely to have many other suiters.

prime-time net, and get their TV at all hours of the day and night. Rights to reruns of network programs are also hot commodities. The first time around is great, but the second is so much sweeter. On their first run, network programs need to recoup the enormous production dollars spent to bring them to the small screen. On the rebound, however, the price is paid, the path paved and the profits pure.

Series	Rating*
1. *Wheel of Fortune*	13.0
2. *Jeopardy!*	10.8
3. *Home Improvement*	10.5
4. *Seinfeld*	8.8
5. *Oprah Winfrey Show*	8.7
6. *National Geographic on Assignment*	8.6
7. *ESPN NFL Regular Season*	7.1
8. *Entertainment Tonight*	7.2
9. *Buena Vista*	7.7
10. *The Simpsons*	6.9

    * through February 2, 1997
Source: Nielsen Media Research, 1997

TELEVISION VIEWING

Most Popular Viewing Days

In many households, every night is TV night. Viewing for many mainstream Americans, in point of fact, has come to closely resemble a second full-time occupation, with the number of hours logged in front of the television rivaling, or even surpassing, that spent in the work place. In any case, those who have assumed this laborious entertainment burden seem to be holding up well as they log their dozens of hours of hardcore viewing each week. These are the most popular days of the week for video viewing, in descending order.

Day	Viewers (millions)
1. Sunday	106.4
2. Tuesday	99.2
3. Monday	95.6
4. Thursday	95.5
5. Wednesday	94.1
6. Friday	89.8
7. Saturday	89.1

Source: Nielsen Media Research.

Most Popular Toys

Following are the 10 best-selling toys of 1996, based on a survey of the nation's retailers by the trade magazine *Playthings*. Three of the top five—Barbie, Star Wars and Batman—also appeared on the 1995 bestseller list. Toys may be just kid stuff, but they are also big business. An honest-to-God marketing hit can mean tens—even hundreds—of millions of dollars in annual revenue. Among the leading toys in the land, Barbie has held tenaciously to her spot as king of the doll hill, finishing second overall. Only the poker-hot Nintendo Video Action system sold better in last year's boom market. Seems toyland is split in a struggle between traditional playthings such as dolls and houses and the new high-tech wizardry of the video system.

Toy/Manufacturer

1. The Barbie Doll /Mattel
2. *Star Wars* merchandise/Hasbro Toy Group

3. Nintendo 64 video games/ Nintendo
4. Baby Go Bye Bye doll/Hasbro Toy Group
5. Batman merchandise/Hasbro Toy Group
6. Saturn video game/Sega
7. Tickle Me Elmo plush toy/Tyco
8. Beanie Babies plush toys/Ty Inc.
9. Wild West building set /Lego
10. Bananas in Pajamas plush toys Tomy America

Source: *Los Angeles Times*, November 22, 1996.

TRAFFIC FATALITIES

Driving Under a Bad Influence

Let's look at the positive side: there are some advantages to age. Comparing 1995 figures with 1985, there was an increase of 47 percent in the number of older drivers, while the total number of licensed drivers increased only 13 percent in the same time period. And these older drivers drove more safely than the younger ones. In 1995, older drivers accounted for a mere five percent of all people injured in traffic accidents, comprising 13 percent of all traffic fatalities and 18 percent of all pedestrian fatalities. In two-vehicle fatal crashes involving an older driver and a younger one, the vehicle driven by the older person was about three times as likely to be the one that was struck. Older drivers involved in fatal crashes had the lowest proportion of intoxication, with blood alcohol concentrations (BAC) of 0.10 grams per deciliter (g/dl) or greater, of all adult drivers. Fatally injured older pedestrians also had the lowest intoxication rate of all adult pedestrian fatalities.

Age Group	Percentage Intoxicated
1. Age 21-34	27.2%
2. Age 35-54	19.9%
3. Age 16-20	12.7%
4. Age 55-69	11.0%
5. Age 16 or younger	4.4%
6. Age 70 or older	4.2%

Source: *Traffic Safety Facts, 1995*, National Highway Traffic Safety Administration.

TRUCKS— MAKES AND MODELS

Most Popular "Light Trucks"

For the last several years, sales of light trucks have dominated the auto industry, as more and more car buyers are opting to purchase trucks instead of their smaller counterparts. To the industry, "light trucks" means pickups, sport-utility vehicles, and minivans. Maybe their robust sales can be traced to their sturdy yet sporty appearance. Or maybe it's all those soccer moms out there—how else can you carpool a troop of kids and all their stuff? Whatever the reasons, here are two lists demonstrating the continued strong demand for these vehicles. The first lists U.S. light truck sales by manufacturer in 1996. The second lists the top-selling light truck models in 1996. It was the third year in a row that the Ford F-Series pickup topped the list of best-selling vehicles, with the Chevrolet C/K pickup right behind, also for the third year in a row. Following are the top selling trucks.

MANUFACTURER

Manufacturer	Units Sold
1. Ford	2,106,186
2. General Motors	1.985,886
3. Chrysler	1,618,193
4. Toyota	366,126
5. Nissan	249,386
6. Isuzu	93,887
7. Honda	57,774
8. Mazda	57,310
9. Suzuki	26,322
10. Land Rover	23,128

TRUCK SALES BY MODEL

Model	Units Sold
1. Ford F-Series	780,838
2. Chevrolet C/K	550,594
3. Ford Explorer	402,663
4. Dodge Ram	383,960
5. Dodge Caravan	300,117
6. Ford Ranger	288,393
7. Jeep Grand Cherokee	279,195
8. Chevrolet S-10 Blazer	246,307
9. Ford Windstar	209,033
10. Chevrolet S-10 Pickup	190,178

Source: Industry sales statistics.

VEGETABLES

Most Calories per Serving

When your mom made you eat your vegetables, she certainly wasn't trying to fatten you up. Vegetables have one of the highest ratios of nutritional value per calorie—the biggest bang for the buck—and most lack the fat and sodium so harmful to the common American diet. These are the vegetables with the most calories per serving; compared to dessert items and fatty meat products, even the top-rated potato comes out smelling sweet.

Vegetable	Calories
1. Potato	145
2. Sweet Potato	115
3. Corn	85
4. Parsnips	63
5. Brussels Sprouts	60
6. Artichoke	55
7. Winter Squash	40
8. Broccoli	40
9. Onion (cooked)	30
10. Carrot	30

Source: Human Nutrition Information Service, U.S. Department of Agriculture.

WARS, DEADLIEST

Most Fatalities in World War II

Total military deaths in World War II are estimated at around 20 to 25 million. The truly shocking fact is that civilian deaths roughly equaled that figure. The reasons are many. In Yugoslavia, two-thirds of all deaths were civilians, the tragedy being that the German invasion of that country sparked a civil war between Communist and Royalist forces, in addition to unleashing inter-ethnic warfare between Croatians, Serbs and other nationalist groups there. In Russia, Yugoslavia, Poland and elsewhere under the Nazi yoke, populations of entire villages and towns were massacred in response to partisan and resistance attacks on German occupation forces. Other civilians died in bombing campaigns against cities—including atomic bombings of Hiroshima and Nagasaki, and the even more devastating fire-bombing of Tokyo, which caused an estimated 100,000 civilian deaths. Of course, the largest number of civilian victims perished in the Holocaust—6 million Jews from all over Europe.

MOST OVERALL DEATHS

Country	Total Dead
1. Soviet Union	15.0 million
2. Poland	6.6 million
3. Germany	6.2 million
4. China	2.2 million
5. Japan	2.0 million
6. Yugoslavia	1.4 million
7. Hungary	850,000
8. France	650,000
9. Romania	640,000
10. Britain	450,000
11. USA	408,000
12. Austria	405,000
13. Czechoslovakia	280,000
14. Italy	220,000
15. Netherlands	206,000
16. Belgium	200,000

MOST MILITARY DEATHS

Country	Military Deaths
1. Soviet Union	7.5 million
2. Germany	4.75 million
3. Japan	1.5 million
4. China	1.35 million
5. Poland	600,000
6. United States	408,000
7. Yugoslavia	400,000
Hungary	400,000
9. Britain	350,000
10. Romania	340,000
11. Austria	280,000
12. Czechoslovakia	250,000
13. France	200,000
14. Italy	150,000
15. Belgium	110,000
16. Netherlands	6,000

MOST CIVILIAN DEATHS

Country	Civilian Deaths
1. Soviet Union	7.5 million
2. Poland	6.0 million
3. Germany	1.47 million
4. Yugoslavia	1 million
5. China	800,000

6. Japan	500,000
7. Hungary	450,000
France	450,000
9. Romania	300,000
10. Netherlands	200,000
11. Austria	125,000
12. Britain	100,000
13. Belgium	90,000
14. Italy	70,000
15. Czechoslovakia	30,000
16. USA	0

Source: World Military and Social Expenditures.

WARS, DEADLIEST

Deadliest U.S. Wars

War is always a great calamity, but it surprises many to learn that one of America's most calamitous losses of men and material came at the hands of its own generals. Beyond the vast global destruction of World War II, the War Between the States has been this country's most devastating conflict. Such is the power and tragedy of a nation of brothers turned to arms.

Conflict	U.S. Battle Deaths
1. World War II	291,557
2. Civil War*	140,414
3. World War I	53,402
4. Vietnam	47,382
5. Korean War	33,629
6. Revolutionary War	4,435
7. War of 1812	2,260
8. Mexican War	1,733
9. Spanish American War	385

* this includes only Union casualties; Confederate deaths are estimated at about the same number, although accurate figures were often not kept by the Confederacy

Source: Department of Defense

WARS, LONGEST

One of the frightening elements of our modern era is the speed at which everything happens. It seems that in the days of yore, people took their time about things, wars included. In the most recent Persian Gulf War, the land battle took 100 hours. The longest continuous conflict in history was the Crusades. In a way, the struggle is still going on, because the contestants are still fighting: Christianity against Islam. The Crusades took place over a period of nearly 200 years, from 1096 to 1291, during which four separate excursions from Europe to the Middle East failed to regain the Holy Lands. Imagine the difficulty CNN would have had continuously broadcasting *that* conflict! Like today's battles between East and West, the Crusades were an indecisive war, with each side claiming its own victory. Of the notable wars through history, the following list is organized by duration.

War	Duration (years)
1. **Crusades**	195
Christianity v. Islam, 1096-1291	
2. **Hundred Years War**	115
England v. France, 1338-1453	
3. **Thirty Years War**	30
Catholics v. Protestants, 1618-1648	
War of the Roses	30
Lancaster v. York, 1655-1685	
5. **Peloponnesian War**	27
Sparta v. Athens, 431-404 B.C.	
6. **First Punic War**	23
Rome v. Carthage, 264-241 B.C.	
7. **Greco-Persian Wars**	21
Greek States v. Persia, 499-478 B.C.	

Second Great Northern War   21
Russia v. Sweden & Baltic Allies,
1700-1721

9. Napoleonic Wars   19
France v. rest of Europe, 1796-
1815

10. Second Punic War   17
Rome v. Carthage, 218-201 B.C.

Source: *Funk & Wagnall's Standard College Dictionary.*

WATER, BOTTLED

Most Popular Brands

The second coming of the "natural
craze" has done wonders for sales
of water. After decades of satisfaction with tap water, many Americans want their water from the
ground, naturally. Below are the
best-selling bottled waters, among
those that sell over $100 million
worth of their product.

Water	Sales, 1995 (millions)
1. Arrowhead	$234.3
2. Poland Spring	$201.9
3. Evian	$170.0
4. Sparkletts	$157.0
5. Hinckley & Schmitt	$113.7

Source: Beverage Marketing Corp.

WEAPONS

Deadliest Weapons in the U.S. Arsenal

Military historian Colonel Trevor
N. Dupuy has devised a formula for
evaluating the relative effectiveness of weapons in war. Using values that are either published or
known by experience, his formula
takes into account a weapon's rate
of fire, number of targets hit per

THEY EVEN SELL IT IN THE PARK, Poland Springs Natural Spring Water, one of
the top-five best-selling brands.

single strike, the incapacitating effect of a single strike from the
weapon and the weapon's effective
range, accuracy and reliability. In
addition, for a mobile weapon such
as a tank or armored personnel car-
rier, the formula considers the
weapon's speed, distance without
refueling, armored protection, ra-
pidity of fire, fire control and
amount of ammunition carried. Aircraft also are affected by their operational ceiling. The resulting
figure—the "Operational Lethality
Index", as Dupuy calls it—can be
used to compare the relative lethality— the killing ability—of weapons systems. According to Dupuy's
formula, ground attack aircraft are
more lethal than tanks—thus dem-

onstrating the value of air superiority in the theatre of combat. One need only look at the devastation visit on Iraqi ground forces in the Persian Gulf War to see an example of the lethality index in practice. The A-10 Warthog's high score results from the incredible array of ground-attack weapons it carries—from bombs and cannons to missiles—combined with its high amount of protective armor and its great mobility. Below are the operational lethality scores for weapons in the U.S. arsenal.

Weapon System	Lethality Score
1. One Megaton Nuclear Airburst	173,846
2. B-52 Bomber	10,063
3. A-10 Ground Attack Plane	2,697
4. F-111E Bomber	1,922
5. A-6E Navy Bomber	1,484
6. F-16 Fighter-Bomber	1,359
7. M1A1 Abrams Tank	1,049
8. A7 Navy Bomber	707
9. M60A3 Tank	650
10. M3 Bradley Fighting Vehicle	597

Source: T.N. Dupuy, *Numbers, Prediction and War: Using History to Evaluate Combat Factors and Predict the Outcome of Battles,* New York: Bobbs-Merrill Co., 1979; and T.N. Dupuy et al, *How to Defeat Saddam Hussein: Scenarios and Strategies for the Gulf War* (New York: Warner Books, 1991.)

WEEKEND ACTIVITIES

Thank God It's Friday and Saturday!

Only about half the world breaks on Saturday and Sunday; outside the Western world, the idea of the weekend has yet to catch on universally. In 1908, the first five-day work week came to America, when a spinning mill in New England arranged its hours to accommodate its Jewish workers, who observed the Sabbath on Saturday. Unionism, which was on the rise in America, had many Jewish leaders, particularly in the garment industries of the manufacturing centers of the North. Hard-goods manufacturers soon followed suit. Henry Ford, an alleged anti-Semite and staunch anti-unionist, was the first industrial baron to launch a five-day week. In 1926 he closed his plants on Saturday. His motives were, however, less than altruistic. At that time, the automobile was no less a recreational item than a mode of transportation for the middel class, and Ford believed the practice would be a boon to the leisure industry. Ford got his way. America took to the weekend—and to the automobile—with a vengeance. Today, few families, even the poorest, don't have an automoible. The list below, compiled by the American Automobile Association, reveals where we stay on our weekend jaunts. The average cost of a weekend for a family of two adults and two children is about $200.

Location	Percent of Travelers
Hotels	54%
Friends or relatives	22%
Campgrounds	17%
Vacation homes	7%

The following list details the most popular weekend pastimes. (Figures add up to more than 100% due to respondents reporting that they participate in many activities.)

MOST POPULAR WEEKEND ACTIVITIES

Activity	Percent Who Participate
1. Spectator outings	76%
2. Visit zoos and fairs	50%
3. Flower gardening	47%
4. Driving for pleasure	43%
5. Photography	35%
6. Sightseeing	34%
Fishing	34%
8. Boating	28%
9. Running/jogging	26%
10. Camping	24%

Where are the "big-three" white-collar sports—tennis, golf and skiing? They came in 11th, 12th and 13th respectively as follows:

Sports	Percent Who Participate
11. Tennis	17%
12. Golfing	13%
13. Skiing	9%

Source: *Sports Illustrated* Sport's Poll; U.S. Census Bureau, *National Recreation Survey*; Harris poll; Gallup poll.

Most Popular Wine Brands

Although we may not be on par with the French or Italians in per capita consumption of wine, the U.S. market is booming. The acceptance of wine as a companion to meals is on the rise, and scads of new and revamped vineyards are competing to quench the national thirst. Leading the bunch are the powerful growers of California's Napa Valley.

Brand	Total Depletions (1,000s)
1. Franzia	13,000
2. Carlo Rossi	11,695
3. Gallo Livingston Cellars	11,230
4. Wine Cellars of E&J Gallo	9,300
5. Inglenook Vineyards	7,550
6. Almaden	7,385
7. Sutter Home	5,345
8. Woodbridge	3,800
9. August Sebastiani	3,600
10. Glen Ellen	3,250

Source: Impact U.S. Wine Market Study, 1996.

WINES, CALIFORNIA

There was a time not long ago when connoisseurs wrinkled their noses at the mention of California wines. Inexpensive? Yes. Drinkable? Perhaps. But fine wine? Never! That began to change with the success of cabernet sauvignon, a wine made from a black Bordeaux grape that took quite well to the California soil and climate. It quickly became known as a less expensive alternative to pricey French Bordeaux, and resulted in both a growing respect for California wineries and a foothold for acceptance of other wines from the Golden State. Today, these domestic wines rival and often exceed the quality of the imports, be they Bordeaux, Burgundy or Chardonnay. In 1994, a California cabernet sauvignon led the list of the world's best wines, according to *Wine Spectator* magazine, and several other California offerings filled out the list, outnumbering imports from France. The list below is the magazine's choice of the top 10 from California, based on quality and price. With the range of varietal grapes and prices it represents, it may not be long before the best of California list becomes the best of the best list.

Rank/Wine/Price

1. **Caymus Cabernet Sauvignon**
   Special Selection (1990):$75
2. **Flora Springs Cabernet**
   Sauvignon Reserve (1991): $33
3. **Ferrari-Carano**
   Chardonnay (1992): $20
4. **Ridge Zinfandel Pagani**
   Ranch Late
   Picked 1992: $16
5. **Mount Veeder Reservecar**
   (1991) Mixed Varietal: $25
6. **Freemark Abbey Edelwein Gold**
   Sweet Johannisberg Riesling
   (1991): $25
7. **Bandiera Cabernet Sauvignon**
   (1990): $8
8. **Villa Mt. Eden Barrel Select**
   Zinfandel (1991): $8
9. **Dry Creek Fume Blanc**
   (1991): $9
10. **Robert Mondavi Woodbridge**
    Chardonnay (1993): $8

Source: *Wine Spectator* magazine, January 1996.

WINES, FRENCH

Best Red Bordeaux and Red Burgundies

Most wine experts agree that France produces the best red wines. There is a considerable difference of opinion as to which country and region produces the best white wine. Naturally, preferences are largely a matter of opinion, but certain red wines from France keep coming up on expert's "best lists." The most famous ranking of red French Bordeau wines, the *Grand Cru* or "Great Growths," officially appeared in 1855 and is still generally valid. But because of wine technology, today's experts have reshuffled the order and added a few of

MIS EN BOUTEILLES AU CHATEAU

CHÂTEAU LAFITE-ROTHSCHILD
1947
APPELLATION PAUILLAC CONTRÔLEE

DÉPOSE

FRANCE

AMONG WINE EXPERTS there is almost no disagreement: Above is the world's greatest wine.

yesteryear's "lesser wines." The following rating is from Frank Schoonmaker, one of the world's most respected wine experts. All are from France, but few independent wine critics will dispute that the French are the undisputed champions at grape growing and winemaking. So Gallic pride should be satisfied.

RED BORDEAUX

Label/Vineyard

1. Chateau Lafite
2. Chateau Margaux
3. Chateau Latour
4. Chateau Haut-Brion
5. Chateau Mouton-Rothschild
6. Chateau Rausan-Segla
7. Chateau Rauzan-Gassies
8. Chateau Leoville-Poyferre
9. Chateau Leoville-Barton
10. Chateau Dufort-Vivens

BURGUNDIES

Label/Vineyard

1. Chambolle Musigny
2. Vougeot
3. Nuit-Saint George
4. Aloxe-Corton
5. Beaune
6. Auxey

THINGS

7. Meursault
8. Puligny-Montrachet
9. Chassagne-Montrachet
10. Santenay
Source: *Frank Schoonmaker's Encyclopedia of Wine*, 1982.

OOS

America's Best Zoos

Almost every city in the country has some kind of zoo or wild animal park. Some are small facilities with a few monkeys or lions pacing back and forth in their cages. Others recreate animals' natural habitats. To rate America's zoos, our editors used four statistics and three ratios. Most important was the ratio of species to budget, that is: How much money could the zoo spend on each type of animal it housed? Next came the ratio of species to acres or: How much land did the animals have in which to roam? The final consideration was crowding: Was the facility too crowded, was it average or were crowds sparse? The following scores are based on a formula using these factors.

Best Zoos	Score
1. San Diego Wild Animal Park	19.39
2. Washington Park (Portland)	7.04
3. Brookfield Zoo (Chicago)	5.56
4. Bronx Zoo (New York City)	4.07
5. San Diego Zoo	4.02
6. Minnesota Zoo	3.58
7. Detroit Zoo	3.41
8. San Francisco Zoo	3.15
9. Miami Metrozoo	3.10
10. National Zoo (Washington, DC)	2.60
11. Phoenix Zoo	2.43
12. Woodland Park (Seattle)	2.26

THE SAVANNAHS OF AFRICA? No, the San Diego Wild Animal Park, the top zoo in the U.S. Photo: Ron Garrison, © San Diego Wild Aminal Park.

BEST ATTENDED ZOOS

1. Lincoln Park Zoo
   (Chicago)   4.0 million
2. San Diego Zoo   3.5 million
3. National Zoo
   (Washington, DC)   3.0 million
4. St. Louis Zoo   2.3 million
5. Bronx Zoo   2.3 million
6. Brookfield Zoo
   (Chicago)   2.0 million
7. Houston Zoo   2.0 million
8. Milwaukee Zoo   1.8 million
9. Los Angeles Zoo   1.7 million
10. Cincinnati Zoo   1.5 million

BIGGEST IN ACREAGE

1. San Diego Wild
   Animal Park   1,800 acres
2. Minnesota Zoo   488 acres
3. Miami Metro. Zoo   290 acres
4. Bronx Zoo
   (New York City)   265 acres

5. Brookfield Zoo
   (Chicago)   204 acres
6. Milwaukee Zoo   185 acres
7. National Zoo,
   (Washington, DC)   163 acres
8. Cleveland Zoo   160 acres
9. Detroit Zoo   125 acres
   San Francisco Zoo   125 acres
   Phoenix Zoo   125 acres

MOST SPECIES

1. San Diego Zoo   800
2. Cincinnati Zoo   735
3. San Antonio Zoo   674
4. Houston Zoo   649
5. Bronx Zoo,(New York City)   644
6. St. Louis Zoo   619
7. Milwaukee Zoo   605
8. Philadelphia   560
9. Oklahoma City Zoo   532
10. Los Angeles Zoo   500

Source: *Best and Worst* original.

INDEX